ה

תשע

סֵדֶר הַתְּפִלּוֹת, סֵדֶר קְרִיאַת הַתּוֹרָה,
הֲלָכוֹת וּמִנְהָגִים לְבֵית הַכְּנֶסֶת וְלַבַּיִת

# Luaḥ Hashanah
# 5779

A guide to prayers, readings,
laws, and customs
for the synagogue and for the home

Rabbi Miles B. Cohen
*and* Leslie Rubin

**Resources for Synagogue and Home**

*Luaḥ Hashanah 5779* was inspired by the vision and endeavors of Kenneth S. Goldrich ז"ל. Ken's efforts provided a comprehensive English *luaḥ* for the Conservative movement beginning in 5755 (1994).

To promote ease of use, we do not list the myriad and legitimate variations in liturgical practices. The congregational rabbi, as the *mara de'atra* (the local authority on Jewish practice), has the ultimate responsibility for such decisions in each community.

This book contains no instance of the Divine name that requires burial (גְּנִיזָה *genizah*). Everywhere that such a name appears, the first letter is separated from the remainder of the letters so that the name never appears as an intact unit (for example, אֵ·ל).



Published by Miles B. Cohen and Leslie Rubin



ISBN (standard edition) 978-0-9968701-5-3
ISBN (electronic edition) 978-0-9968701-6-0
ISBN (large-print/pulpit-size edition, economy version) 978-0-9968701-7-7
ISBN (large-print edition/pulpit-size, deluxe version) 978-0-9968701-8-4

DESIGN AND COMPOSITION BY MILES B. COHEN

PRINTED IN THE UNITED STATES OF AMERICA
BY G&H SOHO, INC.
www.ghsoho.com

## CONTENTS


v Preface
v About the Authors
vi Guide to Transliterations
vii Guide to Symbols and Conventions
viii Jewish Commemorations 5779–5782
x About the Year תשע"ט 5779

1 אֱלוּל Elul 5778
9 תִּשְׁרֵי Tishrey
61 חֶשְׁוָן Ḥeshvan
67 כִּסְלֵו Kislev
82 טֵבֵת Tevet
92 שְׁבָט Shevat
102 אֲדָר רִאשׁוֹן Adar Rishon
110 אֲדָר שֵׁנִי Adar Sheni
123 נִיסָן Nisan
152 אִיָּר Iyyar
165 סִיוָן Sivan
180 תַּמּוּז Tammuz
187 אָב Av
204 אֱלוּל Elul

212 Appendix A: Sefirat Ha'omer
213 Appendix B: Birkat Kohanim
214 Appendix C: Determining the Date of a Yortsayt

## LUAḤ 5779 EDITIONS

### Luaḥ 5779 — *Standard*

This full-color guide—to prayer services, readings (Torah, haftarah, and megillah), and home ceremonies—offers concise yet comprehensive instructions for congregations and individuals.
**www.milesbcohen.com**

### Luaḥ 5779 — *Large-Print/Pulpit-Size*

Measuring 7.5 in. x 11 in., this edition matches the standard print edition page for page, with text that is 25% larger.

- Economy version (text is black and white)
- Deluxe version (text is full color)

**www.milesbcohen.com**

### eLuaḥ™ 5779 — *Electronic*

Download to your PC, Mac, Android phone or tablet, iPhone, iPad, or other device.
Also, access it online from any internet-connected browser.
This edition matches the print editions page for page.
**www.milesbcohen.com**

## LUAḤ EXTRAS

### Additional Resources

Browse supplementary *Luaḥ* resources.
**www.milesbcohen.com/LuahResources**

### Keep Your Luaḥ Up to Date — Register

Join our email list! You will receive *Luaḥ* updates, additions, and corrections during the course of the year.
Register at: **www.milesbcohen.com/LuahUpdates**

*Registered in the past? No need to register again.*

### Questions, Suggestions, and Corrections

We welcome questions, suggestions, and corrections.
Please send your comments to:
**luah@milesbcohen.com**
We post corrections at:
**www.milesbcohen.com/LuahUpdates**

## PREFACE

What is more difficult? Navigating the familiar or the totally unknown? My sense is the totally unknown is easier because we don't know what to expect. In that sense, the familiar is harder because we have an idea of what we may encounter. Of course, often mid-course corrections must be made— they often make the journey more interesting.

So it is with our worship services. We have a good sense of what the expected liturgy is—until we don't. We know what to add or subtract—until we don't. The purpose of the Luah is to gently guide and remind us of additions and deletions from the expected, keeping us on track.

Users of this publication have come to expect that the unexpected will be described and explained. Rabbi Miles Cohen, working with Leslie Rubin, continues to teach and to guide our worship, providing background and exceptional detail. *Luaḥ Hashanah* helps lay leaders, synagogue and school professionals, students, campers and staff, and everyone at services and at home to participate authentically with confidence and understanding.

*Paul Drazen*
RABBI, TEMPLE ADATH YESHURUN
SYRACUSE, NEW YORK

We express our thanks once again to Rabbi Joel Roth of the Jewish Theological Seminary. Rabbi Roth makes himself available throughout the year to clarify and resolve challenging questions of *halakhah* and practice.

## ABOUT THE AUTHORS

RABBI MILES B. COHEN was ordained by the Jewish Theological Seminary of America in 1974. For over twenty years, he worked in curriculum development at the Melton Research Center at JTS, and for many years he taught students preparing to be rabbis, cantors, educators, and lay leaders. He lectures and also conducts workshops all over North America on topics related to synagogue practice. Rabbi Cohen has created guides and interactive software for learning to read Torah, *haftarah,* and *m<sup>e</sup>gillot,* as well as guides for *nusaḥ* skills and Hebrew grammar.

LESLIE RUBIN is a professional editor, specializing in Jewish studies, who has edited and indexed numerous books on technical and academic subjects. In addition, she develops educational and training materials, with an emphasis on usability and concision.

## GUIDE TO TRANSLITERATIONS

Those who use the transliterations find that careful attention to the transliteration system enables accurate pronunciation of the associated Hebrew words. When reading transliterations, use the following guidelines:

### Consonants

ḥ pronounced in many modern dialects like ***ch*** in *Johann Sebastian Ba**ch**;* in other dialects, pronounced like a harsh or raspy ***h***

kh pronounced like ***ch*** in *Johann Sebastian Ba**ch***

' represents *alef* or *ayin* within a word

### Vowels

a pronounced like ***a*** in *father*

ay pronounced like ***ay*** in *k**ay**ak*

e pronounced like ***e*** in *bet*

ey pronounced like ***é*** in *café*

i pronounced like ***ie*** in *f**ie**ld*

o pronounced like ***o*** in *n**o**r*

oy pronounced like ***oy*** in *b**oy***

u pronounced like ***u*** in *fl**u**te*

uy pronounced like ***uey*** in *chop s**uey***

The small, raised vowels $^{a}$, $^{e}$, and $^{o}$ represent the *ḥataf* vowels אֲ אֱ אֳ.
These are hurried counterparts of ***a***, ***e***, and ***o***, the full vowels אַ אֶ אֹ.
Pronounced *sh$^{e}$va* (שְׁוָא נָע *sh$^{e}$va na*), a reduced vowel, is also indicated by $^{e}$.
In general, consonants are doubled to reflect a *dagesh ḥazak* (e.g., *kippur,* not *kipur*) because this often aids in pronunciation of the preceding short vowel. However, consonants are not doubled after prefixes (e.g., *hagadol,* not *haggadol*).

Exceptions to the above conventions are made to improve readability (e.g., *elul,* not *$^{e}$lul; nitsavim,* not *nitstsavim; aliyah,* not *$^{a}$liyyah*).

# GUIDE TO SYMBOLS AND CONVENTIONS

## Symbols

| Symbol | Meaning | Explanation |
| --- | --- | --- |
| + | **Add** | Alerts you to *add* a phrase or prayer that usually we do not recite at the particular service or point in the service |
| ✕ | **Omit** | Alerts you to *omit* a phrase or prayer that usually we recite at the particular service or point in the service |
| ☞ | **Take note** | Alerts you to instructions that require special attention |

## Page Numbers in Various Siddurim

The following notations precede page citations for *siddurim* published by the United Synagogue of Conservative Judaism and The Rabbinical Assembly.

| | |
| --- | --- |
| L | *Lev Shalem* for Shabbat and Festivals |
| S | Shabbat and Festival *Sim Shalom* |
| W | Weekday *Sim Shalom* |
| F | Full Siddur *Sim Shalom* (all editions) |
| P | Personal Edition of Full *Sim Shalom* (Travel Edition) |

## Torah Readings

Verses for each aliyah are provided for the reading of the full parashah and for the triennial-cycle reading. The following notations appear in conjunction with instructions for Torah readings:

| | |
| --- | --- |
| 1 2 3 4 5 6 7 | Aliyah numbers |
| M | Maftir aliyah |
| ° | Aliyah or reading with a special feature that requires attention |
| ☞ ° | Explanation of the special feature marked with ° |

## Color-Coded Boxes

Provides instructions for the stated time period, thus replacing multiple occurrences of identical instructions

Provides historical or other explanatory background material about holidays, fast days, and special occasions

Provides procedures for *halakhot*, rituals, and customs associated with holidays, fast days, and other occasions

# JEWISH COMMEMORATIONS 5779–5782

## 5779 • 2018–2019

### 2018

**Rosh Hashanah Day 1** Mon., Sept. 10
**Rosh Hashanah Day 2** Tue., Sept. 11
**Tsom Gedalyah (fast)** Wed., Sept. 12
**Yom Kippur** Wed., Sept. 19
**Sukkot Day 1** Mon., Sept. 24
**Sukkot Day 2** Tue., Sept. 25
**Hosha'na Rabbah** Sun., Sept. 30
**Shemini Atseret** Mon., Oct. 1
**Simḥat Torah** Tue., Oct. 2
**Ḥanukkah** Mon., Dec. 3–Mon., Dec. 10
**Asarah Betevet (fast)** Tue., Dec. 18

### 2019

**Tu Bishvat** Mon., Jan. 21
**Ta'anit Ester (fast)** Wed., Mar. 20
**Purim** Thu., Mar. 21
**Pesaḥ Day 1** Sat., Apr. 20
**Pesaḥ Day 2** Sun., Apr. 21
**Pesaḥ Day 7** Fri., Apr. 26
**Pesaḥ Day 8** Sat., Apr. 27
**Yom Hasho'ah** Thu., May 2
**Yom Hazikkaron** Wed., May 8
**Yom Ha'atsma'ut** Thu., May 9
**Lag Ba'omer** Thu., May 23
**Yom Yerushalayim** Sun., June 2
**Shavu'ot Day 1** Sun., June 9
**Shavu'ot Day 2** Mon., June 10
**Shiv'ah Asar Betammuz (fast)** Sun., July 21
**Tish'ah Be'av (fast)** Sun., Aug. 11

## 5780 • 2019–2020

### 2019

**Rosh Hashanah Day 1** Mon., Sept. 30
**Rosh Hashanah Day 2** Tue., Oct. 1
**Tsom Gedalyah (fast)** Wed., Oct. 2
**Yom Kippur** Wed., Oct. 9
**Sukkot Day 1** Mon., Oct. 14
**Sukkot Day 2** Tue., Oct. 15
**Hosha'na Rabbah** Sun., Oct. 20
**Shemini Atseret** Mon., Oct. 21
**Simḥat Torah** Tue., Oct. 22
**Ḥanukkah** Mon., Dec. 23–Mon., Dec. 30

### 2020

**Asarah Betevet (fast)** Tue., Jan. 7
**Tu Bishvat** Mon., Feb. 10
**Ta'anit Ester (fast)** Mon., Mar. 9
**Purim** Tue., Mar. 10
**Pesaḥ Day 1** Thu., Apr. 9
**Pesaḥ Day 2** Fri., Apr. 10
**Pesaḥ Day 7** Wed., Apr. 15
**Pesaḥ Day 8** Thu., Apr. 16
**Yom Hasho'ah** Tue., Apr. 21
**Yom Hazikkaron** Tue., Apr. 28
**Yom Ha'atsma'ut** Wed., Apr. 29
**Lag Ba'omer** Tue., May 12
**Yom Yerushalayim** Fri., May 22
**Shavu'ot Day 1** Fri., May 29
**Shavu'ot Day 2** Sat., May 30
**Shiv'ah Asar Betammuz (fast)** Thu., July 9
**Tish'ah Be'av (fast)** Thu., July 30

## 5781 • 2020–2021

### 2020

**Rosh Hashanah Day 1** Sat., Sept. 19
**Rosh Hashanah Day 2** Sun., Sept. 20
**Tsom Gedalyah (fast)** Mon., Sept. 21
**Yom Kippur** Mon., Sept. 28
**Sukkot Day 1** Sat., Oct. 3
**Sukkot Day 2** Sun., Oct. 4
**Hosha'na Rabbah** Fri., Oct. 9
**Shemini Atseret** Sat., Oct. 10
**Simḥat Torah** Sun., Oct. 11
**Ḥanukkah** Fri., Dec. 11–Fri., Dec. 18
**Asarah Betevet (fast)** Fri., Dec. 25

### 2021

**Tu Bishvat** Thu., Jan. 28
**Ta'anit Ester (fast)** Thu., Feb. 25
**Purim** Fri., Feb. 26
**Pesaḥ Day 1** Sun., Mar. 28
**Pesaḥ Day 2** Mon., Mar. 29
**Pesaḥ Day 7** Sat., Apr. 3
**Pesaḥ Day 8** Sun., Apr. 4
**Yom Hasho'ah** Thu., Apr. 8
**Yom Hazikkaron** Wed., Apr. 14
**Yom Ha'atsma'ut** Thu., Apr. 15
**Lag Ba'omer** Fri., Apr. 30
**Yom Yerushalayim** Mon., May 10
**Shavu'ot Day 1** Mon., May 17
**Shavu'ot Day 2** Tue., May 18
**Shiv'ah Asar Betammuz (fast)** Sun., June 27
**Tish'ah Be'av (fast)** Sun., July 18

## 5782 • 2021–2022

### 2021

**Rosh Hashanah Day 1** Tue., Sept. 7
**Rosh Hashanah Day 2** Wed., Sept. 8
**Tsom Gedalyah (fast)** Thu., Sept. 9
**Yom Kippur** Thu., Sept. 16
**Sukkot Day 1** Tue., Sept. 21
**Sukkot Day 2** Wed., Sept. 22
**Hosha'na Rabbah** Mon., Sept. 27
**Shemini Atseret** Tue., Sept. 28
**Simḥat Torah** Wed., Sept. 29
**Ḥanukkah** Mon., Nov. 29–Mon., Dec. 6
**Asarah Betevet (fast)** Tue., Dec. 14

### 2022

**Tu Bishvat** Mon., Jan. 17
**Ta'anit Ester (fast)** Wed., Mar. 16
**Purim** Thu., Mar. 17
**Pesaḥ Day 1** Sat., Apr. 16
**Pesaḥ Day 2** Sun., Apr. 17
**Pesaḥ Day 7** Fri., Apr. 22
**Pesaḥ Day 8** Sat., Apr. 23
**Yom Hasho'ah** Thu., Apr. 28
**Yom Hazikkaron** Wed., May 4
**Yom Ha'atsma'ut** Thu., May 5
**Lag Ba'omer** Thu., May 19
**Yom Yerushalayim** Sun., May 29
**Shavu'ot Day 1** Sun., June 5
**Shavu'ot Day 2** Mon., June 6
**Shiv'ah Asar Betammuz (fast)** Sun., July 17
**Tish'ah Be'av (fast)** Sun., Aug. 7

# ABOUT THE YEAR תשע"ט 5779

## Characteristics of the Year

- Year 3 of the 19-year lunar cycle.
  Years 3, 6, 8, 11, 14, 17, and 19 of the lunar cycle are leap years.
  Leap years have an extra month.
- A 385-day year:
  שָׁנָה מְעֻבֶּרֶת, a *leap* year: a 13-month year, adding 1st Adar with 30 days.
  שָׁנָה שְׁלֵמָה, an *excessive* year: the usual 12 months alternate between 30 and 29 days, except for Ḥeshvan with 30 days.
- Year 11 of the 28-year solar cycle.
- Year 4 of the 7-year שְׁמִטָּה *sheмittah* (Sabbatical Year) cycle.
- Year 3 of the 3-year Torah-reading cycle followed by some congregations.

## Dates to Note

### Major holidays

- **Rosh Hashanah** begins Sunday night, September 9, 2018.
- **Yom Kippur** begins Tuesday night, September 18, 2018.
- **Sukkot** begins Sunday night, September 23, 2018.
- **Sheмini Atseret** begins Sunday night, September 30, 2018.
- **Simḥat Torah** begins Monday night, October 1, 2018.
- **Pesaḥ** begins Friday night, April 19, 2019.
- **Shavu'ot** begins Saturday night, June 8, 2019.

### Minor holidays and observances

- **Hosha'na Rabbah** begins Saturday night, September 29, 2018.
- **Ḥanukkah** begins Sunday night, December 2, 2018.
- **Tu Bishvat** begins Sunday night, January 20, 2019.
- **Purim** begins Wednesday night, March 20, 2019.
- **Yom Hasho'ah** (Holocaust Remembrance Day) begins Wednesday night, May 1, 2019.
- **Yom Hazikkaron** (Israel Memorial Day) begins Tuesday night, May 7, 2019. (always observed on the day preceding Yom Ha'atsma'ut).
- **Yom Ha'atsma'ut** (Israel Independence Day) begins Wednesday night, May 8, 2019 (moved up 1 day to 4 Iyyar).
- **Lag Ba'omer** begins Wednesday night, May 22, 2019.
- **Yom Yerushalayim** (Jerusalem Day) begins Saturday night, June 1, 2019.

### Communal fasts

- **Tsom Gedalyah** begins Wenesday morning, September 12, 2018.
- **Yom Kippur** begins Tuesday night, September 18, 2018.
- **Asarah Betevet** begins Tuesday morning, December 18, 2018.
- **Ta'anit Ester** begins Wednesday morning, March 20, 2019.
- **Shiv'ah Asar Betammuz** begins Sunday morning, July 21, 2019 (delayed 1 day to 18 Tammuz).
- **Tish'ah Be'av** begins Saturday night, August 10, 2019 (delayed 1 day to 10 Av).

| Elul 5778 | | | | | | | Aug \| Sep 2018 | | | | | | |
|---|---|---|---|---|---|---|---|---|---|---|---|---|---|
| 1 | 2 | 3 | 4 | 5 | 6 | 7 | 12 | 13 | 14 | 15 | 16 | 17 | 18 |
| 8 | 9 | 10 | 11 | 12 | 13 | 14 | 19 | 20 | 21 | 22 | 23 | 24 | 25 |
| 15 | 16 | 17 | 18 | 19 | 20 | 21 | 26 | 27 | 28 | 29 | 30 | 31 | 1 |
| 22 | 23 | 24 | 25 | 26 | 27 | 28 | 2 | 3 | 4 | 5 | 6 | 7 | 8 |
| 29 | | | | | | | 9 | | | | | | |



## DURING Elul

### MORNINGS

**If psalm(s) for the day recited early in the service:**

**Every day** Recite psalm(s) for the day, followed by:
קַדִּישׁ יָתוֹם Mourner's Kaddish (some omit) L58 S82 W100 F52
**+** Psalm 27 for the Season of Repentance L59 S80 W92 F40
קַדִּישׁ יָתוֹם Mourner's Kaddish L58 S82 W100 F52

**Weekdays** **+** At the end of the service, sound the shofar* (except on 29 Elul).

**If psalm(s) for the day recited at the end of the service:**

**Every day** Recite psalm(s) for the day, followed by:
קַדִּישׁ יָתוֹם Mourner's Kaddish (some omit) L58 S82 W100 F52

**Weekdays** **+** Sound the shofar* (except on 29 Elul). (Some sound the shofar instead after the last קַדִּישׁ יָתוֹם Mourner's Kaddish.)

**Every day** **+** Psalm 27 for the Season of Repentance L59 S80 W92 F40
קַדִּישׁ יָתוֹם Mourner's Kaddish L58 S82 W100 F52

### EVENINGS

**After עָלֵינוּ Aleynu:**

קַדִּישׁ יָתוֹם Mourner's Kaddish (some omit) L58 S82 W100 F52
**+** Psalm 27 for the Season of Repentance L59 S80 W92 F40
קַדִּישׁ יָתוֹם Mourner's Kaddish L58 S82 W100 F52

---

*Without anyone reciting a בְּרָכָה berakhah or calling out *teki'ah, shevarim*, etc., sound the shofar:
תְּקִיעָה ← שְׁבָרִים ← תְּרוּעָה ← תְּקִיעָה Teki'ah → Shevarim → Teru'ah → Teki'ah

---

## Elul 1 אֱלוּל
**Sat 11 Aug** (evening)

## ראש חֹדֶשׁ אֱלוּל Rosh Ḥodesh Elul — Day 2
מוֹצָאֵי שַׁבָּת Motsa'ey Shabbat Conclusion of Shabbat

**DURING Rosh Ḥodesh**

**Birkat Hamazon:**

**+** יַעֲלֶה וְיָבוֹא Ya'aleh veyavo for Rosh Ḥodesh
L90|95 S340|347 W233|239 F762|780

**+** הָרַחֲמָן Haraḥaman for Rosh Ḥodesh
L92|96 S343|348 W235|240 F768

| Elul 5778 | | | | | | |
|---|---|---|---|---|---|---|
| 1 | 2 | 3 | 4 | 5 | 6 | 7 |
| 8 | 9 | 10 | 11 | 12 | 13 | 14 |
| 15 | 16 | 17 | 18 | 19 | 20 | 21 |
| 22 | 23 | 24 | 25 | 26 | 27 | 28 |
| 29 | | | | | | |

| Aug \| Sep 2018 | | | | | | |
|---|---|---|---|---|---|---|
| 12 | 13 | 14 | 15 | 16 | 17 | 18 |
| 19 | 20 | 21 | 22 | 23 | 24 | 25 |
| 26 | 27 | 28 | 29 | 30 | 31 \| | 1 |
| 2 | 3 | 4 | 5 | 6 | 7 | 8 |
| 9 | | | | | | |

+ Add ✕ Omit ☞ Take note!

**Siddurim**
- **L** Lev Shalem for Shabbat and Festivals
- **S** Shabbat and Festival Sim Shalom
- **W** Weekday Sim Shalom
- **F** Full Sim Shalom (both editions)
- **P** Personal Edition of Full Sim Shalom

---

**עַרְבִית**

Saturday night Arvit as usual until the Amidah L264 S281 W137 F200

**Weekday Amidah:**

+ אַתָּה חוֹנַנְתָּנוּ Attah ḥonantanu L272 S287 W143 F212
+ יַעֲלֶה וְיָבוֹא Ya'aleh veyavo for Rosh Ḥodesh L277 S289 W145 F216

Continue as on a usual Saturday night through קַדִּישׁ שָׁלֵם Full Kaddish L280 S294 W160 F688

Some recite הַבְדָּלָה Havdalah here. L283 S299 W165 F700

עָלֵינוּ Aleynu L281 S297 W163 F696
קַדִּישׁ יָתוֹם Mourner's Kaddish (some omit) L282 S298 W164 F698
+ Psalm 27 for the Season of Repentance L59 S80 W92 F40
קַדִּישׁ יָתוֹם Mourner's Kaddish L58 S82 W100 F52

הַבְדָּלָה Havdalah L283 S299 W165 F700

**Sun 12 Aug שַׁחֲרִית**

**Before מִזְמוֹר שִׁיר Mizmor shir (Psalm 30) or at end of service, recite:** W14 F50

Psalm for Sunday (Psalm 24) W85 F22
קַדִּישׁ יָתוֹם Mourner's Kaddish (some omit) W100 F52
+ Psalm 104 for Rosh Ḥodesh W90 F34
קַדִּישׁ יָתוֹם Mourner's Kaddish (some omit) W100 F52
+ Psalm 27 for the Season of Repentance W92 F40
קַדִּישׁ יָתוֹם Mourner's Kaddish W100 F52"

**Weekday Amidah:**

+ יַעֲלֶה וְיָבוֹא Ya'aleh veyavo for Rosh Ḥodesh W41 F114

✕ ~~תַּחֲנוּן Taḥanun~~

+ חֲצִי הַלֵּל Short Hallel W50 F380
קַדִּישׁ שָׁלֵם Full Kaddish W56 F392

+ **TORAH SERVICE** W65 F138
Remove **1** Torah scroll from ark.

**Torah** 4 aliyot: פִּינְחָס Pineḥas
בְּמִדְבַּר Bemidbar (Numbers) 28:1–15
[1]28:1–3 [2]3–5 [3]6–10 [4]11–15 W320 P943

חֲצִי קַדִּישׁ Short Kaddish W71 F146
Open, raise, display, and wrap scroll.
Return scroll to ark. W76 F150

| ✚ Add | ✘ Omit | ☞ Take note! | **Elul 5778** | **Aug \| Sep 2018** | **אֱלוּל 1** Aug 12 |
|---|---|---|---|---|---|
| | **Siddurim** | | 1 2 3 4 5 6 7 | 12 13 14 15 16 17 18 | |
| **L** | Lev Shalem for Shabbat and Festivals | | 8 9 10 11 12 13 14 | 19 20 21 22 23 24 25 | |
| **S** | Shabbat and Festival Sim Shalom | | 15 16 17 18 19 20 21 | 26 27 28 29 30 31 \| 1 | |
| **W** | Weekday Sim Shalom | | 22 23 24 25 26 27 28 | 2 3 4 5 6 7 8 | |
| **F** | Full Sim Shalom (both editions) | | 29 | 9 | |
| **P** | Personal Edition of Full Sim Shalom | | | | |

        אַשְׁרֵי Ashrey    W78 F152

✘  לַמְנַצֵּחַ Lam<sup>e</sup>natse·aḥ (Psalm 20)

        וּבָא לְצִיּוֹן Uva l<sup>e</sup>tsiyyon    W80 F156

**Some congregations:**
Remove and pack t<sup>e</sup>fillin at this point.
✚  חֲצִי קַדִּישׁ Short Kaddish    W103 F428

**Other congregations:**
✚  חֲצִי קַדִּישׁ Short Kaddish    W103 F428
Remove and cover—but do not pack—t<sup>e</sup>fillin, so that
all begin Musaf Amidah at the same time,
as soon after Kaddish as possible.

מוּסָף    ✚ **Rosh Ḥodesh Amidah for weekdays:**    W104 F486
        Weekday קְדֻשָׁה K<sup>e</sup>dushah    W105 F488

✚  קַדִּישׁ שָׁלֵם Full Kaddish    W82 F158
        עָלֵינוּ Aleynu    W83 F160

**If psalms for the day were recited at Shaḥarit:**
קַדִּישׁ יָתוֹם Mourner's Kaddish    W84 F162
✚ Sound the shofar (see procedure on p. 1).

**If psalms for the day were not recited at Shaḥarit, add here:**
קַדִּישׁ יָתוֹם Mourner's Kaddish (some omit)    W84 F162
Psalm for Sunday (Psalm 24)    W85 F22
קַדִּישׁ יָתוֹם Mourner's Kaddish (some omit)    W100 F52
✚ Psalm 104 for Rosh Ḥodesh    W90 F34
קַדִּישׁ יָתוֹם Mourner's Kaddish (some omit)    W100 F52
✚ Sound the shofar (see procedure on p. 1).
✚ Psalm 27 for the Season of Repentance    W92 F40
קַדִּישׁ יָתוֹם Mourner's Kaddish    W84\|100 F162\|52

מִנְחָה    **Weekday Amidah:**
✚  יַעֲלֶה וְיָבוֹא Ya'aleh v<sup>e</sup>yavo for Rosh Ḥodesh    W127 F178

✘  תַּחֲנוּן Taḥ<sup>a</sup>nun

| Elul 5778 | | | | | | |
|---|---|---|---|---|---|---|
| 1 | 2 | 3 | 4 | 5 | 6 | 7 |
| 8 | 9 | 10 | 11 | 12 | 13 | 14 |
| 15 | 16 | 17 | 18 | 19 | 20 | 21 |
| 22 | 23 | 24 | 25 | 26 | 27 | 28 |
| 29 | | | | | | |

| Aug \| Sep 2018 | | | | | | |
|---|---|---|---|---|---|---|
| 12 | 13 | 14 | 15 | 16 | 17 | 18 |
| 19 | 20 | 21 | 22 | 23 | 24 | 25 |
| 26 | 27 | 28 | 29 | 30 | 31 \| | 1 |
| 2 | 3 | 4 | 5 | 6 | 7 | 8 |
| 9 | | | | | | |

+ Add ✕ Omit ☞ Take note!

**Siddurim**
- **L** Lev Shalem for Shabbat and Festivals
- **S** Shabbat and Festival Sim Shalom
- **W** Weekday Sim Shalom
- **F** Full Sim Shalom (both editions)
- **P** Personal Edition of Full Sim Shalom

## Elul 7 אֱלוּל
Sat 18 Aug

## שַׁבָּת Shabbat פָּרָשַׁת שֹׁפְטִים Parashat Shofetim

**Torah** 7 aliyot (minimum): שֹׁפְטִים Shofetim
דְּבָרִים Devarim (Deuteronomy) 16:18–21:9

| | | | | |
|---|---|---|---|---|
| Annual: | 1 16:18–17:13 | 2 17:14–20 | 3 18:1–5 | 4 18:6–13 |
| | 5 18:14–19:13 | 6 19:14–20:9 | 7 20:10–21:9 | M 21:7–9 |
| Triennial: | 1 18:6–8 | 2 18:9–13 | 3 18:14–17 | 4 18:18–22 |
| | 5 19:1–7 | 6 19:8–10 | 7 19:11–13 | M 19:11–13 |

**Haftarah** יְשַׁעְיָהוּ Yesha'yahu (Isaiah) 51:12–52:12
(4th of 7 haftarot of consolation following Tish'ah Be'av)

מִנְחָה

**Torah** 3 aliyot from כִּי־תֵצֵא Ki tetse
דְּבָרִים Devarim (Deuteronomy) 21:10–21
1 21:10–14 2 15–17 3 18–21 W313 P934

This is also the reading for the coming Monday and Thursday.

## Elul 14 אֱלוּל
Sat 25 Aug

## שַׁבָּת Shabbat פָּרָשַׁת כִּי־תֵצֵא Parashat Ki tetse

**Torah** 7 aliyot (minimum): כִּי־תֵצֵא Ki tetse
דְּבָרִים Devarim (Deuteronomy) 21:10–25:19

| | | | | |
|---|---|---|---|---|
| Annual: | 1 21:10–21 | 2 21:22–22:7 | 3 22:8–23:7 | 4 23:8–24 |
| | 5 23:25–24:4 | 6 24:5–13 | 7 24:14–25:19 | M 25:17–19 |
| Triennial: | 1 23:8–12 | 2 23:13–15 | 3 23:16–19 | 4 23:20–24 |
| | 5 23:25–24:4 | 6 24:5–9 | 7 24:10–13 | M 24:10–13 |

☞ **Haftarah** יְשַׁעְיָהוּ Yesha'yahu (Isaiah) 54:1–10 + °54:11–55:5
(5th + 3rd of 7 haftarot of consolation following Tish'ah Be'av)

☞ °54:1–10 + 54:11–55:5 Because Shabbat Re'eh was Rosh Ḥodesh, the usual 3rd haftarah of consolation was not read. Read the haftarah of Ki tetse and then the haftarah of Re'eh as a single haftarah. In the book of Isaiah these two brief passages are adjacent.

מִנְחָה

**Torah** 3 aliyot from כִּי־תָבוֹא Ki tavo
דְּבָרִים Devarim (Deuteronomy) 26:1–15°
1 26:1–3 2 4–11 3 12–15 W314 P935

This is also the reading for the coming Monday and Thursday.

☞ °26:1–15 The reading extends through verse 15, which enables the correct configuration of the 3 aliyot.

**Elul 21 אֱלוּל**
**Sat 1 Sep**

## שַׁבָּת Shabbat פָּרָשַׁת כִּי־תָבוֹא Parashat Ki tavo

**Torah** 7 aliyot (minimum): כִּי־תָבוֹא Ki tavo
דְּבָרִים Devarim (Deuteronomy) 26:1–29:8

| | | | | |
|---|---|---|---|---|
| Annual: | ¹26:1–11 | ²26:12–15 | ³26:16–19 | ⁴27:1–10 |
| | ⁵27:11–28:6 | ⁶28:7–69° | ⁷29:1–8 | ᴹ29:6–8 |
| Triennial: | ¹26:12–15 | ²26:16–19 | ³27:1–3 | ⁴27:4–8 |
| | ⁵27:6–10° | ⁶27:11–28:3 | ⁷28:4–6 | ᴹ28:4–6 |

☞ °27:6–8 In the triennial reading, these verses, which are part of the 4th aliyah, are read again in the 5th aliyah.

☞ °28:15–69 This is the תּוֹכֵחָה tokheḥah, verses of rebuke and warning. Because of the ominous nature of these verses, do not divide this lengthy passage into shorter aliyot. However, the chanting may be divided among multiple readers. All the readers must be present at the Torah when the oleh/olah recites the first berakhah. This serves as an implicit appointment of all the readers as sheliḥim (agents) of the oleh/olah.
Chant this section in a somewhat **subdued** voice to symbolically minimize the trepidation that the congregation experiences upon hearing the message of these verses. Be sure that all words and te'amim (tropes, cantillations) remain **clearly** audible to the congregation.
However, for verses 7–14, voicing the promise of God's protection and reward, and for the conclusion, verse 69, chant as usual.

**Haftarah** יְשַׁעְיָהוּ Yesha'yahu (Isaiah) 60:1–22
(6th of 7 haftarot of consolation following Tish'ah Be'av)

מִנְחָה

**Torah** 3 aliyot from נִצָּבִים Nitsavim
דְּבָרִים Devarim (Deuteronomy) 29:9–28°
¹29:9–11 ²12–14 ³15–28 ᵂ315 ᴾ936

This is also the reading for the coming Monday and Thursday.

☞ °29:9–28 The reading extends through verse 28, which enables the correct configuration of the 3 aliyot.

**Elul 22 אֱלוּל**
**Sat 1 Sep**

## מוֹצָאֵי שַׁבָּת Motsa'ey Shabbat Conclusion of Shabbat

עַרְבִית

Saturday night Arvit as usual ᴸ264 ˢ281 ᵂ137 ᶠ200

+ Psalm 27 for the Season of Repentance ᴸ59 ˢ80 ᵂ92 ᶠ40
קַדִּישׁ יָתוֹם Mourner's Kaddish ᴸ58 ˢ82 ᵂ100 ᶠ52

| Elul 5778 | | | | | | |
|---|---|---|---|---|---|---|
| 1 | 2 | 3 | 4 | 5 | 6 | 7 |
| 8 | 9 | 10 | 11 | 12 | 13 | 14 |
| 15 | 16 | 17 | 18 | 19 | 20 | 21 |
| 22 | 23 | 24 | 25 | 26 | 27 | 28 |
| 29 | | | | | | |

| Aug \| Sep 2018 | | | | | | |
|---|---|---|---|---|---|---|
| 12 | 13 | 14 | 15 | 16 | 17 | 18 |
| 19 | 20 | 21 | 22 | 23 | 24 | 25 |
| 26 | 27 | 28 | 29 | 30 | 31 | 1 |
| 2 | 3 | 4 | 5 | 6 | 7 | 8 |
| 9 | | | | | | |

+ Add ✕ Omit ☞ Take note!

**Siddurim**
- **L** Lev Shalem for Shabbat and Festivals
- **S** Shabbat and Festival Sim Shalom
- **W** Weekday Sim Shalom
- **F** Full Sim Shalom (both editions)
- **P** Personal Edition of Full Sim Shalom

---

**Elul 22 אֱלוּל**
Sat 1 Sep (night)

## לֵיל סְלִיחוֹת Leyl Seliḥot
Seliḥot at Night

### Seliḥot — Penitential Prayers

We recite סְלִיחוֹת *seliḥot* prayers beginning the Saturday night before Rosh Hashanah to prepare ourselves for the upcoming Days of Repentance.

In a year when Rosh Hashanah begins on a Sunday night or Monday night, as in the coming year, we begin סְלִיחוֹת a week earlier so that we have more time to prepare in advance of Rosh Hashanah.

- Recite the first סְלִיחוֹת at midnight, an expression of our eagerness to begin the process of repentance.
- On subsequent days, recite סְלִיחוֹת before Shaḥarit every morning until Yom Kippur, except Shabbat and Rosh Hashanah.

The standard סְלִיחוֹת liturgy includes:
- אַשְׁרֵי *ashrey* and חֲצִי קַדִּישׁ Short Kaddish
- Various פִּיּוּטִים *piyyutim,* distinct liturgical poems for each day
- The Thirteen Attributes of God, . . . יי יי אֵ·ל רַחוּם וְחַנּוּן *adonay adonay el raḥum veḥannun* (based on Shemot 34:6–7)
- שְׁמַע קוֹלֵנוּ *shema kolenu,* אָשַׁמְנוּ *ashamnu,* and other סְלִיחוֹת prayers that appear in the Yom Kippur liturgy
- Short תַּחֲנוּן *taḥanun*
- קַדִּישׁ שָׁלֵם Full Kaddish

---

**Elul 28 אֱלוּל**
Sat 8 Sep

## שַׁבָּת Shabbat נִצָּבִים Parashat Nitsavim

**Torah** 7 aliyot (minimum): נִצָּבִים Nitsavim
דְּבָרִים Devarim (Deuteronomy) 29:9–30:20

| Annual: | | | | |
|---|---|---|---|---|
| | 1: 29:9–11 | 2: 29:12–14 | 3: 29:15–28 | 4: 30:1–6 |
| | 5: 30:7–10 | 6: 30:11–14 | 7: 30:15–20 | M: 30:15–20 (or 18–20) |

Triennial: Read the full parashah, divided as above.

**Haftarah** יְשַׁעְיָהוּ Yesha'yahu (Isaiah) 61:10–63:9
(last of 7 haftarot of consolation following Tish'ah Be'av)

✕ ~~Birkat Haḥodesh~~

מִנְחָה

**Torah** 3 aliyot from וַיֵּלֶךְ Vayelekh
דְּבָרִים Devarim (Deuteronomy) 31:1–13°
¹31:1–3 ²4–6 ³7–13 W317 P938

This is also the reading for the coming Thursday.

☞°31:1–13 The reading extends through verse 13, which enables the correct configuration of the 3 aliyot.

---

**Elul 29 אֱלוּל**
**Sat 8 Sep (evening)**

**מוֹצָאֵי שַׁבָּת Motsa'ey Shabbat Conclusion of Shabbat**
**עֶרֶב רֹאשׁ הַשָּׁנָה Erev Rosh Hashanah**
**Day before Rosh Hashanah**

עַרְבִית

Saturday night Arvit as usual through the Amidah L264 S281 W137 F200

✕ ~~חֲצִי קַדִּישׁ Short Kaddish~~
✕ ~~וִיהִי נֹעַם Vihi no'am~~
✕ ~~יוֹשֵׁב בְּסֵתֶר עֶלְיוֹן Yoshev beseter elyon~~
✕ ~~וְאַתָּה קָדוֹשׁ Ve'attah kadosh~~

קַדִּישׁ שָׁלֵם Full Kaddish L280 S294 W160 F688

Some recite הַבְדָּלָה Havdalah here. L283 S299 W165 F700

עָלֵינוּ Aleynu L281 S297 W163 F696
קַדִּישׁ יָתוֹם Mourner's Kaddish (some omit) L282 S298 W164 F698
+ Psalm 27 for the Season of Repentance L59 S80 W92 F40
קַדִּישׁ יָתוֹם Mourner's Kaddish L58 S82 W100 F52

הַבְדָּלָה Havdalah L283 S299 W165 F700

**Sun 9 Sep (morning)**

+ סְלִיחוֹת Seliḥot (penitential prayers) (including תַּחֲנוּן Taḥanun)

שַׁחֲרִית

✕ ~~תַּחֲנוּן Taḥanun~~
☞ לַמְנַצֵּחַ Lamenatse·aḥ (Psalm 20) W79 F154

✕ ~~תְּקִיעַת שׁוֹפָר Sounding the shofar~~

+ Psalm 27 for the Season of Repentance W92 F40
קַדִּישׁ יָתוֹם Mourner's Kaddish W100 F52

מִנְחָה ✕ ~~תַּחֲנוּן Taḥanun~~

| Elul 5778 | | | | | | |
|---|---|---|---|---|---|---|
| 1 | 2 | 3 | 4 | 5 | 6 | 7 |
| 8 | 9 | 10 | 11 | 12 | 13 | 14 |
| 15 | 16 | 17 | 18 | 19 | 20 | 21 |
| 22 | 23 | 24 | 25 | 26 | 27 | 28 |
| 29 | | | | | | |

| Aug \| Sep 2018 | | | | | | |
|---|---|---|---|---|---|---|
| 12 | 13 | 14 | 15 | 16 | 17 | 18 |
| 19 | 20 | 21 | 22 | 23 | 24 | 25 |
| 26 | 27 | 28 | 29 | 30 | 31 \| | 1 |
| 2 | 3 | 4 | 5 | 6 | 7 | 8 |
| 9 | | | | | | |

+ Add ✕ Omit ☞ Take note!

**Siddurim**
- **L** Lev Shalem for Shabbat and Festivals
- **S** Shabbat and Festival Sim Shalom
- **W** Weekday Sim Shalom
- **F** Full Sim Shalom (both editions)
- **P** Personal Edition of Full Sim Shalom

## Rosh Hashanah

### Looking Ahead to Rosh Hashanah

**Teki'at Shofar – Hearing the Sounds of the Shofar**

The *mitsvah* of hearing the sounds of the shofar on Rosh Hashanah is not restricted to the synagogue. For a person unable to attend a synagogue service, arrange a shofar blowing wherever the person is located, so the person can fulfill the *mitsvah*.

**Preparing to Celebrate with a New Fruit or with New Clothes**

The 2nd day of Rosh Hashanah is celebrated Monday evening with a "new" fruit (that is, a seasonal fruit that you have not yet tasted this season) or with new clothes, worn for the first time that evening. In preparation, obtain the new fruit or new clothes before Rosh Hashanah begins.

**THROUGH Hosha'na Rabbah (some continue through Shemini Atseret)**

**Mornings** — After Psalm for the Day:
- קַדִּישׁ יָתוֹם Mourner's Kaddish (some omit) L58 S82 W100 F52
- + Psalm 27 for the Season of Repentance L59 S80 W92 F40
- קַדִּישׁ יָתוֹם Mourner's Kaddish L58 S82 W100 F52

**Evenings** — After עָלֵינוּ Aleynu:
- קַדִּישׁ יָתוֹם Mourner's Kaddish (some omit) L58 S82 W100 F52
- + Psalm 27 for the Season of Repentance L59 S80 W92 F40
- קַדִּישׁ יָתוֹם Mourner's Kaddish L58 S82 W100 F52

### Before Rosh Hashanah

**Preparing a Flame for Yom Tov**

On Yom Tov, kindling a *new* fire is not permitted; however, the use of an *existing* fire for cooking or other purposes is permitted.

To light candles for Day 2 of Rosh Hashanah (Monday night), ensure that you have a fire burning before candle-lighting time for Day 1 (Sunday evening) that will continue to burn until after dark on Monday. For example:

- A burning candle that lasts for more than 25 hours
- A pilot light on a gas range (*not* a gas range with an electronic starter)

## Rosh Hashanah — Day 1 and Day 2

### Candle Lighting — Day 1

1. Before lighting candles, prepare a flame. See p. 8.
2. Light the candles at least 18 minutes before sunset.
3. Recite 2 בְּרָכוֹת *berakhot*: L79 S303 F718

בָּרוּךְ אַתָּה יי, אֱ־לֹהֵינוּ מֶלֶךְ הָעוֹלָם, אֲשֶׁר קִדְּשָׁנוּ בְּמִצְוֹתָיו
וְצִוָּנוּ לְהַדְלִיק נֵר שֶׁל יוֹם טוֹב.

Barukh attah adonay, eloheynu melekh ha'olam,
asher kiddeshanu bemitsvotav, vetsivvanu lehadlik ner shel yom tov.

בָּרוּךְ אַתָּה יי, אֱ־לֹהֵינוּ מֶלֶךְ הָעוֹלָם, שֶׁהֶחֱיָנוּ וְקִיְּמָנוּ וְהִגִּיעָנוּ לַזְּמַן הַזֶּה.

Barukh attah adonay, eloheynu melekh ha'olam,
sheheḥeyanu vekiyyemanu vehiggi'anu lazeman hazeh.

### Candle Lighting — Day 2

See p. 11.

### Rosh Hashanah Meals — Day 1 and Day 2

Enjoy festive meals evening and daytime, in the manner of Shabbat meals, with:

- Rosh Hashanah קִדּוּשׁ *kiddush:* Evening L432 S336 F748 Daytime L81 S335 F752
- הַמּוֹצִיא *hamotsi* recited over 2 whole חַלָּה *ḥallah* loaves or rolls L81 S313–14 F744|746

  Round חַלָּה loaves are traditional for Rosh Hashanah.

  After reciting הַמּוֹצִיא, it is customary to dip pieces of חַלָּה in honey (instead of the usual salt) and distribute them to those at the table.
- Apple dipped in honey (evening only, or evening and daytime)

  After eating the חַלָּה:

  1. Dip a piece of apple in honey.
  2. Recite the בְּרָכָה *berakhah* over tree fruit: S336 F715

     בָּרוּךְ אַתָּה יי, אֱ־לֹהֵינוּ מֶלֶךְ הָעוֹלָם, בּוֹרֵא פְּרִי הָעֵץ.

     Barukh attah adonay, eloheynu melekh ha'olam, borey peri ha'ets.
  3. Eat the honey-dipped piece of apple.
  4. Recite the prayer for a sweet year: S336 F750

     יְהִי רָצוֹן מִלְּפָנֶיךָ, יי אֱ־לֹהֵינוּ וֵאלֹהֵי אֲבוֹתֵינוּ,
     שֶׁתְּחַדֵּשׁ עָלֵינוּ שָׁנָה טוֹבָה וּמְתוּקָה.

     Yehi ratson milefanekha, adonay eloheynu veylohey avoteynu,
     sheteḥaddesh aleynu shanah tovah umtukah.
- בִּרְכַּת הַמָּזוֹן *birkat hamazon* with Rosh Hashanah additions (see yellow box, p. 10)
- Festive singing

| Tishrey 5779 | | | | | | |
|---|---|---|---|---|---|---|
| | 1 | 2 | 3 | 4 | 5 | 6 |
| 7 | 8 | 9 | 10 | 11 | 12 | 13 |
| 14 | 15 | 16 | 17 | 18 | 19 | 20 |
| 21 | 22 | 23 | 24 | 25 | 26 | 27 |
| 28 | 29 | 30 | | | | |

| Sep \| Oct 2018 | | | | | | |
|---|---|---|---|---|---|---|
| | 10 | 11 | 12 | 13 | 14 | 15 |
| 16 | 17 | 18 | 19 | 20 | 21 | 22 |
| 23 | 24 | 25 | 26 | 27 | 28 | 29 |
| 30 | 1 | 2 | 3 | 4 | 5 | 6 |
| 7 | 8 | 9 | | | | |

+ Add ✕ Omit ☞ Take note!

**Siddurim**
- **L** Lev Shalem for Shabbat and Festivals
- **S** Shabbat and Festival Sim Shalom
- **W** Weekday Sim Shalom
- **F** Full Sim Shalom (both editions)
- **P** Personal Edition of Full Sim Shalom



## Tishrey 1 תִּשְׁרֵי — רֹאשׁ הַשָּׁנָה Rosh Hashanah — Day 1

**Sun 9 Sep** (evening)

**DURING Rosh Hashanah**

**Birkat Hamazon:**

+ יַעֲלֶה וְיָבוֹא Ya'aleh veyavo for Rosh Hashanah
L90|95 S340|347 W233|239 F762|780

+ הָרַחֲמָן Haraḥaman for Rosh Hashanah
L92|96 S343 W236|240 F768

**עַרְבִית** Follow the service in the maḥzor.

**At home** See "Rosh Hashanah Meals — Day 1 and Day 2," p. 9.

**Mon 10 Sep** (morning) Follow the service in the maḥzor.

**1st scroll** 5 aliyot from וַיֵּרָא Vayera
בְּרֵאשִׁית Bereshit (Genesis) 21:1–34
1 21:1–4 2 5–12 3 13–21 4 22–27 5 28–34

Use Yamim Nora'im cantillation.

**2nd scroll** Maftir aliyah from פִּינְחָס Pineḥas
M בְּמִדְבַּר Bemidbar (Numbers) 29:1–6

Use Yamim Nora'im cantillation.

**Haftarah** for Rosh Hashanah — Day 1
שְׁמוּאֵל א' 1 Shemu'el (1 Samuel) 1:1–2:10

**קִדּוּשָׁא רַבָּא** **Daytime Kiddush for Rosh Hashanah:** L81 S335 F746
תִּקְעוּ בַחֹדֶשׁ שׁוֹפָר Tik'u vaḥodesh shofar (Psalm 81:4–5)
בּוֹרֵא פְּרִי הַגָּפֶן Bo·re peri hagafen

**At home** See "Rosh Hashanah Meals — Day 1 and Day 2," p. 9.

**Tashlikh**

In the afternoon of Day 1 of Rosh Hashanah (if Shabbat, then Day 2), it is customary to walk to a natural body of water for the תַּשְׁלִיךְ *tashlikh* ceremony, which is based on the final three verses in the book of the prophet מִיכָה Mikhah (Micah). Symbolically, we cast away our sins—as if into the depths of the sea—and seek God's forgiveness. Many editions of the maḥzor include the text of the ceremony. If you are unable to accomplish this ritual on Rosh Hashanah, you can perform it until Hosha'na Rabbah, although before Yom Kippur is preferable.

**מִנְחָה** Follow the service in the maḥzor.

**In the afternoon** Walk to a natural body of water, and recite תַּשְׁלִיךְ Tashlikh. For information, see p. 10.

**Candle Lighting for Yom Tov — Day 2**

Day 1 ends after dark: when 3 stars appear, or at least 25 minutes after sunset (at least 43 minutes after the time set for lighting candles on Day 1). Some wait longer. For the appropriate time in your community, consult your rabbi.

1. Wait until Day 1 ends.
2. Do not *strike* a match. Instead, transfer fire to the candles from an *existing* flame (see p. 8) by inserting a match or other stick into the flame.
3. Do not *extinguish* the match or stick. Instead, place it on a non-flammable tray or dish, and let it self-extinguish. Alternately, a wood *safety* match held vertically (flame up) usually self-extinguishes quickly.
4. Recite the 2 בְּרָכוֹת *berakhot* (see p. 9). L79 S303 F718

**Celebrating with a New Fruit or New Clothes**

During candle lighting and Kiddush, have the new fruit on the dinner table or wear the new article of clothing (see p. 8). When you recite שֶׁהֶחֱיָנוּ *sheheḥeyanu*, have in mind that you are reciting it for the new fruit or clothes as well.

## Tishrey 2 תִּשְׁרֵי — רֹאשׁ הַשָּׁנָה Rosh Hashanah — Day 2

**Mon 10 Sep**

**עַרְבִית** Follow the service in the maḥzor.

**At home** See "Candle Lighting — Day 2," above.
See "Rosh Hashanah Meals — Day 1 and Day 2," p. 9.

**Tue 11 Sep (morning)** Follow the service in the maḥzor.

**1st scroll** 5 aliyot from וַיֵּרָא Vayera
בְּרֵאשִׁית Bereshit (Genesis) 22:1–24
[1]22:1–3 [2]4–8 [3]9–14 [4]15–19 [5]20–24

Use Yamim Nora'im cantillation.

**2nd scroll** Maftir aliyah from פִּינְחָס Pineḥas
[M]בְּמִדְבַּר Bemidbar (Numbers) 29:1–6

Use Yamim Nora'im cantillation.

| Tishrey 5779 | | | | | | |
|---|---|---|---|---|---|---|
| | 1 | 2 | 3 | 4 | 5 | 6 |
| 7 | 8 | 9 | 10 | 11 | 12 | 13 |
| 14 | 15 | 16 | 17 | 18 | 19 | 20 |
| 21 | 22 | 23 | 24 | 25 | 26 | 27 |
| 28 | 29 | 30 | | | | |

| Sep \| Oct 2018 | | | | | | |
|---|---|---|---|---|---|---|
| | 10 | 11 | 12 | 13 | 14 | 15 |
| 16 | 17 | 18 | 19 | 20 | 21 | 22 |
| 23 | 24 | 25 | 26 | 27 | 28 | 29 |
| 30 \| | 1 | 2 | 3 | 4 | 5 | 6 |
| 7 | 8 | 9 | | | | |

+ Add ✕ Omit ☞ Take note!

**Siddurim**
- **L** Lev Shalem for Shabbat and Festivals
- **S** Shabbat and Festival Sim Shalom
- **W** Weekday Sim Shalom
- **F** Full Sim Shalom (both editions)
- **P** Personal Edition of Full Sim Shalom



**Haftarah** for Rosh Hashanah — Day 2
יִרְמְיָהוּ Yirmeyahu (Jeremiah) 31:1–19 (31:2–20 in some books)

**קִדּוּשָׁא רַבָּא** — **Daytime Kiddush for Rosh Hashanah:** L81 S335 F746
תִּקְעוּ בַחֹדֶשׁ שׁוֹפָר Tik'u vaḥodesh shofar (Psalm 81:4–5)
בּוֹרֵא פְּרִי הַגָּפֶן Bo·re peri hagafen

**At home** — See "Rosh Hashanah Meals — Day 1 and Day 2," p. 9.

**מִנְחָה** — Follow the service in the maḥzor.

**DURING Aseret Yemey Teshuvah (10 Days of Repentance: Rosh Hashanah – Yom Kippur)**

**Modifications for Aseret Yemey Teshuvah**

**Shabbat and weekdays**

**Every Kaddish (2nd paragraph):**
✕ ~~לְעֵלָּא le'eyla~~
+ לְעֵלָּא לְעֵלָּא le'eyla le'eyla (not לְעֵלָּא וּלְעֵלָּא le'eyla ul'eyla)

**Every Amidah:**
+ In the 1st בְּרָכָה berakhah, add זָכְרֵנוּ Zokhrenu.
+ In the 2nd בְּרָכָה, add מִי כָמוֹךָ Mi khamokha.

Conclusion of the 3rd בְּרָכָה:
✕ ~~הָאֵ־ל הַקָּדוֹשׁ Ha'el hakadosh~~
+ הַמֶּלֶךְ הַקָּדוֹשׁ Hamelekh hakadosh.

+ In the next-to-last בְּרָכָה, add וּכְתֹב Ukhtov.
+ In the last בְּרָכָה, add בְּסֵפֶר חַיִּים Besefer ḥayyim.

Conclusion of the last בְּרָכָה:
✕ ~~הַמְבָרֵךְ . . . בַּשָּׁלוֹם Hamevarekh . . . bashalom~~
+ עוֹשֵׂה הַשָּׁלוֹם Oseh hashalom.

+ **Every Shaharit after יִשְׁתַּבַּח Yishtabbaḥ (some omit):**
Open ark.
Repeat each verse after the sheliaḥ/sheliḥat tsibbur:
שִׁיר הַמַּעֲלוֹת, מִמַּעֲמַקִּים Shir hama'alot, mima'amakkim
(Psalm 130) L450 S254 W62 F134
Close ark.

**Weekdays only** + סְלִיחוֹת Seliḥot (penitential prayers) before Shaharit

**Every weekday Amidah:**
Conclusion of הָשִׁיבָה שׁוֹפְטֵינוּ Hashiva shofeteynu:
✕ ~~מֶלֶךְ אוֹהֵב צְדָקָה וּמִשְׁפָּט Melekh ohev tsedakah umishpat~~
+ הַמֶּלֶךְ הַמִּשְׁפָּט Hamelekh hamishpat.

+ אָבִינוּ מַלְכֵּנוּ Avinu malkenu W57 F124|188
☞ תַּחֲנוּן Taḥanun

**Tishrey 3 תִּשְׁרֵי**
**Tue 11 Sep** (evening)

# צוֹם גְּדַלְיָה Tsom Gedalyah

**Fast of Gedalyah** (communal fast, begins Wednesday at dawn)
**מוֹצָאֵי רֹאשׁ הַשָּׁנָה Motsa'ey Rosh Hashanah**
**Conclusion of Rosh Hashanah**



## Tsom Gedalyah

After Nebuchadnezzar razed Jerusalem in 586 B.C.E., he installed Gedalyah ben Aḥikam as governor of Judah, which was by then a Babylonian province. Later, a Jew was recruited to kill Gedalyah. After the assassination of the governor, the few Jews remaining in Jerusalem dispersed; the last vestiges of Jewish control over Jerusalem ended. Tsom Gedalyah commemorates these events.

- This is a minor fast day, so called because the fast does not begin until dawn.
- The fast (from both eating and drinking) lasts until dark (a minimum of 25 minutes after sunset).
- *Sheliḥey tsibbur,* Torah readers, and those called for *aliyot* should be fasting.
- The preferred fast-day procedures apply when at least six of those who are counted for a *minyan* are fasting.
- If it is ascertained (without causing embarrassment) that fewer than six are fasting, follow the procedures printed in gray and marked with ✦.

**עַרְבִית**

+ Modifications for Aseret Yemey Teshuvah (see p. 12)

Arvit for weekdays L264 S281 W137 F200

**Weekday Amidah:**

+ אַתָּה חוֹנַנְתָּנוּ Attah ḥonantanu L272 S287 W143 F212

קַדִּישׁ שָׁלֵם Full Kaddish L280 S294 W160 F222

Some recite הַבְדָּלָה Havdalah here. L283 S299 W165 F700
For instructions, see below.

עָלֵינוּ Aleynu L281 S297 W163 F696
קַדִּישׁ יָתוֹם Mourner's Kaddish (some omit) L282 S298 W164 F698
+ Psalm 27 for the Season of Repentance L59 S80 W92 F40
קַדִּישׁ יָתוֹם Mourner's Kaddish L58 S82 W100 F52

+ **Havdalah:** L283 S299 W165 F700
✕ ~~הִנֵּה אֵ-ל יְשׁוּעָתִי Hinneh el yeshu'ati~~
בּוֹרֵא פְּרִי הַגָּפֶן Bo·re peri hagafen
✕ ~~בּוֹרֵא מִינֵי בְשָׂמִים Bo·re miney vesamim~~
✕ ~~בּוֹרֵא מְאוֹרֵי הָאֵשׁ Bo·re me'orey ha'esh~~
הַמַּבְדִּיל בֵּין קֹדֶשׁ לְחֹל Hamavdil beyn kodesh leḥol

**Tishrey 5779**

| | | | | | | |
|---|---|---|---|---|---|---|
| | 1 | 2 | 3 | 4 | 5 | 6 |
| 7 | 8 | 9 | 10 | 11 | 12 | 13 |
| 14 | 15 | 16 | 17 | 18 | 19 | 20 |
| 21 | 22 | 23 | 24 | 25 | 26 | 27 |
| 28 | 29 | 30 | | | | |

**Sep | Oct 2018**

| | | | | | | |
|---|---|---|---|---|---|---|
| | 10 | 11 | 12 | 13 | 14 | 15 |
| 16 | 17 | 18 | 19 | 20 | 21 | 22 |
| 23 | 24 | 25 | 26 | 27 | 28 | 29 |
| 30 | 1 | 2 | 3 | 4 | 5 | 6 |
| 7 | 8 | 9 | | | | |

+ Add ✕ Omit ☞ Take note!

**Siddurim**

- **L** Lev Shalem for Shabbat and Festivals
- **S** Shabbat and Festival Sim Shalom
- **W** Weekday Sim Shalom
- **F** Full Sim Shalom (both editions)
- **P** Personal Edition of Full Sim Shalom



## Wed 12 Sep (morning)

+ Modifications for Aseret Yemey Teshuvah (see p. 12)

+ סְלִיחוֹת Seliḥot (penitential prayers) before Shaḥarit.

### שַׁחֲרִית

+ **After יִשְׁתַּבַּח Yishtabbaḥ (some omit):**
Open ark.
Repeat each verse after the sheliaḥ/sheliḥat tsibbur:
שִׁיר הַמַּעֲלוֹת, מִמַּעֲמַקִּים Shir hama'alot, mima'amakkim (Psalm 130) W62 F134
Close ark.

**Silent weekday Amidah:**
Do not add עֲנֵנוּ Anenu.

**Repetition of the weekday Amidah:**

6 or more fasting + עֲנֵנוּ Anenu, before רְפָאֵנוּ Refa'enu W38 F110

Fewer than 6 fasting ✦ Add עֲנֵנוּ Anenu in שׁוֹמֵעַ תְּפִלָּה Shome·a tefillah.
Replace תַּעֲנִיתֵנוּ ta'anitenu (6th word) with הַתַּעֲנִית הַזֶּה hata'anit hazeh. W38 F110

+ אָבִינוּ מַלְכֵּנוּ Avinu malkenu W57 F124
with lines for between Rosh Hashanah and Yom Kippur (omit lines for fast days)

☞ תַּחֲנוּן Taḥanun W62 F132
חֲצִי קַדִּישׁ Short Kaddish W64 F136

Fewer than 6 fasting ✦ Omit the entire Torah service.
Continue with אַשְׁרֵי Ashrey.

6 or more fasting + **TORAH SERVICE** W65 F138
Remove **1** Torah scroll from ark.

**Torah** 3 aliyot from כִּי תִשָּׂא Ki tissa
שְׁמוֹת Shemot (Exodus) 32:11–14, 34:1–10
[1] 32:11–14° [2] 34:1–3 [3] 4–10° W341 P979

☞ °At each of the 3 passages indicated below, follow this procedure:
1. The reader pauses before the indicated text.
2. The congregation recites the indicated text.
3. Afterward, the reader chants the indicated text in the manner of the cantillation of High Holiday Torah reading.

32:12 שׁוּב מֵחֲרוֹן אַפֶּךָ וְהִנָּחֵם עַל־הָרָעָה לְעַמֶּךָ׃

34:6–7 יי | יי אֵ·ל רַחוּם וְחַנּוּן אֶרֶךְ אַפַּיִם וְרַב־חֶסֶד וֶאֱמֶת׃
נֹצֵר חֶסֶד לָאֲלָפִים נֹשֵׂא עָוֺן וָפֶשַׁע וְחַטָּאָה וְנַקֵּה

34:9 וְסָלַחְתָּ לַעֲוֺנֵנוּ וּלְחַטָּאתֵנוּ | וּנְחַלְתָּנוּ׃
To preserve the sense of this passage, maintain the appropriate pause after the טִפְּחָא (וּלְחַטָּאתֵנוּ).

חֲצִי קַדִּישׁ Short Kaddish W71 F146
Open, raise, display, and wrap scroll.
Return scroll to ark. W76 F150

**All minyanim** אַשְׁרֵי Ashrey W78 F152
☞ לַמְנַצֵּחַ Lamenatse·aḥ (Psalm 20) W79 F154
Conclude the service as on a usual weekday.

**מִנְחָה** + Modifications for Aseret Yemey Teshuvah (see p. 12)

אַשְׁרֵי Ashrey W120 F164
חֲצִי קַדִּישׁ Short Kaddish W121 F166

**Fewer than 6 fasting** ✦ Omit the entire Torah service.
Continue with the silent Amidah.

**6 or more fasting** + **TORAH SERVICE** W65 F138

Remove **1** Torah scroll from ark.

**Torah** 3 aliyot from כִּי תִשָּׂא Ki tissa
שְׁמוֹת Shemot (Exodus) 32:11–14, 34:1–10
[1]32:11–14° [2]34:1–3 [M]4–10° W341 P979

☞ °Follow the same procedure as for the morning reading. See p. 14.

☞ Do not recite חֲצִי קַדִּישׁ Short Kaddish after maftir aliyah.
Open, raise, display, and wrap scroll.

Recite the בְּרָכָה berakhah before the haftarah. W74 F410 P989

**Haftarah** יְשַׁעְיָהוּ Yesha'yahu (Isaiah) 55:6–56:8 W342 P980

Recite the 3 concluding haftarah blessings,
through מָגֵן דָּוִד Magen david. W74 F410 P989.

Return scroll to ark. W76 F150
חֲצִי קַדִּישׁ Short Kaddish W121 F166

**All minyanim** **Silent weekday Amidah:**
**If fasting** + עֲנֵנוּ Anenu, in שׁוֹמֵעַ תְּפִלָּה Shome·a tefillah W127 F178
**All** ✕ ~~שָׁלוֹם רָב Shalom rav~~
+ שִׂים שָׁלוֹם Sim shalom W131 F184

| Tishrey 5779 | | | | | | | Sep \| Oct 2018 | | | | | | |
|---|---|---|---|---|---|---|---|---|---|---|---|---|---|
| | 1 | 2 | 3 | 4 | 5 | 6 | | 10 | 11 | 12 | 13 | 14 | 15 |
| 7 | 8 | 9 | 10 | 11 | 12 | 13 | 16 | 17 | 18 | 19 | 20 | 21 | 22 |
| 14 | 15 | 16 | 17 | 18 | 19 | 20 | 23 | 24 | 25 | 26 | 27 | 28 | 29 |
| 21 | 22 | 23 | 24 | 25 | 26 | 27 | 30 \| | 1 | 2 | 3 | 4 | 5 | 6 |
| 28 | 29 | 30 | | | | | 7 | 8 | 9 | | | | |

+ Add ✕ Omit ☞ Take note!

**Siddurim**
- **L** Lev Shalem for Shabbat and Festivals
- **S** Shabbat and Festival Sim Shalom
- **W** Weekday Sim Shalom
- **F** Full Sim Shalom (both editions)
- **P** Personal Edition of Full Sim Shalom



**Repetition of the weekday Amidah:**

6 or more fasting + עֲנֵנוּ Anenu, before רְפָאֵנוּ Refa'enu W124 F172

Fewer than 6 fasting ✦ Add עֲנֵנוּ Anenu in שׁוֹמֵעַ תְּפִלָּה Shome·a tefillah. Replace תַּעֲנִיתֵנוּ ta'anitenu (6th word) with הַתַּעֲנִית הַזֶּה hata'anit hazeh. W127 F172

All minyanim + בִּרְכַּת כֹּהֲנִים Birkat kohanim W131 F184
✕ ~~שָׁלוֹם רָב Shalom rav~~
+ שִׂים שָׁלוֹם Sim shalom W131 F184

+ אָבִינוּ מַלְכֵּנוּ Avinu malkenu W57 F124
with lines for between Rosh Hashanah and Yom Kippur (omit lines for fast days)

☞ תַּחֲנוּן Tahanun W132 F192

קַדִּישׁ שָׁלֵם Full Kaddish W134 F194
Conclude Minhah as on a usual weekday.

---

**Tishrey 4 תִּשְׁרֵי**

Wed 12 Sep (evening) + Modifications for Aseret Yemey Teshuvah (see p. 12)

Thu 13 Sep (daytime) + Modifications for Aseret Yemey Teshuvah (see p. 12)

**Torah** 3 aliyot from וַיֵּלֶךְ Vayelekh
דְּבָרִים Devarim (Deuteronomy) 31:1–13°
¹31:1–3 ²4–6 ³7–13 W317 P938

☞ °31:1–13 The reading extends through verse 13, which enables the correct configuration of the 3 aliyot.

---

**Tishrey 5 תִּשְׁרֵי** **עֶרֶב שַׁבָּת Erev Shabbat Day before Shabbat**

Thu 13 Sep עַרְבִית + Modifications for Aseret Yemey Teshuvah (see p. 12)

Fri 14 Sep שַׁחֲרִית + Modifications for Aseret Yemey Teshuvah (see p. 12)

מִנְחָה + Modifications for Aseret Yemey Teshuvah (see p. 12)
✕ ~~אָבִינוּ מַלְכֵּנוּ Avinu malkenu~~ (as on all Friday afternoons)
✕ ~~תַּחֲנוּן Tahanun~~ (as on all Friday afternoons)

## Tishrey 6 תִּשְׁרֵי
Fri 14 Sep

## שַׁבָּת Shabbat פָּרָשַׁת וַיֵּלֶךְ Parashat Vayelekh
## שַׁבַּת שׁוּבָה Shabbat Shuvah Shabbat of Repentance

**קַבָּלַת שַׁבָּת**

Kabbalat Shabbat as on a usual Shabbat

+ Modifications for Aseret Yemey Teshuvah (see p. 12)

**עַרְבִית**

Shabbat Arvit as usual through
וַיְכֻלּוּ Vaykhullu L53 S47 F314

**מָגֵן אָבוֹת Magen avot:** L53 S47 F314
✕ ~~הָאֵ־ל הַקָּדוֹשׁ Ha'el Hakadosh~~
+ הַמֶּלֶךְ הַקָּדוֹשׁ Hamelekh Hakadosh

Conclude as on a usual Shabbat.

+ Psalm 27 for the Season of Repentance L59 S80 F40
קַדִּישׁ יָתוֹם Mourner's Kaddish L58 S82 F52

Sat 15 Sep

**שַׁחֲרִית**

+ Modifications for Aseret Yemey Teshuvah (see p. 12)

+ **After יִשְׁתַּבַּח Yishtabbaḥ (some omit):**
Open ark.
Repeat each verse after the sheliaḥ/sheliḥat tsibbur:
שִׁיר הַמַּעֲלוֹת, מִמַּעֲמַקִּים Shir hama'alot, mima'amakkim
(Psalm 130) L450 S254 F134
Close ark.

**Torah** 7 aliyot (minimum): וַיֵּלֶךְ Vayelekh
דְּבָרִים Devarim (Deuteronomy) 31:1–30

| | | | | |
|---|---|---|---|---|
| Annual: | 1 31:1–3 | 2 31:4–6 | 3 31:7–9 | 4 31:10–13 |
| | 5 31:14–19 | 6 31:20–24 | 7 31:25–30 | M 31:28–30 |

Triennial: Read the full parashah, divided as above.

**Haftarah** for Shabbat Shuvah (when וַיֵּלֶךְ Vayelekh is read)
הוֹשֵׁעַ Hoshe·a (Hosea) 14:2–10 + מִיכָה Mikhah (Micah) 7:18–20°

☞ °There are other selections found in various ḥumashim. This reading is recommended when the parashah is וַיֵּלֶךְ Vayelekh.

**מוּסָף**

+ Modifications for Aseret Yemey Teshuvah (see p. 12)

**Sep 15** 6 תִשְׁרֵי
**Sep 15** 7 תִּשְׁרֵי
**Sep 16**

| Tishrey 5779 | | | | | | Sep \| Oct 2018 | | | | | |
|---|---|---|---|---|---|---|---|---|---|---|---|
| 1 | 2 | 3 | 4 | 5 | 6 | 10 | 11 | 12 | 13 | 14 | 15 |
| 7 | 8 | 9 | 10 | 11 | 12 | 13 | 16 | 17 | 18 | 19 | 20 | 21 | 22 |
| 14 | 15 | 16 | 17 | 18 | 19 | 20 | 23 | 24 | 25 | 26 | 27 | 28 | 29 |
| 21 | 22 | 23 | 24 | 25 | 26 | 27 | 30 \| 1 | 2 | 3 | 4 | 5 | 6 |
| 28 | 29 | 30 | | | | 7 | 8 | 9 | | | |

**+** Add   **✕** Omit   ☞ Take note!

**Siddurim**
**L** Lev Shalem for Shabbat and Festivals
**S** Shabbat and Festival Sim Shalom
**W** Weekday Sim Shalom
**F** Full Sim Shalom (both editions)
**P** Personal Edition of Full Sim Shalom

---

## Yemey Teshuvah

מִנְחָה **+** Modifications for Aseret Yᵉmey Tᵉshuvah (see p. 12)

> **Torah** 3 aliyot from הַאֲזִינוּ Ha'ᵃzinu
> דְּבָרִים Dᵉvarim (Deuteronomy) 32:1–12°
> ¹32:1–3   ²4–6°   ³7–12          **W**318 **P**939

This is also the reading for the coming Monday and Thursday.

☞°32:1–12  The reading extends through verse 12, which enables the correct configuration of the 3 aliyot.

☞°32:6  Read הַל־אֲדֹנָי hal-adonay. For more information, see p. 25.

☞ צִדְקָתְךָ צֶדֶק Tsidkatᵉkha tsedek   **L**230 **S**239 **W**183 **F**584

---

**Tishrey 7** תִּשְׁרֵי
**Sat 15 Sep**

מוֹצָאֵי שַׁבָּת Motsa'ey Shabbat   Conclusion of Shabbat

עַרְבִית **+** Modifications for Aseret Yᵉmey Tᵉshuvah (see p. 12)

Saturday night Arvit as usual   **L**264 **S**281 **W**137 **F**200
through the Amidah

✕ ~~חֲצִי קַדִּישׁ Short Kaddish~~
✕ ~~וִיהִי נֹעַם Vihi no'am~~
✕ ~~יוֹשֵׁב בְּסֵתֶר עֶלְיוֹן Yoshev bᵉseter elyon~~
✕ ~~וְאַתָּה קָדוֹשׁ Vᵉ'attah kadosh~~

קַדִּישׁ שָׁלֵם Full Kaddish   **L**280 **S**294 **W**160 **F**688

Some recite הַבְדָּלָה Havdalah here.   **L**283 **S**299 **W**165 **F**700

עָלֵינוּ Aleynu   **L**281 **S**297 **W**163 **F**696
קַדִּישׁ יָתוֹם Mourner's Kaddish (some omit)   **L**282 **S**298 **W**164 **F**698
**+** Psalm 27 for the Season of Repentance   **L**59 **S**80 **W**92 **F**40
קַדִּישׁ יָתוֹם Mourner's Kaddish   **L**58 **S**82 **W**100 **F**52
הַבְדָּלָה Havdalah   **L**283 **S**299 **W**165 **F**700

**Sun 16 Sep (daytime)**   **+** Modifications for Aseret Yᵉmey Tᵉshuvah (see p. 12)

**Tishrey 8 תִּשְׁרֵי**
**Sun 16 Sep (evening)** + Modifications for Aseret Yemey Teshuvah (see p. 12)
**Mon 17 Sep (daytime)** + Modifications for Aseret Yemey Teshuvah (see p. 12)

**Torah** 3 aliyot from הַאֲזִינוּ Ha'azinu
דְּבָרִים Devarim (Deuteronomy) 32:1–12°
¹32:1–3 ²4–6° ³7–12 W318 P939

☞°32:1–12 The reading extends through verse 12, which enables the correct configuration of the 3 aliyot.

☞°32:6 Read הַלְאֲ·דֹנָי hal-adonay. For more information, see p. 25.

---

**Tishrey 9 תִּשְׁרֵי**
**Mon 17 Sep**

**עֶרֶב יוֹם כִּפּוּר Erev Yom Kippur**
**Day before Yom Kippur**

**עַרְבִית** + Modifications for Aseret Yemey Teshuvah (see p. 12)

**Tue 18 Sep (morning)** + Modifications for Aseret Yemey Teshuvah (see p. 12)

+ סְלִיחוֹת Seliḥot (penitential prayers)

**שַׁחֲרִית** ✕ ~~מִזְמוֹר לְתוֹדָה Mizmor letodah (Psalm 100)~~

+ **After יִשְׁתַּבַּח Yishtabbaḥ (some omit):**
Open ark.
Repeat each verse after the sheliaḥ/sheliḥat tsibbur:
שִׁיר הַמַּעֲלוֹת, מִמַּעֲמַקִּים Shir hama'alot, mima'amakkim (Psalm 130) L450 W62 F134
Close ark.

✕ ~~אָבִינוּ מַלְכֵּנוּ Avinu malkenu~~
✕ ~~תַּחֲנוּן Taḥanun~~

אַשְׁרֵי Ashrey L214 W78 F152
✕ ~~לַמְנַצֵּחַ Lamenatse·aḥ (Psalm 20)~~
וּבָא לְצִיּוֹן Uva letsiyyon L216 W80 F156
Conclude Shaḥarit as on a usual weekday.

**מִנְחָה** Because of additions to the silent Amidah, use the maḥzor for this Minḥah service.

אַשְׁרֵי Ashrey
חֲצִי קַדִּישׁ Short Kaddish

**Silent weekday Amidah:**

+ אָשַׁמְנוּ Ashamnu
+ עַל חֵטְא Al ḥet

**Repetition of the weekday Amidah:**

✕ ~~אָשַׁמְנוּ Ashamnu~~
✕ ~~עַל חֵטְא Al ḥet~~

✕ ~~אָבִינוּ מַלְכֵּנוּ Avinu malkenu~~
✕ ~~תַּחֲנוּן Taḥanun~~

קַדִּישׁ שָׁלֵם Full Kaddish

Conclude Minḥah as usual.

## Yom Kippur

### Before Yom Kippur

**Last Meal before the Fast**

The Rabbis considered it a *mitsvah* to eat a festive סְעוּדָה מַפְסֶקֶת *se'udah mafseket* (last meal before a fast) before Yom Kippur begins. If possible, attend Minḥah first and then eat.

**Memorial Candle**

If a parent or other close relative has died, before lighting the holiday candles, light a memorial candle that will burn throughout Yom Kippur.

**Resting Candle**

At the conclusion of Yom Kippur, the candle used for Havdalah should be lit from נֵר שֶׁשָּׁבַת *ner sheshavat* "a candle that rested," that is, a flame that was burning before Yom Kippur and burned throughout Yom Kippur. Therefore, before Yom Kippur begins, light a long-burning candle for this purpose.

A candle lit as a memorial candle also may serve as the resting candle. Ensure it is a candle that will burn long enough (about 26 hours) so that it will be available at the conclusion of Yom Kippur. Many memorial candles do not burn long enough.

## Yom Kippur Prohibitions and Practices

The Torah (Vayikra 23:32) refers to Yom Kippur as שַׁבַּת שַׁבָּתוֹן *shabbat shabbaton* (a sabbath of complete rest). Thus, even when Yom Kippur does not fall on Shabbat, cooking, use of fire, and carrying are not permitted. Unlike other Yom Tov days, Yom Kippur always takes on all the restrictions of Shabbat.

In addition, the following are not permitted until dark after Yom Kippur:

- Eating and drinking
- Sexual relations
- Bathing (except for minimal washing to remove dirt or after using the toilet)
- Using skin or bath oils
- Wearing leather shoes

Wearing white is customary. During services, some wear a *kittel* (plain white robe).

## Before Leaving for the Synagogue

### Candle Lighting for Yom Kippur

1. Light the candles at least 18 minutes before sunset.
2. Recite 2 בְּרָכוֹת *berakhot:* S303 F719

בָּרוּךְ אַתָּה יי, אֱ־לֹהֵינוּ מֶלֶךְ הָעוֹלָם, אֲשֶׁר קִדְּשָׁנוּ בְּמִצְוֹתָיו
וְצִוָּנוּ לְהַדְלִיק נֵר שֶׁל יוֹם הַכִּפּוּרִים.

Barukh attah adonay, eloheynu melekh ha'olam, asher kiddeshanu bemitsvotav vetsivvanu lehadlik ner shel yom hakippurim.

בָּרוּךְ אַתָּה יי, אֱ־לֹהֵינוּ מֶלֶךְ הָעוֹלָם, שֶׁהֶחֱיָנוּ וְקִיְּמָנוּ וְהִגִּיעָנוּ לַזְּמַן הַזֶּה.

Barukh attah adonay, eloheynu melekh ha'olam, sheheḥeyanu vekiyyemanu vehiggi'anu lazeman hazeh.

### Blessing the Children

Before leaving for the synagogue, bless the children, L75 S311 F722 even if it is not your custom to do so on Shabbat or Yom Tov.

## Before Kol Nidrey

1. Arrive at the synagogue before sunset, while it is still light.
2. Wear a טַלִּית *tallit*. Before putting it on, recite the בְּרָכָה *berakhah*. L102 S62 W2 F4.

---

**Tishrey 10 תִּשְׁרֵי**
**Tue 18 Sep (evening)**

## יוֹם כִּפּוּר Yom Kippur

**At home**

Before leaving for the synagogue:
Light the candles, and bless the children.
See "Candle Lighting for Yom Kippur" and "Blessing the Children," above.

**In the synagogue**

Before sunset:
☞ Put on a טַלִּית tallit. See "Before Kol Nidrey," above.

| Tishrey 5779 | | | | | | | Sep \| Oct 2018 | | | | | | |
|---|---|---|---|---|---|---|---|---|---|---|---|---|---|
| | 1 | 2 | 3 | 4 | 5 | 6 | | 10 | 11 | 12 | 13 | 14 | 15 |
| 7 | 8 | 9 | 10 | 11 | 12 | 13 | 16 | 17 | 18 | 19 | 20 | 21 | 22 |
| 14 | 15 | 16 | 17 | 18 | 19 | 20 | 23 | 24 | 25 | 26 | 27 | 28 | 29 |
| 21 | 22 | 23 | 24 | 25 | 26 | 27 | 30 \| | 1 | 2 | 3 | 4 | 5 | 6 |
| 28 | 29 | 30 | | | | | 7 | 8 | 9 | | | | |

+ Add ✕ Omit ☞ Take note!

**Siddurim**
- **L** Lev Shalem for Shabbat and Festivals
- **S** Shabbat and Festival Sim Shalom
- **W** Weekday Sim Shalom
- **F** Full Sim Shalom (both editions)
- **P** Personal Edition of Full Sim Shalom



**כָּל־נִדְרֵי**

Remove 2 or more Torah scrolls from ark.
(Some congregations conduct a procession around the sanctuary with all the Torah scrolls and then return all but 2 scrolls to ark.)

Hold 2 Torah scrolls, 1 on each side of the sheliaḥ/sheliḥat tsibbur.

Follow the כָּל־נִדְרֵי Kol nidrey liturgy in the maḥzor.
Recite the כָּל־נִדְרֵי paragraph 3 times, each recitation louder than the previous one.

Recite שֶׁהֶחֱיָנוּ sheheḥeyanu.

Return scrolls to ark.

**עַרְבִית**

Follow the service in the maḥzor.

☞ After reciting the line שְׁמַע יִשְׂרָאֵל Shema Yisra'el, recite . . . בָּרוּךְ שֵׁם כְּבוֹד barukh shem kevod . . . *aloud* (rather than in the usual undertone).

**Wed 19 Sep שַׁחֲרִית**

Follow the service in the maḥzor.

☞ After reciting the line שְׁמַע יִשְׂרָאֵל Shema Yisra'el, recite . . . בָּרוּךְ שֵׁם כְּבוֹד barukh shem kevod . . . *aloud* (rather than in the usual undertone).

**1st scroll** 6 aliyot from אַחֲרֵי מוֹת Aḥarey mot
וַיִּקְרָא Vayikra (Leviticus) 16:1–34
1: 16:1–6 2: 7–11 3: 12–17 4: 18–24 5: 25–30 6: 31–34

Use Yamim Nora'im cantillation.

**2nd scroll** Maftir aliyah from פִּינְחָס Pineḥas
בְּמִדְבַּר M Bemidbar (Numbers) 29:7–11

Use Yamim Nora'im cantillation.

**Haftarah** for Yom Kippur morning
יְשַׁעְיָהוּ Yesha'yahu (Isaiah) 57:14–58:14

**מוּסָף**

Follow the service in the maḥzor.

**Repetition of the Amidah:**
Some congregations include בִּרְכַּת כֹּהֲנִים Birkat kohanim, the Priestly Blessing by the Kohanim (*dukhenen*).
For procedures, see p. 213.

**מִנְחָה** Follow the service in the maḥzor.

**Torah** 3 aliyot from אַחֲרֵי מוֹת Aḥarey mot
וַיִּקְרָא Vayikra (Leviticus) 18:1–30
[1]18:1–5 [2]6–21 [M]22–30

Use weekday cantillation, not Yamim Nora'im cantillation.

**Haftarah** for Yom Kippur afternoon
יוֹנָה Yonah (Jonah) 1:1–4:11 + מִיכָה Mikhah (Micah) 7:18–20

**נְעִילָה** Follow the service in the maḥzor.

**THROUGH HOSHA'NA RABBAH (some continue through Shemini Atseret)**

**Evenings** (at the end of Arvit)
**Mornings** (after psalms for the day)
+ Psalm 27 for the Season of Repentance L59 S80 W92 F40
קַדִּישׁ יָתוֹם Mourner's Kaddish L58 S82 W100 F52

**THROUGH 24 TISHREY (others omit through 1 Ḥeshvan)**
✕ ~~תַּחֲנוּן Taḥanun~~

---

**Tishrey 11 תִּשְׁרֵי**
**Wed 19 Sep**

**מוֹצָאֵי יוֹם כִּפּוּר Motsa'ey Yom Kippur**
**Conclusion of Yom Kippur**

**עַרְבִית** Arvit for weekdays L264 S281 W137 F200

**Weekday Amidah:**
+ אַתָּה חוֹנַנְתָּנוּ Attah ḥonantanu L272 S287 W143 F212

✕ ~~חֲצִי קַדִּישׁ Short Kaddish~~
✕ ~~וִיהִי נֹעַם Vihi no'am~~
✕ ~~יוֹשֵׁב בְּסֵתֶר עֶלְיוֹן Yoshev beseter elyon~~
✕ ~~וְאַתָּה קָדוֹשׁ Ve'attah kadosh~~

קַדִּישׁ שָׁלֵם Full Kaddish L280 S294 W160 F222

Some recite הַבְדָּלָה Havdalah here. L283 S299 W165 F700
For instructions, see below.

עָלֵינוּ Aleynu L281 S297 W163 F696
קַדִּישׁ יָתוֹם Mourner's Kaddish (some omit) L282 S298 W164 F698
+ Psalm 27 for the Season of Repentance L59 S80 W92 F40
קַדִּישׁ יָתוֹם Mourner's Kaddish L58 S82 W100 F52

| Tishrey 5779 | | | | | | | Sep \| Oct 2018 | | | | | | |
|---|---|---|---|---|---|---|---|---|---|---|---|---|---|
| | 1 | 2 | 3 | 4 | 5 | 6 | | 10 | 11 | 12 | 13 | 14 | 15 |
| 7 | 8 | 9 | 10 | 11 | 12 | 13 | 16 | 17 | 18 | 19 | 20 | 21 | 22 |
| 14 | 15 | 16 | 17 | 18 | 19 | 20 | 23 | 24 | 25 | 26 | 27 | 28 | 29 |
| 21 | 22 | 23 | 24 | 25 | 26 | 27 | 30 | 1 | 2 | 3 | 4 | 5 | 6 |
| 28 | 29 | 30 | | | | | 7 | 8 | 9 | | | | |

+ Add ✕ Omit ☞ Take note!

**Siddurim**
- **L** Lev Shalem for Shabbat and Festivals
- **S** Shabbat and Festival Sim Shalom
- **W** Weekday Sim Shalom
- **F** Full Sim Shalom (both editions)
- **P** Personal Edition of Full Sim Shalom

+ **Havdalah:** L283 S299 W165 F700

☞ Light the candle from a flame burning since before Yom Kippur, if available. See "Resting Candle," p. 20.

✕ ~~הִנֵּה אֵ·ל יְשׁוּעָתִי Hinneh el yeshu'ati~~
בּוֹרֵא פְּרִי הַגָּפֶן Bo·re peri hagafen
✕ ~~בּוֹרֵא מִינֵי בְשָׂמִים Bo·re miney vesamim~~
בּוֹרֵא מְאוֹרֵי הָאֵשׁ Bo·re me'orey ha'esh
הַמַּבְדִּיל בֵּין קֹדֶשׁ לְחֹל Hamavdil beyn kodesh lehol

**At home** Begin immediately to build your סֻכָּה sukkah, even if you can do only a small first step. See "Looking Ahead to Sukkot," below.

**Thu 20 Sep**

**Torah** 3 aliyot from הַאֲזִינוּ Ha'azinu
דְּבָרִים Devarim (Deuteronomy) 32:1–12°
¹32:1–3 ²4–6° ³7–12 W318 P939

☞ °32:1–12 The reading extends through verse 12, which enables the correct configuration of the 3 aliyot.

☞ °32:6 Read הַלְאֲ·דֹנָי hal-adonay. For more information, see p. 25.

## Sukkot

### Looking Ahead to Sukkot

**Building a Sukkah**

- Immediately after Yom Kippur ends (or as soon thereafter as possible), begin to build your סֻכָּה *sukkah*—even if you can do only a small first step.
  This concrete act symbolizes our firm commitment, expressed throughout Yom Kippur, to build *mitsvot* into our everyday lives.
- During the days leading up to Sukkot, complete the *sukkah*.
  It is considered an act of הִדּוּר מִצְוָה *hiddur mitsvah* (beautification of the *mitsvah*) to build and decorate your סֻכָּה in a manner that enhances your enjoyment of the festival.

**Acquiring Lulav and Etrog**

The *mitsvah* of נְטִילַת לוּלָב *netilat lulav* (taking the *lulav*) requires אַרְבָּעָה מִינִים *arba'ah minim* (4 species): לוּלָב *lulav* (1 palm branch), אֶתְרוֹג *etrog* (1 citron), הֲדַסִּים *hadassim* (3 myrtle branches), and עֲרָבוֹת *aravot* (2 willow branches).

Another act of הִדּוּר מִצְוָה (see above) is to acquire אַרְבָּעָה מִינִים as fresh and unblemished as available and affordable so that their beauty enhances your enjoyment of the festival.

All the branches are placed in a special holder made of woven palm fronds and tied with side fronds from this or another *lulav*. See instructions, p. 26.

**Tishrey 13 תִּשְׁרֵי**
**Sat 22 Sep**

## שַׁבָּת Shabbat פָּרָשַׁת הַאֲזִינוּ Parashat Ha'azinu

**Torah** 7 aliyot (minimum): הַאֲזִינוּ Ha'azinu
דְּבָרִים Devarim (Deuteronomy) 32:1–52°

☞°Do not subdivide any of the first 6 aliyot. The divisions below are indicated in the Talmud by the mnemonic הזי״ו ל״ך, which denotes the first letter of each of the 6 aliyot in the poetry section. No other parashah has aliyah divisions mandated by rabbinic tradition.

Annual: ¹32:1–6° (ה) ²32:7–12 (ז) ³32:13–18 (י) ⁴32:19–28 (ו)
⁵32:29–39 (ל) ⁶32:40–43 (ך) ⁷32:44–52 ᴹ32:48–52

Triennial: Read the full parashah, divided as above.

☞°32:6 Read הַלְאֲ·דֹנָי hal-adonay.
The קְרֵי kerey, the manner in which this word is *read*, is governed by the Masorah, written in the Aleppo Codex (www.aleppocodex.org) and described in Masoretic commentaries such as Minḥat Shay: (1) Read this as a single word, (2) pronouce the 1st syllable as הַל hal, and (3) then pronounce God's name, *adonay*.
Most books present הַ לְיְ·הֹוָה improperly. As noted in some books, the ה is to appear as a word standing by itself. This is a feature only of the כְּתִיב ketiv, the manner in which the word is *written* in the Torah scroll; it does not affect the *pronunciation* of the word.

**Haftarah** שְׁמוּאֵל ב׳ 2 Shemu'el (2 Samuel) 22:1–51

✕ ~~אַב הָרַחֲמִים Av Haraḥamim~~

מִנְחָה

**Torah** 3 aliyot from וְזֹאת הַבְּרָכָה Vezot haberakhah
דְּבָרִים Devarim (Deuteronomy) 33:1–17
¹33:1–7 ²8–12 ³13–17 W319 P940

☞These verses are not read publicly again until next Shabbat.

✕ ~~צִדְקָתְךָ צֶדֶק Tsidkatekha tsedek~~

**Tishrey 14 תִּשְׁרֵי**
**Sat 22 Sep**

## מוֹצָאֵי שַׁבָּת Motsa'ey Shabbat Conclusion of Shabbat
## עֶרֶב סֻכּוֹת Erev Sukkot Day before Sukkot

עַרְבִית

Saturday night Arvit as usual through the Amidah L264 S281 W137 F200

✕ ~~חֲצִי קַדִּישׁ Short Kaddish~~
✕ ~~וִיהִי נֹעַם Vihi no'am~~
✕ ~~יֹשֵׁב בְּסֵתֶר עֶלְיוֹן Yoshev beseter elyon~~
✕ ~~וְאַתָּה קָדוֹשׁ Ve'attah kadosh~~

**Sep 22** תִשְׁרֵי 14  
**Sep 23**

| Tishrey 5779 | Sep \| Oct 2018 | | |
|---|---|---|---|
| 1 2 3 4 5 6 | 10 11 12 13 14 15 | ✚ Add  ✖ Omit  ☞ Take note! | |
| 7 8 9 10 11 12 13 | 16 17 18 19 20 21 22 | **Siddurim** | |
| 14 15 16 17 18 19 20 | 23 24 25 26 27 28 29 | **L** Lev Shalem for Shabbat and Festivals | |
| 21 22 23 24 25 26 27 | 30 \| 1 2 3 4 5 6 | **S** Shabbat and Festival Sim Shalom | |
| 28 29 30 | 7 8 9 | **W** Weekday Sim Shalom | |
| | | **F** Full Sim Shalom (both editions) | |
| | | **P** Personal Edition of Full Sim Shalom | |

סוכות Sukkot

קַדִּישׁ שָׁלֵם Full Kaddish  **L**280 **S**294 **W**160 **F**688

Some recite הַבְדָּלָה Havdalah here.  **L**283 **S**299 **W**165 **F**700

עָלֵינוּ Aleynu  **L**281 **S**297 **W**163 **F**696

קַדִּישׁ יָתוֹם Mourner's Kaddish (some omit)  **L**282 **S**298 **W**164 **F**698

✚ Psalm 27 for the Season of Repentance  **L**59 **S**80 **W**92 **F**40

קַדִּישׁ יָתוֹם Mourner's Kaddish  **L**58 **S**82 **W**100 **F**52

הַבְדָּלָה Havdalah  **L**283 **S**299 **W**165 **F**700

**Sun 23 Sep** שַׁחֲרִית  Weekday Shaḥarit as usual

✖ ~~תַּחֲנוּן~~ ~~Taḥanun~~

☞ לַמְנַצֵּחַ Lamᵉnatse·aḥ (Psalm 20)  **W**79 **F**154

מִנְחָה  ✖ ~~תַּחֲנוּן~~ ~~Taḥanun~~

---

### Preparing for Sukkot

**The Lulav Assembly**

Prepare the 3 kinds of branches of the אַרְבָּעָה מִינִים *arba'ah minim* (4 species) for the performance of the *mitsvah* on Sukkot:

1. Hold the לוּלָב *lulav* (palm branch) with the tip pointing up and the thick spine facing toward you.
2. Slide the לוּלָב into the opening in the center of the special holder.
3. Insert 3 הֲדַסִּים *hᵃdassim* (myrtle branches) into the right sleeve of the holder.
4. Insert 2 עֲרָבוֹת *aravot* (willow branches) into the left sleeve of the holder.
5. Adjust the branches so that the tips of the עֲרָבוֹת (on the left) do not reach as high as the tips of the הֲדַסִּים (on the right). Trim any excess at the bottom of the holder.
6. Using a palm frond from this or another palm branch, tie around the middle of the holder to bind the 3 kinds of branches together.
7. Using additional fronds, tie around the *lulav* in 2 additional places to keep the fronds together. The highest tie must be at least 4 inches from the tip.

For joining the branches with the *etrog* and performing the *mitsvah*, see p. 27.

**Preparing a Flame for Yom Tov**

On Yom Tov, kindling a *new* fire is not permitted; however, the use of an *existing* fire for cooking or other purposes is permitted.

To light candles for Day 2 of Yom Tov (Monday night), ensure that you have a fire burning before candle-lighting time for Day 1 (Sunday evening) that will continue to burn until after dark on Monday. For example:

- A burning candle that lasts for more than 25 hours
- A pilot light on a gas range (*not* a gas range with an electronic starter)

## Mitsvot throughout Sukkot

### Eating in the Sukkah

During Sukkot, it is a *mitsvah* for all eating to be done in the סֻכָּה *sukkah.* (The obligation is suspended in the case of inclement weather.)

**For Kiddush in the sukkah,** see blue box, p. 28.

**For other occasions,** as a symbol of our dwelling in the סֻכָּה, while seated:

1. Recite the בְּרָכָה *berakhah* appropriate for the food you will eat. W228 F714
   - If eating bread or other grain products, add the בְּרָכָה for dwelling in the סֻכָּה:

     בָּרוּךְ אַתָּה יי, אֱ·לֹהֵינוּ מֶלֶךְ הָעוֹלָם, אֲשֶׁר קִדְּשָׁנוּ בְּמִצְוֹתָיו
     וְצִוָּנוּ לֵישֵׁב בַּסֻּכָּה.

     Barukh attah adonay, eloheynu melekh ha'olam,
     asher kiddeshanu bemitsvotav vetsivvanu leshev basukkah.
   - If this is your first time eating in the סֻכָּה this season, add:

     בָּרוּךְ אַתָּה יי, אֱ·לֹהֵינוּ מֶלֶךְ הָעוֹלָם, שֶׁהֶחֱיָנוּ וְקִיְּמָנוּ וְהִגִּיעָנוּ לַזְּמַן הַזֶּה.

     Barukh attah adonay, eloheynu melekh ha'olam,
     sheheḥeyanu vekiyyemanu vehiggi'anu lazeman hazeh.
2. Then eat some of the food.

Upon entering the סֻכָּה for each evening meal, some recite אֻשְׁפִּיזִין *ushpizin,* inviting our revered ancestors to join us in the סֻכָּה as our honored guests. L424 S330

### Taking the Lulav and Waving the Lulav (not on Shabbat)

Each day of Sukkot except Shabbat, perform the *mitsvah* of נְטִילַת לוּלָב *netilat lulav* (taking the *lulav*): L315 S131 W49 F379

1. Take the *lulav* assembly in the right hand (if left-handed, in the left hand).
   Note: Make sure the thick spine of the *lulav* is facing you, with the 3 *hadassim* (myrtles) on the right and the 2 *aravot* (willows) on the left.
2. Hold the *etrog* in your other hand **stem-end up** for reciting the בְּרָכָה *berakhah.*
3. Hold *lulav* and *etrog* together in front of you, and recite the בְּרָכָה:

   בָּרוּךְ אַתָּה יי, אֱ·לֹהֵינוּ מֶלֶךְ הָעוֹלָם, אֲשֶׁר קִדְּשָׁנוּ בְּמִצְוֹתָיו
   וְצִוָּנוּ עַל נְטִילַת לוּלָב.

   Barukh attah adonay, eloheynu melekh ha'olam,
   asher kiddeshanu bemitsvotav vetsivvanu al netilat lulav.

   Note: If this is your first time this season, add שֶׁהֶחֱיָנוּ *sheheḥeyanu* (see above).
4. For the נִעֲנוּעִים *ni'nu'im* (waving movements), turn the *etrog* **stem-end down.**
5. Hold *lulav* and *etrog* together. To perform the *mitsvah,* "wave"—that is, extend arms and retract 3 times—in each of 6 directions, as follows:
   a. At home, face east; in the synagogue, face the wall holding the ark.
   b. Wave (1st) to the front, then (2nd) to the right, then (3rd) to the back, and then (4th) to the left, thus proceding in a clockwise direction.
   c. Wave (5th) up (keep *lulav* vertical), and then (6th) down (*lulav* still vertical).

## Sukkot — Day 1 and Day 2

### Candle Lighting for Yom Tov — Day 1

1. Before lighting candles, prepare a flame. See p. 26.
2. Light the candles at least 18 minutes before sunset.
3. Recite 2 בְּרָכוֹת *berakhot:* L79 S303 F718

בָּרוּךְ אַתָּה יי, אֱ־לֹהֵינוּ מֶלֶךְ הָעוֹלָם, אֲשֶׁר קִדְּשָׁנוּ בְּמִצְוֹתָיו
וְצִוָּנוּ לְהַדְלִיק נֵר שֶׁל יוֹם טוֹב.

Barukh attah adonay, eloheynu melekh ha'olam,
asher kiddeshanu bemitsvotav vetsivvanu lehadlik ner shel yom tov.

בָּרוּךְ אַתָּה יי, אֱ־לֹהֵינוּ מֶלֶךְ הָעוֹלָם, שֶׁהֶחֱיָנוּ וְקִיְּמָנוּ וְהִגִּיעָנוּ לַזְּמַן הַזֶּה.

Barukh attah adonay, eloheynu melekh ha'olam,
sheheḥeyanu vekiyyemanu vehiggi'anu lazeman hazeh.

### Candle Lighting for Yom Tov — Day 2

See p. 33.

### Kiddush — Day 1, Day 2, and Shabbat Ḥol Hamo'ed

Recite קִדּוּשׁ *kiddush* in the סֻכָּה *sukkah.* If your usual custom is to stand for קִדּוּשׁ, recite all בְּרָכוֹת while standing, and then sit to drink.

- If this is your first time eating in the סֻכָּה this season:
  Add the בְּרָכָה *berakhah* for dwelling in the סֻכָּה, and then add שֶׁהֶחֱיָנוּ *sheheḥeyanu* (see p. 27).
- If you have already eaten in the סֻכָּה this season:
  **Yom Tov evening only:** Add שֶׁהֶחֱיָנוּ *sheheḥeyanu* (see p. 27).
  **All occasions:** Add the בְּרָכָה *berakhah* for dwelling in the סֻכָּה (see p. 27).

### Yom Tov Meals — Day 1 and Day 2

In the סֻכָּה (see procedures above and on p. 27), enjoy festive meals evening and daytime, in the manner of Shabbat meals, with:

- Yom Tov קִדּוּשׁ *kiddush:* Evening L79 S334 F742 Daytime L81 S335 F746
- הַמּוֹצִיא *hamotsi* recited over 2 whole חַלָּה *ḥallah* loaves or rolls L81 S313–14 F744|746
- בִּרְכַּת הַמָּזוֹן *birkat hamazon* with Sukkot additions (see yellow box, p. 29)
- Festive singing

**DURING SUKKOT**

Every Shaḥarit, Minḥah, and Arvit Amidah:

Days 1–7 + יַעֲלֶה וְיָבוֹא Ya'aleh veyavo for Sukkot

Birkat Hamazon:

Days 1–7 + יַעֲלֶה וְיָבוֹא Ya'aleh veyavo for Sukkot L90|95 S340|347 W233|239 F762|780

Days 1 and 2 only + הָרַחֲמָן Haraḥaman for Yom Tov L92|96 S343|348 W236|240 F768

Days 1–7 (some: only Days 3–7) + הָרַחֲמָן Haraḥaman for Sukkot L92|96 S343 W236|240 F768



## Tishrey 15 תִּשְׁרֵי — סֻכּוֹת Sukkot — Day 1

Sun 23 Sep

עַרְבִית Arvit for Yom Tov L39 S28 F279

+ וַיְדַבֵּר מֹשֶׁה Vaydabber mosheh (Vayikra 23:44) L46 S34 F294

חֲצִי קַדִּישׁ Short Kaddish L46 S34 F294

Yom Tov Amidah: L306 S41 F304

+ Insertions for Sukkot

קַדִּישׁ שָׁלֵם Full Kaddish L54 S48 F316

✕ ~~קִדּוּשׁ Kiddush during Arvit~~

עָלֵינוּ Aleynu L56 S51 F320

קַדִּישׁ יָתוֹם Mourner's Kaddish (some omit) L58 S52 F324

+ Psalm 27 for the Season of Repentance L59 S80 F40

קַדִּישׁ יָתוֹם Mourner's Kaddish L58 S82 F52

☞ At the conclusion of Arvit, in the sukkah:

+ קִדּוּשׁ Kiddush for Yom Tov with insertions for Sukkot L79 S50 F318

+ לֵישֵׁב בַּסֻּכָּה Leshev basukkah L80 S50 F320

+ שֶׁהֶחֱיָנוּ Sheheḥeyanu L80 S50 F320

At home

See "Eating in the Sukkah," p. 27.
See "Yom Tov Meals — Day 1 and Day 2," p. 28.

Mon 24 Sep שַׁחֲרִית

At the end of the preliminary service, begin formal chanting at הָאֵ-ל בְּתַעֲצוּמוֹת עֻזֶּךָ Ha'el beta'atsumot uzzekha. L147 S105 F336

סֻכּוֹת
Sukkot

✕ ~~הַכֹּל יוֹדוּךָ Hakol yodukha~~
✕ ~~אֵ־ל אָדוֹן El adon~~
✕ ~~לָאֵ־ל אֲשֶׁר שָׁבַת La'el asher shavat~~
+ הַמֵּאִיר לָאָרֶץ Hame'ir la'arets L152 S109 F342

**Yom Tov Amidah:** L306 S123 F366
+ Insertions for Sukkot

For instructions on taking the lulav and etrog, see p. 27. For waving the lulav during Hallel, see p. 31.

+ הַלֵּל שָׁלֵם Full Hallel, including waving the lulav L316 S133 F380

Some congregations recite הוֹשַׁע־נָא Hosha'na and conduct the procession with lulav and etrog here, rather than after the Musaf Amidah. See instructions, p. 32.

קַדִּישׁ שָׁלֵם Full Kaddish L321 S138 F392

## YOM TOV TORAH SERVICE L322 S139 F394

+ יי יי אֵ־ל רַחוּם וְחַנּוּן
Adonay adonay el raḥum veḥannun (3 times) L323 S140 F394
+ רִבּוֹנוֹ שֶׁל עוֹלָם Ribbono shel olam L323 S140 F396
+ וַאֲנִי תְפִלָּתִי לְךָ Va'ani tefillati lekha (3 times) L323 S140 F396

Remove **2** Torah scrolls from ark.

**1st scroll** 5 aliyot from אֱמֹר Emor
וַיִּקְרָא Vayikra (Leviticus) 22:26–23:44
1 22:26–23:3 2 23:4–14 3 15–22 4 23–32 5 33–44

Place 2nd scroll on table next to 1st scroll.
חֲצִי קַדִּישׁ Short Kaddish L327 S146 F408
Open, raise, display, and wrap 1st scroll.

**2nd scroll** Maftir aliyah from פִּינְחָס Pineḥas
M בְּמִדְבַּר Bemidbar (Numbers) 29:12–16

Open, raise, display, and wrap 2nd scroll.

**Haftarah** for Sukkot — Day 1
זְכַרְיָה Zekharyah (Zechariah) 14:1–21

**Haftarah blessings:**
✕ ~~Concluding Shabbat בְּרָכָה berakhah~~
+ Concluding Yom Tov בְּרָכָה berakhah with insertions for Sukkot L329 S147 F412

## Waving the Lulav during Hallel (not on Shabbat)

At 3 points during Hallel, wave the *lulav* (that is, extend arms and retract 3 times) in each of 6 directions. These נִעְנוּעִים *ni'nu'im* (waving movements) are described more fully in the blue box on p. 27, steps 4–5.

When we chant the name of God, we hold the *lulav* erect, out of respect.

1. At the 4-verse section הוֹדוּ לַייָ כִּי טוֹב *hodu ladonay ki tov:* L319 S136 W53 F386

   The *sheliaḥ/sheliḥat tsibbur* chants each verse (waving the *lulav* only during the first 2) and waits for the response from the congregation.

   After the *sheliaḥ/sheliḥat tsibbur* recites each verse, the congregation responds with the following refrain and waving:

| חַסְדּוֹ. | לְעוֹלָם | כִּי | טוֹב | כִּי | לַייָ | הוֹדוּ | **Refrain** |
|---|---|---|---|---|---|---|---|
| down | up | left | back | right | hold erect | front | |

| חַסְדּוֹ. | לְעוֹלָם | כִּי | טוֹב | כִּי | לַייָ | הוֹדוּ | **Verse 1** |
|---|---|---|---|---|---|---|---|
| down | up | left | back | right | hold erect | front | |

**Refrain** (see above)

| חַסְדּוֹ. | לְעוֹלָם | כִּי | יִשְׂרָאֵל | נָא | יֹאמַר | **Verse 2** |
|---|---|---|---|---|---|---|
| down | up | left | back | right | front | |

**Refrain** (see above)

יֹאמְרוּ נָא בֵית אַהֲרֹן, כִּי לְעוֹלָם חַסְדּוֹ. **Verse 3**

Sheliaḥ/sheliḥat tsibbur does not wave the lulav.

**Refrain** (see above)

יֹאמְרוּ נָא יִרְאֵי יְיָ, כִּי לְעוֹלָם חַסְדּוֹ. **Verse 4**

Sheliaḥ/sheliḥat tsibbur does not wave the lulav.

**Refrain** (see above)

2. At the verse אָנָּא יְיָ, הוֹשִׁיעָה נָּא *anna adonay, hoshi'ah na:* L320 S137 W55 F388

   The *sheliaḥ/sheliḥat* tsibbur chants the verse, waving the *lulav* as follows:

| נָּא. | הוֹשִׁיעָה | יְיָ | אָנָּא |
|---|---|---|---|
| up, then down | back, then left | hold erect | front, then right |

   The congregation repeats that verse and the waving.

   The *sheliaḥ/sheliḥat tsibbur* again chants that verse and waves, as does the congregation.

3. Upon reaching the next הוֹדוּ לַייָ כִּי טוֹב *hodu ladonay ki tov,* L320 S137 W55 F388 each congregant chants the verse, waving the *lulav* as before:

| חַסְדּוֹ. | לְעוֹלָם | כִּי | טוֹב | כִּי | לַייָ | הוֹדוּ |
|---|---|---|---|---|---|---|
| down | up | left | back | right | hold erect | front |

   Then chant the verse again, waving in the same manner.

| Tishrey 5779 | | | | | | |
|---|---|---|---|---|---|---|
| | 1 | 2 | 3 | 4 | 5 | 6 |
| 7 | 8 | 9 | 10 | 11 | 12 | 13 |
| 14 | 15 | 16 | 17 | 18 | 19 | 20 |
| 21 | 22 | 23 | 24 | 25 | 26 | 27 |
| 28 | 29 | 30 | | | | |

| Sep \| Oct 2018 | | | | | | |
|---|---|---|---|---|---|---|
| | 10 | 11 | 12 | 13 | 14 | 15 |
| 16 | 17 | 18 | 19 | 20 | 21 | 22 |
| 23 | 24 | 25 | 26 | 27 | 28 | 29 |
| 30 \| 1 | 2 | 3 | 4 | 5 | 6 | |
| 7 | 8 | 9 | | | | |

+ Add ✕ Omit ☞ Take note!

**Siddurim**
- **L** Lev Shalem for Shabbat and Festivals
- **S** Shabbat and Festival Sim Shalom
- **W** Weekday Sim Shalom
- **F** Full Sim Shalom (both editions)
- **P** Personal Edition of Full Sim Shalom

✕ ~~יְקוּם פֻּרְקָן Yekum purkan~~
✕ ~~אַב הָרַחֲמִים Av Harahamim~~

אַשְׁרֵי Ashrey L339 S151 F420
Return scrolls to ark. L340 S153 F422
חֲצִי קַדִּישׁ Short Kaddish L342 S155 F428

מוּסָף

**Yom Tov Amidah:** L343 S166 F456
+ Insertions for Sukkot

Some congregations include in the repetition of the Amidah the Priestly Blessing by the Kohanim (*dukhenen*).
בִּרְכַּת כֹּהֲנִים Birkat kohanim L353 S177 F472
For procedures, see p. 213.

For procedures for reciting הוֹשַׁע־נָא Hosha'na, including procession with lulav and etrog, see the blue box, below.

### Circling the Sanctuary with Lulav and Etrog

Each day of Sukkot, except Shabbat, remove a Torah scroll from the ark and hold it at the reading table. Congregants with *lulav* and *etrog* form a procession, reminiscent of the processions of the priests around the altar of the Temple in ancient times. The ark remains open during the procession.

1. Before beginning the procession, chant the introductory הוֹשַׁע־נָא *hosha'na* lines. L383 S200 W116 F530
2. Proceed counterclockwise, making a circle around the reading table, Torah scroll, and sanctuary.
3. During the procession, chant the הוֹשַׁע־נָא poem designated for the particular day. Precede and follow each phrase of the poem (or small groups of phrases) with the word הוֹשַׁע־נָא.

+ הוֹשַׁע־נָא Hosha'na for Day 1:
לְמַעַן אֲמִתָּךְ Lema'an amittakh L383 S200 F530+531

+ כְּהוֹשַׁעְתָּ Kehosha'ta L385 S201 F534
+ הוֹשִׁיעָה אֶת־עַמֶּךָ Hoshi'ah et ammekha L386 S201 F535

קַדִּישׁ שָׁלֵם Full kaddish L203 S181 F506
Continue with אֵין כֵּא·לֹהֵינוּ Eyn keloheynu. L204 S182 F508

קִדּוּשָׁא רַבָּא

**Daytime Kiddush for Yom Tov, in the sukkah:** L81 S335 F746
וַיְדַבֵּר מֹשֶׁה Vaydabber mosheh (Vayikra 23:44)
בּוֹרֵא פְּרִי הַגָּפֶן Bo·re peri hagafen
+ לֵישֵׁב בַּסֻּכָּה Leshev basukkah L80 S50 F320

**At home** See “Eating in the Sukkah,” p. 27.
See “Yom Tov Meals — Day 1 and Day 2,” p. 28.

**מִנְחָה**

אַשְׁרֵי Ashrey L214 S226 W170 F558
וּבָא לְצִיּוֹן Uva letsiyyon L216 S227 W171 F560
חֲצִי קַדִּישׁ Short Kaddish L217 S229 W173 F564

**Yom Tov Amidah:** L306 S242 W184 F586
+ Insertions for Sukkot

קַדִּישׁ שָׁלֵם Full Kaddish L230 S247 W189 F596
עָלֵינוּ Aleynu L231 S248 W190 F598
קַדִּישׁ יָתוֹם Mourner’s Kaddish L232 S249 W191 F600

**Candle Lighting for Yom Tov — Day 2**

Day 1 ends after dark: when 3 stars appear, or at least 25 minutes after sunset (at least 43 minutes after the time set for lighting candles on Day 1). Some wait longer. For the appropriate time in your community, consult your rabbi.

1. Wait until Day 1 ends.
2. Do not *strike* a match. Instead, transfer fire to the candles from an *existing* flame (see p. 26) by inserting a match or other stick into the flame.
3. Do not *extinguish* the match or stick. Instead, place it on a non-flammable tray or dish, and let it self-extinguish. Alternately, a wood *safety* match held vertically (flame up) usually self-extinguishes quickly.
4. Recite the 2 בְּרָכוֹת *berakhot* (see p. 28). L79 S303 F718

## Tishrey 16 תִּשְׁרֵי Mon 24 Sep — סֻכּוֹת Sukkot — Day 2

**עַרְבִית**

Arvit for Yom Tov L39 S28 F279
+ וַיְדַבֵּר מֹשֶׁה Vaydabber mosheh (Vayikra 23:44) L46 S34 F294
חֲצִי קַדִּישׁ Short Kaddish L46 S34 F294

**Yom Tov Amidah:** L306 S41 F304
+ Insertions for Sukkot

קַדִּישׁ שָׁלֵם Full Kaddish L54 S48 F316

✕ ~~קִדּוּשׁ Kiddush during Arvit~~

עָלֵינוּ Aleynu L56 S51 F320
קַדִּישׁ יָתוֹם Mourner’s Kaddish (some omit) L58 S52 F324
+ Psalm 27 for the Season of Repentance L59 S80 F40
קַדִּישׁ יָתוֹם Mourner’s Kaddish L58 S82 F52

| Tishrey 5779 | | | | | | | Sep \| Oct 2018 | | | | | | |
|---|---|---|---|---|---|---|---|---|---|---|---|---|---|
| | 1 | 2 | 3 | 4 | 5 | 6 | | 10 | 11 | 12 | 13 | 14 | 15 |
| 7 | 8 | 9 | 10 | 11 | 12 | 13 | 16 | 17 | 18 | 19 | 20 | 21 | 22 |
| 14 | 15 | 16 | 17 | 18 | 19 | 20 | 23 | 24 | 25 | 26 | 27 | 28 | 29 |
| 21 | 22 | 23 | 24 | 25 | 26 | 27 | 30 \| | 1 | 2 | 3 | 4 | 5 | 6 |
| 28 | 29 | 30 | | | | | 7 | 8 | 9 | | | | |

+ Add ✕ Omit ☞ Take note!

**Siddurim**
**L** Lev Shalem for Shabbat and Festivals
**S** Shabbat and Festival Sim Shalom
**W** Weekday Sim Shalom
**F** Full Sim Shalom (both editions)
**P** Personal Edition of Full Sim Shalom

☞ **At the conclusion of Arvit, in the sukkah:**
+ קִדּוּשׁ Kiddush for Yom Tov with insertions for Sukkot L79 S50 F318
+ שֶׁהֶחֱיָנוּ Sheheḥeyanu L80 S50 F320
+ לֵישֵׁב בַּסֻּכָּה Leshev basukkah L80 S50 F320

**At home**
See “Candle Lighting for Yom Tov — Day 2, p. 33.
See “Eating in the Sukkah,” p. 27.
See “Yom Tov Meals — Day 1 and Day 2,” p. 28.

**Tue 25 Sep** **שַׁחֲרִית**

At the end of the preliminary service, begin formal chanting at הָאֵ·ל בְּתַעֲצוּמוֹת עֻזֶּךָ Ha’el beta’atsumot uzzekha. L147 S105 F336

✕ ~~הַכֹּל יוֹדוּךָ Hakol yodukha~~
✕ ~~אֵ·ל אָדוֹן El adon~~
✕ ~~לָאֵ·ל אֲשֶׁר שָׁבַת La’el asher shavat~~
+ הַמֵּאִיר לָאָרֶץ Hame’ir la’arets L152 S109 F342

**Yom Tov Amidah:** L306 S123 F366
+ Insertions for Sukkot

For instructions on taking the lulav and etrog, see p. 27.
For waving the lulav during Hallel, see p. 31.

+ הַלֵּל שָׁלֵם Full Hallel, including waving the lulav L316 S133 F380

Some congregations recite הוֹשַׁע־נָא Hosha’na and conduct the procession with lulav and etrog here, rather than after the Musaf Amidah. See instructions, p. 35.

קַדִּישׁ שָׁלֵם Full Kaddish L321 S138 F392

**YOM TOV TORAH SERVICE** L322 S139 F394
+ יי יי אֵ·ל רַחוּם וְחַנּוּן Adonay adonay el raḥum veḥannun (3 times) L323 S140 F394
+ רִבּוֹנוֹ שֶׁל עוֹלָם Ribbono shel olam L323 S140 F396
+ וַאֲנִי תְפִלָּתִי לְךָ Va’ani tefillati lekha (3 times) L323 S140 F396

Remove **2** Torah scrolls from ark.

**1st scroll** 5 aliyot from אֱמֹר Emor
וַיִּקְרָא Vayikra (Leviticus) 22:26–23:44
[1]22:26–23:3 [2]23:4–14 [3]15–22 [4]23–32 [5]33–44

סֻכּוֹת Sukkot

Place 2nd scroll on table next to 1st scroll.
חֲצִי קַדִּישׁ Short Kaddish L327 S146 F408
Open, raise, display, and wrap 1st scroll.

**2nd scroll** Maftir aliyah from פִּינְחָס Pineḥas
בְּמִדְבַּר M Bemidbar (Numbers) 29:12–16

Open, raise, display, and wrap 2nd scroll.

**Haftarah** for Sukkot — Day 2
מְלָכִים א׳ 1 Melakhim (1 Kings) 8:2–21

**Haftarah blessings:**
✕ ~~Concluding Shabbat בְּרָכָה berakhah~~
+ Concluding Yom Tov בְּרָכָה berakhah with insertions for Sukkot L329 S147 F412

✕ ~~יְקוּם פֻּרְקָן Yekum purkan~~
✕ ~~אַב הָרַחֲמִים Av Haraḥamim~~

אַשְׁרֵי Ashrey L339 S151 F420
Return scrolls to ark. L340 S153 F422
חֲצִי קַדִּישׁ Short Kaddish L342 S155 F428

מוּסָף

**Yom Tov Amidah:** L343 S166 F456
+ Insertions for Sukkot

Some congregations include in the repetition of the Amidah the Priestly Blessing by the Kohanim (*dukhenen*).
בִּרְכַּת כֹּהֲנִים Birkat kohanim L353 S177 F472
For procedures, see p. 213.

For procedures for reciting הוֹשַׁע־נָא Hosha'na, including procession with lulav and etrog, see p. 32.

+ הוֹשַׁע־נָא Hosha'na for Day 2:
אֶבֶן שְׁתִיָּה Even shetiyyah L383+384 S200 F530+531

+ כְּהוֹשַׁעְתָּ Kehosha'ta L385 S201 F534
+ הוֹשִׁיעָה אֶת־עַמֶּךָ Hoshi'ah et ammekha L386 S201 F535

קַדִּישׁ שָׁלֵם Full kaddish L203 S181 F506
Continue with אֵין כֵּא·לֹהֵינוּ Eyn keloheynu. L204 S182 F508

קִדּוּשָׁא רַבָּא

**Daytime Kiddush for Yom Tov, in the sukkah:** L81 S335 F746
וַיְדַבֵּר מֹשֶׁה Vaydabber mosheh (Vayikra 23:44)
בּוֹרֵא פְּרִי הַגָּפֶן Bo·re peri hagafen
+ לֵישֵׁב בַּסֻּכָּה Leshev basukkah L80 S50 F320

Tishrey 5779

| | | | | | | |
|---|---|---|---|---|---|---|
| | 1 | 2 | 3 | 4 | 5 | 6 |
| 7 | 8 | 9 | 10 | 11 | 12 | 13 |
| 14 | 15 | 16 | 17 | 18 | 19 | 20 |
| 21 | 22 | 23 | 24 | 25 | 26 | 27 |
| 28 | 29 | 30 | | | | |

Sep | Oct 2018

| | | | | | | |
|---|---|---|---|---|---|---|
| | 10 | 11 | 12 | 13 | 14 | 15 |
| 16 | 17 | 18 | 19 | 20 | 21 | 22 |
| 23 | 24 | 25 | 26 | 27 | 28 | 29 |
| 30 \| | 1 | 2 | 3 | 4 | 5 | 6 |
| 7 | 8 | 9 | | | | |

+ Add ✕ Omit ☞ Take note!

**Siddurim**
- **L** Lev Shalem for Shabbat and Festivals
- **S** Shabbat and Festival Sim Shalom
- **W** Weekday Sim Shalom
- **F** Full Sim Shalom (both editions)
- **P** Personal Edition of Full Sim Shalom



**At home** See “Eating in the Sukkah,” p. 27.
See “Yom Tov Meals — Day 1 and Day 2,” p. 28.

**מִנְחָה**
אַשְׁרֵי Ashrey L214 S226 W170 F558
וּבָא לְצִיּוֹן Uva letsiyyon L216 S227 W171 F560
חֲצִי קַדִּישׁ Short Kaddish L217 S229 W173 F564

**Yom Tov Amidah:** L306 S242 W184 F586
+ Insertions for Sukkot

קַדִּישׁ שָׁלֵם Full Kaddish L230 S247 W189 F596
עָלֵינוּ Aleynu L231 S248 W190 F598
קַדִּישׁ יָתוֹם Mourner’s Kaddish L232 S249 W191 F600

---

**Tishrey 17 תִּשְׁרֵי**
**Tue 25 Sep** (evening)
through
**Tishrey 19 תִּשְׁרֵי**
**Fri 28 Sep** (daytime)

## חֹל הַמּוֹעֵד סֻכּוֹת Ḥol Hamo’ed Sukkot Weekdays

**חֹל הַמּוֹעֵד Ḥol Hamo’ed (ḤH) — Days 1–3**

ḤH Day 1 Tue 25 Sep — **מוֹצָאֵי יוֹם טוֹב Motsa’ey Yom Tov Conclusion of Yom Tov**
**חֹל הַמּוֹעֵד Ḥol Hamo’ed (ḤH) — Day 1**

ḤH Day 2 Wed 26 Sep — **חֹל הַמּוֹעֵד Ḥol Hamo’ed (ḤH) — Day 2**
ḤH Day 3 Thu 27 Sep — **חֹל הַמּוֹעֵד Ḥol Hamo’ed (ḤH) — Day 3**

**עַרְבִית** Arvit for weekdays L264 S281 W137 F200

**Weekday Amidah:**
ḤH Day 1 Tue 25 Sep + אַתָּה חוֹנַנְתָּנוּ Attah ḥonantanu L272 S287 W143 F212
All evenings + יַעֲלֶה וְיָבוֹא Ya’aleh veyavo for Sukkot L277 S289 W145 F216

All evenings קַדִּישׁ שָׁלֵם Full Kaddish L280 S294 W160 F222
עָלֵינוּ Aleynu L281 S297 W163 F696
קַדִּישׁ יָתוֹם Mourner’s Kaddish (some omit) L282 S298 W164 F698
+ Psalm 27 for the Season of Repentance L59 S80 W92 F40
קַדִּישׁ יָתוֹם Mourner’s Kaddish L58 S82 W100 F52

ḤH Day 1 Tue 25 Sep + **Havdalah, in the sukkah:** L283 S299 W165 F700
✕ ~~הִנֵּה אֵ-ל יְשׁוּעָתִי Hinneh el yeshu’ati~~
בּוֹרֵא פְּרִי הַגָּפֶן Bo·re peri hagafen
✕ ~~בּוֹרֵא מִינֵי בְשָׂמִים Bo·re miney vesamim~~
✕ ~~בּוֹרֵא מְאוֹרֵי הָאֵשׁ Bo·re me’orey ha’esh~~
הַמַּבְדִּיל בֵּין קֹדֶשׁ לְחֹל Hamavdil beyn kodesh leḥol
✕ ~~לֵישֵׁב בַּסֻּכָּה Leshev basukkah~~

## Tefillin during Ḥol Hamo'ed

Whether or not to wear תְּפִלִּין *tefillin* during Ḥol Hamo'ed is a long-standing controversy. Ashkenazic Jews tend to wear תְּפִלִּין; Sephardic and Hasidic Jews tend not to wear תְּפִלִּין. The practice in Israel is not to wear them. Some who wear תְּפִלִּין do not recite the בְּרָכוֹת *berakhot*.

1. Determine your individual practice according to the following instructions:
   - If there is an established custom in your family, follow it.
   - If there is no established custom in your family, consult your rabbi.
   - Regardless of your custom, when you are in Israel, do not wear תְּפִלִּין.
2. If you wear תְּפִלִּין, remove them just before the beginning of Hallel.

**ḤH Day 1 Wed 26 Sep**
**ḤH Day 2 Thu 27 Sep**
**ḤH Day 3 Fri 28 Sep**

שַׁחֲרִית Shaḥarit for weekdays W1 F2

**Weekday Amidah:**

+ יַעֲלֶה וְיָבוֹא Ya'aleh veyavo for Sukkot W41 F114

✕ ~~תַּחֲנוּן Taḥanun~~

☞ Those wearing תְּפִלִּין tefillin now remove and pack them.

For instructions on taking the lulav and etrog, see p. 27. For waving the lulav during Hallel, see p. 31.

+ הַלֵּל שָׁלֵם Full Hallel, including waving the lulav W50 F380

Some congregations recite הוֹשַׁע־נָא Hosha'na and conduct the procession with lulav and etrog here, rather than after the Musaf Amidah. See instructions, p. 38.

קַדִּישׁ שָׁלֵם Full Kaddish W56 F392

+ **WEEKDAY TORAH SERVICE** W65 F138
Remove **1** Torah scroll from ark.

**Torah** 4 aliyot from: פָּרָשַׁת פִּינְחָס Parashat Pineḥas
בְּמִדְבַּר Bemidbar (Numbers) 29

| | | | | | |
|---|---|---|---|---|---|
| ḤH Day 1 Wed 26 Sep | 1 29:17–19 | 2 20–22 | 3 23–25 | 4 17–22 | W321 P967 |
| ḤH Day 2 Thu 27 Sep | 1 29:20–22 | 2 23–25 | 3 26–28 | 4 20–25 | W322 P968 |
| ḤH Day 3 Fri 28 Sep | 1 29:23–25 | 2 26–28 | 3 29–31 | 4 23–28 | W323 P969 |

חֲצִי קַדִּישׁ Short Kaddish W71 F146

Open, raise, display, and wrap scroll.
Return scroll to ark. W76 F150

אַשְׁרֵי Ashrey W78 F152
✕ ~~לַמְנַצֵּחַ Lamenatse·aḥ (Psalm 20)~~
וּבָא לְצִיּוֹן Uva letsiyyon W80 F156

\+ חֲצִי קַדִּישׁ Short Kaddish W103 F428

מוּסָף + **Yom Tov Amidah:** W104+110 F456+462
Weekday קְדֻשָּׁה Kedushah W105 F460
\+ Insertions for Sukkot

ḤH Day **1** Wed **26** Sep + Insertions for Ḥol Hamo'ed Sukkot — Day 1 W111 F466
ḤH Day **2** Thu **27** Sep + Insertions for Ḥol Hamo'ed Sukkot — Day 2 W111 F467
ḤH Day **3** Fri **28** Sep + Insertions for Ḥol Hamo'ed Sukkot — Day 3 W111 F467

For procedures for reciting הוֹשַׁע־נָא Hosha'na, including procession with lulav and etrog, see p. 32.

Open ark and remove **1** Torah scroll.

\+ הוֹשַׁע־נָא Hosha'na W116 F530

ḤH Day **1** Wed **26** Sep + אֶעֱרֹךְ שׁוּעִי E'erokh shu'i W116 F532
ḤH Day **2** Thu **27** Sep + אוֹם אֲנִי חוֹמָה Om ani ḥomah W117 F532
ḤH Day **3** Fri **28** Sep + אֵ·ל לְמוֹשָׁעוֹת El lemosha'ot W118 F533

\+ כְּהוֹשַׁעְתָּ Kehosha'ta W119 F534
\+ הוֹשִׁיעָה אֶת־עַמֶּךָ Hoshi'ah et ammekha W119 F535
Return scroll to ark, and close ark.

קַדִּישׁ שָׁלֵם Full Kaddish W82 F158
עָלֵינוּ Aleynu W83 F160
Conclude as on a usual weekday.
\+ Psalm 27 for the Season of Repentance W92 F40
קַדִּישׁ יָתוֹם Mourner's Kaddish W100 F52

At home — See "Eating in the sukkah," p. 27.

מִנְחָה — Minḥah for weekdays L289 S1 W120 F164

**Weekday Amidah:**
\+ יַעֲלֶה וְיָבוֹא Ya'aleh veyavo for Sukkot L298 S7 W127 F178

✕ ~~תַּחֲנוּן Taḥanun~~

ḤH Day **3** Fri **28** Sep
At home — Light Shabbat candles as for a usual Shabbat.

| | | | |
|---|---|---|---|
| ✚ Add    ✗ Omit    ☞ Take note! | Tishrey 5779 | Sep \| Oct 2018 | 20 תִּשְׁרֵי  Sep 28 |
| | | | Sep 29 |

**Siddurim**
- **L** Lev Shalem for Shabbat and Festivals
- **S** Shabbat and Festival Sim Shalom
- **W** Weekday Sim Shalom
- **F** Full Sim Shalom (both editions)
- **P** Personal Edition of Full Sim Shalom

Calendar:
- 1 2 3 4 5 6 / 10 11 12 13 14 15
- 7 8 9 10 11 12 13 / 16 17 18 19 20 21 22
- 14 15 16 17 18 19 20 / 23 24 25 26 27 28 29
- 21 22 23 24 25 26 27 / 30 | 1 2 3 4 5 6
- 28 29 30 / 7 8 9

---

## Tishrey 20 תִּשְׁרֵי
**Fri 28 Sep (evening)**

### שַׁבַּת חֹל הַמּוֹעֵד סֻכּוֹת Shabbat Ḥol Hamo'ed Sukkot
### Ḥol Hamo'ed — Day 4

קַבָּלַת שַׁבָּת ✗ ~~Kabbalat Shabbat~~
through
✗ ~~לְכָה דוֹדִי Lekhah dodi~~

Begin with מִזְמוֹר שִׁיר לְיוֹם הַשַּׁבָּת
Mizmor shir leyom hashabbat (Psalm 92).   L27 S23 F266

עַרְבִית   Arvit as on a usual Shabbat

✗ ~~וַיְדַבֵּר מֹשֶׁה Vaydabber mosheh~~

**Shabbat Amidah:**
✚ יַעֲלֶה וְיָבוֹא Ya'aleh veyavo for Sukkot   L50 S36 F298

וַיְכֻלּוּ Vaykhullu   L53 S41 F314

Continue as on a usual Shabbat through
קַדִּישׁ שָׁלֵם Full Kaddish   L54 S48 F316

✗ ~~קִדּוּשׁ Kiddush during Arvit~~

עָלֵינוּ Aleynu   L56 S51 F320
קַדִּישׁ יָתוֹם Mourner's Kaddish (some omit)   L58 S52 F324
✚ Psalm 27 for the Season of Repentance   L59 S80 F40
קַדִּישׁ יָתוֹם Mourner's Kaddish   L58 S82 F52

☞ **At the conclusion of Arvit, in the sukkah:**
קִדּוּשׁ Kiddush for Shabbat   L55 S49 F318
✚ לֵישֵׁב בַּסֻּכָּה Leshev basukkah   L80 S50 F320

**Sat 29 Sep**   שַׁחֲרִית   Shaḥarit for Shabbat   L99 S61 F2

**Shabbat Amidah:**
✚ יַעֲלֶה וְיָבוֹא Ya'aleh veyavo for Sukkot   L163 S118 F360

✗ ~~Lulav and etrog~~

✚ הַלֵּל שָׁלֵם Full Hallel   L316 S133 F380

Some congregations recite הוֹשַׁע־נָא Hosha'na here, rather than after Musaf. See instructions, p. 41.

קַדִּישׁ שָׁלֵם Full Kaddish   L321 S138 F392

סֻכּוֹת Sukkot

+ **Megillah reading:**
Some congregations read
מְגִלַּת קֹהֶלֶת Megillat Kohelet (Scroll of Ecclesiastes), without reciting a בְּרָכָה berakhah.
Some read selections in English. L426 S373 F794

קַדִּישׁ יָתוֹם Mourner's Kaddish L121 S82 F52

## SHABBAT TORAH SERVICE L168 S139 F394

✕ ~~יי יי אֵ-ל רַחוּם וְחַנּוּן Adonay adonay el raḥum veḥannun~~
✕ ~~רִבּוֹנוֹ שֶׁל עוֹלָם Ribbono shel olam~~
✕ ~~וַאֲנִי תְפִלָּתִי לְךָ Va'ani tefillati lekha~~

Remove **2** Torah scrolls from ark.

**1st scroll** 7 aliyot from כִּי תִשָּׂא Ki tissa
שְׁמוֹת Shemot (Exodus) 33:12–34:26
1 33:12–16 2 33:17–19 3 33:20–23 4 34:1–3
5 34:4–10° 6 34:11–17 7 34:18–26

☞ °34:6–7, 9 Chant these verses in the usual manner. Do not chant them in the manner they are chanted on fast days.

Place 2nd scroll on table next to 1st scroll.
חֲצִי קַדִּישׁ Short Kaddish L174 S146 F408
Open, raise, display, and wrap 1st scroll.

+ **2nd scroll** Maftir aliyah from פִּינְחָס Pineḥas
M בְּמִדְבַּר Bemidbar (Numbers) 29:26–31

Open, raise, display, and wrap 2nd scroll.

**Haftarah** for Shabbat Ḥol Hamo'ed Sukkot
יְחֶזְקֵאל Yeḥezkel (Ezekiel) 38:18–39:16

**Haftarah blessings:**
✕ ~~Concluding Shabbat בְּרָכָה berakhah~~
+ Concluding Yom Tov בְּרָכָה berakhah with
☞ insertions for Shabbat and for Sukkot L329 S147 F412

יְקוּם פֻּרְקָן Yekum purkan L176 S148 F412
✕ ~~אַב הָרַחֲמִים Av Haraḥamim~~

אַשְׁרֵי Ashrey L181 S151 F420
Return scrolls to ark. L183 S153 F422

חֲצִי קַדִּישׁ Short Kaddish L184 S155 F428

**מוּסָף**

☞ **Yom Tov Amidah:** L343 S166 F456
קְדֻשָּׁה Kedushah for Shabbat L345 S167 F458
✕ ~~אַדִּיר אַדִּירֵנוּ Addir addirenu~~

+ Insertions for Shabbat
+ Insertions for Sukkot
+ Insertions for Ḥol Hamo'ed Sukkot — Day 4 L350 S172 F467

+ Open ark. Do not remove a Torah scroll.
✕ ~~Lulav and etrog~~
✕ ~~Procession~~

+ הוֹשַׁע־נָא Hosha'na L387 S202 F535
+ אוֹם נְצוּרָה Om netsurah L387 S202 F536
+ כְּהוֹשַׁעְתָּ Kehosha'ta for Shabbat L388 S202 F536
+ הוֹשִׁיעָה אֶת־עַמֶּךָ Hoshi'ah et ammekha L391 S204 F538
Close ark.

קַדִּישׁ שָׁלֵם Full Kaddish L203 S181 F506
Continue with אֵין כֵּא·לֹהֵינוּ Eyn keloheynu. L204 S182 F508

**קִדּוּשָׁא רַבָּא**

**Daytime Kiddush for Shabbat, in the sukkah:** L81 S335 F746
וְשָׁמְרוּ Veshameru
זָכוֹר Zakhor (many omit)
עַל־כֵּן בֵּרַךְ Al ken berakh
✕ ~~וַיְדַבֵּר מֹשֶׁה Vaydabber mosheh (Vayikra 23:44)~~
בּוֹרֵא פְּרִי הַגָּפֶן Bo·re peri hagafen
+ לֵישֵׁב בַּסֻּכָּה Leshev basukkah

**At home**

See "Eating in the Sukkah," p. 27.

**מִנְחָה**

Minḥah for Shabbat L214 S226 W170 F558

**Torah** 3 aliyot from וְזֹאת הַבְּרָכָה Vezot haberakhah
דְּבָרִים Devarim (Deuteronomy) 33:1–17
1 33:1–7 2 8–12 3 13–17 W319 P940

**Shabbat Amidah:** L223 S234 W178 F574
+ יַעֲלֶה וְיָבוֹא Ya'aleh veyavo for Sukkot L227 S237 W181 F580

✕ ~~צִדְקָתְךָ צֶדֶק Tsidkatekha tsedek~~

סכות Sukkot

| Tishrey 5779 | | | | | | |
|---|---|---|---|---|---|---|
| | 1 | 2 | 3 | 4 | 5 | 6 |
| 7 | 8 | 9 | 10 | 11 | 12 | 13 |
| 14 | 15 | 16 | 17 | 18 | 19 | 20 |
| 21 | 22 | 23 | 24 | 25 | 26 | 27 |
| 28 | 29 | 30 | | | | |

| Sep \| Oct 2018 | | | | | | |
|---|---|---|---|---|---|---|
| 10 | 11 | 12 | 13 | 14 | 15 | |
| 16 | 17 | 18 | 19 | 20 | 21 | 22 |
| 23 | 24 | 25 | 26 | 27 | 28 | 29 |
| 30 \| 1 | 2 | 3 | 4 | 5 | 6 | |
| 7 | 8 | 9 | | | | |

+ Add ✕ Omit ☞ Take note!

**Siddurim**
- **L** Lev Shalem for Shabbat and Festivals
- **S** Shabbat and Festival Sim Shalom
- **W** Weekday Sim Shalom
- **F** Full Sim Shalom (both editions)
- **P** Personal Edition of Full Sim Shalom

## Hosha'na Rabbah

Hosha'na Rabbah, the last day of Sukkot, is the final day of the intense period of reflection and self-evaluation that began on Rosh Hashanah. This day is considered the time of the final sealing of God's judgment. Thus, this day shares with Yom Kippur some themes of repentance and forgiveness. The *sheliaḥ/sheliḥat tsibbur* wears a *kittel* (plain white robe) for the מוּסָף *musaf* service.

The Hosha'na Rabbah service is very complex, combining elements of weekday, festival, and High Holiday services. The נֻסַּח *nusaḥ* (traditional musical chant) for the different sections also reflects the wide range of holiday moods expressed. A proper נֻסַּח for each section is noted. For some sections, it is understood that there are differing cantorial traditions.

### Hosha'na Prayers and Processions

The procedures are the same as those for the previous days (see p. 32). However, there are 7 Hosha'na prayers and 7 processions around the sanctuary. Many congregations remove all the Torah scrolls from the ark at this point. The ark remains open during the processions.

1. Before beginning the first procession, chant the introductory הוֹשַׁע־נָא *hosha'na* lines. L392 S200 W116 F530
2. For each procession, proceed counterclockwise, making a circle around the reading table, Torah scroll, and sanctuary.
3. During each procession, chant the הוֹשַׁע־נָא poem designated for that procession. Precede and follow each phrase of the poem (or small groups of phrases) with the word הוֹשַׁע־נָא.

### Aravot — The 5 Willow Branches

1. Just before תַּעֲנֶה אֱמוּנִים *ta'aneh emunim,* L397 S210 F544 set aside the *lulav* and *etrog*.
2. Take a bundle of 5 עֲרָבוֹת *aravot* (willow branches).
3. Return Torah scrolls to the ark and close the ark before beating the עֲרָבוֹת. (Some return the scrolls after beating the עֲרָבוֹת.)
4. Beat the bundle of עֲרָבוֹת against the floor or other hard surface, stripping off some of the leaves.
   Do *not* beat more than 5 times.

---

**Tishrey 21 תִּשְׁרֵי**
**Sat 29 Sep**

## הוֹשַׁעְנָא רַבָּה Hosha'na Rabbah

**Last day of Ḥol Hamo'ed**

**מוֹצָאֵי שַׁבָּת Motsa'ey Shabbat Conclusion of Shabbat**

עַרְבִית — Arvit for Saturday night L264 S281 W137 F200

**Weekday Amidah:**

+ אַתָּה חוֹנַנְתָּנוּ Attah ḥonantanu L272 S287 W143 F212
+ יַעֲלֶה וְיָבוֹא Ya'aleh veyavo for Sukkot L277 S289 W145 F216

| + Add | ✗ Omit | ☞ Take note! | **Tishrey 5779** | Sep \| Oct 2018 | תִּשְׁרֵי 21 | Sep 29 |
|---|---|---|---|---|---|---|

**Siddurim**
- **L** Lev Shalem for Shabbat and Festivals
- **S** Shabbat and Festival Sim Shalom
- **W** Weekday Sim Shalom
- **F** Full Sim Shalom (both editions)
- **P** Personal Edition of Full Sim Shalom

Sep 30

סֻכּוֹת Sukkot

✗ חֲצִי קַדִּישׁ Short Kaddish

✗ וִיהִי נֹעַם Vihi no'am

✗ יוֹשֵׁב בְּסֵתֶר עֶלְיוֹן Yoshev bᵉseter elyon

✗ וְאַתָּה קָדוֹשׁ Vᵉ'attah kadosh

    קַדִּישׁ שָׁלֵם Full Kaddish    ᴸ280 ˢ294 ᵂ160 ᶠ688

✗ הַבְדָּלָה Havdalah during Arvit

    עָלֵינוּ Aleynu    ᴸ281 ˢ297 ᵂ163 ᶠ696
    קַדִּישׁ יָתוֹם Mourner's Kaddish (some omit)    ᴸ282 ˢ298 ᵂ164 ᶠ698
+ Psalm 27 for the Season of Repentance    ᴸ59 ˢ80 ᵂ92 ᶠ40
    קַדִּישׁ יָתוֹם Mourner's Kaddish    ᴸ58 ˢ82 ᵂ100 ᶠ52

    Havdalah for the end of a usual Shabbat,
    in the sukkah    ᴸ283 ˢ299 ᵂ165 ᶠ700

✗ לֵישֵׁב בַּסֻּכָּה Leshev basukkah

**Sun 30 Sep**    שַׁחֲרִית    Shaḥarit for weekdays    ᵂ1 ᶠ2

    בִּרְכוֹת הַשַּׁחַר Birkhot hashaḥar    ᵂ6 ᶠ2
    Use Yamim Nora'im nusaḥ.

    **Before מִזְמוֹר שִׁיר Mizmor shir (Psalm 30)**    ᵂ14 ᶠ50
    **or at end of service, recite:**
    Psalm for Sunday (Psalm 24)    ᵂ85 ᶠ22
    Use weekday minor nusaḥ for the psalms.
    קַדִּישׁ יָתוֹם Mourner's Kaddish (some omit)    ᵂ100 ᶠ52
+ Psalm 27 for the Season of Repentance    ᵂ92 ᶠ40
    קַדִּישׁ יָתוֹם Mourner's Kaddish    ᵂ100 ᶠ52

    מִזְמוֹר שִׁיר (Psalm 30)    ᵂ14 ᶠ50
    קַדִּישׁ יָתוֹם Mourner's Kaddish    ᵂ15 ᶠ52

    בָּרוּךְ שֶׁאָמַר Barukh she'amar    ᵂ16 ᶠ54
    Use Yamim Nora'im nusaḥ.

    הוֹדוּ לַיי Hodu ladonay    ᵂ17 ᶠ54
    Use weekday minor nusaḥ up to יִשְׁתַּבַּח.

☞ מִזְמוֹר לְתוֹדָה Mizmor lᵉtodah    ᴸ446 ˢ205 ᵂ20 ᶠ60

+ Psalms recited on Shabbat and Yom Tov:
☞ Psalms 19, 34, 90, 91, 135, 136, 33, 92, 93    ᴸ127–34 ˢ87–95 ᶠ60–78

    Continue with the usual weekday service from
    יְהִי כְבוֹד יי Yᵉhi khᵉvod adonay    ᵂ20 ᶠ80

יִשְׁתַּבַּח Yishtabbaḥ W29 F94
Use weekday Ahavah Rabbah nusaḥ.

Open ark.
Repeat each verse after the sheliaḥ/sheliḥat tsibbur:
+ שִׁיר הַמַּעֲלוֹת, מִמַּעֲמַקִּים Shir hama'alot, mima'amakkim (Psalm 130): W62 F134
Use Seliḥot nusaḥ.
Close ark.

חֲצִי קַדִּישׁ Short Kaddish W29 F94
Use weekday Ahavah Rabbah nusaḥ.

בָּרְכוּ Barekhu and response W30 F96
Use weekday Ahavah Rabbah nusaḥ.

בָּרוּךְ . . . יוֹצֵר אוֹר Barukh . . . yotser or W30 F96
Use Yamim Nora'im nusaḥ through בָּרוּךְ . . . גָּאַל יִשְׂרָאֵל.

**Weekday Amidah:** W36 F106
Use weekday Amidah (pentatonic) nusaḥ.
+ יַעֲלֶה וְיָבוֹא Ya'aleh veyavo for Sukkot W41 F114

✕ ~~תַּחֲנוּן Taḥanun~~

☞ Those wearing תְּפִלִּין tefillin now remove and pack them.

For instructions on taking the lulav and etrog, see p. 27.
For waving the lulav during Hallel, see p. 31.

+ הַלֵּל שָׁלֵם Full Hallel, including waving the lulav W50 F380
Chant the regular Shalosh Regalim Hallel.

Some congregations recite הוֹשַׁע־נָא Hosha'na and conduct the processions with lulav and etrog here, rather than after the Musaf Amidah. See instructions, p. 46.

קַדִּישׁ שָׁלֵם Full Kaddish L321 S138 F392
Chant quickly in major, as on Shabbat.

## ☞ YOM TOV TORAH SERVICE

Chant as on Yom Tov.

+ אֵין כָּמוֹךָ Eyn Kamokha L322 S139 F394
+ יי יי אֵ-ל רַחוּם וְחַנּוּן
Adonay adonay el raḥum veḥannun (3 times) L323 S140 F394
+ רִבּוֹנוֹ שֶׁל עוֹלָם Ribbono shel olam L323 S140 F396
+ וַאֲנִי תְפִלָּתִי לְךָ Va'ani tefillati lekha (3 times) L323 S140 F396

Remove **1** Torah scroll from ark.

שְׁמַע Shema and אֶחָד Eḥad L325 S141 F398
Conclude אֶחָד Eḥad as on High Holidays, with קָדוֹשׁ וְנוֹרָא שְׁמוֹ Kadosh venora shemo.
Chant as on Yamim Nora'im.

גַּדְּלוּ Gaddelu L325 S141 F398
Chant as on Shabbat.

☞ וְיַעֲזֹר Veya'azor L325 S141 F400

**Torah** 4 aliyot from: פָּרָשַׁת פִּינְחָס Parashat Pineḥas
בְּמִדְבַּר Bemidbar (Numbers) 29:26–34°
1 29:26–28  2 29–31  3 32–34  4 29–34  W324 P971

☞ °Use Yamim Nora'im cantillation for all 4 aliyot.

חֲצִי קַדִּישׁ Short Kaddish W71 F146
Use weekday minor nusaḥ.

Open, raise, display, and wrap scroll.

Return scroll to ark. W76 F150

אַשְׁרֵי Ashrey L214 S226 W78 F152
Use weekday minor nusaḥ through וּבָא לְצִיּוֹן.

✕ ~~לַמְנַצֵּחַ Lamenatse·aḥ (Psalm 20)~~
וּבָא לְצִיּוֹן Uva letsiyyon L216 S227 W80 F156

☞ Sheliaḥ/sheliḥat tsibbur customarily wears a *kittel* (plain white robe) for Musaf.

+ חֲצִי קַדִּישׁ Short Kaddish L217 S155 W103 F428
Chant in major as on Shabbat.

מוּסָף

**Silent Yom Tov Amidah:** L343 S166 F456
+ Insertions for Sukkot
+ Insertions for Hosha'na Rabbah L350 S173 F467

**Repetition of the Yom Tov Amidah:** L343 S166 F456
Chant as on Shabbat up to קְדֻשָּׁה.
קְדֻשָּׁה Kedushah for Yom Tov (including אַדִּיר אַדִּירֵנוּ Addir addirenu) L345 S167 F458
Chant as on Yamim Nora'im.
לְדוֹר וָדוֹר Ledor vador, to the end of the Amidah
Use Shalosh Regalim nusaḥ.
+ Insertions for Sukkot
+ Insertions for Hosha'na Rabbah L350 S173 F467

| Tishrey 5779 | | | | | | | Sep \| Oct 2018 | | | | | | |
|---|---|---|---|---|---|---|---|---|---|---|---|---|---|
| | 1 | 2 | 3 | 4 | 5 | 6 | | 10 | 11 | 12 | 13 | 14 | 15 |
| 7 | 8 | 9 | 10 | 11 | 12 | 13 | 16 | 17 | 18 | 19 | 20 | 21 | 22 |
| 14 | 15 | 16 | 17 | 18 | 19 | 20 | 23 | 24 | 25 | 26 | 27 | 28 | 29 |
| 21 | 22 | 23 | 24 | 25 | 26 | 27 | 30 | 1 | 2 | 3 | 4 | 5 | 6 |
| 28 | 29 | 30 | | | | | 7 | 8 | 9 | | | | |

+ Add ✕ Omit ☞ Take note!

**Siddurim**
- **L** Lev Shalem for Shabbat and Festivals
- **S** Shabbat and Festival Sim Shalom
- **W** Weekday Sim Shalom
- **F** Full Sim Shalom (both editions)
- **P** Personal Edition of Full Sim Shalom

For procedures specific to Hosha'na Rabbah for reciting הוֹשַׁע־נָא Hosha'na prayers, including processions with lulav and etrog, see p. 42.

Open ark and remove all the Torah scrolls.

+ Recite 7 הוֹשַׁע־נָא Hosha'na prayers during 7 processions. L392–96 S206–8 F538–42
  Chant in minor.

+ אֲנִי וָהוֹ הוֹשִׁיעָה־נָּא L385 S209 F542
  Chant in major.
  כְּהוֹשַׁעְתָּ Kehosha'ta L385 S209 F542
  Chant in minor.

Put aside the lulav and etrog.
Take a bundle of 5 עֲרָבוֹת aravot (willow branches).

+ תַּעֲנֶה אֱמוּנִים Ta'aneh emunim L397 S210 F544

Return scrolls to ark, and close ark.
(Some return the scrolls after beating the עֲרָבוֹת.)

+ Sheliaḥ/sheliḥat tsibbur, then congregation:
  קוֹל מְבַשֵּׂר, מְבַשֵּׂר וְאוֹמֵר
  Kol mevasser, mevasser ve'omer L399 S211 F545
  Chant in major.
  Repeat two more times.

+ Beat the עֲרָבוֹת against the floor or other hard surface.
☞ Do *not* beat more than 5 times.

+ הוֹשִׁיעָה אֶת־עַמֶּךָ Hoshi'ah et ammekha L401 S212 F546
  Chant in major.

+ יְהִי רָצוֹן Yehi ratson L401 S212 F547

קַדִּישׁ שָׁלֵם Full Kaddish L203 S181 F506
Chant quickly in major, as on Shabbat. Continue as on Shabbat.

+ אֵין כֵּא·לֹהֵינוּ Eyn keloheynu L204 S182 F508
  עָלֵינוּ Aleynu L281 S183 F510

**If psalms for the day were not recited at Shaḥarit, add here:**
קַדִּישׁ יָתוֹם Mourner's Kaddish (some omit) L282 S184 F512
Psalm for Sunday (Psalm 24) W85 F22
Use weekday minor nusaḥ for the psalms.

קַדִּישׁ יָתוֹם Mourner's Kaddish (some omit) L58 S82 F52
+ Psalm 27 for the Season of Repentance L59 S80 F40
קַדִּישׁ יָתוֹם Mourner's Kaddish L282|58 S184|82 F512|52

**At home** See “Eating in the Sukkah,” p. 27.

**מִנְחָה** Minḥah for weekdays L289 S1 W120 F164

**Weekday Amidah:**

+ יַעֲלֶה וְיָבוֹא Ya’aleh veyavo for Sukkot L298 S7 W127 F178

✕ ~~תַּחֲנוּן Taḥanun~~

## Shemini Atseret and Simḥat Torah

### Preparing for Yom Tov

**Preparing a Flame for Yom Tov**

Before candle lighting for Shemini Atseret (Sunday), prepare a flame. See p. 26.

### Yom Tov — Day 1 and Day 2

**Candle Lighting**

- **Shemini Atseret:** See “Candle Lighting for Yom Tov — Day 1,” p. 28.
- **Simḥat Torah:** See “Candle Lighting for Yom Tov — Day 2,” p. 33.

**Yom Tov Meals — Day 1 and Day 2**

- **Shemini Atseret:** Continue to eat meals in the *sukkah*, but do not say the בְּרָכָה *berakhah* for dwelling in the *sukkah*.
- **Simḥat Torah:** Do not eat in the *sukkah*.

Enjoy festive meals evening and daytime, in the manner of Shabbat meals, with:

- Yom Tov קִדּוּשׁ *kiddush:* Evening L79 S334 F742 Daytime L81 S335 F746
- הַמּוֹצִיא *hamotsi* recited over 2 whole חַלָּה *ḥallah* loaves or rolls L81 S313–14 F744|746
- בִּרְכַּת הַמָּזוֹן *birkat hamazon* with additions for Shemini Atseret and Simḥat Torah (see yellow box, p. 48)
- Festive singing

## Tishrey 22 תִּשְׁרֵי Sun 30 Sep — שְׁמִינִי עֲצֶרֶת Shemini Atseret

**עַרְבִית** Arvit for Yom Tov L39 S28 F279

+ וַיְדַבֵּר מֹשֶׁה Vaydabber mosheh (Vayikra 23:44) L46 S34 F294

חֲצִי קַדִּישׁ Short Kaddish L46 S34 F294

**Yom Tov Amidah:** L306 S41 F304

+ Insertions for Shemini Atseret

קַדִּישׁ שָׁלֵם Full Kaddish L54 S48 F316

Tishrey 5779

| | | | | | | |
|---|---|---|---|---|---|---|
| | 1 | 2 | 3 | 4 | 5 | 6 |
| 7 | 8 | 9 | 10 | 11 | 12 | 13 |
| 14 | 15 | 16 | 17 | 18 | 19 | 20 |
| 21 | 22 | 23 | 24 | 25 | 26 | 27 |
| 28 | 29 | 30 | | | | |

Sep | Oct 2018

| | | | | | | |
|---|---|---|---|---|---|---|
| | 10 | 11 | 12 | 13 | 14 | 15 |
| 16 | 17 | 18 | 19 | 20 | 21 | 22 |
| 23 | 24 | 25 | 26 | 27 | 28 | 29 |
| 30 | 1 | 2 | 3 | 4 | 5 | 6 |
| 7 | 8 | 9 | | | | |

+ Add ✕ Omit ☞ Take note!

**Siddurim**
- **L** Lev Shalem for Shabbat and Festivals
- **S** Shabbat and Festival Sim Shalom
- **W** Weekday Sim Shalom
- **F** Full Sim Shalom (both editions)
- **P** Personal Edition of Full Sim Shalom



✕ ~~קִדּוּשׁ Kiddush during Arvit~~

Conclude as on Shabbat.

Some continue to recite:
Psalm 27 for the Season of Repentance L59 S80 F40
קַדִּישׁ יָתוֹם Mourner's Kaddish L58 S82 F52

☞ **At the conclusion of Arvit, in the sukkah:**
+ קִדּוּשׁ Kiddush for Yom Tov with insertions for Shemini Atseret L79 S50 F318
+ שֶׁהֶחֱיָנוּ Sheheḥeyanu L80 S50 F320
✕ ~~לֵישֵׁב בַּסֻּכָּה Leshev basukkah~~

**At home** See "Yom Tov Meals — Day 1 and Day 2," p. 47.

**DURING Shemini Atseret and Simḥat Torah**

**Birkat Hamazon:**
+ יַעֲלֶה וְיָבוֹא Ya'aleh veyavo for Shemini Atseret L90|95 S340|347 W233|239 F762|780
+ הָרַחֲמָן Haraḥaman for Yom Tov L92|96 S343|348 W236|240 F768
✕ ~~הָרַחֲמָן Haraḥaman for Sukkot~~

**Mon 1 Oct** שַׁחֲרִית

At the end of the preliminary service, begin formal chanting at
הָאֵ·ל בְּתַעֲצוּמוֹת עֻזֶּךָ Ha'el beta'atsumot uzzekha. L147 S105 F336

✕ ~~הַכֹּל יוֹדוּךָ Hakol yodukha~~
✕ ~~אֵ·ל אָדוֹן El adon~~
✕ ~~לָאֵ·ל אֲשֶׁר שָׁבַת La'el asher shavat~~
+ הַמֵּאִיר לָאָרֶץ Hame'ir la'arets L152 S109 F342

**Yom Tov Amidah:** L306 S123 F366
+ Insertions for Shemini Atseret

+ הַלֵּל שָׁלֵם Full Hallel L316 S133 F380

קַדִּישׁ שָׁלֵם Full Kaddish L321 S138 F392

**YOM TOV TORAH SERVICE** L322 S139 F394
+ יי יי אֵ·ל רַחוּם וְחַנּוּן Adonay adonay el raḥum veḥannun (3 times) L323 S140 F394
+ רִבּוֹנוֹ שֶׁל עוֹלָם Ribbono shel olam L323 S140 F396
+ וַאֲנִי תְפִלָּתִי לְךָ Va'ani tefillati lekha (3 times) L323 S140 F396

Remove **2** Torah scrolls from ark.

**1st scroll** 5 aliyot from רְאֵה Re'eh
דְּבָרִים Devarim (Deuteronomy) 14:22–16:17
[1]14:22–29 [2]15:1–18 [3]15:19–16:3 [4]16:4–8 [5]16:9–17
Some divide as follows:
[1]14:22–15:23 [2]16:1–3 [3]16:4–8 [4]16:9–12 [5]16:13–17

Place 2nd scroll on table next to 1st scroll.
חֲצִי קַדִּישׁ Short Kaddish L327 S146 F408
Open, raise, display, and wrap 1st scroll.

**2nd scroll** Maftir aliyah from פִּינְחָס Pineḥas
M בְּמִדְבַּר Bemidbar (Numbers) 29:35–30:1

Open, raise, display, and wrap 2nd scroll.

**Haftarah** for Shemini Atseret
מְלָכִים א׳ 1 Melakhim (1 Kings) 8:54–66

**Haftarah blessings:**
✕ ~~Concluding Shabbat בְּרָכָה berakhah~~
+ Concluding Yom Tov בְּרָכָה berakhah
with insertions for Shemini Atseret L329 S147 F412

✕ ~~יְקוּם פֻּרְקָן Yekum purkan~~

+ יִזְכֹּר Yizkor L330 S188 F516
☞ אַב הָרַחֲמִים Av Haraḥamim L446 S151 F420

אַשְׁרֵי Ashrey L339 S151 F420
Return scrolls to ark. L340 S153 F422

**Mashiv Haruaḥ**
Announce before the silent Amidah: "In the silent Amidah, add מַשִּׁיב הָרוּחַ וּמוֹרִיד הַגָּשֶׁם *mashiv haruaḥ umorid hagashem.*"

For congregations that follow the tradition of Erets Yisra'el to add מוֹרִיד הַטָּל *morid hatal* during the summer, instead announce before the silent Amidah: "In the silent Amidah, replace מוֹרִיד הַטָּל *morid hatal* with מַשִּׁיב הָרוּחַ וּמוֹרִיד הַגָּשֶׁם *mashiv haruaḥ umorid hagashem.*"

☞ Sheliaḥ/sheliḥat tsibbur customarily wears a *kittel* (plain white robe) for Musaf.

| Tishrey 5779 | | | | | | |
|---|---|---|---|---|---|---|
| | 1 | 2 | 3 | 4 | 5 | 6 |
| 7 | 8 | 9 | 10 | 11 | 12 | 13 |
| 14 | 15 | 16 | 17 | 18 | 19 | 20 |
| 21 | 22 | 23 | 24 | 25 | 26 | 27 |
| 28 | 29 | 30 | | | | |

| Sep \| Oct 2018 | | | | | | |
|---|---|---|---|---|---|---|
| | 10 | 11 | 12 | 13 | 14 | 15 |
| 16 | 17 | 18 | 19 | 20 | 21 | 22 |
| 23 | 24 | 25 | 26 | 27 | 28 | 29 |
| 30 | 1 | 2 | 3 | 4 | 5 | 6 |
| 7 | 8 | 9 | | | | |

+ Add ✕ Omit ☞ Take note!

**Siddurim**
- **L** Lev Shalem for Shabbat and Festivals
- **S** Shabbat and Festival Sim Shalom
- **W** Weekday Sim Shalom
- **F** Full Sim Shalom (both editions)
- **P** Personal Edition of Full Sim Shalom



חֲצִי קַדִּישׁ Short Kaddish L342 S155 F428
The distinctive traditional melody of this Kaddish anticipates the opening melody of the repetition of the Amidah.

**מוּסָף**

**Silent Yom Tov Amidah:** L343 S166 F456
+ מַשִּׁיב הָרוּחַ Mashiv haruaḥ L344 S166 F456
+ Insertions for Shemini Atseret

Open ark.

**Repetition of the Yom Tov Amidah:** L374 S217 F482
+ תְּפִלַּת גֶּשֶׁם Tefillat geshem L377 S218 F482

Close ark.

Continue with מְכַלְכֵּל חַיִּים Mekhalkel ḥayyim L344 S166 F456
+ Insertions for Shemini Atseret

Some congregations include in the repetition of the Amidah the Priestly Blessing by the Kohanim (*dukhenen*).
בִּרְכַּת כֹּהֲנִים Birkat kohanim L353 S177 F472
For procedures, see p. 213.

קַדִּישׁ שָׁלֵם Full Kaddish L203 S181 F506
Continue with אֵין כֵּא·לֹהֵינוּ Eyn keloheynu. L204 S182 F508

Some continue to recite:
Psalm 27 for the Season of Repentance L59 S80 F40
קַדִּישׁ יָתוֹם Mourner's Kaddish L58 S82 F52

**קִדּוּשָׁא רַבָּא**

☞ **Daytime Kiddush for Yom Tov, in the sukkah:** L81 S335 F746
וַיְדַבֵּר מֹשֶׁה Vaydabber mosheh (Vayikra 23:44)
בּוֹרֵא פְּרִי הַגָּפֶן Bo·re peri hagafen
✕ ~~לֵישֵׁב בַּסֻּכָּה Leshev basukkah~~

**At home**

See "Yom Tov Meals — Day 1 and Day 2," p. 47.

**UNTIL Pesaḥ**

**Every Amidah:**
+ מַשִּׁיב הָרוּחַ וּמוֹרִיד הַגֶּשֶׁם Mashiv haruaḥ umorid hagashem

**מִנְחָה**

אַשְׁרֵי Ashrey L214 S226 W170 F558
וּבָא לְצִיּוֹן Uva letsiyyon L216 S227 W171 F560
חֲצִי קַדִּישׁ Short Kaddish L217 S229 W173 F564

**Yom Tov Amidah:** L306 S242 W184 F586
+ מַשִּׁיב הָרוּחַ Mashiv haruaḥ
+ Insertions for Shemini Atseret

קַדִּישׁ שָׁלֵם Full Kaddish L230 S247 W189 F596
עָלֵינוּ Aleynu L231 S248 W190 F598
קַדִּישׁ יָתוֹם Mourner's Kaddish L232 S249 W191 F600



## Celebrating with the Torah on Simḥat Torah

**Attah Hor'eyta**

Whenever we remove the Torah from the ark, we first recite several biblical verses in praise of God. On Simḥat Torah we recite a much larger collection of verses, known as אַתָּה הָרְאֵתָ *attah hor'eyta.* L402 S213 F548

Traditionally, a person recites a verse, and the congregation repeats it. In many congregations, various people take turns leading this recitation.

In congregations where the verses are repeated to accommodate more leaders:

1. Recite the first 10 verses sequentially, through . . . וְיִהְיוּ נָא *veyihyu na. . . .*
2. Repeat this block of 10 verses as necessary.
3. Open the ark, and recite the remaining 9 verses from וַיְהִי בִּנְסֹעַ *vayhi binsoa.*

**Hakkafot**

Throughout the year, before we read the Torah, we carry the scroll(s) around the sanctuary in procession. On Simḥat Torah, both evening and morning, we carry *all* the Torah scrolls in 7 הַקָּפוֹת *hakkafot* (processions around the sanctuary). These are reminiscent of the processions of the priests around the altar of the Temple in ancient times. The ark remains open during the processions.

For each הַקָּפָה *hakkafah:*

1. Ask a different congregant to lead.
2. Proceed counterclockwise, making a circle around the reading table and sanctuary.
3. During the procession, chant the assigned liturgical lines, sung phrase by phrase and repeated by the congregation. L404 S214 F550
4. Encourage festive singing and dancing.

## Tishrey 23 תִּשְׁרֵי — שִׂמְחַת תּוֹרָה Simḥat Torah

Mon 1 Oct

עַרְבִית Arvit for Yom Tov L39 S28 F279

+ וַיְדַבֵּר מֹשֶׁה Vaydabber mosheh (Vayikra 23:44) L46 S34 F294

חֲצִי קַדִּישׁ Short Kaddish L46 S34 F294

| Tishrey 5779 | | | | | | | Sep \| Oct 2018 | | | | | | |
|---|---|---|---|---|---|---|---|---|---|---|---|---|---|
| | 1 | 2 | 3 | 4 | 5 | 6 | | 10 | 11 | 12 | 13 | 14 | 15 |
| 7 | 8 | 9 | 10 | 11 | 12 | 13 | 16 | 17 | 18 | 19 | 20 | 21 | 22 |
| 14 | 15 | 16 | 17 | 18 | 19 | 20 | 23 | 24 | 25 | 26 | 27 | 28 | 29 |
| 21 | 22 | 23 | 24 | 25 | 26 | 27 | 30 | 1 | 2 | 3 | 4 | 5 | 6 |
| 28 | 29 | 30 | | | | | 7 | 8 | 9 | | | | |

+ Add ✕ Omit ☞ Take note!

**Siddurim**
- **L** Lev Shalem for Shabbat and Festivals
- **S** Shabbat and Festival Sim Shalom
- **W** Weekday Sim Shalom
- **F** Full Sim Shalom (both editions)
- **P** Personal Edition of Full Sim Shalom

שִׂמְחַת תּוֹרָה Simḥat Torah

Yom Tov Amidah: L306 S41 F304
+ Insertions for Simḥat Torah

קַדִּישׁ שָׁלֵם Full Kaddish L54 S48 F316

**TORAH SERVICE FOR SIMḤAT TORAH** L402 S213 F548

אַתָּה הָרְאֵתָ Attah hor'eyta L402 S213 F548
For procedures, see p. 51.

Remove all Torah scrolls from ark.

Perform 7 הַקָּפוֹת hakkafot around the sanctuary.
For procedures, see p. 51. L404 S214 F550

Return all but 1 Torah scroll to ark.

שְׁמַע Shema and אֶחָד Eḥad L325 S141 F398
Conclude אֶחָד Eḥad as on High Holidays, with קָדוֹשׁ וְנוֹרָא שְׁמוֹ Kadosh venora shemo.
Chant as on Yamim Nora'im.

Continue with גַּדְּלוּ Gaddelu, and carry the Torah in a procession, as usual.

☞ וְיַעֲזֹר Veya'azor L325 S141 F400

**Torah** 3 aliyot from וְזֹאת הַבְּרָכָה Vezot haberakhah
דְּבָרִים Devarim (Deuteronomy) 33:1–17
¹33:1–7 ²8–12 ³13–17 W319 P940

Use Yamim Nora'im cantillation for this reading.

☞ חֲצִי קַדִּישׁ Short Kaddish L327 S146 F408
Open, raise, display, and wrap the scroll.

Return scroll to ark as at Shabbat Minḥah. L221 S232 F570

+ קִדּוּשׁ Kiddush for Yom Tov
with insertions for Simḥat Torah L79 S50 F318
+ שֶׁהֶחֱיָנוּ Sheheḥeyanu L80 S50 F319

עָלֵינוּ Aleynu L56 S51 F320
Conclude as on Shabbat.

✕ ~~Psalm 27 for the Season of Repentance~~

**At home** See "Candle Lighting" and "Yom Tov Meals," p. 47.

## Reading the Torah on Simḥat Torah Morning

### The 1st Scroll: Completing the Reading of the Torah

After 7 הַקָּפוֹת *hakkafot,* traditionally everyone is called to the Torah. Repeat the first 5 readings until all are called except those to be called for the 2 special *aliyot* (see below) and the מַפְטִיר *maftir aliyah.* If כֹּהֵן *kohen* and לֵוִי *levi* are usually called for the first 2 *aliyot,* call them for the first 2 *aliyot* of each round of 5, until all of them are called. Call the last adult together with all the children (עִם כָּל־הַנְּעָרִים ... יַעֲמֹד *ya'amod . . . im kol hane'arim*). Spread a large טַלִּית *tallit* above the children. The adult recites the בְּרָכוֹת *berakhot.* Before the second בְּרָכָה, bless the children with הַמַּלְאָךְ הַגֹּאֵל אֹתִי (Bereshit 48:16) S295 F692.

Many congregations hold concurrent Torah readings. After everyone has been called to the Torah, gather again as a single congregation. In some congregations people are called to the Torah as families or other small groups.

Whether there is one Torah reading or several readings at different stations, there must be at all times, at each reading, at least 10 adults attending to the reading.

Recite מֵרְשׁוּת *mereshut* to call חֲתַן הַתּוֹרָה *ḥatan hatorah* ("groom" of the Torah) or כַּלַּת הַתּוֹרָה *kallat hatorah* ("bride" of the Torah), the person called for the *aliyah* that completes the reading of the Torah. See p. 55.

Chant the parashah using the cantillation of the High Holidays. As we complete the reading of the Torah, we complete the holiday season as well.

### The 2nd Scroll: Beginning the Reading of the Torah Anew

After we complete the reading of the Torah, we immediately begin reading it again, a symbolic act expressing our continuing dedication to the study of Torah.

Recite מֵרְשׁוּת *mereshut* to call חֲתַן בְּרֵאשִׁית *ḥatan bereshit* ("groom" of Bereshit) or כַּלַּת בְּרֵאשִׁית *kallat bereshit* ("bride" of Bereshit), the person called for the *aliyah* that begins the reading of the Torah anew. See p. 55.

The congregation participates in the festive reading of this section in two ways.

1. Each day of creation ends with the refrain ... וַיְהִי־עֶרֶב וַיְהִי־בֹקֶר יוֹם *vayhi erev vayhi voker yom . . .* ("then was evening, then was morning, the 1st [2nd, 3rd . . .] day"). For each of the 6 occurrences of the refrain (1:5, 8, 13, 19, 23, and 31), follow this procedure:
   a. At the phrase preceding the refrain, the Torah reader uses a prompting melody to alert the congregation.
   b. After the prompt, the reader pauses.
   c. The congregation chants ... וַיְהִי־עֶרֶב וַיְהִי־בֹקֶר יוֹם, the refrain for that day.
   d. When the congregation finishes, the reader chants the refrain from the Torah using the concluding melody phrase of the Shirat Hayam melody.
   e. The reader continues reading.
2. When the reader reaches וַיְכֻלּוּ (2:1), the reader pauses.
   a. The congregation chants the וַיְכֻלּוּ passage (2:1–3).
   b. After the congregation finishes, the reader chants the passage.

| Tishrey 5779 | | | | | | |
|---|---|---|---|---|---|---|
| | 1 | 2 | 3 | 4 | 5 | 6 |
| 7 | 8 | 9 | 10 | 11 | 12 | 13 |
| 14 | 15 | 16 | 17 | 18 | 19 | 20 |
| 21 | 22 | 23 | 24 | 25 | 26 | 27 |
| 28 | 29 | 30 | | | | |

| Sep \| Oct 2018 | | | | | | |
|---|---|---|---|---|---|---|
| | 10 | 11 | 12 | 13 | 14 | 15 |
| 16 | 17 | 18 | 19 | 20 | 21 | 22 |
| 23 | 24 | 25 | 26 | 27 | 28 | 29 |
| 30 \| | 1 | 2 | 3 | 4 | 5 | 6 |
| 7 | 8 | 9 | | | | |

+ Add ✕ Omit ☞ Take note!

**Siddurim**
- **L** Lev Shalem for Shabbat and Festivals
- **S** Shabbat and Festival Sim Shalom
- **W** Weekday Sim Shalom
- **F** Full Sim Shalom (both editions)
- **P** Personal Edition of Full Sim Shalom



## Tue 2 Oct שַׁחֲרִית

At the end of the preliminary service, begin formal chanting at
הָאֵ-ל בְּתַעֲצוּמוֹת עֻזֶּךָ Ha'el beta'atsumot uzzekha. L147 S105 F336

✕ ~~הַכֹּל יוֹדוּךָ Hakol yodukha~~
✕ ~~אֵ-ל אָדוֹן El adon~~
✕ ~~לָאֵ-ל אֲשֶׁר שָׁבַת La'el asher shavat~~

+ הַמֵּאִיר לָאָרֶץ Hame'ir la'arets L152 S109 F342

**Yom Tov Amidah:** L306 S123 F366
+ Insertions for Simḥat Torah

Some congregations include in the repetition of the Amidah the Priestly Blessing by the Kohanim (*dukhenen*).
☞ On Simḥat Torah, perform this at Shaḥarit.
בִּרְכַּת כֹּהֲנִים Birkat kohanim L353 S177 F472
For procedures, see p. 213.

+ הַלֵּל שָׁלֵם Full Hallel L316 S133 F380

קַדִּישׁ שָׁלֵם Full Kaddish L321 S138 F392

**TORAH SERVICE FOR SIMḤAT TORAH** L402 S213 F548

אַתָּה הָרְאֵתָ Attah hor'eyta L402 S213 F548
For procedures, see p. 51.

Remove all Torah scrolls from ark.

Perform 7 הַקָּפוֹת around the sanctuary.
For procedures, see p. 51. L404 S214 F550

Return all but 3 Torah scrolls to ark.
(For concurrent readings, retain additional scrolls.)

שְׁמַע Shema and אֶחָד Eḥad L325 S141 F398
Conclude אֶחָד Eḥad as on High Holidays, with
קָדוֹשׁ וְנוֹרָא שְׁמוֹ Kadosh venora shemo.
Chant as on Yamim Nora'im.

Continue with גַּדְּלוּ Gaddelu, and carry the Torah in a procession, as usual.

**1st scroll** 5 aliyot from וְזֹאת הַבְּרָכָה Vezot haberakhah
דְּבָרִים Devarim (Deuteronomy) 33:1–26
[1]33:1–7 [2]8–12 [3]13–17 [4]18–21 [5]22–26

Use Yamim Nora'im cantillation for this reading.

Repeat these 5 aliyot until all except those designated for the two ḥatan/kallah aliyot and the person reading the haftarah have been called to the Torah. For procedures for this reading, see p. 53.

Call חֲתַן הַתּוֹרָה ḥatan hatorah or כַּלַּת הַתּוֹרָה kallat hatorah:
מֵרְשׁוּת Me^reshut L406 S215 F552
Use the melody of אַקְדָּמוּת, as chanted on Shavu'ot.

**1st scroll** Read the concluding section of the Torah.
דְּבָרִים Devarim (Deuteronomy) 33:27–34:12°

Use Yamim Nora'im cantillation for this reading.

☞ °34:12 When the Torah reader concludes a book of the Torah:

1. Close the Torah scroll.
2. **For Oleh:** Congregation chants חֲזַק חֲזַק וְנִתְחַזֵּק ḥazak ḥazak venitḥazzek; oleh remains silent.
   **For Olah:** Congregation chants חִזְקִי חִזְקִי וְנִתְחַזֵּק ḥizki ḥizki venitḥazzek; olah remains silent.
3. Torah reader repeats congregation's words (oleh/olah remains silent; if Torah reader is the oleh/olah, omit this repetition).
4. Open the Torah scroll.
5. The oleh/olah kisses the Torah scroll, closes it, and continues with the usual concluding berakhah.

Place 2nd scroll on table next to 1st scroll.
Open, raise, display, and wrap 1st scroll.

Call חֲתַן בְּרֵאשִׁית ḥatan bereshit or
כַּלַּת בְּרֵאשִׁית kallat bereshit:
מֵרְשׁוּת Mereshut L407 S216 F554
Use the melody of אַקְדָּמוּת, as chanted on Shavu'ot.

**2nd scroll** Read the opening section of the Torah.
בְּרֵאשִׁית Bereshit (Genesis) °1:1–2:3

Use regular Shabbat cantillation for this reading.

☞ °1:1–2:3 Use special procedures for this reading. See p. 53.

Place 3rd scroll on table next to 2nd scroll.
Place or hold 1st scroll near other scrolls at table.
(Some do not return the 1st scroll to table.)

חֲצִי קַדִּישׁ Short Kaddish L327 S146 F408
Open, raise, display, and wrap 2nd scroll.

| Tishrey 5779 | | | | | | |
|---|---|---|---|---|---|---|
| | 1 | 2 | 3 | 4 | 5 | 6 |
| 7 | 8 | 9 | 10 | 11 | 12 | 13 |
| 14 | 15 | 16 | 17 | 18 | 19 | 20 |
| 21 | 22 | 23 | 24 | 25 | 26 | 27 |
| 28 | 29 | 30 | | | | |

| Sep \| Oct 2018 | | | | | | |
|---|---|---|---|---|---|---|
| | 10 | 11 | 12 | 13 | 14 | 15 |
| 16 | 17 | 18 | 19 | 20 | 21 | 22 |
| 23 | 24 | 25 | 26 | 27 | 28 | 29 |
| 30 | 1 | 2 | 3 | 4 | 5 | 6 |
| 7 | 8 | 9 | | | | |

+ Add ✕ Omit ☞ Take note!

**Siddurim**
- **L** Lev Shalem for Shabbat and Festivals
- **S** Shabbat and Festival Sim Shalom
- **W** Weekday Sim Shalom
- **F** Full Sim Shalom (both editions)
- **P** Personal Edition of Full Sim Shalom

+ **3rd scroll** Maftir aliyah from פִּינְחָס Pineḥas
בְּמִדְבַּר[M] Bemidbar (Numbers) 29:35–30:1

Open, raise, display, and wrap 3rd scroll.

**Haftarah** for Simḥat Torah
יְהוֹשֻׁעַ Yehoshua (Joshua) 1:1–18

**Haftarah blessings:**
✕ ~~Concluding Shabbat בְּרָכָה berakhah~~
+ Concluding Yom Tov בְּרָכָה berakhah
with insertions for Simḥat Torah L329 S147 F412

✕ ~~יְקוּם פֻּרְקָן Yekum purkan~~
✕ ~~אַב הָרַחֲמִים Av Haraḥamim~~

אַשְׁרֵי Ashrey L339 S151 F420
Return scrolls to ark. L340 S153 F422
חֲצִי קַדִּישׁ Short Kaddish L342 S155 F428

**מוּסָף**

**Yom Tov Amidah:** L343 S166 F456
+ Insertions for Simḥat Torah

☞ In congregations where the Kohanim recite the Priestly Blessing (*dukhenen*), on Simḥat Torah recite at Shaḥarit, not at Musaf.

קַדִּישׁ שָׁלֵם Full Kaddish L203 S181 F506
Continue with אֵין כֵּא·לֹהֵינוּ Eyn keloheynu. L204 S182 F508

**קִדּוּשָׁא רַבָּא**

**Daytime Kiddush for Yom Tov:** L81 S335 F746
וַיְדַבֵּר מֹשֶׁה Vaydabber mosheh (Vayikra 23:44)
בּוֹרֵא פְּרִי הַגָּפֶן Bo·re peri hagafen

**At home**

See "Yom Tov Meals — Day 1 and Day 2," p. 47.

**מִנְחָה**

אַשְׁרֵי Ashrey L214 S226 W170 F558
וּבָא לְצִיּוֹן Uva letsiyyon L216 S227 W171 F560
חֲצִי קַדִּישׁ Short Kaddish L217 S229 W173 F564

**Yom Tov Amidah:** L306 S242 W184 F586
+ Insertions for Simḥat Torah

קַדִּישׁ שָׁלֵם Full Kaddish L230 S247 W189 F596
עָלֵינוּ Aleynu L231 S248 W190 F598
קַדִּישׁ יָתוֹם Mourner's Kaddish L232 S249 W191 F600

**Tishrey 24 תִּשְׁרֵי**
**Tue 2 Oct**

## מוֹצָאֵי יוֹם טוֹב Motsa'ey Yom Tov
## Conclusion of Yom Tov
## אִסְרוּ חַג Isru Ḥag The Day after Yom Tov

עַרְבִית Arvit for weekdays L264 S281 W137 F200

**Weekday Amidah:**
+ אַתָּה חוֹנַנְתָּנוּ Attah ḥonantanu L272 S281 W143 F212

קַדִּישׁ שָׁלֵם Full Kaddish L280 S294 W160 F222

Some recite הַבְדָּלָה Havdalah here. L283 S299 W165 F700
For instructions, see below.

עָלֵינוּ Aleynu L281 S297 W163 F696
קַדִּישׁ יָתוֹם Mourner's Kaddish L282 S298 W164 F698

+ **Havdalah:** L283 S299 W165 F700
✕ ~~הִנֵּה אֵ־ל יְשׁוּעָתִי Hinneh el yeshu'ati~~
בּוֹרֵא פְּרִי הַגָּפֶן Bo·re peri hagafen
✕ ~~בּוֹרֵא מִינֵי בְשָׂמִים Bo·re miney vesamim~~
✕ ~~בּוֹרֵא מְאוֹרֵי הָאֵשׁ Bo·re me'orey ha'esh~~
הַמַּבְדִּיל בֵּין קֹדֶשׁ לְחֹל Hamavdil beyn kodesh leḥol

**Wed 3 Oct** שַׁחֲרִית Shaḥarit for weekdays W1 F2

✕ ~~תַּחֲנוּן Taḥanun~~

☞ לַמְנַצֵּחַ Lamenatse·aḥ (Psalm 20) W79 F154

מִנְחָה ✕ ~~תַּחֲנוּן Taḥanun~~

---

**Tishrey 25 תִּשְׁרֵי**
**Thu 4 Oct** (daytime)

**BEGINNING 25 Tishrey** Some resume reciting תַּחֲנוּן Taḥanun.
Others do not resume until 2 Ḥeshvan.

**Torah** 3 aliyot from בְּרֵאשִׁית Bereshit
בְּרֵאשִׁית Bereshit (Genesis) 1:1–13
1 1:1–5 2 6–8 3 9–13 W264 P885

# Oct 6  27 תִּשְׁרֵי

| Tishrey 5779 | | | | | | Sep \| Oct 2018 | | | | |
|---|---|---|---|---|---|---|---|---|---|---|
| 1 | 2 | 3 | 4 | 5 | 6 | 10 | 11 | 12 | 13 | 14 | 15 |
| 7 | 8 | 9 | 10 | 11 | 12 | 13 | 16 | 17 | 18 | 19 | 20 | 21 | 22 |
| 14 | 15 | 16 | 17 | 18 | 19 | 20 | 23 | 24 | 25 | 26 | 27 | 28 | 29 |
| 21 | 22 | 23 | 24 | 25 | 26 | 27 | 30 \| 1 | 2 | 3 | 4 | 5 | 6 |
| 28 | 29 | 30 | | | | 7 | 8 | 9 | | | |

**+** Add   **✗** Omit   ☞ Take note!

**Siddurim**
- **L** Lev Shalem for Shabbat and Festivals
- **S** Shabbat and Festival Sim Shalom
- **W** Weekday Sim Shalom
- **F** Full Sim Shalom (both editions)
- **P** Personal Edition of Full Sim Shalom

---

**Tishrey 27  תִּשְׁרֵי**
Sat **6** Oct

**שַׁבָּת Shabbat   פָּרָשַׁת בְּרֵאשִׁית Parashat Bereshit**
**שַׁבָּת מְבָרְכִים הַחֹדֶשׁ Shabbat Mevarekhim Haḥodesh**

**Torah** 7 aliyot (minimum):  בְּרֵאשִׁית Bereshit
בְּרֵאשִׁית Bereshit (Genesis) 1:1–6:8

Annual:    **¹**1:1–2:3°   **²**2:4–19   **³**2:20–3:21   **⁴**3:22–4:18
           **⁵**4:19–26    **⁶**5:1–24   **⁷**5:25–6:8°   **ᴹ**6:5–8

Triennial: **¹**5:1–5    **²**5:6–8     **³**5:9–14      **⁴**5:15–20
           **⁵**5:21–24  **⁶**5:25–31°  **⁷**5:32–6:8    **ᴹ**6:5–8

☞°1:1–2:3  Unlike on Simḥat Torah, the congregation does not recite aloud during this reading.
Use only the usual Torah reading melody.

☞°5:29  Note the rare occurrence of the te'amim (tropes) (אֿ) גֵּרְשַׁ֞יִם and תְּלִישָׁא־גְדוֹלָ֕ה (אֿ) on the same word זֶ֞ה. Chant first the melody of גֵּרְשַׁ֞יִם and then the melody of תְּלִישָׁא־גְדוֹלָ֕ה consecutively on the 1 syllable of the word. Do **not** chant the word twice.

### Haftarah
Ashkenazic: יְשַׁעְיָ֫הוּ Yesha'yahu (Isaiah) 42:5–43:10
Sephardic: יְשַׁעְיָ֫הוּ Yesha'yahu (Isaiah) 42:5–21

**+ Birkat Haḥodesh:**   **ᴸ**180 **ˢ**150 **ᶠ**418
Announce Rosh Ḥodesh Marḥeshvan:
Do not announce the month as "Ḥeshvan."

רֹאשׁ חֹדֶשׁ מַרְחֶשְׁוָן יִהְיֶה בְּיוֹם שְׁלִישִׁי וּבְיוֹם רְבִיעִי . . .
Rosh ḥodesh Marḥeshvan yihyeh beyom shelishi uvyom revi'i . . .
(Monday night, Tuesday, and Wednesday)

**✗** אַב הָרַחֲמִים ~~Av Haraḥamim~~

---

**מִנְחָה**

**Torah** 3 aliyot from נֹחַ Noaḥ
בְּרֵאשִׁית Bereshit (Genesis) 6:9–22
**¹**6:9–16   **²**17–19   **³**20–22                    **ᵂ**265 **ᴾ**886

This is also the reading for the coming Monday and Thursday.

☞ Congregations that have not yet resumed reciting תַּחֲנוּן Taḥanun omit צִדְקָתְךָ צֶדֶק Tsidkatekha tsedek.

## Tishrey 29 תִּשְׁרֵי — Mon 8 Oct

## עֶרֶב רֹאשׁ חֹדֶשׁ Erev Rosh Hodesh
Day before Rosh Hodesh

**מִנְחָה**
✕ ~~תַּחֲנוּן Tahanun~~

## Tishrey 30 תִּשְׁרֵי — Mon 8 Oct (evening)

## רֹאשׁ חֹדֶשׁ חֶשְׁוָן Rosh Hodesh Heshvan — Day 1

**DURING Rosh Hodesh**

**Birkat Hamazon:**
+ יַעֲלֶה וְיָבוֹא Ya'aleh veyavo for Rosh Hodesh L90|95 S340|347 W233|239 F762|780
+ הָרַחֲמָן Harahaman for Rosh Hodesh L92|96 S343|348 W235|240 F768

**עַרְבִית**

**Weekday Amidah:**
+ יַעֲלֶה וְיָבוֹא Ya'aleh veyavo for Rosh Hodesh W145 F216

## Tue 9 Oct

**שַׁחֲרִית**

**Before מִזְמוֹר שִׁיר Mizmor shir (Psalm 30)** W14 F50
**or at end of service, recite:**
Psalm for Tuesday (Psalm 82) W87 F26
קַדִּישׁ יָתוֹם Mourner's Kaddish (some omit) W100 F52
+ Psalm 104 for Rosh Hodesh W90 F34
קַדִּישׁ יָתוֹם Mourner's Kaddish W100 F52

**Weekday Amidah:**
+ יַעֲלֶה וְיָבוֹא Ya'aleh veyavo for Rosh Hodesh W41 F114

✕ ~~תַּחֲנוּן Tahanun~~

+ חֲצִי הַלֵּל Short Hallel W50 F380
קַדִּישׁ שָׁלֵם Full Kaddish W56 F392

+ **TORAH SERVICE** W65 F138
Remove **1** Torah scroll from ark.

**Torah** 4 aliyot: פִּינְחָס Pinehas
בְּמִדְבַּר Bemidbar (Numbers) 28:1–15
[1]28:1–3 [2]3–5 [3]6–10 [4]11–15 W320 P943

חֲצִי קַדִּישׁ Short Kaddish W71 F146
Open, raise, display, and wrap scroll.
Return scroll to ark. W76 F150

Oct 9  30  תִּשְׁרֵי           Tishrey 5779      Sep | Oct 2018       **+** Add    **✗** Omit    ☞ Take note!

|   |   |   |   |   |   |   |   |   |   |   |   |
|---|---|---|---|---|---|---|---|---|---|---|---|
|   | 1 | 2 | 3 | 4 | 5 | 6 | 10 | 11 | 12 | 13 | 14 | 15 |

**Siddurim**

| 7 | 8 | 9 | 10 | 11 | 12 | 13 | 16 | 17 | 18 | 19 | 20 | 21 | 22 | **L** Lev Shalem for Shabbat and Festivals |
| 14 | 15 | 16 | 17 | 18 | 19 | 20 | 23 | 24 | 25 | 26 | 27 | 28 | 29 | **S** Shabbat and Festival Sim Shalom |
| 21 | 22 | 23 | 24 | 25 | 26 | 27 | 30 | 1 | 2 | 3 | 4 | 5 | 6 | **W** Weekday Sim Shalom |
| 28 | 29 | 30 |   |   |   |   | 7 | 8 | 9 |   |   |   |   | **F** Full Sim Shalom (both editions) |
|   |   |   |   |   |   |   |   |   |   |   |   |   |   | **P** Personal Edition of Full Sim Shalom |

אַשְׁרֵי Ashrey    **W**78 **F**152

**✗** ~~לַמְנַצֵּחַ Lamenatse·aḥ (Psalm 20)~~

וּבָא לְצִיּוֹן Uva letsiyyon    **W**80 **F**156

**Some congregations:**
Remove and pack tefillin at this point.

**+** חֲצִי קַדִּישׁ Short Kaddish    **W**103 **F**428

**Other congregations:**

**+** חֲצִי קַדִּישׁ Short Kaddish    **W**103 **F**428
Remove and cover—but do not pack—tefillin, so that all begin Musaf Amidah at the same time, as soon after Kaddish as possible.

מוּסָף    **+** **Rosh Ḥodesh Amidah for weekdays:**    **W**104 **F**486
Weekday קְדֻשָּׁה Kedushah    **W**105 **F**488
**+** וּלְכַפָּרַת פֶּשַׁע Ulkhapparat pasha    **W**107 **F**494
Add these words only through Rosh Ḥodesh Adar Sheni.

**+** קַדִּישׁ שָׁלֵם Full Kaddish    **W**82 **F**158
עָלֵינוּ Aleynu    **W**83 **F**160

**If psalms for the day were not recited at Shaḥarit, add here:**
קַדִּישׁ יָתוֹם Mourner's Kaddish (some omit)    **W**84 **F**162
Psalm for Tuesday (Psalm 82)    **W**87 **F**26
קַדִּישׁ יָתוֹם Mourner's Kaddish (some omit)    **W**100 **F**52
**+** Psalm 104 for Rosh Ḥodesh    **W**90 **F**34

קַדִּישׁ יָתוֹם Mourner's Kaddish    **W**84|100 **F**162|52

מִנְחָה    **Weekday Amidah:**
**+** יַעֲלֶה וְיָבֹא Ya'aleh veyavo for Rosh Ḥodesh    **W**127 **F**178

**✗** ~~תַּחֲנוּן Taḥanun~~

---

**Luaḥ 5779 — Large-Print/Pulpit-Size Edition**

Measuring 7.5 in. x 11 in., this edition matches the standard print edition page for page, but the text is 25% larger.
- Economy version (text is black and white)
- Deluxe version (text is full color)

Visit: www.milesbcohen.com

## Ḥeshvan 1 חֶשְׁוָן — רֹאשׁ חֹדֶשׁ חֶשְׁוָן Rosh Ḥodesh Ḥeshvan — Day 2

Tue **9** Oct (evening)

**DURING Rosh Ḥodesh**

**Birkat Hamazon:**

+ יַעֲלֶה וְיָבוֹא Ya'aleh veyavo for Rosh Ḥodesh L90|95 S340|347 W233|239 F762|780

+ הָרַחֲמָן Haraḥaman for Rosh Ḥodesh L92|96 S343|348 W235|240 F768

**עַרְבִית**

**Weekday Amidah:**

+ יַעֲלֶה וְיָבוֹא Ya'aleh veyavo for Rosh Ḥodesh W145 F216

Wed **10** Oct **שַׁחֲרִית**

**Before מִזְמוֹר שִׁיר Mizmor shir (Psalm 30)** W14 F50
**or at end of service, recite:**

Psalm for Wednesday (Psalms 94:1–95:3) W87 F26
קַדִּישׁ יָתוֹם Mourner's Kaddish (some omit) W100 F52
+ Psalm 104 for Rosh Ḥodesh W90 F34
קַדִּישׁ יָתוֹם Mourner's Kaddish W100 F52

**Weekday Amidah:**

+ יַעֲלֶה וְיָבוֹא Ya'aleh veyavo for Rosh Ḥodesh W41 F114

✕ ~~תַּחֲנוּן Taḥanun~~

+ חֲצִי הַלֵּל Short Hallel W50 F380
קַדִּישׁ שָׁלֵם Full Kaddish W56 F392

+ **TORAH SERVICE** W65 F138
Remove **1** Torah scroll from ark.

**Torah** 4 aliyot: פִּינְחָס Pineḥas
בְּמִדְבַּר Bemidbar (Numbers) 28:1–15
[1]28:1–3 [2]3–5 [3]6–10 [4]11–15 W320 P943

חֲצִי קַדִּישׁ Short Kaddish W71 F146
Open, raise, display, and wrap scroll.
Return scroll to ark. W76 F150

אַשְׁרֵי Ashrey W78 F152
✕ ~~לַמְנַצֵּחַ Lamenatse·aḥ (Psalm 20)~~
וּבָא לְצִיּוֹן Uva letsiyyon W80 F156

**Oct 10** 1 חֶשְׁוָן
**Oct 11** 2 חֶשְׁוָן

| Ḥeshvan 5779 | | | | Oct \| Nov 2018 | | | | |
|---|---|---|---|---|---|---|---|---|
| | 1 | 2 | 3 | 4 | | 10 | 11 | 12 | 13 |
| 5 | 6 | 7 | 8 | 9 | 10 | 11 | 14 | 15 | 16 | 17 | 18 | 19 | 20 |
| 12 | 13 | 14 | 15 | 16 | 17 | 18 | 21 | 22 | 23 | 24 | 25 | 26 | 27 |
| 19 | 20 | 21 | 22 | 23 | 24 | 25 | 28 | 29 | 30 | 31 \| 1 | 2 | 3 |
| 26 | 27 | 28 | 29 | 30 | | | 4 | 5 | 6 | 7 | 8 | | |

**+** Add    **✕** Omit    ☞ Take note!

**Siddurim**
- **L** Lev Shalem for Shabbat and Festivals
- **S** Shabbat and Festival Sim Shalom
- **W** Weekday Sim Shalom
- **F** Full Sim Shalom (both editions)
- **P** Personal Edition of Full Sim Shalom

---

### Some congregations:
Remove and pack tefillin at this point.
- **+** חֲצִי קַדִּישׁ Short Kaddish    W103 F428

### Other congregations:
- **+** חֲצִי קַדִּישׁ Short Kaddish    W103 F428

Remove and cover—but do not pack—tefillin, so that all begin Musaf Amidah at the same time, as soon after Kaddish as possible.

**מוּסָף**  **+** **Rosh Ḥodesh Amidah for weekdays:**    W104 F486
  Weekday קְדֻשָּׁה Kedushah    W105 F488
- **+** וּלְכַפָּרַת פָּשַׁע Ulkhapparat pasha    W107 F494
  Add these words only through Rosh Ḥodesh Adar Sheni.

- **+** קַדִּישׁ שָׁלֵם Full Kaddish    W82 F158
  עָלֵינוּ Aleynu    W83 F160

**If psalms for the day were not recited at Shaḥarit, add here:**
  קַדִּישׁ יָתוֹם Mourner's Kaddish (some omit)    W84 F162
  Psalm for Wednesday (Psalms 94:1–95:3)    W87 F26
  קַדִּישׁ יָתוֹם Mourner's Kaddish (some omit)    W100 F52
- **+** Psalm 104 for Rosh Ḥodesh    W90 F34

  קַדִּישׁ יָתוֹם Mourner's Kaddish    W84|100 F162|52

**מִנְחָה**  **Weekday Amidah:**
- **+** יַעֲלֶה וְיָבוֹא Ya'aleh veyavo for Rosh Ḥodesh    W127 F178

- **✕** תַּחֲנוּן ~~Taḥanun~~

---

## Ḥeshvan 2 חֶשְׁוָן
### Thu 11 Oct

> **BEGINNING 2 Ḥeshvan**   Those who have not yet resumed reciting תַּחֲנוּן Taḥanun resume now.

| ✚ Add   ✗ Omit   ☞ Take note! | Ḥeshvan 5779 | Oct \| Nov 2018 | חֶשְׁוָן 4 **Oct 13** |
| | 1 2 3 4 | 10 11 12 13 | חֶשְׁוָן 11 **Oct 20** |
| **Siddurim** | 5 6 7 8 9 10 11 | 14 15 16 17 18 19 20 | |
| L Lev Shalem for Shabbat and Festivals | 12 13 14 15 16 17 18 | 21 22 23 24 25 26 27 | |
| S Shabbat and Festival Sim Shalom | 19 20 21 22 23 24 25 | 28 29 30 31 \| 1 2 3 | |
| W Weekday Sim Shalom | 26 27 28 29 30 | 4 5 6 7 8 | |
| F Full Sim Shalom (both editions) | | | |
| P Personal Edition of Full Sim Shalom | | | |

## Ḥeshvan 4 חֶשְׁוָן
Sat 13 Oct

## שַׁבָּת Shabbat פָּרָשַׁת נֹחַ Parashat Noaḥ

**Torah** 7 aliyot (minimum): נֹחַ Noaḥ
בְּרֵאשִׁית Bereshit (Genesis) 6:9–11:32

| | | | | |
|---|---|---|---|---|
| Annual: | 1 6:9–22 | 2 7:1–16 | 3 7:17–8:14 | 4 8:15–9:7 |
| | 5 9:8–17 | 6 9:18–10:32 | 7 11:1–32 | M 11:29–32 |
| Triennial: | 1 11:1–4 | 2 11:5–9 | 3 11:10–13 | 4 11:14–17 |
| | 5 11:18–21 | 6 11:22–25 | 7 11:26–32 | M 11:29–32 |

**Haftarah**
Ashkenazic: יְשַׁעְיָהוּ Yesha'yahu (Isaiah) 54:1–55:5
Sephardic: יְשַׁעְיָהוּ Yesha'yahu (Isaiah) 54:1–10

מִנְחָה

**Torah** 3 aliyot from לֶךְ־לְךָ Lekh lekha
בְּרֵאשִׁית Bereshit (Genesis) 12:1–13
1 12:1–3 2 4–9 3 10–13 W266 P887

This is also the reading for the coming Monday and Thursday.

## Ḥeshvan 11 חֶשְׁוָן
Sat 20 Oct

## שַׁבָּת Shabbat פָּרָשַׁת לֶךְ־לְךָ Parashat Lekh lekha

**Torah** 7 aliyot (minimum): לֶךְ־לְךָ Lekh lekha
בְּרֵאשִׁית Bereshit (Genesis) 12:1–17:27

| | | | | |
|---|---|---|---|---|
| Annual: | 1 12:1–13 | 2 12:14–13:4 | 3 13:5–18 | 4 14:1–20 |
| | 5 14:21–15:6 | 6 15:7–17:6 | 7 17:7–27 | M 17:24–27 |
| Triennial: | 1 16:1–6 | 2 16:7–9 | 3 16:10–16 | 4 17:1–6 |
| | 5 17:7–17 | 6 17:18–23 | 7 17:24–27 | M 17:24–27 |

**Haftarah** יְשַׁעְיָהוּ Yesha'yahu (Isaiah) 40:27–41:16°

☞ °40:31 Read וְקוֹיֵ vekoyey (not vekovey, as printed in many books).

מִנְחָה

**Torah** 3 aliyot from וַיֵּרָא Vayera
בְּרֵאשִׁית Bereshit (Genesis) 18:1–14
1 18:1–5 2 6–8 3 9–14 W267 P888

This is also the reading for the coming Monday and Thursday.

Oct 27 **18** חֶשְׁוָן
Nov 3 **25** חֶשְׁוָן

Ḥeshvan 5779
| | 1 | 2 | 3 | 4 |
| 5 | 6 | 7 | 8 | 9 | 10 | 11 |
| 12 | 13 | 14 | 15 | 16 | 17 | 18 |
| 19 | 20 | 21 | 22 | 23 | 24 | 25 |
| 26 | 27 | 28 | 29 | 30 |

Oct | Nov 2018
| | | | | 10 | 11 | 12 | 13 |
| 14 | 15 | 16 | 17 | 18 | 19 | 20 |
| 21 | 22 | 23 | 24 | 25 | 26 | 27 |
| 28 | 29 | 30 | 31 | 1 | 2 | 3 |
| 4 | 5 | 6 | 7 | 8 |

✚ Add  ✖ Omit  ☞ Take note!

**Siddurim**
**L** Lev Shalem for Shabbat and Festivals
**S** Shabbat and Festival Sim Shalom
**W** Weekday Sim Shalom
**F** Full Sim Shalom (both editions)
**P** Personal Edition of Full Sim Shalom

---

## Ḥeshvan 18 חֶשְׁוָן
Sat **27** Oct

שַׁבָּת Shabbat  פָּרָשַׁת וַיֵּרָא Parashat Vayera

**Torah** 7 aliyot (minimum): וַיֵּרָא Vayera
בְּרֵאשִׁית Bereshit (Genesis) 18:1–22:24

Annual:     ¹18:1–14      ²18:15–33     ³19:1–20°    ⁴19:21–21:4
            ⁵21:5–21      ⁶21:22–34     ⁷22:1–24     ᴹ22:20–24

Triennial:  ¹21:1–4       ²21:5–13      ³21:14–21    ⁴21:22–34
            ⁵22:1–8       ⁶22:9–19      ⁷22:20–24    ᴹ22:20–24

☞ °19:16  Note the rare ta'am (trope) | (ז|): שַׁלְשֶׁלֶת (וַיִּתְמַהְמָהּ

**Haftarah**
Ashkenazic: מְלָכִים ב׳ 2 Melakhim (2 Kings) 4:1–37
Sephardic: מְלָכִים ב׳ 2 Melakhim (2 Kings) 4:1–23

מִנְחָה     **Torah** 3 aliyot from חַיֵּי שָׂרָה Ḥayyey sarah
            בְּרֵאשִׁית Bereshit (Genesis) 23:1–16
            ¹23:1–7    ²8–12    ³13–16                    **W**268  **P**888

This is also the reading for the coming Monday and Thursday.

---

## Ḥeshvan 25 חֶשְׁוָן
Sat **3** Nov

שַׁבָּת Shabbat  פָּרָשַׁת חַיֵּי שָׂרָה Parashat Ḥayyey sarah
שַׁבָּת מְבָרְכִים הַחֹדֶשׁ Shabbat Mevarekhim Haḥodesh

**Torah** 7 aliyot (minimum): חַיֵּי שָׂרָה Ḥayyey sarah
בְּרֵאשִׁית Bereshit (Genesis) 23:1–25:18

Annual:     ¹23:1–16      ²23:17–24:9    ³24:10–26°   ⁴24:27–52
            ⁵24:53–67     ⁶25:1–11       ⁷25:12–18    ᴹ25:16–18

Triennial:  ¹24:53–58     ²24:59–61      ³24:62–67    ⁴25:1–6
            ⁵25:7–11      ⁶25:12–15      ⁷25:16–18    ᴹ25:16–18

☞ °24:12  Note the rare ta'am (trope) | (ז|): שַׁלְשֶׁלֶת (וַיֹּאמַר

**Haftarah** מְלָכִים א׳ 1 Melakhim (1 Kings) 1:1–31

✚ **Birkat Haḥodesh:**  **L**180 **S**150 **F**418
Announce Rosh Ḥodesh Kislev:
רֹאשׁ חֹדֶשׁ כִּסְלֵו יִהְיֶה בְּיוֹם חֲמִישִׁי וּבְיוֹם שִׁשִּׁי . . .
Rosh ḥodesh Kislev yihyeh beyom ḥamishi
uvyom shishi . . .
(Wednesday night, Thursday, and Friday)

✖ ~~אַב הָרַחֲמִים Av Haraḥamim~~

מִנְחָה

**Torah** 3 aliyot from תּוֹלְדֹת Toledot
בְּרֵאשִׁית Bereshit (Genesis) 25:19–26:5
[1]25:19–22 [2]23–26 [3]25:27–26:5 W269 P890

This is also the reading for the coming Monday.

---

**Heshvan 29 חֶשְׁוָן**
**Wed 7 Nov**

## עֶרֶב רֹאשׁ חֹדֶשׁ Erev Rosh Ḥodesh
Day before Rosh Ḥodesh

מִנְחָה ✕ ~~תַּחֲנוּן Taḥanun~~

---

**Heshvan 30 חֶשְׁוָן**
**Wed 7 Nov (evening)**

## רֹאשׁ חֹדֶשׁ כִּסְלֵו Rosh Ḥodesh Kislev — Day 1

For determining the *yortsayt* of a death on 30 Ḥeshvan, see p. 214.

**DURING Rosh Ḥodesh**

**Birkat Hamazon:**
+ יַעֲלֶה וְיָבוֹא Ya'aleh veyavo for Rosh Ḥodesh
L90|95 S340|347 W233|239 F762|780
+ הָרַחֲמָן Haraḥaman for Rosh Ḥodesh
L92|96 S343|348 W235|240 F768

עַרְבִית

**Weekday Amidah:**
+ יַעֲלֶה וְיָבוֹא Ya'aleh veyavo for Rosh Ḥodesh W145 F216

**Thu 8 Nov** שַׁחֲרִית

**Before מִזְמוֹר שִׁיר Mizmor shir (Psalm 30)** W14 F50
**or at end of service, recite:**
Psalm for Thursday (Psalm 81) W89 F30
קַדִּישׁ יָתוֹם Mourner's Kaddish (some omit) W100 F52
+ Psalm 104 for Rosh Ḥodesh W90 F34
קַדִּישׁ יָתוֹם Mourner's Kaddish W100 F52

**Weekday Amidah:**
+ יַעֲלֶה וְיָבוֹא Ya'aleh veyavo for Rosh Ḥodesh W41 F114

✕ ~~תַּחֲנוּן Taḥanun~~

+ חֲצִי הַלֵּל Short Hallel W50 F380
קַדִּישׁ שָׁלֵם Full Kaddish W56 F392

| Ḥeshvan 5779 | | | | | | | Oct \| Nov 2018 | | | | | | |
|---|---|---|---|---|---|---|---|---|---|---|---|---|---|
| | | 1 | 2 | 3 | 4 | | | | | 10 | 11 | 12 | 13 |
| 5 | 6 | 7 | 8 | 9 | 10 | 11 | 14 | 15 | 16 | 17 | 18 | 19 | 20 |
| 12 | 13 | 14 | 15 | 16 | 17 | 18 | 21 | 22 | 23 | 24 | 25 | 26 | 27 |
| 19 | 20 | 21 | 22 | 23 | 24 | 25 | 28 | 29 | 30 | 31 \| | 1 | 2 | 3 |
| 26 | 27 | 28 | 29 | 30 | | | 4 | 5 | 6 | 7 | 8 | | |

\+ Add ✕ Omit ☞ Take note!

**Siddurim**
- **L** Lev Shalem for Shabbat and Festivals
- **S** Shabbat and Festival Sim Shalom
- **W** Weekday Sim Shalom
- **F** Full Sim Shalom (both editions)
- **P** Personal Edition of Full Sim Shalom

## TORAH SERVICE W65 F138

Remove **1** Torah scroll from ark.

**Torah** 4 aliyot: פִּינְחָס Pineḥas
בְּמִדְבַּר Bemidbar (Numbers) 28:1–15
1 28:1–3 2 3–5 3 6–10 4 11–15 W320 P943

חֲצִי קַדִּישׁ Short Kaddish W71 F146
Open, raise, display, and wrap scroll.
Return scroll to ark. W76 F150

אַשְׁרֵי Ashrey W78 F152
✕ ~~לַמְנַצֵּחַ Lamenatse·aḥ (Psalm 20)~~
וּבָא לְצִיּוֹן Uva letsiyyon W80 F156

**Some congregations:**
Remove and pack tefillin at this point.
\+ חֲצִי קַדִּישׁ Short Kaddish W103 F428

**Other congregations:**
\+ חֲצִי קַדִּישׁ Short Kaddish W103 F428
Remove and cover—but do not pack—tefillin, so that all begin Musaf Amidah at the same time, as soon after Kaddish as possible.

מוּסָף
\+ **Rosh Ḥodesh Amidah for weekdays:** W104 F486
Weekday קְדֻשָּׁה Kedushah W105 F488
\+ וּלְכַפָּרַת פָּשַׁע Ulkhapparat pasha W107 F494
Add these words only through Rosh Ḥodesh Adar Sheni.

\+ קַדִּישׁ שָׁלֵם Full Kaddish W82 F158
עָלֵינוּ Aleynu W83 F160

**If psalms for the day were not recited at Shaḥarit, add here:**
קַדִּישׁ יָתוֹם Mourner's Kaddish (some omit) W84 F162
Psalm for Thursday (Psalm 81) W89 F30
קַדִּישׁ יָתוֹם Mourner's Kaddish (some omit) W100 F52
\+ Psalm 104 for Rosh Ḥodesh W90 F34

קַדִּישׁ יָתוֹם Mourner's Kaddish W84|100 F162|52

מִנְחָה
**Weekday Amidah:**
\+ יַעֲלֶה וְיָבוֹא Ya'aleh veyavo for Rosh Ḥodesh W127 F178

✕ ~~תַּחֲנוּן Taḥanun~~

| | | | |
|---|---|---|---|
| ➕ Add  ❌ Omit  ☞ Take note! | Kislev 5779 | Nov \| Dec 2018 | כִּסְלֵו 1 **Nov 8** |
| | | | **Nov 9** |

**Siddurim**
- **L** Lev Shalem for Shabbat and Festivals
- **S** Shabbat and Festival Sim Shalom
- **W** Weekday Sim Shalom
- **F** Full Sim Shalom (both editions)
- **P** Personal Edition of Full Sim Shalom

| | | | | | | |
|---|---|---|---|---|---|---|
| | | | | 1 | 2 | 9  10 |
| 3 | 4 | 5 | 6 | 7 | 8 | 9 |
| 10 | 11 | 12 | 13 | 14 | 15 | 16 |
| 17 | 18 | 19 | 20 | 21 | 22 | 23 |
| 24 | 25 | 26 | 27 | 28 | 29 | 30 |

(Nov/Dec: 11 12 13 14 15 16 17 / 18 19 20 21 22 23 24 / 25 26 27 28 29 30 \| 1 / 2 3 4 5 6 7 8)

## Kislev 1 כִּסְלֵו   רֹאשׁ חֹדֶשׁ כִּסְלֵו  Rosh Ḥodesh Kislev — Day 2
**Thu 8 Nov** (evening)

**DURING Rosh Ḥodesh**   **Birkat Hamazon:**
➕ יַעֲלֶה וְיָבוֹא Ya'aleh v<sup>e</sup>yavo for Rosh Ḥodesh
   <sup>L</sup>90|95 <sup>S</sup>340|347 <sup>W</sup>233|239 <sup>F</sup>762|780

➕ הָרַחֲמָן Haraḥaman for Rosh Ḥodesh
   <sup>L</sup>92|96 <sup>S</sup>343|348 <sup>W</sup>235|240 <sup>F</sup>768

עַרְבִית   **Weekday Amidah:**
➕ יַעֲלֶה וְיָבוֹא Ya'aleh v<sup>e</sup>yavo for Rosh Ḥodesh   <sup>W</sup>145 <sup>F</sup>216

**Fri 9 Nov**   שַׁחֲרִית
Before מִזְמוֹר שִׁיר Mizmor shir (Psalm 30)   <sup>W</sup>14 <sup>F</sup>50
or at end of service, recite:
Psalm for Friday (Psalm 93)   <sup>W</sup>90 <sup>F</sup>32
קַדִּישׁ יָתוֹם Mourner's Kaddish (some omit)   <sup>W</sup>100 <sup>F</sup>52
➕ Psalm 104 for Rosh Ḥodesh   <sup>W</sup>90 <sup>F</sup>34
קַדִּישׁ יָתוֹם Mourner's Kaddish   <sup>W</sup>100 <sup>F</sup>52

**Weekday Amidah:**
➕ יַעֲלֶה וְיָבוֹא Ya'aleh v<sup>e</sup>yavo for Rosh Ḥodesh   <sup>W</sup>41 <sup>F</sup>114
❌ תַּחֲנוּן ~~Taḥanun~~
➕ חֲצִי הַלֵּל Short Hallel   <sup>W</sup>50 <sup>F</sup>380
   קַדִּישׁ שָׁלֵם Full Kaddish   <sup>W</sup>56 <sup>F</sup>392

➕ **TORAH SERVICE**   <sup>W</sup>65 <sup>F</sup>138
Remove **1** Torah scroll from ark.

> **Torah** 4 aliyot: פִּינְחָס Pineḥas
> בְּמִדְבַּר B<sup>e</sup>midbar (Numbers) 28:1–15
> <sup>1</sup>28:1–3  <sup>2</sup>3–5  <sup>3</sup>6–10  <sup>4</sup>11–15
> <sup>W</sup>320 <sup>P</sup>943

חֲצִי קַדִּישׁ Short Kaddish   <sup>W</sup>71 <sup>F</sup>146
Open, raise, display, and wrap scroll.
Return scroll to ark.   <sup>W</sup>76 <sup>F</sup>150

אַשְׁרֵי Ashrey   <sup>W</sup>78 <sup>F</sup>152
❌ לַמְנַצֵּחַ ~~Lam<sup>e</sup>natse·aḥ (Psalm 20)~~
וּבָא לְצִיּוֹן Uva l<sup>e</sup>tsiyyon   <sup>W</sup>80 <sup>F</sup>156

**Some congregations:**
Remove and pack t<sup>e</sup>fillin at this point.
➕ חֲצִי קַדִּישׁ Short Kaddish   <sup>W</sup>103 <sup>F</sup>428

**Other congregations:**
+ חֲצִי קַדִּישׁ Short Kaddish W103 F428
Remove and cover—but do not pack—tefillin, so that all begin Musaf Amidah at the same time, as soon after Kaddish as possible.

**מוּסָף**

+ **Rosh Ḥodesh Amidah for weekdays:** W104 F486
Weekday קְדֻשָּׁה Kedushah W105 F488
+ וּלְכַפָּרַת פָּשַׁע Ulkhapparat pasha W107 F494
Add these words only through Rosh Ḥodesh Adar Sheni.

+ קַדִּישׁ שָׁלֵם Full Kaddish W82 F158
עָלֵינוּ Aleynu W83 F160

**If psalms for the day were not recited at Shaḥarit, add here:**
קַדִּישׁ יָתוֹם Mourner's Kaddish (some omit) W84 F162
Psalm for Friday (Psalm 93) W90 F32
קַדִּישׁ יָתוֹם Mourner's Kaddish (some omit) W100 F52
+ Psalm 104 for Rosh Hodesh W90 F34

קַדִּישׁ יָתוֹם Mourner's Kaddish W84|100 F162|52

**מִנְחָה**

**Weekday Amidah:**
+ יַעֲלֶה וְיָבוֹא Ya'aleh veyavo for Rosh Ḥodesh W127 F178

✕ ~~תַּחֲנוּן Taḥanun~~

## Kislev 2 כִּסְלֵו
**Sat 10 Nov**

## שַׁבָּת Shabbat פָּרָשַׁת תּוֹלְדֹת Parashat Toledot

**Torah** 7 aliyot (minimum): תּוֹלְדֹת Toledot
בְּרֵאשִׁית Bereshit (Genesis) 25:19–28:9

| | | | | |
|---|---|---|---|---|
| Annual: | 1 25:19–26:5 | 2 26:6–12 | 3 26:13–22 | 4 26:23–29 |
| | 5 26:30–27:27° | 6 27:28–28:4 | 7 28:5–28:9° | M 28:7–9° |
| Triennial: | 1 27:28–30 | 2 27:31–33 | 3 27:34–37 | 4 27:38–40 |
| | 5 27:41–46 | 6 28:1–4 | 7 28:5–9° | M 28:7–9° |

☞ °27:25 Note the rare ta'am (trope) מֵירְכָא־כְפוּלָה (֦):
וַיָּבֵא לוֹ יַיִן Connect לוֹ to the preceding and following words without a pause; then pause after the טִפְחָא (יַיִן), as usual.

☞ °28:9 Note the unusual use of the ta'am | מֻנַּח־לְגַרְמֵיהּ (= | מֻנַּח־מַפְסִיק): אֶת־מָחֲלַת

**Haftarah** מַלְאָכִי Mal'akhi (Malachi) 1:1–2:7

+ Add ✕ Omit ☞ Take note!

**Siddurim**
**L** Lev Shalem for Shabbat and Festivals
**S** Shabbat and Festival Sim Shalom
**W** Weekday Sim Shalom
**F** Full Sim Shalom (both editions)
**P** Personal Edition of Full Sim Shalom

Kislev 5779

| | | | | | | |
|---|---|---|---|---|---|---|
| | | | | | 1 | 2 |
| 3 | 4 | 5 | 6 | 7 | 8 | 9 |
| 10 | 11 | 12 | 13 | 14 | 15 | 16 |
| 17 | 18 | 19 | 20 | 21 | 22 | 23 |
| 24 | 25 | 26 | 27 | 28 | 29 | 30 |

Nov | Dec 2018

| | | | | | | |
|---|---|---|---|---|---|---|
| | | | | | 9 | 10 |
| 11 | 12 | 13 | 14 | 15 | 16 | 17 |
| 18 | 19 | 20 | 21 | 22 | 23 | 24 |
| 25 | 26 | 27 | 28 | 29 | 30 | 1 |
| 2 | 3 | 4 | 5 | 6 | 7 | 8 |

2 כִּסְלֵו Nov 10
9 כִּסְלֵו Nov 17
16 כִּסְלֵו Nov 24

מִנְחָה

**Torah** 3 aliyot from וַיֵּצֵא Vayetse
בְּרֵאשִׁית Bereshit (Genesis) 28:10–22
[1]28:10–12 [2]13–17 [3]18–22 W270 P891

This is also the reading for the coming Monday and Thursday.

## Kislev 9 כִּסְלֵו
**Sat 17 Nov**

## שַׁבָּת Shabbat פָּרָשַׁת וַיֵּצֵא Parashat Vayetse

**Torah** 7 aliyot (minimum): וַיֵּצֵא Vayetse
בְּרֵאשִׁית Bereshit (Genesis) 28:10–32:3

| | | | | |
|---|---|---|---|---|
| Annual: | [1]28:10–22 | [2]29:1–17 | [3]29:18–30:13 | [4]30:14–27 |
| | [5]30:28–31:16 | [6]31:17–42 | [7]31:43–32:3 | [M]32:1–3 |
| Triennial: | [1]31:17–21 | [2]31:22–24 | [3]31:25–35 | [4]31:36–42 |
| | [5]31:43–45 | [6]31:46–50 | [7]31:51–32:3 | [M]32:1–3 |

**Haftarah**
Ashkenazic: הוֹשֵׁעַ Hoshe·a (Hosea) 12:13–14:10
Sephardic: הוֹשֵׁעַ Hoshe·a (Hosea) 11:7–12:12

מִנְחָה

**Torah** 3 aliyot from וַיִּשְׁלַח Vayishlaḥ
בְּרֵאשִׁית Bereshit (Genesis) 32:4–13
[1]32:4–6 [2]7–9 [3]10–13 W271 P892

This is also the reading for the coming Monday and Thursday.

## Kislev 16 כִּסְלֵו
**Sat 24 Nov**

## שַׁבָּת Shabbat פָּרָשַׁת וַיִּשְׁלַח Parashat Vayishlaḥ

**Torah** 7 aliyot (minimum): וַיִּשְׁלַח Vayishlaḥ
בְּרֵאשִׁית Bereshit (Genesis) 32:4–36:43

| | | | | |
|---|---|---|---|---|
| Annual: | [1]32:4–13 | [2]32:14–30 | [3]32:31–33:5 | [4]33:6–20 |
| | [5]34:1–35:11 | [6]35:12–36:19° | [7]36:20–43 | [M]36:40–43 |
| Triennial: | [1]35:16–26° | [2]35:27–29 | [3]36:1–8 | [4]36:9–19 |
| | [5]36:20–30 | [6]36:31–39 | [7]36:40–43 | [M]36:40–43 |

☞ °35:22 Read as 1 continuous verse. Do not break into 2 verses before וַיִּהְיוּ. Use the teʼamim (tropes) indicated below:

וַיְהִי בִּשְׁכֹּן יִשְׂרָאֵל בָּאָרֶץ הַהִוא וַיֵּלֶךְ רְאוּבֵן וַיִּשְׁכַּב אֶת־בִּלְהָה
פִּילֶגֶשׁ אָבִיו וַיִּשְׁמַע יִשְׂרָאֵל וַיִּהְיוּ בְנֵי־יַעֲקֹב שְׁנֵים עָשָׂר׃

**Haftarah** עֹבַדְיָה Ovadyah (Obadiah) 1:1–21

| Nov 24 **16 כִּסְלֵו** | Kislev 5779 | Nov \| Dec 2018 | ✚ Add   ✗ Omit   ☞ Take note! |
|---|---|---|---|
| Dec 1 **23 כִּסְלֵו** | 1 2 | 9 10 | **Siddurim** |
| | 3 4 5 6 7 8 9 | 11 12 13 14 15 16 17 | **L** Lev Shalem for Shabbat and Festivals |
| | 10 11 12 13 14 15 16 | 18 19 20 21 22 23 24 | **S** Shabbat and Festival Sim Shalom |
| | 17 18 19 20 21 22 23 | 25 26 27 28 29 30\|1 | **W** Weekday Sim Shalom |
| | 24 25 26 27 28 29 30 | 2 3 4 5 6 7 8 | **F** Full Sim Shalom (both editions) |
| | | | **P** Personal Edition of Full Sim Shalom |

### מִנְחָה

**Torah** 3 aliyot from וַיֵּשֶׁב Vayeshev
בְּרֵאשִׁית Bereshit (Genesis) 37:1–11
¹37:1–3   ²4–7   ³8–11                                        **W**272 **P**893

This is also the reading for the coming Monday and Thursday.

### Kislev 23 כִּסְלֵו
### Sat 1 Dec

שַׁבָּת **Shabbat**   פָּרָשַׁת וַיֵּשֶׁב **Parashat Vayeshev**
שַׁבַּת מְבָרְכִים הַחֹדֶשׁ **Shabbat Mevarekhim Haḥodesh**

**Torah** 7 aliyot (minimum): וַיֵּשֶׁב Vayeshev
בְּרֵאשִׁית Bereshit (Genesis) 37:1–40:23

Annual:      ¹37:1–11     ²37:12–22    ³37:23–36    ⁴38:1–30
             ⁵39:1–6      ⁶39:7–23°    ⁷40:1–23     **M**40:20–23

Triennial:   ¹39:1–6      ²39:7–10°    ³39:11–18    ⁴39:19–23
             ⁵40:1–8      ⁶40:9–15     ⁷40:16–23    **M**40:20–23

☞ °39:8  Note the rare ta'am (trope) \| שַׁלְשֶׁלֶת (|ˣ) וַיְמָאֵן

**Haftarah** עָמוֹס Amos (Amos) 2:6–3:8

✚ **Birkat Haḥodesh:**   **L**180 **S**150 **F**418
Announce Rosh Ḥodesh Tevet:
רֹאשׁ חֹדֶשׁ טֵבֵת יִהְיֶה בְּיוֹם שַׁבַּת קֹדֶשׁ
וּלְמָחֳרָתוֹ בְּיוֹם רִאשׁוֹן . . .
Rosh ḥodesh Tevet yihyeh beyom shabbat kodesh
ulmoḥorato beyom rishon . . .
(Friday night, Saturday, and Sunday)

✗ אַב הָרַחֲמִים ~~Av Haraḥamim~~

### מִנְחָה

**Torah** 3 aliyot from מִקֵּץ Mikkets
בְּרֵאשִׁית Bereshit (Genesis) 41:1–14
¹41:1–4   ²5–7   ³8–14                                        **W**273 **P**894

☞ These verses are not read publicly again until next Shabbat.

| ✚ Add | ✘ Omit | ☞ Take note! | **Kislev 5779** | **Nov \| Dec 2018** | **Dec 1** כִּסְלֵו **24** |
|---|---|---|---|---|---|
| | Siddurim | | 1 2 | 9 10 | |
| L | Lev Shalem for Shabbat and Festivals | | 3 4 5 6 7 8 9 | 11 12 13 14 15 16 17 | |
| S | Shabbat and Festival Sim Shalom | | 10 11 12 13 14 15 16 | 18 19 20 21 22 23 24 | |
| W | Weekday Sim Shalom | | 17 18 19 20 21 22 23 | 25 26 27 28 29 30 \| 1 | |
| F | Full Sim Shalom (both editions) | | 24 25 26 27 28 29 30 | 2 3 4 5 6 7 8 | |
| P | Personal Edition of Full Sim Shalom | | | | |

## Kislev 24 כִּסְלֵו
## Sat 1 Dec

**מוֹצָאֵי שַׁבָּת Motsa'ey Shabbat — Conclusion of Shabbat**
**עֶרֶב חֲנֻכָּה Erev Ḥanukkah — Day before Ḥanukkah**

**עַרְבִית**

Saturday night Arvit as usual through the Amidah L264 S281 W137 F200

☞ חֲצִי קַדִּישׁ Short Kaddish L279 S292 W158 F682

☞ וִיהִי נֹעַם Vihi no'am L279 S292 W158 F684
יוֹשֵׁב בְּסֵתֶר עֶלְיוֹן Yoshev beseter elyon L279 S292 W158 F684
וְאַתָּה קָדוֹשׁ Ve'attah kadosh L216 S293 W159 F684

קַדִּישׁ שָׁלֵם Full Kaddish L280 S294 W160 F688

Conclude as on a usual Saturday night.

**מִנְחָה** ✕ ~~תַּחֲנוּן Taḥanun~~

# Ḥanukkah

## General Instructions for Candle Lighting at Home

### Candle Lighting Times

- Except before and after Shabbat, light Ḥanukkah candles (solid, or oil and wicks) as soon after dark as possible.
- Ḥanukkah candles must burn for at least ½ hour (on Shabbat, 1½ hours).
- Before Shabbat:
  1. Before Shabbat candle lighting time, light Ḥanukkah candles that burn for 1½ hours.
  2. Then light Shabbat candles at least 18 minutes before sunset.
- After Shabbat:

  In the synagogue, light the Ḥanukkah candles *before* Havdalah.
  At home, light the Ḥanukkah candles *after* Havdalah.

### Setup for the Ḥanukkiyyah (Menorah, Candelabra)

1. At home, place the חֲנֻכִּיָּה *ḥanukkiyyah* so that it is visible from outside.
2. Place the candles into the חֲנֻכִּיָּה.
   a. Start at the right end, placing candles from right to left.
   b. Place 1 candle the 1st night, 2 the 2nd night, and so forth.
3. Place the additional שַׁמָּשׁ *shammash* candle into its distinct location.

**Lighting and Berakhot**

1. Light the שַׁמָּשׁ first.
2. Before lighting the other candles, recite the בְּרָכוֹת *berakhot*: L429 S307 W192 F242

בָּרוּךְ אַתָּה יי, אֱ·לֹהֵינוּ מֶלֶךְ הָעוֹלָם, אֲשֶׁר קִדְּשָׁנוּ בְּמִצְוֹתָיו
וְצִוָּנוּ לְהַדְלִיק נֵר שֶׁל חֲנֻכָּה.

Barukh attah adonay, eloheynu melekh ha'olam,
asher kiddeshanu bemitsvotav vetsivvanu lehadlik ner shel ḥanukkah.

בָּרוּךְ אַתָּה יי, אֱ·לֹהֵינוּ מֶלֶךְ הָעוֹלָם,
שֶׁעָשָׂה נִסִּים לַאֲבוֹתֵינוּ בַּיָּמִים הָהֵם וּבַזְּמַן הַזֶּה.

Barukh attah adonay, eloheynu melekh ha'olam,
she'asah nissim la'avoteinu bayamim hahem uvazeman hazeh.

On the 1st night only, add:

בָּרוּךְ אַתָּה יי, אֱ·לֹהֵינוּ מֶלֶךְ הָעוֹלָם,
שֶׁהֶחֱיָנוּ וְקִיְּמָנוּ וְהִגִּיעָנוּ לַזְּמַן הַזֶּה.

Barukh attah adonay, eloheynu melekh ha'olam,
sheheḥeyanu vekiyyemanu vehiggi'anu lazeman hazeh.

3. Use the שַׁמָּשׁ to light the 1st (left-most) candle.
4. Proceeding left to right, use the שַׁמָּשׁ to light the remaining candles,
   - while reciting הַנֵּרוֹת הַלָּלוּ if reciting from memory.
   - before reciting הַנֵּרוֹת הַלָּלוּ if reading from a text. L429 S308 W193 F242
5. Chant מָעוֹז צוּר. L429 S308 W193 F242

**Special Instructions for the Synagogue**

Follow the general instructions above, but observe the following modifications:

- Place the חֲנֻכִּיָּה *ḥanukkiyyah* along the southern wall of the room for prayer.
- Before Arvit, light the Ḥanukkah candles as described in the preceding instructions, *except:*
  1. On Friday afternoon, light the Ḥanukkah candles after Minḥah.
     If Minḥah is delayed, be sure to light the Ḥanukkah candles before Shabbat candle-lighting time (at least 18 minutes before sunset).
  2. After Shabbat, light the Ḥanukkah candles *before* Havdalah.
- Before Shaḥarit (except on Shabbat), light the candles in the manner of the previous evening, but omit the בְּרָכוֹת *berakhot*.

**DURING Ḥanukkah**

**Every Shaḥarit and Minḥah**

✕ ~~תַּחֲנוּן Taḥanun~~

**Birkat Hamazon:**

+ עַל הַנִּסִּים Al Hanissim for Ḥanukkah L430 S338|345 W231|237 F758

**Every Amidah:**

+ עַל הַנִּסִּים Al Hanissim for Ḥanukkah

## Kislev 25 כִּסְלֵו חֲנֻכָּה Ḥanukkah — Day 1

Sun **2** Dec

עַרְבִית + In the synagogue, before Arvit, light Ḥanukkah candles (see p. 72). W192 F242

**Weekday Amidah:**

+ עַל הַנִּסִּים Al Hanissim for Ḥanukkah W146 F218

קַדִּישׁ שָׁלֵם Full Kaddish W149 F222
עָלֵינוּ Aleynu W150 F224
קַדִּישׁ יָתוֹם Mourner's Kaddish W151 F226

Mon **3** Dec שַׁחֲרִית + In the synagogue, before Shaḥarit, light Ḥanukkah candles (see p. 72). W192 F242

**Weekday Amidah:**

+ עַל הַנִּסִּים Al Hanissim for Ḥanukkah W42 F116

✕ ~~תַּחֲנוּן Taḥanun~~

+ הַלֵּל שָׁלֵם Full Hallel W50 F380
חֲצִי קַדִּישׁ Short Kaddish W64 F390

**TORAH SERVICE** W65 F138
Remove **1** Torah scroll from ark.

**Torah** 3 aliyot from נָשֹׂא Naso
בְּמִדְבַּר Bemidbar (Numbers) 7:1–17
°1 7:1–11 °2 12–14 °3 15–17 W331 P945

☞°These aliyah divisions are preferable to the ones indicated in many siddurim.

חֲצִי קַדִּישׁ Short Kaddish W71 F146
Open, raise, display, and wrap scroll.
Return scroll to ark. W76 F150

אַשְׁרֵי Ashrey W78 F152
✕ ~~לַמְנַצֵּחַ Lamenatse·aḥ (Psalm 20)~~
וּבָא לְצִיּוֹן Uva letsiyyon W80 F156
קַדִּישׁ שָׁלֵם Full Kaddish W82 F158
עָלֵינוּ Aleynu W83 F160
קַדִּישׁ יָתוֹם Mourner's Kaddish (some omit) W84 F162

**If the Psalm for the Day was not recited earlier, add here:**
Psalm for Monday (Psalm 48) W86 F24
קַדִּישׁ יָתוֹם Mourner's Kaddish (some omit) W100 F52

| Kislev 5779 | | | | | | | Nov \| Dec 2018 | | | | | | |
|---|---|---|---|---|---|---|---|---|---|---|---|---|---|
| | | | | | 1 | 2 | | | | | | 9 | 10 |
| 3 | 4 | 5 | 6 | 7 | 8 | 9 | 11 | 12 | 13 | 14 | 15 | 16 | 17 |
| 10 | 11 | 12 | 13 | 14 | 15 | 16 | 18 | 19 | 20 | 21 | 22 | 23 | 24 |
| 17 | 18 | 19 | 20 | 21 | 22 | 23 | 25 | 26 | 27 | 28 | 29 | 30 \| | 1 |
| 24 | 25 | 26 | 27 | 28 | 29 | 30 | 2 | 3 | 4 | 5 | 6 | 7 | 8 |

+ Add ✕ Omit ☞ Take note!

**Siddurim**
- **L** Lev Shalem for Shabbat and Festivals
- **S** Shabbat and Festival Sim Shalom
- **W** Weekday Sim Shalom
- **F** Full Sim Shalom (both editions)
- **P** Personal Edition of Full Sim Shalom

+ Psalm 30 for Ḥanukkah W14 F50
קַדִּישׁ יָתוֹם Mourner's Kaddish W100|15 F162|52

מִנְחָה

**Weekday Amidah:**
+ עַל הַנִּסִּים Al Hanissim for Ḥanukkah W128 F180

✕ ~~תַּחֲנוּן Taḥanun~~

## Kislev 26 כִּסְלֵו
Mon 3 Dec

## חֲנֻכָּה Ḥanukkah — Day 2

עַרְבִית

+ In the synagogue, before Arvit, light Ḥanukkah candles (see p. 72). W192 F242

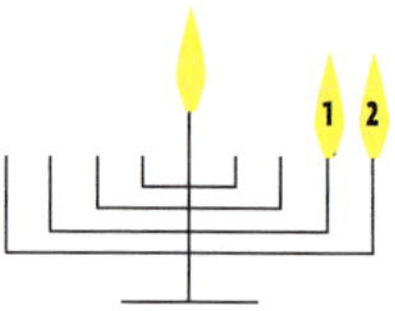


**Weekday Amidah:**
+ עַל הַנִּסִּים Al Hanissim for Ḥanukkah W146 F218

קַדִּישׁ שָׁלֵם Full Kaddish W149 F222
עָלֵינוּ Aleynu W150 F224
קַדִּישׁ יָתוֹם Mourner's Kaddish W151 F226

Tue 4 Dec שַׁחֲרִית

+ In the synagogue, before Shaḥarit, light Ḥanukkah candles (see p. 72). W192 F242

**Weekday Amidah:**
+ עַל הַנִּסִּים Al Hanissim for Ḥanukkah W42 F116

✕ ~~תַּחֲנוּן Taḥanun~~

+ הַלֵּל שָׁלֵם Full Hallel W50 F380
חֲצִי קַדִּישׁ Short Kaddish W64 F390

+ **TORAH SERVICE** W65 F138
Remove **1** Torah scroll from ark.

**Torah** 3 aliyot from נָשֹׂא Naso
בְּמִדְבַּר Bemidbar (Numbers) 7:18–29
¹7:18–20 ²21–23 ³24–29 W332 P946

חֲצִי קַדִּישׁ Short Kaddish W71 F146
Open, raise, display, and wrap scroll.
Return scroll to ark. W76 F150

אַשְׁרֵי Ashrey W78 F152
✕ ~~לַמְנַצֵּחַ Lamenatse·aḥ (Psalm 20)~~
וּבָא לְצִיּוֹן Uva letsiyyon W80 F156

קַדִּישׁ שָׁלֵם Full Kaddish W82 F158
עָלֵינוּ Aleynu W83 F160
קַדִּישׁ יָתוֹם Mourner's Kaddish (some omit) W84 F162

**If the Psalm for the Day was not recited earlier, add here:**
Psalm for Tuesday (Psalm 82) W87 F26
קַדִּישׁ יָתוֹם Mourner's Kaddish (some omit) W100 F52

\+ Psalm 30 for Ḥanukkah W14 F50
קַדִּישׁ יָתוֹם Mourner's Kaddish W100|15 F162|52

**מִנְחָה**

**Weekday Amidah:**
\+ עַל הַנִּסִּים Al Hanissim for Ḥanukkah W128 F180

✗ ~~תַּחֲנוּן Taḥanun~~

---

**UNTIL Pesaḥ**

**Every weekday Amidah:**
\+ וְתֵן טַל וּמָטָר לִבְרָכָה Veten tal umatar livrakhah
✗ ~~וְתֵן בְּרָכָה Veten berakhah~~

| | |
|---|---|
| עַרְבִית | W144 F214 |
| שַׁחֲרִית | W39 F112 |
| מִנְחָה | W125 F174 |

---

## Kislev 27 כִּסְלֵו
Tue 4 Dec

## חֲנֻכָּה Hanukkah — Day 3

**עַרְבִית**

\+ In the synagogue, before Arvit, light Ḥanukkah candles (see p. 72). W192 F242

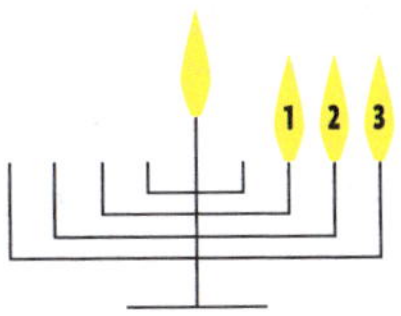


**Weekday Amidah:**
\+ עַל הַנִּסִּים Al Hanissim for Ḥanukkah W146 F218

קַדִּישׁ שָׁלֵם Full Kaddish W149 F222
עָלֵינוּ Aleynu W150 F224
קַדִּישׁ יָתוֹם Mourner's Kaddish W151 F226

Wed 5 Dec **שַׁחֲרִית**

\+ In the synagogue, before Shaḥarit, light Ḥanukkah candles (see p. 72). W192 F242

**Weekday Amidah:**
\+ עַל הַנִּסִּים Al Hanissim for Ḥanukkah W42 F116

✗ ~~תַּחֲנוּן Taḥanun~~

| Kislev 5779 | | | | | | |
|---|---|---|---|---|---|---|
| | | | | | 1 | 2 |
| 3 | 4 | 5 | 6 | 7 | 8 | 9 |
| 10 | 11 | 12 | 13 | 14 | 15 | 16 |
| 17 | 18 | 19 | 20 | 21 | 22 | 23 |
| 24 | 25 | 26 | 27 | 28 | 29 | 30 |

| Nov \| Dec 2018 | | | | | | |
|---|---|---|---|---|---|---|
| | | | | | 9 | 10 |
| 11 | 12 | 13 | 14 | 15 | 16 | 17 |
| 18 | 19 | 20 | 21 | 22 | 23 | 24 |
| 25 | 26 | 27 | 28 | 29 | 30 \| | 1 |
| 2 | 3 | 4 | 5 | 6 | 7 | 8 |

+ Add ✕ Omit ☞ Take note!

**Siddurim**
**L** Lev Shalem for Shabbat and Festivals
**S** Shabbat and Festival Sim Shalom
**W** Weekday Sim Shalom
**F** Full Sim Shalom (both editions)
**P** Personal Edition of Full Sim Shalom

+ הַלֵּל שָׁלֵם Full Hallel W50 F380
חֲצִי קַדִּישׁ Short Kaddish W64 F390

+ **TORAH SERVICE** W65 F138
Remove **1** Torah scroll from ark.

**Torah** 3 aliyot from נָשֹׂא Naso
בְּמִדְבַּר Bemidbar (Numbers) 7:24–35
[1]7:24–26 [2]27–29 [3]30–35 W332 P947

חֲצִי קַדִּישׁ Short Kaddish W71 F146
Open, raise, display, and wrap scroll.
Return scroll to ark. W76 F150

אַשְׁרֵי Ashrey W78 F152
✕ ~~לַמְנַצֵּחַ Lamenatse-aḥ (Psalm 20)~~
וּבָא לְצִיּוֹן Uva letsiyyon W80 F156
קַדִּישׁ שָׁלֵם Full Kaddish W82 F158
עָלֵינוּ Aleynu W83 F160
קַדִּישׁ יָתוֹם Mourner's Kaddish (some omit) W84 F162

**If the Psalm for the Day was not recited earlier, add here:**
Psalm for Wednesday (Psalms 94:1–95:3) W87 F26
קַדִּישׁ יָתוֹם Mourner's Kaddish (some omit) W100 F52

+ Psalm 30 for Ḥanukkah W14 F50
קַדִּישׁ יָתוֹם Mourner's Kaddish W100|15 F162|52

מִנְחָה
**Weekday Amidah:**
+ עַל הַנִּסִּים Al Hanissim for Ḥanukkah W128 F180

✕ ~~תַּחֲנוּן Taḥanun~~

חנכה Hanukkah

## Kislev 28 כִּסְלֵו
Wed 5 Dec

## חֲנֻכָּה Ḥanukkah — Day 4

עַרְבִית
+ In the synagogue, before Arvit, light Ḥanukkah candles (see p. 72). W192 F242

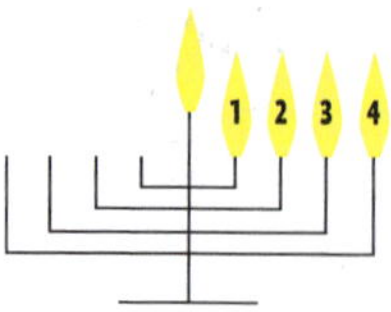


**Weekday Amidah:**
+ עַל הַנִּסִּים Al Hanissim for Ḥanukkah W146 F218

קַדִּישׁ שָׁלֵם Full Kaddish W149 F222
עָלֵינוּ Aleynu W150 F224
קַדִּישׁ יָתוֹם Mourner's Kaddish W151 F226

## Thu 6 Dec

### שַׁחֲרִית

+ In the synagogue, before Shaḥarit, light Ḥanukkah candles (see p. 72). W192 F242

**Weekday Amidah:**

+ עַל הַנִּסִּים Al Hanissim for Ḥanukkah W42 F116

✕ ~~תַּחֲנוּן Taḥanun~~

+ הַלֵּל שָׁלֵם Full Hallel W50 F380

חֲצִי קַדִּישׁ Short Kaddish W64 F390

**TORAH SERVICE** W65 F138

Remove **1** Torah scroll from ark.

**Torah** 3 aliyot from נָשֹׂא Naso
בְּמִדְבַּר Bemidbar (Numbers) 7:30–41
¹7:30–32 ²33–35 ³36–41 W333 P948

חֲצִי קַדִּישׁ Short Kaddish W71 F146

Open, raise, display, and wrap scroll.

Return scroll to ark. W76 F150

אַשְׁרֵי Ashrey W78 F152

✕ ~~לַמְנַצֵּחַ Lamenatse·aḥ (Psalm 20)~~

וּבָא לְצִיּוֹן Uva letsiyyon W80 F156

קַדִּישׁ שָׁלֵם Full Kaddish W82 F158

עָלֵינוּ Aleynu W83 F160

קַדִּישׁ יָתוֹם Mourner's Kaddish (some omit) W84 F162

**If the Psalm for the Day was not recited earlier, add here:**

Psalm for Thursday (Psalm 81) W89 F30

קַדִּישׁ יָתוֹם Mourner's Kaddish (some omit) W100 F52

+ Psalm 30 for Ḥanukkah W14 F50

קַדִּישׁ יָתוֹם Mourner's Kaddish W100|15 F162|52

### מִנְחָה

**Weekday Amidah:**

+ עַל הַנִּסִּים Al Hanissim for Ḥanukkah W128 F180

✕ ~~תַּחֲנוּן Taḥanun~~

| Kislev 5779 | | | | | | |
|---|---|---|---|---|---|---|
| | | | | | 1 | 2 |
| 3 | 4 | 5 | 6 | 7 | 8 | 9 |
| 10 | 11 | 12 | 13 | 14 | 15 | 16 |
| 17 | 18 | 19 | 20 | 21 | 22 | 23 |
| 24 | 25 | 26 | 27 | 28 | 29 | 30 |

| Nov \| Dec 2018 | | | | | | |
|---|---|---|---|---|---|---|
| | | | | | 9 | 10 |
| 11 | 12 | 13 | 14 | 15 | 16 | 17 |
| 18 | 19 | 20 | 21 | 22 | 23 | 24 |
| 25 | 26 | 27 | 28 | 29 | 30 \| | 1 |
| 2 | 3 | 4 | 5 | 6 | 7 | 8 |

+ Add ✕ Omit ☞ Take note!

**Siddurim**
- **L** Lev Shalem for Shabbat and Festivals
- **S** Shabbat and Festival Sim Shalom
- **W** Weekday Sim Shalom
- **F** Full Sim Shalom (both editions)
- **P** Personal Edition of Full Sim Shalom

## Kislev 29 כִּסְלֵו
Thu 6 Dec

## חֲנֻכָּה Ḥanukkah — Day 5

**עַרְבִית**

+ In the synagogue, before Arvit, light Ḥanukkah candles (see p. 72). W192 F242

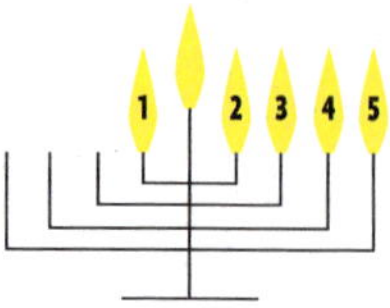


**Weekday Amidah:**

+ עַל הַנִּסִּים Al Hanissim for Ḥanukkah W146 F218

קַדִּישׁ שָׁלֵם Full Kaddish W149 F222
עָלֵינוּ Aleynu W150 F224
קַדִּישׁ יָתוֹם Mourner's Kaddish W151 F226

Fri 7 Dec

**שַׁחֲרִית**

+ In the synagogue, before Shaḥarit, light Ḥanukkah candles (see p. 72). W192 F242

**Weekday Amidah:**

+ עַל הַנִּסִּים Al Hanissim for Ḥanukkah W42 F116

✕ ~~תַּחֲנוּן Taḥanun~~

+ הַלֵּל שָׁלֵם Full Hallel W50 F380
חֲצִי קַדִּישׁ Short Kaddish W64 F390

+ **TORAH SERVICE** W65 F138
Remove **1** Torah scroll from ark.

**Torah** 3 aliyot from נָשֹׂא Naso
בְּמִדְבַּר Bemidbar (Numbers) 7:36–47
[1]7:36–38 [2]39–41 [3]42–47 W333 P949

חֲצִי קַדִּישׁ Short Kaddish W71 F146
Open, raise, display, and wrap scroll.
Return scroll to ark. W76 F150

אַשְׁרֵי Ashrey W78 F152
✕ ~~לַמְנַצֵּחַ Lamenatse·aḥ (Psalm 20)~~
וּבָא לְצִיּוֹן Uva letsiyyon W80 F156
קַדִּישׁ שָׁלֵם Full Kaddish W82 F158
עָלֵינוּ Aleynu W83 F160
קַדִּישׁ יָתוֹם Mourner's Kaddish (some omit) W84 F162

**If the Psalm for the Day was not recited earlier, add here:**
Psalm for Friday (Psalm 93) W90 F32
קַדִּישׁ יָתוֹם Mourner's Kaddish (some omit) W100 F52

+ Psalm 30 for Ḥanukkah W14 F50
קַדִּישׁ יָתוֹם Mourner's Kaddish W100|15 F162|52

**מִנְחָה**

**Weekday Amidah:**

+ עַל הַנִּסִּים Al Hanissim for Ḥanukkah W128 F180

✕ ~~תַּחֲנוּן Taḥanun~~

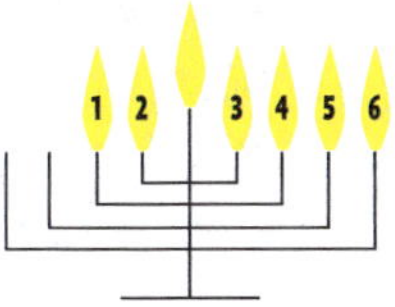


**At home** + Before lighting Shabbat candles, light Ḥanukkah candles (see p. 71). L429 S307 W192 F242

**In the synagogue** + Before Kabbalat Shabbat, light Ḥanukkah candles (see p. 72). L429 S307 W192 F242

## Kislev 30 כִּסְלֵו
**Fri 7 Dec** (evening)

**שַׁבָּת Shabbat** פָּרָשַׁת מִקֵּץ **Parashat Mikkets**
**רֹאשׁ חֹדֶשׁ טֵבֵת Rosh Ḥodesh Tevet — Day 1**
**Ḥanukkah — Day 6**

For determining the *yortsayt* of a death on 30 Kislev, see p. 214.

**DURING Rosh Hodesh**

**Birkat Hamazon:**

+ יַעֲלֶה וְיָבוֹא Ya'aleh veyavo for Rosh Ḥodesh
L90|95 S340|347 W233|239 F762|780

+ הָרַחֲמָן Haraḥaman for Rosh Ḥodesh
L92|96 S343|348 W235|240 F768

☞ Ensure that Ḥanukkah candles are lit before Shabbat. See blue boxes, pp. 71–72.

**קַבָּלַת שַׁבָּת** ☞ Recite Kabbalat Shabbat as on a usual Shabbat. L6 S15 F254

**עַרְבִית**

**Shabbat Amidah:**

+ יַעֲלֶה וְיָבוֹא Ya'aleh veyavo for Rosh Ḥodesh L50 S36 F298
+ עַל הַנִּסִּים Al Hanissim for Ḥanukkah L430 S37 F300

Continue Shabbat Arvit service as usual.

עָלֵינוּ Aleynu L56 S51 F320
קַדִּישׁ יָתוֹם Mourner's Kaddish L58 S52 F324

| Kislev 5779 | | | | | | | Nov \| Dec 2018 | | | | | | |
|---|---|---|---|---|---|---|---|---|---|---|---|---|---|
| | | | | | 1 | 2 | | | | | | 9 | 10 |
| 3 | 4 | 5 | 6 | 7 | 8 | 9 | 11 | 12 | 13 | 14 | 15 | 16 | 17 |
| 10 | 11 | 12 | 13 | 14 | 15 | 16 | 18 | 19 | 20 | 21 | 22 | 23 | 24 |
| 17 | 18 | 19 | 20 | 21 | 22 | 23 | 25 | 26 | 27 | 28 | 29 | 30 | 1 |
| 24 | 25 | 26 | 27 | 28 | 29 | 30 | 2 | 3 | 4 | 5 | 6 | 7 | 8 |

+ Add ✕ Omit ☞ Take note!

**Siddurim**
- **L** Lev Shalem for Shabbat and Festivals
- **S** Shabbat and Festival Sim Shalom
- **W** Weekday Sim Shalom
- **F** Full Sim Shalom (both editions)
- **P** Personal Edition of Full Sim Shalom

## Sat 8 Dec שַׁחֲרִית

**Before מִזְמוֹר שִׁיר Mizmor shir (Psalm 30)** L120 S81 F50
**or after Aleynu, recite:**
Psalm for Shabbat (Psalm 92) L112 S72 F32
קַדִּישׁ יָתוֹם Mourner's Kaddish (some omit) L121 S82 F52
+ Psalm 104 for Rosh Ḥodesh L114 S78 F34
קַדִּישׁ יָתוֹם Mourner's Kaddish L121 S82 F52

**Shabbat Amidah:**
+ יַעֲלֶה וְיָבוֹא Ya'aleh veyavo for Rosh Ḥodesh L163 S118 F360
+ עַל הַנִּסִּים Al Hanissim for Ḥanukkah L430 S119 F362

+ הַלֵּל שָׁלֵם Full Hallel L316 S133 F380
קַדִּישׁ שָׁלֵם Full Kaddish L167 S138 F392

**TORAH SERVICE** L168 S139 F394

☞ Remove **3** Torah scrolls from ark.

**1st scroll** 6 aliyot (minimum): מִקֵּץ Mikkets
בְּרֵאשִׁית Bereshit (Genesis) 41:1–44:17

| | | | | |
|---|---|---|---|---|
| Annual: | [1] 41:1–14 | [2] 41:15–38 | [3] 41:39–52 | [4] 41:53–42:18 |
| | [5] 42:19–43:15 | [6] 43:16–44:17 | | |
| Triennial: | [1] 43:16–18 | [2] 43:19–25 | [3] 43:26–29 | [4] 43:30–34 |
| | [5] 44:1–6 | [6] 44:7–17 | | |

Place 2nd scroll on table next to 1st scroll.
Open, raise, display, and wrap 1st scroll.

+ **2nd scroll** 7th aliyah from פִּינְחָס Pineḥas
בְּמִדְבַּר Bemidbar (Numbers) 28:9–15

Place 3rd scroll on table next to 2nd scroll.
Place or hold 1st scroll near other scrolls at table.
(Some do not return the 1st scroll to table.)

חֲצִי קַדִּישׁ Short Kaddish L174 S146 F408
Open, raise, display, and wrap 2nd scroll.

**3rd scroll** Maftir aliyah from נָשֹׂא Naso
M בְּמִדְבַּר Bemidbar (Numbers) 7:42–47°

☞ °Read only these 6 verses, not 12 as on most days of Ḥanukkah.

Open, raise, display, and wrap 3rd scroll.

☞ **Haftarah** for Shabbat Ḥanukkah
זְכַרְיָה Zekharyah (Zechariah) 2:14–4:7

|  |  |
|---|---|
| ✚ Add  ✗ Omit  ☞ Take note! | **Kislev 5779**    Nov \| Dec 2018    **30 כִּסְלֵו Dec 8** |

| Siddurim |
|---|
| **L** Lev Shalem for Shabbat and Festivals |
| **S** Shabbat and Festival Sim Shalom |
| **W** Weekday Sim Shalom |
| **F** Full Sim Shalom (both editions) |
| **P** Personal Edition of Full Sim Shalom |

| | | | | | | | |
|---|---|---|---|---|---|---|---|
| | | | | 1 | 2 | 9 | 10 |
| 3 | 4 | 5 | 6 | 7 | 8 | 9 | 11 12 13 14 15 16 17 |
| 10 | 11 | 12 | 13 | 14 | 15 | 16 | 18 19 20 21 22 23 24 |
| 17 | 18 | 19 | 20 | 21 | 22 | 23 | 25 26 27 28 29 30 \| 1 |
| 24 | 25 | 26 | 27 | 28 | 29 | 30 | 2 3 4 5 6 7 8 |

✗ אַב הָרַחֲמִים Av Haraḥamim

אַשְׁרֵי Ashrey    L181 S151 F420
Return scrolls to ark.    L183 S153 F422

חֲצִי קַדִּישׁ Short Kaddish    L184 S155 F428

**מוּסָף**    **Rosh Ḥodesh Amidah for Shabbat:**    L193 S166 F486
Shabbat קְדֻשָּׁה Kedushah    L195 S167 F490
Continuation of Amidah    L196 S168 F496
✚ וּלְכַפָּרַת פָּשַׁע Ulkhapparat pasha    L199 S169 F498
   Add these words only through Rosh Ḥodesh Adar Sheni.

✚ עַל הַנִּסִּים Al Hanissim for Ḥanukkah    L430 S176 F438

קַדִּישׁ שָׁלֵם Full Kaddish    L203 S181 F506
אֵין כֵּאלֹהֵינוּ Eyn keloheynu    L204 S182 F508
עָלֵינוּ Aleynu    L205 S183 F510
קַדִּישׁ יָתוֹם Mourner's Kaddish (some omit)    L207 S184 F512

**If the Psalm for the Day was not recited at Shaḥarit, add here:**
Psalm for Shabbat (Psalm 92)    L112 S72 F32
קַדִּישׁ יָתוֹם Mourner's Kaddish (some omit)    L121 S82 F52
✚ Psalm 104 for Rosh Ḥodesh    L114 S78 F34
קַדִּישׁ יָתוֹם Mourner's Kaddish (some omit)    L121 S82 F52

✚ Psalm 30 for Ḥanukkah    L120 S81 F50
קַדִּישׁ יָתוֹם Mourner's Kaddish    L207\|121 S184\|82 F512\|52

**מִנְחָה**    **Torah** 3 aliyot from וַיִּגַּשׁ Vayiggash
בְּרֵאשִׁית Bereshit (Genesis) 44:18–30
¹44:18–20    ²21–24    ³25–30      W274 P895
This is also the reading for the coming Thursday.

**Shabbat Amidah:**
✚ יַעֲלֶה וְיָבוֹא Ya'aleh veyavo for Rosh Ḥodesh    L227 S237 F580
✚ עַל הַנִּסִּים Al Hanissim for Ḥanukkah    L430 S238 F582

✗ צִדְקָתְךָ צֶדֶק Tsidkatekha tsedek

Ḥanukkah   חֲנֻכָּה

---

**Register to Keep Up to Date**
Join our email list! You will receive *Luaḥ* updates, additions, and corrections during the course of the year.
Register at: **www.milesbcohen.com/LuahUpdates**
*Registered in the past? No need to register again.*

# Dec 8　טֵבֵת 1

**Tevet 5779** | **Dec 2018 | Jan 2019**

| 1 | 2 | 3 | 4 | 5 | 6 | 7 | 9 | 10 | 11 | 12 | 13 | 14 | 15 |
| 8 | 9 | 10 | 11 | 12 | 13 | 14 | 16 | 17 | 18 | 19 | 20 | 21 | 22 |
| 15 | 16 | 17 | 18 | 19 | 20 | 21 | 23 | 24 | 25 | 26 | 27 | 28 | 29 |
| 22 | 23 | 24 | 25 | 26 | 27 | 28 | 30 | 31 | 1 | 2 | 3 | 4 | 5 |
| 29 | | | | | | | 6 | | | | | | |

✚ Add　✘ Omit　☞ Take note!

**Siddurim**
- **L** Lev Shalem for Shabbat and Festivals
- **S** Shabbat and Festival Sim Shalom
- **W** Weekday Sim Shalom
- **F** Full Sim Shalom (both editions)
- **P** Personal Edition of Full Sim Shalom

---

**DURING Ḥanukkah**　Continue:

**Every Shaḥarit and Minḥah**
✘ ~~תַּחֲנוּן~~ ~~Taḥanun~~

**Birkat Hamazon:**
✚ עַל הַנִּסִּים Al Hanissim for Ḥanukkah
　　　　　　　　　　**L**430 **S**338|345 **W**231|237 **F**758

**Every Amidah:**
✚ עַל הַנִּסִּים Al Hanissim for Ḥanukkah

---

**Tevet 1　טֵבֵת 1**
**Sat 8 Dec (evening)**

רֹאשׁ חֹדֶשׁ טֵבֵת　**Rosh Ḥodesh Tevet — Day 2**
חֲנֻכָּה　**Ḥanukkah — Day 7**
מוֹצָאֵי שַׁבָּת　**Motsa'ey Shabbat　Conclusion of Shabbat**

**DURING Rosh Ḥodesh**　**Birkat Hamazon:**
✚ יַעֲלֶה וְיָבוֹא Ya'aleh veyavo for Rosh Ḥodesh
　　　　　　　　　　**L**90|95 **S**340|347 **W**233|239 **F**762|780

✚ הָרַחֲמָן Haraḥaman for Rosh Ḥodesh
　　　　　　　　　　**L**92|96 **S**343|348 **W**235|240 **F**768

---

עַרְבִית　Saturday night Arvit as usual　**L**264 **S**281 **W**137 **F**200
until the Amidah

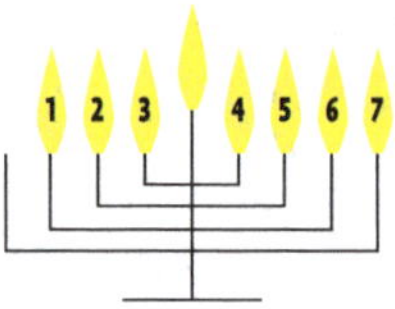

**Weekday Amidah:**
✚ אַתָּה חוֹנַנְתָּנוּ Attah ḥonantanu　**L**272 **S**287 **W**143 **F**212
✚ יַעֲלֶה וְיָבוֹא Ya'aleh veyavo for Rosh Ḥodesh　**L**277 **S**289 **W**145 **F**216
✚ עַל הַנִּסִּים Al Hanissim for Ḥanukkah　**L**430 **S**290 **W**146 **F**218

☞ חֲצִי קַדִּישׁ Short Kaddish　**L**269 **S**292 **W**158 **F**682
☞ וִיהִי נֹעַם Vihi no'am　**L**279 **S**292 **W**158 **F**684
☞ יוֹשֵׁב בְּסֵתֶר עֶלְיוֹן Yoshev beseter elyon　**L**279 **S**292 **W**158 **F**684
☞ וְאַתָּה קָדוֹשׁ Ve'attah kadosh　**L**216 **S**293 **W**159 **F**684 .
קַדִּישׁ שָׁלֵם Full Kaddish　**L**280 **S**294 **W**160 **F**688

Those who recite הַבְדָּלָה Havdalah here:
First light Ḥanukkah candles (see p. 72),　**L**429 **S**307 **W**192 **F**242
then recite הַבְדָּלָה.　**L**283 **S**299 **W**165 **F**700

עָלֵינוּ Aleynu　**L**281 **S**297 **W**163 **F**696
קַדִּישׁ יָתוֹם Mourner's Kaddish　**L**121 **S**82 **W**15 **F**51

+ Light Ḥanukkah candles (see p. 72). L429 S307 W192 F242
הַבְדָּלָה Havdalah L283 S299 W165 F700

At home ☞ הַבְדָּלָה Havdalah L283 S299 W165 F700
+ Light Ḥanukkah candles (see p. 71). L429 S307 W192 F242

**Sun 9 Dec** שַׁחֲרִית + In the synagogue, before Shaḥarit, light Ḥanukkah candles (see p. 72). W192 F242

**Before מִזְמוֹר שִׁיר Mizmor shir (Psalm 30)** W14 F50
**or at end of service, recite:**
Psalm for Sunday (Psalm 24) W85 F22
קַדִּישׁ יָתוֹם Mourner's Kaddish (some omit) W100 F52
+ Psalm 104 for Rosh Ḥodesh W90 F34
קַדִּישׁ יָתוֹם Mourner's Kaddish W100 F52

**Weekday Amidah:**
+ יַעֲלֶה וְיָבוֹא Ya'aleh veyavo for Rosh Ḥodesh W41 F114
+ עַל הַנִּסִּים Al Hanissim for Ḥanukkah W42 F116

✕ ~~תַּחֲנוּן Taḥanun~~

+ הַלֵּל שָׁלֵם Full Hallel W50 F380
קַדִּישׁ שָׁלֵם Full Kaddish W56 F392

+ **TORAH SERVICE** W65 F138
Remove **2** Torah scrolls from ark.

**1st scroll** 3 aliyot from פִּינְחָס Pineḥas
בְּמִדְבַּר Bemidbar (Numbers) 28:1–15
[1] 28:1–5 [2] 6–10 [3] 11–15 W336 P943

Place 2nd scroll on table next to the 1st.
(Do not recite חֲצִי קַדִּישׁ Short Kaddish here.)

Open, raise, display, and wrap 1st scroll.

**2nd scroll** 1 aliyah from נָשֹׂא Naso
[4] בְּמִדְבַּר Bemidbar (Numbers) 7:48–53° W333 P951
☞ °Read only these 6 verses, not 12 as on most days of Ḥanukkah.

Place 1st scroll on table next to 2nd scroll.
חֲצִי קַדִּישׁ Short Kaddish W71 F146

Dec 9 **טֵבֵת 1**   Tevet 5779   Dec 2018 | Jan 2019   ✚ Add   ✖ Omit   ☞ Take note!

| | | | | | | | | | | | | | | |
|---|---|---|---|---|---|---|---|---|---|---|---|---|---|---|
| 1 | 2 | 3 | 4 | 5 | 6 | 7 | 9 | 10 | 11 | 12 | 13 | 14 | 15 | |
| 8 | 9 | 10 | 11 | 12 | 13 | 14 | 16 | 17 | 18 | 19 | 20 | 21 | 22 | |
| 15 | 16 | 17 | 18 | 19 | 20 | 21 | 23 | 24 | 25 | 26 | 27 | 28 | 29 | |
| 22 | 23 | 24 | 25 | 26 | 27 | 28 | 30 | 31 | 1 | 2 | 3 | 4 | 5 | |
| 29 | | | | | | | 6 | | | | | | | |

**Siddurim**
- **L** Lev Shalem for Shabbat and Festivals
- **S** Shabbat and Festival Sim Shalom
- **W** Weekday Sim Shalom
- **F** Full Sim Shalom (both editions)
- **P** Personal Edition of Full Sim Shalom

---

Open, raise, display, and wrap 2nd scroll.
Return scrolls to ark.    W76 F150

אַשְׁרֵי Ashrey    W78 F152

✖ ~~לַמְנַצֵּחַ Lamenatse·aḥ (Psalm 20)~~

וּבָא לְצִיּוֹן Uva letsiyyon    W80 F156

*Some congregations:*
Remove and pack tefillin at this point.
✚ חֲצִי קַדִּישׁ Short Kaddish    W103 F428

*Other congregations:*
✚ חֲצִי קַדִּישׁ Short Kaddish    W103 F428
Remove and cover—but do not pack—tefillin, so that
all begin Musaf Amidah at the same time,
as soon after Kaddish as possible.

מוּסָף ✚ **Rosh Ḥodesh Amidah for weekdays:**    W104 F486
Weekday קְדֻשָּׁה Kedushah    W105 F488
✚ וּלְכַפָּרַת פֶּשַׁע Ulkhapparat pasha    W107 F494
Add these words only through Rosh Ḥodesh Adar Sheni.
✚ עַל הַנִּסִּים Al Hanissim for Ḥanukkah    W108 F500

✚ קַדִּישׁ שָׁלֵם Full Kaddish    W82 F158
עָלֵינוּ Aleynu    W83 F160
קַדִּישׁ יָתוֹם Mourner's Kaddish (some omit)    W84 F162

*If psalms for the day were not recited at Shaḥarit, add here:*
Psalm for Sunday (Psalm 24)    W85 F22
קַדִּישׁ יָתוֹם Mourner's Kaddish (some omit)    W100 F52
✚ Psalm 104 for Rosh Ḥodesh    W90 F34
קַדִּישׁ יָתוֹם Mourner's Kaddish (some omit)    W100 F52
✚ Psalm 30 for Ḥanukkah    W14 F50
קַדִּישׁ יָתוֹם Mourner's Kaddish    W84|100 F162|52

מִנְחָה **Weekday Amidah:**
✚ יַעֲלֶה וְיָבוֹא Ya'aleh veyavo for Rosh Ḥodesh    W127 F178
✚ עַל הַנִּסִּים Al Hanissim for Ḥanukkah    W128 F180

✖ ~~תַּחֲנוּן Taḥanun~~

## Tevet 2 טֵבֵת
Sun 9 Dec

# חֲנֻכָּה Ḥanukkah — Day 8

**עַרְבִית**

+ In the synagogue, before Arvit, light Ḥanukkah candles (see p. 72). W192 F242

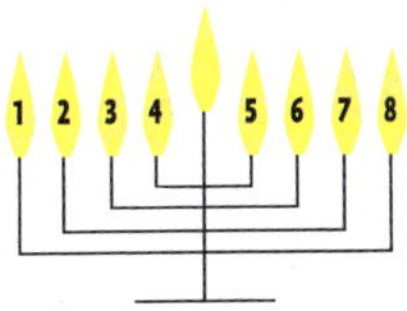


**Weekday Amidah:**

+ עַל הַנִּסִּים Al Hanissim for Ḥanukkah W146 F218

קַדִּישׁ שָׁלֵם Full Kaddish W149 F222
עָלֵינוּ Aleynu W150 F224
קַדִּישׁ יָתוֹם Mourner's Kaddish W151 F226

Mon 10 Dec **שַׁחֲרִית**

+ In the synagogue, before Shaḥarit, light Ḥanukkah candles (see p. 72). W192 F242

**Weekday Amidah:**

+ עַל הַנִּסִּים Al Hanissim for Ḥanukkah W42 F116

✕ ~~תַּחֲנוּן Taḥanun~~

+ הַלֵּל שָׁלֵם Full Hallel W50 F380
חֲצִי קַדִּישׁ Short Kaddish W64 F390

**TORAH SERVICE** W65 F138
Remove **1** Torah scroll from ark.

☞ **Torah** 3 aliyot from נָשֹׂא Naso + בְּהַעֲלֹתְךָ Beha'alotekha
בְּמִדְבַּר Bemidbar (Numbers) 7:54–8:4
[1]7:54–56 [2]57–59 [3]7:60–8:4 W334–35 P952–54 + 919

חֲצִי קַדִּישׁ Short Kaddish W71 F146
Open, raise, display, and wrap scroll.
Return scroll to ark. W76 F150

אַשְׁרֵי Ashrey W78 F152
✕ ~~לַמְנַצֵּחַ Lamenatse·aḥ (Psalm 20)~~
וּבָא לְצִיּוֹן Uva letsiyyon W80 F156
קַדִּישׁ שָׁלֵם Full Kaddish W82 F158
עָלֵינוּ Aleynu W83 F160
קַדִּישׁ יָתוֹם Mourner's Kaddish (some omit) W84 F162

| Tevet 5779 | | | | | | |
|---|---|---|---|---|---|---|
| 1 | 2 | 3 | 4 | 5 | 6 | 7 |
| 8 | 9 | 10 | 11 | 12 | 13 | 14 |
| 15 | 16 | 17 | 18 | 19 | 20 | 21 |
| 22 | 23 | 24 | 25 | 26 | 27 | 28 |
| 29 | | | | | | |

| Dec 2018 \| Jan 2019 | | | | | | |
|---|---|---|---|---|---|---|
| 9 | 10 | 11 | 12 | 13 | 14 | 15 |
| 16 | 17 | 18 | 19 | 20 | 21 | 22 |
| 23 | 24 | 25 | 26 | 27 | 28 | 29 |
| 30 | 31 \| 1 | 2 | 3 | 4 | 5 | |
| 6 | | | | | | |

+ Add  ✕ Omit  ☞ Take note!

**Siddurim**
- **L** Lev Shalem for Shabbat and Festivals
- **S** Shabbat and Festival Sim Shalom
- **W** Weekday Sim Shalom
- **F** Full Sim Shalom (both editions)
- **P** Personal Edition of Full Sim Shalom

**If the Psalm for the Day was not recited earlier, add here:**
Psalm for Monday (Psalm 48) W86 F24
קַדִּישׁ יָתוֹם Mourner's Kaddish (some omit) W100 F52

+ Psalm 30 for Ḥanukkah W14 F50
קַדִּישׁ יָתוֹם Mourner's Kaddish W100|15 F162|52

מִנְחָה

**Weekday Amidah:**
+ עַל הַנִּסִּים Al Hanissim for Ḥanukkah W128 F180

✕ ~~תַּחֲנוּן Taḥanun~~

## Tevet 7 טֵבֵת
Sat 15 Dec

חֲנֻכָּה Hanukkah

## שַׁבָּת Shabbat פָּרָשַׁת וַיִּגַּשׁ Parashat Vayiggash

**Torah** 7 aliyot (minimum): וַיִּגַּשׁ Vayiggash
בְּרֵאשִׁית Bereshit (Genesis) 44:18–47:27

| | | | | |
|---|---|---|---|---|
| Annual: | 1 44:18–30 | 2 44:31–45:7 | 3 45:8–18 | 4 45:19–27 |
| | 5 45:28–46:27 | 6 46:28–47:10 | 7 47:11–27 | M 47:25–27 |
| Triennial: | 1 46:28–30 | 2 46:31–34 | 3 47:1–6 | 4 47:7–10 |
| | 5 47:11–19 | 6 47:20–22 | 7 47:23–27 | M 47:25–27 |

**Haftarah** יְחֶזְקֵאל Yeḥezkel (Ezekiel) 37:15–28

מִנְחָה

**Torah** 3 aliyot from וַיְחִי Vayḥi
בְּרֵאשִׁית Bereshit (Genesis) 47:28–48:9
1 47:28–31  2 48:1–3  3 48:4–9  W275 P896

This is also the reading for the coming Monday and Thursday.

## Tevet 10 טֵבֵת — עֲשָׂרָה בְּטֵבֵת Asarah Betevet

**Tue 18 Dec (morning)** — **10th of Tevet** (communal fast, begins at dawn)

### Asarah Betevet

Asarah Betevet marks the beginning of the siege of Jerusalem by Nebuchadnezzar of Babylonia, which ended 18 months later with the destruction of Jerusalem and the First Temple.

- This is a minor fast day, so called because the fast does not begin until dawn.
- The fast (from both eating and drinking) lasts until dark (a minimum of 25 minutes after sunset).
- *Sheliḥey tsibbur,* Torah readers, and those called for *aliyot* should be fasting.
- The preferred fast-day procedures apply when at least 6 of those who are counted for a *minyan* are fasting.
- If it is ascertained (without causing embarrassment) that fewer than 6 are fasting, follow the procedures printed in gray and marked with ✦.

Following the suggestion of the Chief Rabbinate in Israel, some observe Asarah Betevet as a Holocaust memorial day by:

- Adding a special memorial prayer at the morning Torah service for those killed in the Holocaust.
  The text of the memorial prayer of the Chief Rabbinate, with translation and explanation, can be found at www.milesbcohen.com/LuahResources.
- Designating a Mourner's Kaddish at the end of the service as a קַדִּישׁ כְּלָלִי *kaddish kelali*, a general Mourner's Kaddish (recited by those having lost one or both parents).

**שַׁחֲרִית**

**Silent weekday Amidah:**
Do not add עֲנֵנוּ Anenu.

**Repetition of the weekday Amidah:**

**6 or more fasting** + עֲנֵנוּ Anenu, before רְפָאֵנוּ Refa'enu W38 F110

**Fewer than 6 fasting** ✦ Add עֲנֵנוּ Anenu in שׁוֹמֵעַ תְּפִלָּה Shome·a tefillah.
Replace תַּעֲנִיתֵנוּ ta'anitenu (6th word) with הַתַּעֲנִית הַזֶּה hata'anit hazeh. W38 F110

**6 or more fasting** + אָבִינוּ מַלְכֵּנוּ Avinu malkenu W57 F124

**Fewer than 6 fasting** ✦ Those fasting recite אָבִינוּ מַלְכֵּנוּ individually.

☞ תַּחֲנוּן Taḥanun W62 F132

חֲצִי קַדִּישׁ Short Kaddish W64 F136

Tevet 5779

| | | | | | | |
|---|---|---|---|---|---|---|
| 1 | 2 | 3 | 4 | 5 | 6 | 7 |
| 8 | 9 | 10 | 11 | 12 | 13 | 14 |
| 15 | 16 | 17 | 18 | 19 | 20 | 21 |
| 22 | 23 | 24 | 25 | 26 | 27 | 28 |
| 29 | | | | | | |

Dec 2018 | Jan 2019

| | | | | | | |
|---|---|---|---|---|---|---|
| 9 | 10 | 11 | 12 | 13 | 14 | 15 |
| 16 | 17 | 18 | 19 | 20 | 21 | 22 |
| 23 | 24 | 25 | 26 | 27 | 28 | 29 |
| 30 | 31 | 1 | 2 | 3 | 4 | 5 |
| 6 | | | | | | |

+ Add ✕ Omit ☞ Take note!

**Siddurim**

- **L** Lev Shalem for Shabbat and Festivals
- **S** Shabbat and Festival Sim Shalom
- **W** Weekday Sim Shalom
- **F** Full Sim Shalom (both editions)
- **P** Personal Edition of Full Sim Shalom

---

Fewer than 6 fasting ✦ Omit the entire Torah service.
Continue with אַשְׁרֵי Ashrey.

6 or more fasting + **TORAH SERVICE** W65 F138

Remove **1** Torah scroll from ark.

**Torah** 3 aliyot from כִּי תִשָּׂא Ki tissa
**שְׁמוֹת** Shemot (Exodus) 32:11–14, 34:1–10
[1]32:11–14° [2]34:1–3 [3]4–10° W341 P979

☞ °At each of the 3 passages indicated below, follow this procedure:

1. The reader pauses before the indicated text.
2. The congregation recites the indicated text.
3. Afterward, the reader chants the indicated text in the manner of the cantillation of High Holiday Torah reading.

32:12 שׁוּב מֵחֲרוֹן אַפֶּךָ וְהִנָּחֵם עַל־הָרָעָה לְעַמֶּךָ׃

34:6–7 יְיָ | יְיָ אֵ־ל רַחוּם וְחַנּוּן אֶרֶךְ אַפַּיִם וְרַב־חֶסֶד וֶאֱמֶת׃
נֹצֵר חֶסֶד לָאֲלָפִים נֹשֵׂא עָוֺן וָפֶשַׁע וְחַטָּאָה וְנַקֵּה

34:9 וְסָלַחְתָּ לַעֲוֺנֵנוּ וּלְחַטָּאתֵנוּ | וּנְחַלְתָּנוּ׃

To preserve the sense of this passage, maintain the appropriate pause after the טִפְּחָא (וּלְחַטָּאתֵנוּ).

חֲצִי קַדִּישׁ Short Kaddish W71 F146
Open, raise, display, and wrap scroll.
Return scroll to ark. W76 F150

All minyanim אַשְׁרֵי Ashrey W78 F152
☞ לַמְנַצֵּחַ Lamenatse·aḥ (Psalm 20) W79 F154
Conclude the service in the usual manner.

מִנְחָה אַשְׁרֵי Ashrey W120 F164
חֲצִי קַדִּישׁ Short Kaddish W121 F166

Fewer than 6 fasting ✦ Omit the entire Torah service.
Continue with the silent Amidah.

6 or more fasting + **TORAH SERVICE** W65 F138

Remove **1** Torah scroll from ark.

**Torah** 3 aliyot from כִּי תִשָּׂא Ki tissa
**שְׁמוֹת** Shemot (Exodus) 32:11–14, 34:1–10
[1]32:11–14° [2]34:1–3 [M]4–10° W341 P979

☞ °Follow the same procedure as for the morning reading. See above.

☞ Do not recite חֲצִי קַדִּישׁ Short Kaddish after maftir aliyah.

Open, raise, display, and wrap scroll.

Recite the בְּרָכָה berakhah before the haftarah. W74 F410 P989

**Haftarah** יְשַׁעְיָהוּ Yesha'yahu (Isaiah) 55:6–56:8 W342 P980

Recite the 3 concluding haftarah blessings, through מָגֵן דָּוִד Magen david. W74 F410 P989.

Return scroll to ark. W76 F150
חֲצִי קַדִּישׁ Short Kaddish W121 F166

**Silent weekday Amidah:**

All minyanim
If fasting + עֲנֵנוּ Anenu, in שׁוֹמֵעַ תְּפִלָּה Shome·a tefillah W127 F178
All ✕ ~~שָׁלוֹם רָב Shalom rav~~
+ שִׂים שָׁלוֹם Sim shalom W131 F184

**Repetition of the weekday Amidah:**

6 or more fasting + עֲנֵנוּ Anenu, before רְפָאֵנוּ Refa'enu W124 F172
Fewer than 6 fasting ✦ Add עֲנֵנוּ Anenu in שׁוֹמֵעַ תְּפִלָּה Shome·a tefillah. Replace תַּעֲנִיתֵנוּ ta'anitenu (6th word) with הַתַּעֲנִית הַזֶּה hata'anit hazeh. W127 F172
All minyanim + בִּרְכַּת כֹּהֲנִים Birkat kohanim W131 F184
✕ ~~שָׁלוֹם רָב Shalom rav~~
+ שִׂים שָׁלוֹם Sim shalom W131 F184

6 or more fasting + אָבִינוּ מַלְכֵּנוּ Avinu malkenu W57 F188
Fewer than 6 fasting ✦ Those fasting recite אָבִינוּ מַלְכֵּנוּ individually.

☞ תַּחֲנוּן Taḥanun W132 F192

קַדִּישׁ שָׁלֵם Full Kaddish W134 F194
עָלֵינוּ Aleynu W135 F196
קַדִּישׁ יָתוֹם Mourner's Kaddish W136 F198

| Tevet 5779 | | | | | | |
|---|---|---|---|---|---|---|
| 1 | 2 | 3 | 4 | 5 | 6 | 7 |
| 8 | 9 | 10 | 11 | 12 | 13 | 14 |
| 15 | 16 | 17 | 18 | 19 | 20 | 21 |
| 22 | 23 | 24 | 25 | 26 | 27 | 28 |
| 29 | | | | | | |

| Dec 2018 \| Jan 2019 | | | | | | |
|---|---|---|---|---|---|---|
| 9 | 10 | 11 | 12 | 13 | 14 | 15 |
| 16 | 17 | 18 | 19 | 20 | 21 | 22 |
| 23 | 24 | 25 | 26 | 27 | 28 | 29 |
| 30 | 31 \| 1 | 2 | 3 | 4 | 5 | |
| 6 | | | | | | |

+ Add ✕ Omit ☞ Take note!

**Siddurim**
- **L** Lev Shalem for Shabbat and Festivals
- **S** Shabbat and Festival Sim Shalom
- **W** Weekday Sim Shalom
- **F** Full Sim Shalom (both editions)
- **P** Personal Edition of Full Sim Shalom

## Tevet 14 טֵבֵת
Sat 22 Dec

## שַׁבָּת Shabbat פָּרָשַׁת וַיְחִי Parashat Vayḥi

**Torah** 7 aliyot (minimum): וַיְחִי Vayḥi
בְּרֵאשִׁית Bereshit (Genesis) 47:28–50:26

| | | | | |
|---|---|---|---|---|
| Annual: | 1 47:28–48:9 | 2 48:10–16 | 3 48:17–22 | 4 49:1–18 |
| | 5 49:19–26 | 6 49:27–50:20 | 7 50:21–26 ▮ | M 50:23–26 |
| Triennial: | 1 49:27–30 | 2 49:31–33 | 3 50:1–6 | 4 50:7–9 |
| | 5 50:10–14 | 6 50:15–20 | 7 50:21–26 ▮ | M 50:23–26 |

▮ חזק When the Torah reader concludes a book of the Torah:
1. Close the Torah scroll.
2. **For Oleh:** Congregation chants חֲזַק חֲזַק וְנִתְחַזֵּק ḥazak ḥazak venitḥazzek; oleh remains silent.
   **For Olah:** Congregation chants חִזְקִי חִזְקִי וְנִתְחַזֵּק ḥizki ḥizki venitḥazzek; olah remains silent.
3. Torah reader repeats congregation's words (oleh/olah remains silent; if Torah reader is the oleh/olah, omit this repetition).
4. Open the Torah scroll.
5. The oleh/olah kisses the Torah scroll, closes it, and continues with the usual concluding berakhah.

**Haftarah** מְלָכִים א׳ 1 Melakhim (1 Kings) 2:1–12

מִנְחָה

**Torah** 3 aliyot from שְׁמוֹת Shemot
שְׁמוֹת Shemot (Exodus) 1:1–17
1 1:1–7 2 8–12 3 13–17 W276 P897

This is also the reading for the coming Monday and Thursday.

## Tevet 21 טֵבֵת
Sat 29 Dec

## שַׁבָּת Shabbat פָּרָשַׁת שְׁמוֹת Parashat Shemot

**Torah** 7 aliyot (minimum): שְׁמוֹת Shemot
שְׁמוֹת Shemot (Exodus) 1:1–6:1

| | | | | |
|---|---|---|---|---|
| Annual: | 1 1:1–17 | 2 1:18–2:10 | 3 2:11–25 | 4 3:1–15 |
| | 5 3:16–4:17 | 6 4:18–31 | 7 5:1–6:1° | M 5:22–6:1 |
| Triennial: | 1 4:18–20 | 2 4:21–26 | 3 4:27–31 | 4 5:1–5 |
| | 5 5:6–9 | 6 5:10–14 | 7 5:15–6:1° | M 5:22–6:1 |

☞ °5:15 Note the rare ta'am (trope) מֵירְכָא־כְפוּלָה (֮): לָ֣מָּה תַעֲשֶׂ֥֥ה כֹה
Connect תַעֲשֶׂ֥֥ה to the preceding and following words, without a pause; then pause, as usual, after the טִפְּחָא (כֹה).

**Haftarah**
Ashkenazic: יְשַׁעְיָהוּ Yesha'yahu (Isaiah) 27:6–28:13; 29:22–23
Sephardic: יִרְמְיָהוּ Yirmeyahu (Jeremiah) 1:1–2:3

מִנְחָה

**Torah** 3 aliyot from וָאֵרָא Va'era
שְׁמוֹת Shemot (Exodus) 6:2–13
¹6:2–5 ²6–9 ³10–13 W277 P898

This is also the reading for the coming Monday and Thursday.

## Tevet 28 טֵבֵת
## Sat 5 Jan

**שַׁבָּת Shabbat** פָּרָשַׁת וָאֵרָא Parashat Va'era
שַׁבַּת מְבָרְכִים הַחֹדֶשׁ Shabbat Mevarekhim Haḥodesh

**Torah** 7 aliyot (minimum): וָאֵרָא Va'era
שְׁמוֹת Shemot (Exodus) 6:2–9:35

| | | | | |
|---|---|---|---|---|
| Annual: | ¹6:2–13 | ²6:14–28 | ³6:29–7:7 | ⁴7:8–8:6 |
| | ⁵8:7–18 | ⁶8:19–9:16 | ⁷9:17–35 | M9:33–35 |
| Triennial: | ¹8:16–23 | ²8:24–28 | ³9:1–7 | ⁴9:8–16 |
| | ⁵9:17–21 | ⁶9:22–26 | ⁷9:27–35 | M9:33–35 |

**Haftarah** יְחֶזְקֵאל Yeḥezkel (Ezekiel) 28:25–29:21

+ **Birkat Haḥodesh:** L180 S150 F418
Announce Rosh Ḥodesh Shevat:
רֹאשׁ חֹדֶשׁ שְׁבָט יִהְיֶה בְּיוֹם שֵׁנִי . . .
Rosh ḥodesh Shevat yihyeh beyom sheni . . .
(Sunday night and Monday)

✕ ~~אַב הָרַחֲמִים Av Haraḥamim~~

מִנְחָה

**Torah** 3 aliyot from בֹּא Bo
שְׁמוֹת Shemot (Exodus) 10:1–11
¹10:1–3 ²4–6 ³7–11 W278 P899

This is also the reading for the coming Thursday.

## Tevet 29 טֵבֵת
## Sun 6 Jan

עֶרֶב רֹאשׁ חֹדֶשׁ Erev Rosh Ḥodesh
Day before Rosh Ḥodesh

מִנְחָה ✕ ~~תַּחֲנוּן Taḥanun~~

| Shevat 5779 | | | | | | |
|---|---|---|---|---|---|---|
| | 1 | 2 | 3 | 4 | 5 | 6 |
| 7 | 8 | 9 | 10 | 11 | 12 | 13 |
| 14 | 15 | 16 | 17 | 18 | 19 | 20 |
| 21 | 22 | 23 | 24 | 25 | 26 | 27 |
| 28 | 29 | 30 | | | | |

| Jan \| Feb 2019 | | | | | | |
|---|---|---|---|---|---|---|
| | 7 | 8 | 9 | 10 | 11 | 12 |
| 13 | 14 | 15 | 16 | 17 | 18 | 19 |
| 20 | 21 | 22 | 23 | 24 | 25 | 26 |
| 27 | 28 | 29 | 30 | 31 | 1 | 2 |
| 3 | 4 | 5 | | | | |

+ Add ✗ Omit ☞ Take note!

**Siddurim**
- **L** Lev Shalem for Shabbat and Festivals
- **S** Shabbat and Festival Sim Shalom
- **W** Weekday Sim Shalom
- **F** Full Sim Shalom (both editions)
- **P** Personal Edition of Full Sim Shalom

## Shevat 1 שְׁבָט
Sun 6 Jan (evening)

# רֹאשׁ חֹדֶשׁ שְׁבָט Rosh Hodesh Shevat

**DURING Rosh Hodesh**

**Birkat Hamazon:**
+ יַעֲלֶה וְיָבוֹא Ya'aleh veyavo for Rosh Hodesh L90|95 S340|347 W233|239 F762|780
+ הָרַחֲמָן Harahaman for Rosh Hodesh L92|96 S343|348 W235|240 F768

**עַרְבִית**

**Weekday Amidah:**
+ יַעֲלֶה וְיָבוֹא Ya'aleh veyavo for Rosh Hodesh W145 F216

**Mon 7 Jan** **שַׁחֲרִית**

**Before מִזְמוֹר שִׁיר Mizmor shir (Psalm 30)** W14 F50
**or at end of service, recite:**
Psalm for Monday (Psalm 48) W86 F24
קַדִּישׁ יָתוֹם Mourner's Kaddish (some omit) W100 F52
+ Psalm 104 for Rosh Hodesh W90 F34
קַדִּישׁ יָתוֹם Mourner's Kaddish W100 F52

**Weekday Amidah:**
+ יַעֲלֶה וְיָבוֹא Ya'aleh veyavo for Rosh Hodesh W41 F114

✗ ~~תַּחֲנוּן Tahanun~~

+ חֲצִי הַלֵּל Short Hallel W50 F380
קַדִּישׁ שָׁלֵם Full Kaddish W56 F392

**TORAH SERVICE** W65 F138
Remove **1** Torah scroll from ark.

**Torah** 4 aliyot: פִּינְחָס Pinehas
בְּמִדְבַּר Bemidbar (Numbers) 28:1–15
¹28:1–3 ²3–5 ³6–10 ⁴11–15 W320 P943

חֲצִי קַדִּישׁ Short Kaddish W71 F146
Open, raise, display, and wrap scroll.
Return scroll to ark. W76 F150

אַשְׁרֵי Ashrey W78 F152
✗ ~~לַמְנַצֵּחַ Lamenatse·ah (Psalm 20)~~
וּבָא לְצִיּוֹן Uva letsiyyon W80 F156

**Some congregations:**
Remove and pack tefillin at this point.
+ חֲצִי קַדִּישׁ Short Kaddish W103 F428

**Other congregations:**

+ חֲצִי קַדִּישׁ Short Kaddish W103 F428

Remove and cover—but do not pack—tefillin, so that all begin Musaf Amidah at the same time, as soon after Kaddish as possible.

מוּסָף

+ **Rosh Hodesh Amidah for weekdays:** W104 F486

Weekday קְדֻשָּׁה Kedushah W105 F488

+ וּלְכַפָּרַת פָּשַׁע Ulkhapparat pasha W107 F494

Add these words only through Rosh Hodesh Adar Sheni.

+ קַדִּישׁ שָׁלֵם Full Kaddish W82 F158

עָלֵינוּ Aleynu W83 F160

**If psalms for the day were not recited at Shaharit, add here:**

קַדִּישׁ יָתוֹם Mourner's Kaddish (some omit) W84 F162

Psalm for Monday (Psalm 48) W86 F24

קַדִּישׁ יָתוֹם Mourner's Kaddish (some omit) W100 F52

+ Psalm 104 for Rosh Hodesh W90 F34

קַדִּישׁ יָתוֹם Mourner's Kaddish W84|100 F162|52

מִנְחָה

**Weekday Amidah:**

+ יַעֲלֶה וְיָבוֹא Ya'aleh veyavo for Rosh Hodesh W127 F178

✕ ~~תַּחֲנוּן Tahanun~~

---

## Shevat 6 שְׁבָט
Sat 12 Jan

## שַׁבָּת Shabbat פָּרָשַׁת בֹּא Parashat Bo

**Torah** 7 aliyot (minimum): בֹּא Bo

שְׁמוֹת Shemot (Exodus) 10:1–13:16

| | | | | |
|---|---|---|---|---|
| Annual: | 1 10:1–11 | 2 10:12–23 | 3 10:24–11:3 | 4 11:4–12:20 |
| | 5 12:21–28 | 6 12:29–51 | 7 13:1–16 | M 13:14–16 |
| Triennial: | 1 12:29–32 | 2 12:33–36 | 3 12:37–42 | 4 12:43–51 |
| | 5 13:1–4 | 6 13:5–10 | 7 13:11–16 | M 13:14–16 |

**Haftarah** יִרְמְיָהוּ Yirmeyahu (Jeremiah) 46:13–28

מִנְחָה

**Torah** 3 aliyot from בְּשַׁלַּח Beshallah

שְׁמוֹת Shemot (Exodus) 13:17–14:8

1 13:17–22 2 14:1–4 3 14:5–8 W279 P900

This is also the reading for the coming Monday and Thursday.

| Shevat 5779 | | | | | |
|---|---|---|---|---|---|
| | 1 | 2 | 3 | 4 | 5 | 6 |
| 7 | 8 | 9 | 10 | 11 | 12 | 13 |
| 14 | 15 | 16 | 17 | 18 | 19 | 20 |
| 21 | 22 | 23 | 24 | 25 | 26 | 27 |
| 28 | 29 | 30 | | | | |

| Jan \| Feb 2019 | | | | | | |
|---|---|---|---|---|---|---|
| | 7 | 8 | 9 | 10 | 11 | 12 |
| 13 | 14 | 15 | 16 | 17 | 18 | 19 |
| 20 | 21 | 22 | 23 | 24 | 25 | 26 |
| 27 | 28 | 29 | 30 | 31 | 1 | 2 |
| 3 | 4 | 5 | | | | |

+ Add ✕ Omit ☞ Take note!

**Siddurim**

**L** Lev Shalem for Shabbat and Festivals
**S** Shabbat and Festival Sim Shalom
**W** Weekday Sim Shalom
**F** Full Sim Shalom (both editions)
**P** Personal Edition of Full Sim Shalom

# Chanting Shirat Hayam

## Parashat Beshallaḥ and Pesaḥ — Day 7

The congregation stands during the reading of שִׁירַת הַיָּם *shirat hayam,* as if to reenact the celebration following the crossing of the Sea of Reeds.

According to Ashkenazic practice, we highlight certain verses with the distinctive Shirat Hayam melody. Although traditions differ as to which verses to highlight, a common tradition is: Shemot 15:1b, 2a, 3, 6, 11, 16b, 18, and 21b (a = up to and including the word with ֔; b = after ֔).

In addition, we distinguish parts of three verses (14:22b, 29b, and 31b) that precede the Shirah itself with the same melody. These serve to alert the congregation that something special follows.

Many congregations observe a very old practice. The congregation participates in the chanting of the highlighted verses, as if reenacting the events of Shemot 15:1: "Then Moses and the people Israel sang this song."

There are two common patterns of congregational participation. Both rely on the division of the poetic verses into short phrases and the division of the special melody into two melody phrases.

### Call and Repeat

The Torah reader chants a phrase, and then the congregation repeats that phrase and melody. The reader chants the next phrase, and then the congregation repeats that phrase. For example:

Torah reader chants: אָשִׁירָה לַייָ כִּי־גָאֹה גָּאָה
Congregation *repeats:* אָשִׁירָה לַייָ כִּי־גָאֹה גָּאָה

Torah reader chants: סוּס וְרֹכְבוֹ רָמָה בַיָּם׃
Congregation *repeats:* סוּס וְרֹכְבוֹ רָמָה בַיָּם׃

### Call and Respond

The Torah reader chants a phrase; then the congregation chants the following phrase, which (in most cases) completes the verse. The reader then repeats the phrase that the congregation chanted so that the congregation hears every word read directly from the Torah. For example:

Torah reader chants: אָשִׁירָה לַייָ כִּי־גָאֹה גָּאָה
Congregation *responds:* סוּס וְרֹכְבוֹ רָמָה בַיָּם׃
Torah reader *repeats:* סוּס וְרֹכְבוֹ רָמָה בַיָּם׃

Whichever procedure your congregation follows, observe carefully the following restrictions so that congregants hear every word read directly from the Torah. Congregants must wait for the Torah reader to stop before they begin to chant. Similarly, the Torah reader must not begin again until congregants have completed their chanting.

## Shevat 13 שְׁבָט Sat 19 Jan (morning)

## שַׁבָּת Shabbat פָּרָשַׁת בְּשַׁלַּח Parashat Beshallaḥ
## שַׁבַּת שִׁירָה Shabbat Shirah

**Shabbat Shirah** is the Shabbat of Song. The parashah contains שִׁירַת הַיָּם *shirat hayam,* the song of celebration that Moses, Miriam, and the people Israel sang after the successful crossing of the Sea of Reeds and the defeat of the Egyptian army by the hand of God.
For instructions for the special chanting of this passage, see p. 94.

**Torah** 7 aliyot (minimum): בְּשַׁלַּח Beshallaḥ
שְׁמוֹת Shemot (Exodus) 13:17–17:16

| | | | | |
|---|---|---|---|---|
| Annual: | 1 13:17–14:8 | 2 14:9–14 | 3 14:15–25° | 4 14:26–15:26° |
| | 5 15:27–16:10 | 6 16:11–36 | 7 17:1–16 | M 17:14–16 |
| Triennial: | 1 14:26–15:21° | 2 15:22–26 | 3 15:27–16:10 | 4 16:11–27 |
| | 5 16:28–36 | 6 17:1–7 | 7 17:8–16 | M 17:14–16 |

☞ °14:22, 29, 31; 15:1–21 For instructions for the special chanting of שִׁירַת הַיָּם Shirat Hayam and of parts of the preceding sections, see p. 94.

☞ °15:11, 16 To preserve the sense of these phrases, maintain the proper pauses after the te'amim (tropes) פַּשְׁטָא ( ) and טִפְּחָא ( ):

15:11 מִי־כָמֹכָה בָּאֵלִם | יי | מִי כָּמֹכָה | נֶאְדָּר בַּקֹּדֶשׁ . . .
15:16 . . . עַד־יַעֲבֹר עַמְּךָ | יי | עַד־יַעֲבֹר | עַם־זוּ קָנִיתָ׃

**Haftarah**
Ashkenazic: שׁוֹפְטִים Shofetim (Judges) 4:4–5:31
Sephardic: שׁוֹפְטִים Shofetim (Judges) 5:1–5:31

מִנְחָה

**Torah** 3 aliyot from יִתְרוֹ Yitro
שְׁמוֹת Shemot (Exodus) 18:1–12
1 18:1–4 2 5–8 3 9–12 W280 P901

This is also the reading for the coming Monday and Thursday.

## Shevat 14 שְׁבָט Sun 20 Jan

## עֶרֶב ט״וּ בִּשְׁבָט Erev Tu Bishvat
## Day before Tu Bishvat

מִנְחָה ✕ ~~תַּחֲנוּן Taḥanun~~

| Shevat 5779 | | | | | | |
|---|---|---|---|---|---|---|
| | 1 | 2 | 3 | 4 | 5 | 6 |
| 7 | 8 | 9 | 10 | 11 | 12 | 13 |
| 14 | 15 | 16 | 17 | 18 | 19 | 20 |
| 21 | 22 | 23 | 24 | 25 | 26 | 27 |
| 28 | 29 | 30 | | | | |

| Jan \| Feb 2019 | | | | | | |
|---|---|---|---|---|---|---|
| | 7 | 8 | 9 | 10 | 11 | 12 |
| 13 | 14 | 15 | 16 | 17 | 18 | 19 |
| 20 | 21 | 22 | 23 | 24 | 25 | 26 |
| 27 | 28 | 29 | 30 | 31 \| 1 | 2 | |
| 3 | 4 | 5 | | | | |

+ Add ✕ Omit ☞ Take note!

**Siddurim**
**L** Lev Shalem for Shabbat and Festivals
**S** Shabbat and Festival Sim Shalom
**W** Weekday Sim Shalom
**F** Full Sim Shalom (both editions)
**P** Personal Edition of Full Sim Shalom

## Shevat 15 שְׁבָט ט"ו בִּשְׁבָט Tu Bishvat — 15th of Shevat

Sun 20 Jan (evening)

**Tu Bishvat** is referred to as the New Year for trees because the fruits of trees that blossom after the 15th of Shevat were counted in ancient times as belonging to the next year for purposes of tithing.

To celebrate, we eat a tree fruit that we have not yet tasted this season, reciting the *berakhot* בּוֹרֵא פְּרִי הָעֵץ *bo·re peri ha'ets* and שֶׁהֶחֱיָנוּ *sheheḥeyanu.* Other customs include holding a Tu Bishvat seder and eating fruits from Israel.

Mon 21 Jan שַׁחֲרִית ✕ ~~תַּחֲנוּן Taḥanun~~
☞ לַמְנַצֵּחַ Lamenatse·aḥ (Psalm 20) W/9 F154

מִנְחָה ✕ ~~תַּחֲנוּן Taḥanun~~

## Chanting Aseret Hadibberot

**Parashat Yitro, and Shavu'ot — Day 1**

The congregation stands as they hear this section read, just as the people Israel stood at the foot of Mount Sinai and listened to the voice of God.

The proper chanting of עֲשֶׂרֶת הַדִּבְּרוֹת *aseret hadibberot* requires exceptional attention because this passage is marked with 2 sets of verse divisions and 2 sets of *te'amim* (tropes, cantillation marks). One set, for private study, divides the passage into verses of a usual length, suitable for study. The 2nd set, for public reading, divides the passage into exactly *10* verses. Each verse corresponds to 1 of the 10 pronouncements. The congregation listens to exactly *10* pronouncements, reenacting the events experienced by the people Israel at Mount Sinai.

For the public reading, a long pronouncement, such as that commanding observance of Shabbat, joins several verses into a single long verse. On the other hand, a verse containing 4 very brief pronouncements breaks into 4 separate, very short verses for the public reading.

Over the centuries, the complexity of the task of separating 2 sets of verse divisions and 2 sets of *te'amim* resulted in countless errors in printed *ḥumashim.* The 2 sets of verse divisions led to a confusion in verse *numbering,* which in fact should follow the private reading. There are 22 verses in the chapter, but many editions erroneously count 23. This leads to confusion in labeling the *aliyah* divisions. See Torah reading information on p. 98.

The correct verse divisions and *te'amim* for the public reading appear on p. 97. Only this version, supported by the earliest manuscripts and the most authoritative printed editions, presents *10* pronouncements in *10* verses.

# עֲשֶׂרֶת הַדִּבְּרוֹת — פָּרָשַׁת יִתְרוֹ

**For Public Reading** — טַעֲמָא תְנִינָא (טַעַם עֶלְיוֹן)

## דִּבְּרוֹת

1 אָנֹכִ֖י
יְ·הוָ֣ה אֱ·לֹהֶ֑יךָ אֲשֶׁ֧ר הוֹצֵאתִ֛יךָ מֵאֶ֥רֶץ מִצְרַ֖יִם מִבֵּ֣ית
2 עֲבָדִ֑ים: לֹ֣א יִהְיֶה־לְךָ֩ אֱלֹהִ֨ים אֲחֵרִ֜ים עַל־פָּנַ֗י לֹ֣א
תַעֲשֶׂה־לְךָ֣ פֶ֣סֶל | וְכָל־תְּמוּנָ֡ה אֲשֶׁ֣ר בַּשָּׁמַ֣יִם | מִמַּ֡עַל
וַאֲשֶׁר֩ בָּאָ֨רֶץ מִתַּ֜חַת וַאֲשֶׁ֥ר בַּמַּ֣יִם | מִתַּ֣חַת לָאָ֗רֶץ לֹֽא־
°Read: **to'ovdem** תִשְׁתַּחֲוֶ֥ה לָהֶם֮ וְלֹ֣א תָעָבְדֵם֒ כִּ֣י אָנֹכִ֞י יְ·הוָ֤ה אֱ·לֹהֶ֙יךָ֙
אֵ֣·ל קַנָּ֔א פֹּ֠קֵד עֲוֺ֨ן אָבֹ֧ת עַל־בָּנִ֛ים עַל־שִׁלֵּשִׁ֥ים
וְעַל־רִבֵּעִ֖ים לְשֹׂנְאָ֑י וְעֹ֤שֶׂה חֶ֙סֶד֙ לַאֲלָפִ֔ים לְאֹהֲבַ֖י
3 וּלְשֹׁמְרֵ֥י מִצְוֺתָֽי׃ לֹ֥א תִשָּׂ֛א אֶת־
שֵֽׁם־יְ·הוָ֥ה אֱ·לֹהֶ֖יךָ לַשָּׁ֑וְא כִּ֣י לֹ֤א יְנַקֶּה֙ יְ·הוָ֔ה אֵ֛ת
אֲשֶׁר־יִשָּׂ֥א אֶת־שְׁמ֖וֹ לַשָּֽׁוְא׃
4 זָכ֛וֹר֩ אֶת־י֨וֹם הַשַּׁבָּ֜ת לְקַדְּשׁ֗וֹ שֵׁ֤שֶׁת יָמִים֙ תַּעֲבֹד֮
וְעָשִׂ֣יתָ כָל־מְלַאכְתֶּךָ֒ וְי֨וֹם הַשְּׁבִיעִ֜י שַׁבָּ֣ת | לַ·יהוָ֣ה
אֱ·לֹהֶ֗יךָ לֹ֣א תַעֲשֶׂ֣ה כָל־מְלָאכָ֡ה אַתָּ֣ה וּבִנְךָ֩־וּבִתֶּ֨ךָ
עַבְדְּךָ֤ וַאֲמָֽתְךָ֙ וּבְהֶמְתֶּ֔ךָ וְגֵרְךָ֖ אֲשֶׁ֣ר בִּשְׁעָרֶ֑יךָ
כִּ֣י שֵֽׁשֶׁת־יָמִ֡ים עָשָׂ֣ה יְ·הוָ֣ה אֶת־הַשָּׁמַ֣יִם וְאֶת־
הָאָ֗רֶץ אֶת־הַיָּם֙ וְאֶת־כָּל־אֲשֶׁר־בָּ֔ם וַיָּ֖נַח בַּיּ֣וֹם
הַשְּׁבִיעִ֑י עַל־כֵּ֗ן בֵּרַ֛ךְ יְ·הוָ֛ה אֶת־י֥וֹם הַשַּׁבָּ֖ת
5 וַֽיְקַדְּשֵֽׁהוּ׃ כַּבֵּ֥ד אֶת־אָבִ֖יךָ וְאֶת־אִמֶּ֑ךָ
לְמַ֙עַן֙ יַאֲרִכ֣וּן יָמֶ֔יךָ עַ֚ל הָאֲדָמָ֔ה אֲשֶׁר־יְ·הוָ֥ה אֱ·לֹהֶ֖יךָ
7 | 6 נֹתֵ֥ן לָֽךְ׃ לֹ֖א תִּרְצָֽח׃ לֹ֖א
9 | 8 תִּנְאָֽף׃ לֹ֖א תִּגְנֹֽב׃ לֹֽא־
10 תַעֲנֶ֥ה בְרֵעֲךָ֖ עֵ֥ד שָֽׁקֶר׃ לֹ֥א
תַחְמֹ֖ד בֵּ֣ית רֵעֶ֑ךָ לֹֽא־
תַחְמֹ֞ד אֵ֣שֶׁת רֵעֶ֗ךָ וְעַבְדּ֤וֹ וַאֲמָתוֹ֙ וְשׁוֹר֣וֹ וַחֲמֹר֔וֹ
וְכֹ֖ל אֲשֶׁ֥ר לְרֵעֶֽךָ׃

| Shevat 5779 | | | | | | | Jan \| Feb 2019 | | | | | | |
|---|---|---|---|---|---|---|---|---|---|---|---|---|---|
| | 1 | 2 | 3 | 4 | 5 | 6 | | 7 | 8 | 9 | 10 | 11 | 12 |
| 7 | 8 | 9 | 10 | 11 | 12 | 13 | 13 | 14 | 15 | 16 | 17 | 18 | 19 |
| 14 | 15 | 16 | 17 | 18 | 19 | 20 | 20 | 21 | 22 | 23 | 24 | 25 | 26 |
| 21 | 22 | 23 | 24 | 25 | 26 | 27 | 27 | 28 | 29 | 30 | 31 | 1 | 2 |
| 28 | 29 | 30 | | | | | 3 | 4 | 5 | | | | |

+ Add ✕ Omit ☞ Take note!

**Siddurim**

- **L** Lev Shalem for Shabbat and Festivals
- **S** Shabbat and Festival Sim Shalom
- **W** Weekday Sim Shalom
- **F** Full Sim Shalom (both editions)
- **P** Personal Edition of Full Sim Shalom

## Aseret Hadibberot in the Triennial Cycle

- **Triennial Option A:** The full parashah. The congregation thus experiences עֲשֶׂרֶת הַדִּבְּרוֹת every year.
- **Triennial Option B:** An abbreviated reading. The congregation experiences עֲשֶׂרֶת הַדִּבְּרוֹת only in years 2 and 3 of the cycle.

For details, see below.

## Shevat 20 שְׁבָט Sat 26 Jan — שַׁבָּת Shabbat פָּרָשַׁת יִתְרוֹ Parashat Yitro

The עֲשֶׂרֶת הַדִּבְּרוֹת *aseret hadibberot* section, which appears in Parashat Yitro, is usually called "the 10 commandments." But the Hebrew phrase actually means "the 10 pronouncements."

For the correct text and *te'amim* (tropes, cantillation marks), see p. 97. For special instructions for the chanting of this passage, see p. 96.

**Torah** 7 aliyot (minimum): יִתְרוֹ Yitro
שְׁמוֹת Shemot (Exodus) 18:1–20:22

| | | | | |
|---|---|---|---|---|
| Annual: | 1 18:1–12 | 2 18:13–23 | 3 18:24–27 | 4 19:1–6 |
| | 5 19:7–19 | °6 19:20–20:13 | °7 20:14–22 | °M 20:18–22 |

Triennial:

| | | | | |
|---|---|---|---|---|
| °Option A | Read the full parashah, dividing as above. | | | |
| °Option B | 1 19:1–6 | 2 19:7–9 | 3 19:10–13 | 4 19:14–19 |
| | °5 19:20–20:13 | °6 20:14–17 | °7 20:18–22 | °M 20:20–22 |

☞ °**Verse numbers in chapter 20:** The verses are misnumbered in many editions. Use these guidelines to properly divide the reading:

**Annual and Triennial Option A**
Aliyah **6**: ends לְרֵעֶךָ (20:14 in many books)
Aliyah **7**: וְכָל־הָעָם through עָלָיו (20:15–23 in many books)
Maftir aliyah: וַיֹּאמֶר יי through עָלָיו (20:19–23 in many books)

**Triennial Option B**
Aliyah **5**: ends לְרֵעֶךָ (20:14 in many books)
Aliyah **6**: וְכָל־הָעָם through הָאֱלֹהִים (20:15–18 in many books)
Aliyah **7**: וַיֹּאמֶר יי through עָלָיו (20:19–23 in many books)
Maftir aliyah: מִזְבַּח אֲדָמָה through עָלָיו (20:21–23 in many books)

☞ °20:1–13 Follow the te'amim (tropes) for the public reading of עֲשֶׂרֶת הַדִּבְּרוֹת, on p. 97. For additional instructions for this passage, see p. 96.

☞ °Triennial Option B excludes Aseret Hadibberot in year 1 (next year).

**Haftarah**
Ashkenazic: יְשַׁעְיָהוּ Yesha'yahu (Isaiah) 6:1–7:6; 9:5–6
Sephardic: יְשַׁעְיָהוּ Yesha'yahu (Isaiah) 6:1–13

מִנְחָה

**Torah** 3 aliyot from מִשְׁפָּטִים Mishpatim
שְׁמוֹת Shemot (Exodus) 21:1–19
¹21:1–6 ²7–11 ³12–19 W281 P901

This is also the reading for the coming Monday and Thursday.

---

## Shevat 27 שְׁבָט
## Sat 2 Feb

## שַׁבָּת Shabbat פָּרָשַׁת מִשְׁפָּטִים Parashat Mishpatim
## שַׁבַּת מְבָרְכִים הַחֹדֶשׁ Shabbat Mevarekhim Haḥodesh

**Torah** 7 aliyot (minimum): מִשְׁפָּטִים Mishpatim
שְׁמוֹת Shemot (Exodus) 21:1–24:18

| | | | | |
|---|---|---|---|---|
| Annual: | ¹21:1–19 | ²21:20–22:3 | ³22:4–26 | ⁴22:27–23:5 |
| | ⁵23:6–19 | ⁶23:20–25 | ⁷23:26–24:18 | M24:16–18 |
| Triennial: | ¹23:20–25 | ²23:26–30 | ³23:31–33 | ⁴24:1–6 |
| | ⁵24:7–11 | ⁶24:12–14 | ⁷24:15–18 | M24:15–18 |

**Haftarah** יִרְמְיָהוּ Yirmeyahu (Jeremiah) 34:8–22, 33:25–26

+ **Birkat Haḥodesh:** L180 S150 F418
Announce Rosh Ḥodesh Adar Rishon:
Do not announce the month as "Adar Alef."
רֹאשׁ חֹדֶשׁ אֲדָר רִאשׁוֹן יִהְיֶה בְּיוֹם שְׁלִישִׁי וּבְיוֹם רְבִיעִי . . .
Rosh ḥodesh Adar Rishon yihyeh beyom shelishi uvyom revi'i . . .
(Monday night, Tuesday, and Wednesday)

✕ ~~אַב הָרַחֲמִים Av Haraḥamim~~

מִנְחָה

**Torah** 3 aliyot from תְּרוּמָה Terumah
שְׁמוֹת Shemot (Exodus) 25:1–16
¹25:1–5 ²6–9 ³10–16 W282 P902

This is also the reading for the coming Monday and Thursday.

| Shevat 5779 | | | | | | | Jan \| Feb 2019 | | | | | | |
|---|---|---|---|---|---|---|---|---|---|---|---|---|---|
| | 1 | 2 | 3 | 4 | 5 | 6 | | 7 | 8 | 9 | 10 | 11 | 12 |
| 7 | 8 | 9 | 10 | 11 | 12 | 13 | 13 | 14 | 15 | 16 | 17 | 18 | 19 |
| 14 | 15 | 16 | 17 | 18 | 19 | 20 | 20 | 21 | 22 | 23 | 24 | 25 | 26 |
| 21 | 22 | 23 | 24 | 25 | 26 | 27 | 27 | 28 | 29 | 30 | 31 | 1 | 2 |
| 28 | 29 | 30 | | | | | 3 | 4 | 5 | | | | |

+ Add ✕ Omit ☞ Take note!

**Siddurim**
- **L** Lev Shalem for Shabbat and Festivals
- **S** Shabbat and Festival Sim Shalom
- **W** Weekday Sim Shalom
- **F** Full Sim Shalom (both editions)
- **P** Personal Edition of Full Sim Shalom

---

**Shevat 29 שְׁבָט**
**Mon 4 Feb**

## עֶרֶב רֹאשׁ חֹדֶשׁ Erev Rosh Ḥodesh
Day before Rosh Ḥodesh

מִנְחָה ✕ ~~תַּחֲנוּן Taḥanun~~

---

**Shevat 30 שְׁבָט**
**Mon 4 Feb (evening)**

## רֹאשׁ חֹדֶשׁ אֲדָר רִאשׁוֹן
## Rosh Ḥodesh Adar Rishon — Day 1

**DURING Rosh Ḥodesh** — **Birkat Hamazon:**

+ יַעֲלֶה וְיָבוֹא Ya'aleh veyavo for Rosh Ḥodesh L90|95 S340|347 W233|239 F762|780

+ הָרַחֲמָן Haraḥaman for Rosh Ḥodesh L92|96 S343|348 W235|240 F768

עַרְבִית **Weekday Amidah:**
+ יַעֲלֶה וְיָבוֹא Ya'aleh veyavo for Rosh Ḥodesh W145 F216

**Tue 5 Feb** שַׁחֲרִית

**Before מִזְמוֹר שִׁיר Mizmor shir (Psalm 30)** W14 F50
**or at end of service, recite:**
Psalm for Tuesday (Psalm 82) W87 F26
קַדִּישׁ יָתוֹם Mourner's Kaddish (some omit) W100 F52
+ Psalm 104 for Rosh Ḥodesh W90 F34
קַדִּישׁ יָתוֹם Mourner's Kaddish W100 F52

**Weekday Amidah:**
+ יַעֲלֶה וְיָבוֹא Ya'aleh veyavo for Rosh Ḥodesh W41 F114

✕ ~~תַּחֲנוּן Taḥanun~~

+ חֲצִי הַלֵּל Short Hallel W50 F380
קַדִּישׁ שָׁלֵם Full Kaddish W56 F392

+ **TORAH SERVICE** W65 F138
Remove **1** Torah scroll from ark.

**Torah** 4 aliyot: פִּינְחָס Pineḥas
בְּמִדְבַּר Bemidbar (Numbers) 28:1–15
[1]28:1–3 [2]3–5 [3]6–10 [4]11–15 W320 P943

חֲצִי קַדִּישׁ Short Kaddish W71 F146
Open, raise, display, and wrap scroll.
Return scroll to ark. W76 F150

אַשְׁרֵי Ashrey W78 F152

✕ ~~לַמְנַצֵּחַ Lamenatse·ah (Psalm 20)~~

וּבָא לְצִיּוֹן Uva letsiyyon W80 F156

**Some congregations:**

Remove and pack tefillin at this point.

+ חֲצִי קַדִּישׁ Short Kaddish W103 F428

**Other congregations:**

+ חֲצִי קַדִּישׁ Short Kaddish W103 F428

Remove and cover—but do not pack—tefillin, so that all begin Musaf Amidah at the same time, as soon after Kaddish as possible.

מוּסָף

+ **Rosh Hodesh Amidah for weekdays:** W104 F486

Weekday קְדֻשָּׁה Kedushah W105 F488

+ וּלְכַפָּרַת פָּשַׁע Ulkhapparat pasha W107 F494

Add these words only through Rosh Hodesh Adar Sheni.

+ קַדִּישׁ שָׁלֵם Full Kaddish W82 F158

עָלֵינוּ Aleynu W83 F160

**If psalms for the day were not recited at Shaharit, add here:**

קַדִּישׁ יָתוֹם Mourner's Kaddish (some omit) W84 F162

Psalm for Tuesday (Psalm 82) W87 F26

קַדִּישׁ יָתוֹם Mourner's Kaddish (some omit) W100 F52

+ Psalm 104 for Rosh Hodesh W90 F34

קַדִּישׁ יָתוֹם Mourner's Kaddish W84|100 F162|52

מִנְחָה

**Weekday Amidah:**

+ יַעֲלֶה וְיָבוֹא Ya'aleh veyavo for Rosh Hodesh W127 F178

✕ ~~תַּחֲנוּן Tahanun~~

| 1st Adar 5779 | | | | | | | Feb \| Mar 2019 | | | | | | |
|---|---|---|---|---|---|---|---|---|---|---|---|---|---|
| | | | 1 | 2 | 3 | 4 | | | | 6 | 7 | 8 | 9 |
| 5 | 6 | 7 | 8 | 9 | 10 | 11 | 10 | 11 | 12 | 13 | 14 | 15 | 16 |
| 12 | 13 | 14 | 15 | 16 | 17 | 18 | 17 | 18 | 19 | 20 | 21 | 22 | 23 |
| 19 | 20 | 21 | 22 | 23 | 24 | 25 | 24 | 25 | 26 | 27 | 28 | 1 | 2 |
| 26 | 27 | 28 | 29 | 30 | | | 3 | 4 | 5 | 6 | 7 | | |

+ Add ✕ Omit ☞ Take note!

**Siddurim**
- **L** Lev Shalem for Shabbat and Festivals
- **S** Shabbat and Festival Sim Shalom
- **W** Weekday Sim Shalom
- **F** Full Sim Shalom (both editions)
- **P** Personal Edition of Full Sim Shalom

## 1st Adar 1 אֲדָר א׳
Tue 5 Feb (evening)

# רֹאשׁ חֹדֶשׁ אֲדָר רִאשׁוֹן
## Rosh Ḥodesh Adar Rishon — Day 2

For determining the *yortsayt* of a death during Adar, 1st Adar, or 2nd Adar, see p. 214.

**DURING Rosh Ḥodesh**

**Birkat Hamazon:**

+ יַעֲלֶה וְיָבוֹא Ya'aleh veyavo for Rosh Ḥodesh L90|95 S340|347 W233|239 F762|780

+ הָרַחֲמָן Haraḥaman for Rosh Ḥodesh L92|96 S343|348 W235|240 F768

**עַרְבִית**

**Weekday Amidah:**

+ יַעֲלֶה וְיָבוֹא Ya'aleh veyavo for Rosh Ḥodesh W145 F216

**Wed 6 Feb שַׁחֲרִית**

**Before מִזְמוֹר שִׁיר Mizmor shir (Psalm 30)** W14 F50
**or at end of service, recite:**

Psalm for Wednesday (Psalms 94:1–95:3) W87 F26
קַדִּישׁ יָתוֹם Mourner's Kaddish (some omit) W100 F52
+ Psalm 104 for Rosh Ḥodesh W90 F34
קַדִּישׁ יָתוֹם Mourner's Kaddish W100 F52

**Weekday Amidah:**

+ יַעֲלֶה וְיָבוֹא Ya'aleh veyavo for Rosh Ḥodesh W41 F114

✕ ~~תַּחֲנוּן Taḥanun~~

+ חֲצִי הַלֵּל Short Hallel W50 F380
קַדִּישׁ שָׁלֵם Full Kaddish W56 F392

+ **TORAH SERVICE** W65 F138
Remove **1** Torah scroll from ark.

**Torah** 4 aliyot: פִּינְחָס Pineḥas
בְּמִדְבַּר Bemidbar (Numbers) 28:1–15
¹28:1–3 ²3–5 ³6–10 ⁴11–15 W320 P943

חֲצִי קַדִּישׁ Short Kaddish W71 F146
Open, raise, display, and wrap scroll.
Return scroll to ark. W76 F150

אַשְׁרֵי Ashrey W78 F152
✕ ~~לַמְנַצֵּחַ Lamenatse·aḥ (Psalm 20)~~
וּבָא לְצִיּוֹן Uva letsiyyon W80 F156

**Some congregations:**
Remove and pack tefillin at this point.
+ חֲצִי קַדִּישׁ Short Kaddish W103 F428

**Other congregations:**
+ חֲצִי קַדִּישׁ Short Kaddish W103 F428
Remove and cover—but do not pack—tefillin, so that all begin Musaf Amidah at the same time, as soon after Kaddish as possible.

מוּסָף
+ **Rosh Ḥodesh Amidah for weekdays:** W104 F486
Weekday קְדֻשָּׁה Kedushah W105 F488
+ וּלְכַפָּרַת פָּשַׁע Ulkhapparat pasha W107 F494
Add these words only through Rosh Ḥodesh Adar Sheni.

+ קַדִּישׁ שָׁלֵם Full Kaddish W82 F158
עָלֵינוּ Aleynu W83 F160

**If psalms for the day were not recited at Shaḥarit, add here:**
קַדִּישׁ יָתוֹם Mourner's Kaddish (some omit) W84 F162
Psalm for Wednesday (Psalms 94:1–95:3) W87 F26
קַדִּישׁ יָתוֹם Mourner's Kaddish (some omit) W100 F52
+ Psalm 104 for Rosh Ḥodesh W90 F34

קַדִּישׁ יָתוֹם Mourner's Kaddish W84|100 F162|52

מִנְחָה
**Weekday Amidah:**
+ יַעֲלֶה וְיָבוֹא Ya'aleh veyavo for Rosh Ḥodesh W127 F178

✗ ~~תַּחֲנוּן Taḥanun~~

---

## 1st Adar 4 אֲדָר א׳ Sat 9 Feb

## שַׁבָּת Shabbat פָּרָשַׁת תְּרוּמָה Parashat Terumah

**Torah** 7 aliyot (minimum): תְּרוּמָה Terumah
שְׁמוֹת Shemot (Exodus) 25:1–27:19

| | | | | |
|---|---|---|---|---|
| Annual: | [1] 25:1–16 | [2] 25:17–40 | [3] 26:1–14 | [4] 26:15–30 |
| | [5] 26:31–37 | [6] 27:1–8 | [7] 27:9–19 | [M] 27:17–19 |
| Triennial: | [1] 26:31–33 | [2] 26:34–37 | [3] 27:1–3 | [4] 27:4–8 |
| | [5] 27:9–12 | [6] 27:13–16 | [7] 27:17–19 | [M] 27:17–19 |

**Haftarah** מְלָכִים א׳ 1 Melakhim (1 Kings) 5:26–6:13

Feb 9 4 אֲדָר א׳
Feb 16 11 אֲדָר א׳
Feb 18 13 אֲדָר א׳
Feb 19 14 אֲדָר א׳

1st Adar 5779

| | | | | | | |
|---|---|---|---|---|---|---|
| | | | 1 | 2 | 3 | 4 |
| 5 | 6 | 7 | 8 | 9 | 10 | 11 |
| 12 | 13 | 14 | 15 | 16 | 17 | 18 |
| 19 | 20 | 21 | 22 | 23 | 24 | 25 |
| 26 | 27 | 28 | 29 | 30 | | |

Feb | Mar 2019

| | | | | | | |
|---|---|---|---|---|---|---|
| | | | 6 | 7 | 8 | 9 |
| 10 | 11 | 12 | 13 | 14 | 15 | 16 |
| 17 | 18 | 19 | 20 | 21 | 22 | 23 |
| 24 | 25 | 26 | 27 | 28 | 1 | 2 |
| 3 | 4 | 5 | 6 | 7 | | |

+ Add ✕ Omit ☞ Take note!

**Siddurim**
- **L** Lev Shalem for Shabbat and Festivals
- **S** Shabbat and Festival Sim Shalom
- **W** Weekday Sim Shalom
- **F** Full Sim Shalom (both editions)
- **P** Personal Edition of Full Sim Shalom

מִנְחָה

**Torah** 3 aliyot from תְּצַוֶּה Tetsavveh
שְׁמוֹת Shemot (Exodus) 27:20–28:12
¹27:20–28:5 ²6–9 ³10–12 W283 P903

This is also the reading for the coming Monday and Thursday.

---

## 1st Adar 11 אֲדָר א׳ Sat 16 Feb

## שַׁבָּת Shabbat פָּרָשַׁת תְּצַוֶּה Parashat Tetsavveh

**Torah** 7 aliyot (minimum): תְּצַוֶּה Tetsavveh
שְׁמוֹת Shemot (Exodus) 27:20–30:10

| | | | | |
|---|---|---|---|---|
| Annual: | ¹27:20–28:12 | ²28:13–30 | ³28:31–43 | ⁴29:1–18 |
| | ⁵29:19–37 | ⁶29:38–46 | ⁷30:1–10 | ᴹ30:8–10 |
| Triennial: | ¹29:19–21 | ²29:22–25 | ³29:26–30 | ⁴29:31–34 |
| | ⁵29:35–37 | ⁶29:38–46 | ⁷30:1–10 | ᴹ30:8–10 |

**Haftarah** יְחֶזְקֵאל Yeḥezkel (Ezekiel) 43:10–27

מִנְחָה

**Torah** 3 aliyot from כִּי־תִשָּׂא Ki tissa
שְׁמוֹת Shemot (Exodus) 30:11–21°
¹30:11–13 ²14–16 ³17–21 W284 P904

This is also the reading for the coming Monday and Thursday.

☞ °30:11–21 Read only these verses. Do not read to the end of the 1st Shabbat aliyah.

---

## 1st Adar 13 אֲדָר א׳ Mon 18 Feb

## עֶרֶב פּוּרִים קָטָן Erev Purim Katan
## Day before Purim Katan

מִנְחָה ✕ ~~תַּחֲנוּן Taḥanun~~

---

## 1st Adar 14 אֲדָר א׳ Tue 19 Feb

## פּוּרִים קָטָן Purim Katan
## Fourteenth of 1st Adar

שַׁחֲרִית ✕ ~~תַּחֲנוּן Taḥanun~~

✕ ~~לַמְנַצֵּחַ Lamenatse·aḥ (Psalm 20)~~

מִנְחָה ✕ ~~תַּחֲנוּן Taḥanun~~

## 1st Adar 15 אֲדָר א׳ Wed 20 Feb

## פּוּרִים שׁוּשָׁן קָטָן Shushan Purim Katan
**15th of 1st Adar**

שַׁחֲרִית ✕ ~~תַּחֲנוּן Taḥanun~~

✕ ~~לַמְנַצֵּחַ Lamenatse·aḥ (Psalm 20)~~

מִנְחָה ✕ ~~תַּחֲנוּן Taḥanun~~

## 1st Adar 18 אֲדָר א׳ Sat 23 Feb

## שַׁבָּת Shabbat פָּרָשַׁת כִּי תִשָּׂא Parashat Ki tissa

**Torah** 7 aliyot (minimum): כִּי תִשָּׂא Ki tissa
שְׁמוֹת Shemot (Exodus) 30:11–34:35

| | | | | |
|---|---|---|---|---|
| Annual: | 1 30:11–31:17 | °2 31:18–33:11 | 3 33:12–16 | 4 33:17–23 |
| | 5 34:1–9° | 6 34:10–26 | 7 34:27–35 | M 34:33–35 |
| Triennial: | 1 33:12–16 | 2 33:17–23 | 3 34:1–9° | 4 34:10–17 |
| | 5 34:18–21 | 6 34:22–26 | 7 34:27–35 | M 34:33–35 |

**Annual Reading**

☞°**Aliyah 2** It is traditional to call a **levi** (Levite, descendant of the tribe of Levi) for this aliyah. Only the tribe of Levi remained loyal to Moses and to God (32:26); only a descendant of the tribe of Levi can stand at the Torah with head held high for this aliyah. This practice should be followed even in congregations that do not regularly call a **levi** in the traditional sequence.
Because of the shameful nature of these verses, do not divide this lengthy passage into shorter aliyot. However, the chanting may be divided among multiple readers. All the readers must be present at the Torah when the oleh/olah recites the first berakhah. This serves as an implicit appointment of all the readers as sheliḥim (agents) of the oleh/olah.

☞°31:18–33:11 Chant most of the story of the golden calf in a somewhat **subdued** voice to symbolically minimize the embarrassment the congregants experience upon hearing the terrible misdeeds of their ancestors. Be sure that all words and te'amim (tropes, cantillations) remain clearly audible to the congregation.
However, chant the following verses as usual:
Shemot 31:18, 32:11–14, 33:1–2, 33:3 only through וּדְבָשׁ, 33:7–11

☞°32:12, 34:6–7, 9 Chant these verses in the usual manner. Do **not** chant them as chanted on fast days.

| 1st Adar 5779 | | | | | | |
|---|---|---|---|---|---|---|
| | | | 1 | 2 | 3 | 4 |
| 5 | 6 | 7 | 8 | 9 | 10 | 11 |
| 12 | 13 | 14 | 15 | 16 | 17 | 18 |
| 19 | 20 | 21 | 22 | 23 | 24 | 25 |
| 26 | 27 | 28 | 29 | 30 | | |

| Feb \| Mar 2019 | | | | | | |
|---|---|---|---|---|---|---|
| | | | 6 | 7 | 8 | 9 |
| 10 | 11 | 12 | 13 | 14 | 15 | 16 |
| 17 | 18 | 19 | 20 | 21 | 22 | 23 |
| 24 | 25 | 26 | 27 | 28 | 1 | 2 |
| 3 | 4 | 5 | 6 | 7 | | |

+ Add ✕ Omit ☞ Take note!

**Siddurim**
**L** Lev Shalem for Shabbat and Festivals
**S** Shabbat and Festival Sim Shalom
**W** Weekday Sim Shalom
**F** Full Sim Shalom (both editions)
**P** Personal Edition of Full Sim Shalom

**Haftarah**
Ashkenazic: מְלָכִים א׳ 1 Melakhim (1 Kings) 18:1–39
Sephardic: מְלָכִים א׳ 1 Melakhim (1 Kings) 18:20–39

מִנְחָה

**Torah** 3 aliyot from וַיַּקְהֵל Vayak·hel
שְׁמוֹת Shemot (Exodus) 35:1–20
¹35:1–3 ²4–10 ³11–20 W285 P905

This is also the reading for the coming Monday and Thursday.

## 1st Adar 25 אֲדָר א׳ — שַׁבָּת Shabbat פָּרָשַׁת וַיַּקְהֵל Parashat Vayak·hel
Sat **2** Mar (morning)
שַׁבַּת שְׁקָלִים Shabbat Shekalim
שַׁבַּת מְבָרְכִים הַחֹדֶשׁ Shabbat Mevarekhim Haḥodesh

**Shabbat Shekalim** is the 1st of 4 special Shabbatot before Pesaḥ. Its name comes from the *maftir aliyah* reading, Shemot 30:11–16, which describes the obligation of every Israelite man to contribute a half shekel.

The contribution served 2 purposes. It provided funds to support the operation of the *mishkan* (portable sanctuary). At the same time, it accomplished a census of Israelite men.

In Temple days, this tax was instituted as an annual obligation, to be paid during the month of Adar. Shabbat Shekalim was scheduled to fall before or on the 1st day of Adar as a reminder of the upcoming obligation. In a leap year it falls before the start of 2nd Adar.

Today we observe this obligation by collecting *maḥatsit hashekel* before Purim (see p. 115). The funds support Jewish institutions or other charitable endeavors.

**TORAH SERVICE** L168 S139 F394

Remove **2** Torah scrolls from ark.

**1st scroll** 7 aliyot (minimum): וַיַּקְהֵל Vayak·hel
שְׁמוֹת Shemot (Exodus) 35:1–38:20

Annual: ¹35:1–20 ²35:21–29 ³35:30–36:7 ⁴36:8–19 ⁵36:20–37:16 ⁶37:17–29 ⁷38:1–20

Triennial: ¹35:1–3 ²35:4–10 ³35:11–20 ⁴35:21–29 ⁵35:30–35 ⁶36:1–7 ⁷36:8–19

Place 2nd scroll on table next to 1st scroll.
חֲצִי קַדִּישׁ Short Kaddish L174 S146 F408
Open, raise, display, and wrap 1st scroll.

+ **2nd scroll** Maftir aliyah from כִּי תִשָּׂא Ki tissa
שְׁמוֹת[M] Shemot (Exodus) 30:11–16

Open, raise, display, and wrap 2nd scroll.

☞ **Haftarah** for Shabbat Shekalim
Ashkenazic: מְלָכִים ב׳ 2 Melakhim (2 Kings) 12:1–17
Sephardic: מְלָכִים ב׳ 2 Melakhim (2 Kings) 11:17–12:17

+ **Birkat Haḥodesh:** L180 S150 F418
Announce Rosh Ḥodesh Adar Sheni:
Do not announce the month as “Adar Bet.”
רֹאשׁ חֹדֶשׁ אֲדָר שֵׁנִי יִהְיֶה בְּיוֹם חֲמִישִׁי וּבְיוֹם שִׁשִּׁי . . .
Rosh ḥodesh Adar Sheni yihyeh beyom ḥamishi uvyom shishi . . .
(Wednesday night, Thursday, and Friday)

✕ ~~אַב הָרַחֲמִים Av Haraḥamim~~

אַשְׁרֵי Ashrey L181 S151 F420
Return scrolls to ark. L183 S153 F422

חֲצִי קַדִּישׁ Short Kaddish L184 S155 F428

Continue as on a usual Shabbat.

מִנְחָה

**Torah** 3 aliyot from פְקוּדֵי Pekudey
שְׁמוֹת Shemot (Exodus) 38:21–39:1
[1]38:21–23 [2]24–27 [3]38:28–39:1 W286 P906

This is also the reading for the coming Monday.

☞ צִדְקָתְךָ צֶדֶק Tsidkatekha tsedek L230 S239 W183 F584

---

**1st Adar 29 אֲדָר א׳**
**Wed 6 Mar**

**עֶרֶב רֹאשׁ חֹדֶשׁ Erev Rosh Ḥodesh**
**Day before Rosh Ḥodesh**

מִנְחָה ✕ ~~תַּחֲנוּן Taḥanun~~

| 1st Adar 5779 | | | | | | |
|---|---|---|---|---|---|---|
| | | 1 | 2 | 3 | 4 | |
| 5 | 6 | 7 | 8 | 9 | 10 | 11 |
| 12 | 13 | 14 | 15 | 16 | 17 | 18 |
| 19 | 20 | 21 | 22 | 23 | 24 | 25 |
| 26 | 27 | 28 | 29 | 30 | | |

| Feb \| Mar 2019 | | | | | | |
|---|---|---|---|---|---|---|
| | | | 6 | 7 | 8 | 9 |
| 10 | 11 | 12 | 13 | 14 | 15 | 16 |
| 17 | 18 | 19 | 20 | 21 | 22 | 23 |
| 24 | 25 | 26 | 27 | 28 \| | 1 | 2 |
| 3 | 4 | 5 | 6 | 7 | | |

+ Add ✕ Omit ☞ Take note!

**Siddurim**
- **L** Lev Shalem for Shabbat and Festivals
- **S** Shabbat and Festival Sim Shalom
- **W** Weekday Sim Shalom
- **F** Full Sim Shalom (both editions)
- **P** Personal Edition of Full Sim Shalom

## 1st Adar 30 אֲדָר א׳ ראשׁ חֹדֶשׁ אֲדָר שֵׁנִי Rosh Hodesh Adar Sheni – Day 1

Wed **6** Mar (evening)

**DURING Rosh Hodesh**

**Birkat Hamazon:**

+ יַעֲלֶה וְיָבוֹא Ya'aleh veyavo for Rosh Hodesh
L90|95 S340|347 W233|239 F762|780

+ הָרַחֲמָן Harahaman for Rosh Hodesh
L92|96 S343|348 W235|240 F768

**עַרְבִית**

**Weekday Amidah:**

+ יַעֲלֶה וְיָבוֹא Ya'aleh veyavo for Rosh Hodesh W145 F216

Thu **7** Mar **שַׁחֲרִית**

**Before מִזְמוֹר שִׁיר Mizmor shir (Psalm 30)** W14 F50
**or at end of service, recite:**

Psalm for Thursday (Psalm 81) W89 F30
קַדִּישׁ יָתוֹם Mourner's Kaddish (some omit) W100 F52
+ Psalm 104 for Rosh Hodesh W90 F34
קַדִּישׁ יָתוֹם Mourner's Kaddish W100 F52

**Weekday Amidah:**

+ יַעֲלֶה וְיָבוֹא Ya'aleh veyavo for Rosh Hodesh W41 F114

✕ ~~תַּחֲנוּן Tahanun~~

+ חֲצִי הַלֵּל Short Hallel W50 F380
קַדִּישׁ שָׁלֵם Full Kaddish W56 F392

**TORAH SERVICE** W65 F138
Remove **1** Torah scroll from ark.

**Torah** 4 aliyot: פִּינְחָס Pinehas
בְּמִדְבַּר Bemidbar (Numbers) 28:1–15
¹28:1–3 ²3–5 ³6–10 ⁴11–15 W320 P943

חֲצִי קַדִּישׁ Short Kaddish W71 F146
Open, raise, display, and wrap scroll.
Return scroll to ark. W76 F150

אַשְׁרֵי Ashrey W78 F152
✕ ~~לַמְנַצֵּחַ Lamenatse-ah (Psalm 20)~~
וּבָא לְצִיּוֹן Uva letsiyyon W80 F156

**Some congregations:**
Remove and pack t^e^fillin at this point.
+ חֲצִי קַדִּישׁ Short Kaddish W103 F428

**Other congregations:**
+ חֲצִי קַדִּישׁ Short Kaddish W103 F428
Remove and cover—but do not pack—t^e^fillin, so that all begin Musaf Amidah at the same time, as soon after Kaddish as possible.

מוּסָף
+ **Rosh Ḥodesh Amidah for weekdays:** W104 F486
Weekday קְדֻשָּׁה K^e^dushah W105 F488
+ וּלְכַפָּרַת פָּשַׁע Ulkhapparat pasha W107 F494
Add these words only through Rosh Ḥodesh Adar Sheni.

+ קַדִּישׁ שָׁלֵם Full Kaddish W82 F158
עָלֵינוּ Aleynu W83 F160

**If psalms for the day were not recited at Shaḥarit, add here:**
קַדִּישׁ יָתוֹם Mourner's Kaddish (some omit) W84 F162
Psalm for Thursday (Psalm 81) W89 F30
קַדִּישׁ יָתוֹם Mourner's Kaddish (some omit) W100 F52
+ Psalm 104 for Rosh Ḥodesh W90 F34

קַדִּישׁ יָתוֹם Mourner's Kaddish W84|100 F162|52

מִנְחָה
**Weekday Amidah:**
+ יַעֲלֶה וְיָבוֹא Ya'aleh veyavo for Rosh Ḥodesh W127 F178

× ~~תַּחֲנוּן Taḥanun~~

## 2nd Adar 1 אֲדָר ב׳ — רֹאשׁ חֹדֶשׁ אֲדָר שֵׁנִי Rosh Hodesh Adar Sheni – Day 2

Thu **7** Mar (evening)

For determining the *yortsayt* of a death during Adar, 1st Adar, or 2nd Adar, see p. 214.

מִשֶּׁנִּכְנַס אֲדָר מַרְבִּין בְּשִׂמְחָה *mishenikhnas adar marbin besimḥah.*
The Rabbis instructed: "From the moment Adar arrives, we are to increase our joy." For a leap year, most authorities apply this dictum only to 2nd Adar, the Adar in which Purim is celebrated. Purim is still 2 weeks away. Yet our mood already begins to change as we anticipate its upcoming celebration.

**DURING Rosh Hodesh**

**Birkat Hamazon:**
+ יַעֲלֶה וְיָבוֹא Ya'aleh veyavo for Rosh Hodesh — L90|95 S340|347 W233|239 F762|780
+ הָרַחֲמָן Harahaman for Rosh Hodesh — L92|96 S343|348 W235|240 F768

**עַרְבִית**

**Weekday Amidah:**
+ יַעֲלֶה וְיָבוֹא Ya'aleh veyavo for Rosh Hodesh — W145 F216

Fri **8** Mar **שַׁחֲרִית**

**Before מִזְמוֹר שִׁיר Mizmor shir (Psalm 30)** W14 F50
**or at end of service, recite:**
Psalm for Friday (Psalm 93) W90 F32
קַדִּישׁ יָתוֹם Mourner's Kaddish (some omit) W100 F52
+ Psalm 104 for Rosh Hodesh W90 F34
קַדִּישׁ יָתוֹם Mourner's Kaddish W100 F52

**Weekday Amidah:**
+ יַעֲלֶה וְיָבוֹא Ya'aleh veyavo for Rosh Hodesh W41 F114

✕ ~~תַּחֲנוּן Tahanun~~

+ חֲצִי הַלֵּל Short Hallel W50 F380
קַדִּישׁ שָׁלֵם Full Kaddish W56 F392

+ **TORAH SERVICE** W65 F138
Remove **1** Torah scroll from ark.

**Torah** 4 aliyot: פִּינְחָס Pinehas
בְּמִדְבַּר Bemidbar (Numbers) 28:1–15
1 28:1–3 2 3–5 3 6–10 4 11–15 — W320 P943

חֲצִי קַדִּישׁ Short Kaddish W71 F146
Open, raise, display, and wrap scroll.
Return scroll to ark. W76 F150

אַשְׁרֵי Ashrey W78 F152
✕ ~~לַמְנַצֵּחַ Lamenatse·aḥ (Psalm 20)~~
וּבָא לְצִיּוֹן Uva letsiyyon W80 F156

**Some congregations:**
Remove and pack tefillin at this point.
+ חֲצִי קַדִּישׁ Short Kaddish W103 F428

**Other congregations:**
+ חֲצִי קַדִּישׁ Short Kaddish W103 F428
Remove and cover—but do not pack—tefillin, so that all begin Musaf Amidah at the same time, as soon after Kaddish as possible.

מוּסָף

+ **Rosh Ḥodesh Amidah for weekdays:** W104 F486
Weekday קְדֻשָּׁה Kedushah W105 F488
+ וּלְכַפָּרַת פָּשַׁע Ulkhapparat pasha W107 F494
Add these words only through Rosh Ḥodesh Adar Sheni.

+ קַדִּישׁ שָׁלֵם Full Kaddish W82 F158
עָלֵינוּ Aleynu W83 F160

**If psalms for the day were not recited at Shaḥarit, add here:**
קַדִּישׁ יָתוֹם Mourner's Kaddish (some omit) W84 F162
Psalm for Friday (Psalm 93) W90 F32
קַדִּישׁ יָתוֹם Mourner's Kaddish (some omit) W100 F52
+ Psalm 104 for Rosh Ḥodesh W90 F34

קַדִּישׁ יָתוֹם Mourner's Kaddish W84|100 F162|52

מִנְחָה

**Weekday Amidah:**
+ יַעֲלֶה וְיָבוֹא Ya'aleh veyavo for Rosh Ḥodesh W127 F178

✕ ~~תַּחֲנוּן Taḥanun~~

## 2nd Adar 2 אֲדָר ב׳ Sat 9 Mar

## שַׁבָּת Shabbat פָּרָשַׁת פְּקוּדֵי Parashat Pekudey

**Torah** 7 aliyot (minimum): פְּקוּדֵי Pekudey
שְׁמוֹת Shemot (Exodus) 38:21–40:38

| | | | | |
|---|---|---|---|---|
| Annual: | 1 38:21–39:1 | 2 39:2–21 | 3 39:22–32 | 4 39:33–43 |
| | 5 40:1–16 | 6 40:17–27 | 7 40:28–38 ▮ | M 40:34–38 |
| Triennial: | 1 39:22–26 | 2 39:27–32 | 3 39:33–43 | 4 40:1–8 |
| | 5 40:9–16 | 6 40:17–27 | 7 40:28–38 ▮ | M 40:34–38 |

▮ חזק When the Torah reader concludes a book of the Torah:

1. Close the Torah scroll.
2. **For Oleh:** Congregation chants חֲזַק חֲזַק וְנִתְחַזֵּק ḥazak ḥazak venitḥazzek; oleh remains silent.
   **For Olah:** Congregation chants חִזְקִי חִזְקִי וְנִתְחַזֵּק ḥizki ḥizki venitḥazzek; olah remains silent.
3. Torah reader repeats congregation's words (oleh/olah remains silent; if Torah reader is the oleh/olah, omit this repetition).
4. Open the Torah scroll.
5. The oleh/olah kisses the Torah scroll, closes it, and continues with the usual concluding berakhah.

**Haftarah**
Ashkenazic: מְלָכִים א׳ 1 Melakhim (1 Kings) 7:51–8:21
Sephardic: מְלָכִים א׳ 1 Melakhim (1 Kings) 7:40–50

### מִנְחָה

**Torah** 3 aliyot from וַיִּקְרָא Vayikra
וַיִּקְרָא Vayikra (Leviticus) 1:1–13
1 1:1–4 2 5–9 3 10–13 W287 P907

This is also the reading for the coming Monday and Thursday.

| + Add | ✗ Omit | ☞ Take note! | **2nd Adar 5779** | **Mar | Apr 2019** | **אֲדָר ב׳ 9** Mar 16 |
|---|---|---|---|---|---|
| | Siddurim | | 1 2 | 8 9 | |
| L | Lev Shalem for Shabbat and Festivals | | 3 4 5 6 7 8 9 | 10 11 12 13 14 15 16 | |
| S | Shabbat and Festival Sim Shalom | | 10 11 12 13 14 15 16 | 17 18 19 20 21 22 23 | |
| W | Weekday Sim Shalom | | 17 18 19 20 21 22 23 | 24 25 26 27 28 29 30 | |
| F | Full Sim Shalom (both editions) | | 24 25 26 27 28 29 | 31 | 1 2 3 4 5 | |
| P | Personal Edition of Full Sim Shalom | | | | |

## 2nd Adar 9 אֲדָר ב׳ Sat 16 Mar (morning)

## שַׁבָּת Shabbat פָּרָשַׁת וַיִּקְרָא Parashat Vayikra
## שַׁבַּת זָכוֹר Shabbat Zakhor

**Shabbat Zakhor**, the 2nd of 4 special Shabbatot before Pesaḥ, is named after the first word of the *maftir aliyah* reading, Devarim 25:17–19. It recalls Amalek's cowardly attack upon the weak and weary of the people Israel as they traveled in the wilderness. The people Israel is commanded to remember what Amalek did and to wipe out Amalek's memory.

The Rabbis prescribed that we fulfill this commandment once a year by reading this passage publicly from a Torah scroll. They chose the Shabbat before Purim for this reading to connect the wiping out of the memory of Amalek to the Purim practice of "blotting out" the name of Haman, who was a descendant of Amalek.

**TORAH SERVICE** L168 S139 F394

Remove **2** Torah scrolls from ark.

**1st scroll** 7 aliyot (minimum): וַיִּקְרָא Vayikra
וַיִּקְרָא Vayikra (Leviticus) 1:1–5:26

| | | | | |
|---|---|---|---|---|
| Annual: | [1]1:1–13 | [2]1:14–2:6 | [3]2:7–16 | [4]3:1–17 |
| | [5]4:1–26 | [6]4:27–5:10 | [7]5:11–26 | |
| Triennial: | [1]4:27–31 | [2]4:32–35 | [3]5:1–10 | [4]5:11–13 |
| | [5]5:14–16 | [6]5:17–19 | [7]5:20–26 | |

Place 2nd scroll on table next to 1st scroll.
חֲצִי קַדִּישׁ Short Kaddish L174 S146 F408
Open, raise, display, and wrap 1st scroll.

+ **2nd scroll** Maftir aliyah from כִּי־תֵצֵא Ki tetse
דְּבָרִים[M] Devarim (Deuteronomy) 25:17–19°

☞°25:19 There should be **no** repetition of this verse or any of its words, despite a widespread practice of reading part or all of this verse twice using variant readings of the 6th-to-last word. The proper reading of this word is זֵכֶר, as it appears in the most reliable manuscripts and in almost all printed editions. For more information, see www.milesbcohen.com/LuahResources.

Open, raise, display, and wrap 2nd scroll.

☞**Haftarah** for Shabbat Zakhor
Ashkenazic: שְׁמוּאֵל א׳ 1 Shemu'el (1 Samuel) 15:2–34
Sephardic: שְׁמוּאֵל א׳ 1 Shemu'el (1 Samuel) 15:1–34

✕ ~~אַב הָרַחֲמִים Av Haraḥamim~~

| 2nd Adar 5779 | | | | | | | Mar \| Apr 2019 | | | | | | |
|---|---|---|---|---|---|---|---|---|---|---|---|---|---|
| | | | | | 1 | 2 | | | | | | 8 | 9 |
| 3 | 4 | 5 | 6 | 7 | 8 | 9 | 10 | 11 | 12 | 13 | 14 | 15 | 16 |
| 10 | 11 | 12 | 13 | 14 | 15 | 16 | 17 | 18 | 19 | 20 | 21 | 22 | 23 |
| 17 | 18 | 19 | 20 | 21 | 22 | 23 | 24 | 25 | 26 | 27 | 28 | 29 | 30 |
| 24 | 25 | 26 | 27 | 28 | 29 | | 31 \| | 1 | 2 | 3 | 4 | 5 | |

+ Add ✕ Omit ☞ Take note!

**Siddurim**
**L** Lev Shalem for Shabbat and Festivals
**S** Shabbat and Festival Sim Shalom
**W** Weekday Sim Shalom
**F** Full Sim Shalom (both editions)
**P** Personal Edition of Full Sim Shalom

אַשְׁרֵי Ashrey L181 S151 F420
Return scrolls to ark. L183 S153 F422

חֲצִי קַדִּישׁ Short Kaddish L184 S155 F428

Continue as on a usual Shabbat.

מִנְחָה

**Torah** 3 aliyot from צַו Tsav
וַיִּקְרָא Vayikra (Leviticus) 6:1–11
¹6:1–3 ²4–6 ³7–11 W288 P908

This is also the reading for the coming Monday.

☞ צִדְקָתְךָ צֶדֶק Tsidkatekha tsedek L230 S239 W183 F584

## 2nd Adar 13 אֲדָר ב׳ תַּעֲנִית אֶסְתֵּר Ta'anit Ester

Wed 20 Mar (morning) Fast of Esther (communal fast, begins at dawn)

### Ta'anit Ester

Ta'anit Ester commemorates the fasting by the Jews before commencing their defensive battle against Haman's forces. The fast day is named for Esther in remembrance of the 3-day fast she proclaimed for all the Jews in advance of her perilous seeking of an audience with the king to plead for the Jews.

- This is a minor fast day, so called because the fast does not begin until dawn.
- The fast (from both eating and drinking) lasts until dark (a minimum of 25 minutes after sunset).
- *Sheliḥey tsibbur,* Torah readers, and those called for *aliyot* should be fasting.
- The preferred fast-day procedures apply when at least 6 of those who are counted for a *minyan* are fasting.
- If it is ascertained (without causing embarrassment) that fewer than 6 are fasting, follow the procedures printed in gray and marked with ✦.

שַׁחֲרִית

**Silent Weekday Amidah:**
Do not add עֲנֵנוּ Anenu.

**Repetition of the Weekday Amidah:**

6 or more fasting + עֲנֵנוּ Anenu before רְפָאֵנוּ Refa'enu W38 F110

Fewer than 6 fasting ✦ Add עֲנֵנוּ Anenu in שׁוֹמֵעַ תְּפִלָּה Shome·a tefillah. Replace תַּעֲנִיתֵנוּ ta'anitenu (6th word) with הַתַּעֲנִית הַזֶּה hata'anit hazeh. W38 F110

6 or more fasting + אָבִינוּ מַלְכֵּנוּ Avinu malkenu W57 F124

Fewer than 6 fasting ✦ Those fasting recite אָבִינוּ מַלְכֵּנוּ individually.

☞ תַּחֲנוּן Taḥanun W62 F132
חֲצִי קַדִּישׁ Short Kaddish W64 F136

**Fewer than 6 fasting** ✦ Omit the entire Torah service.
Continue with אַשְׁרֵי Ashrey.

**6 or more fasting** + **TORAH SERVICE** W65 F138
Remove **1** Torah scroll from ark.

**Torah** 3 aliyot from כִּי תִשָּׂא Ki tissa
שְׁמוֹת Shemot (Exodus) 32:11–14, 34:1–10
¹32:11–14° ²34:1–3 ³4–10° W341 P979

☞ °At each of the 3 passages indicated below, follow this procedure:
1. The reader pauses before the indicated text.
2. The congregation recites the indicated text.
3. Afterward, the reader chants the indicated text in the manner of the cantillation of High Holiday Torah reading.

32:12 שׁוּב מֵחֲרוֹן אַפֶּךָ וְהִנָּחֵם עַל־הָרָעָה לְעַמֶּךָ׃

34:6–7 יי | יי אֵ·ל רַחוּם וְחַנּוּן אֶרֶךְ אַפַּיִם וְרַב־חֶסֶד וֶאֱמֶת׃
נֹצֵר חֶסֶד לָאֲלָפִים נֹשֵׂא עָוֺן וָפֶשַׁע וְחַטָּאָה וְנַקֵּה

34:9 וְסָלַחְתָּ לַעֲוֺנֵנוּ וּלְחַטָּאתֵנוּ | וּנְחַלְתָּנוּ׃

To preserve the sense of this passage, maintain the appropriate pause after the טִפְחָא (וּלְחַטָּאתֵנוּ).

חֲצִי קַדִּישׁ Short Kaddish W71 F146
Open, raise, display, and wrap scroll.
Return scroll to ark. W76 F150

**All minyanim** אַשְׁרֵי Ashrey W78 F152
☞ לַמְנַצֵּחַ Lamenatse·aḥ (Psalm 20) W79 F154
Conclude the service in the usual manner.

מַחֲצִית הַשֶּׁקֶל ***maḥatsit hashekel***, in common practice, is half the basic unit of currency in use in a Jewish community. At Purim time, it is customary to contribute 3 half-shekels (e.g., $1.50 in the United States or Canada). This is because in the Torah, the phrase מַחֲצִית הַשֶּׁקֶל appears 3 times in the description of this obligation to contribute (Shemot 30:11–16).

In the Torah, the half-shekel collection was to support operation of the *mishkan*. Later the funds were used for Temple upkeep. This was a tax, instituted as an annual obligation to be paid during the month of Adar.

Currently, the funds support Jewish institutions or other charitable endeavors.

| 2nd Adar 5779 | | | | | | | Mar \| Apr 2019 | | | | | | |
|---|---|---|---|---|---|---|---|---|---|---|---|---|---|
| | | | | | 1 | 2 | | | | | | 8 | 9 |
| 3 | 4 | 5 | 6 | 7 | 8 | 9 | 10 | 11 | 12 | 13 | 14 | 15 | 16 |
| 10 | 11 | 12 | 13 | 14 | 15 | 16 | 17 | 18 | 19 | 20 | 21 | 22 | 23 |
| 17 | 18 | 19 | 20 | 21 | 22 | 23 | 24 | 25 | 26 | 27 | 28 | 29 | 30 |
| 24 | 25 | 26 | 27 | 28 | 29 | | 31 \| | 1 | 2 | 3 | 4 | 5 | |

+ Add ✕ Omit ☞ Take note!

**Siddurim**
- **L** Lev Shalem for Shabbat and Festivals
- **S** Shabbat and Festival Sim Shalom
- **W** Weekday Sim Shalom
- **F** Full Sim Shalom (both editions)
- **P** Personal Edition of Full Sim Shalom

---

**מִנְחָה** Before or at Minḥah, we give מַחֲצִית הַשֶּׁקֶל maḥatsit hashekel (see green box, p. 115).

אַשְׁרֵי Ashrey W120 F164
חֲצִי קַדִּישׁ Short Kaddish W121 F166

Fewer than 6 fasting ✦ Omit the entire Torah service. Continue with the silent Amidah.

6 or more fasting + **TORAH SERVICE** W65 F138

Remove **1** Torah scroll from ark.

**Torah** 3 aliyot from כִּי תִשָּׂא Ki tissa
שְׁמוֹת Shemot (Exodus) 32:11–14, 34:1–10
[1]32:11–14° [2]34:1–3 [M]4–10° W341 P979

☞ °Follow the same procedure as for the morning reading. See p. 115.

☞ Do not recite חֲצִי קַדִּישׁ Short Kaddish after maftir aliyah.

Open, raise, display, and wrap scroll.

Recite the בְּרָכָה berakhah before the haftarah. W74 F410 P989

**Haftarah** יְשַׁעְיָהוּ Yesha'yahu (Isaiah) 55:6–56:8 W342 P980

Recite the 3 concluding haftarah blessings, through מָגֵן דָּוִד Magen david. W74 F410 P989.

Return scroll to ark. W76 F150
חֲצִי קַדִּישׁ Short Kaddish W121 F166

All minyanim **Silent weekday Amidah:**
If fasting + עֲנֵנוּ Anenu, in שׁוֹמֵעַ תְּפִלָּה Shome·a tefillah W127 F178
All ✕ ~~שָׁלוֹם רָב Shalom rav~~
+ שִׂים שָׁלוֹם Sim shalom W131 F184

**Repetition of the weekday Amidah:**
6 or more fasting + עֲנֵנוּ Anenu, before רְפָאֵנוּ Refa'enu W124 F172
Fewer than 6 fasting ✦ Add עֲנֵנוּ Anenu in שׁוֹמֵעַ תְּפִלָּה Shome·a tefillah. Replace תַּעֲנִיתֵנוּ ta'anitenu (6th word) with הַתַּעֲנִית הַזֶּה hata'anit hazeh. W127 F172
All minyanim + בִּרְכַּת כֹּהֲנִים Birkat kohanim W131 F184
✕ ~~שָׁלוֹם רָב Shalom rav~~
+ שִׂים שָׁלוֹם Sim shalom W131 F184

✕ ~~אָבִינוּ מַלְכֵּנוּ Avinu malkenu~~
✕ ~~תַּחֲנוּן Taḥanun~~

קַדִּישׁ שָׁלֵם Full Kaddish W134 F194
עָלֵינוּ Aleynu W135 F196
קַדִּישׁ יָתוֹם Mourner's Kaddish W136 F198

## Purim

### The 5 Mitsvot of Purim

Five מִצְוֹת *mitsvot* are associated with the celebration of Purim:

1. מִקְרָא מְגִלָּה בְּעַרְבִית *mikra megillah be'arvit.* All Jewish men, women, and children are to listen to the reading of the מְגִלָּה *megillah* at the Arvit service.
2. מִקְרָא מְגִלָּה בְּשַׁחֲרִית *mikra megillah beshaḥarit.* It is an additional and separate מִצְוָה *mitsvah* for all Jewish men, women, and children to listen to the reading of the מְגִלָּה at the Shaḥarit service.
3. מַתָּנוֹת לָאֶבְיוֹנִים *mattanot la'evyonim.* To express our joy on Purim, we give gifts of food, drink, money, or clothing to poor people. Fulfill the מִצְוָה by giving at least 1 gift each to 2 poor people during Purim day.
4. מִשְׁלוֹחַ מָנוֹת *mishloaḥ manot.* Another way to express the joy of Purim is to give gifts of food and drink to family and friends. Fulfill the מִצְוָה by giving 2 kinds of food to 1 person during Purim day. More gifts may be given, but it is preferable to maximize gifts to poor people (מַתָּנוֹת לָאֶבְיוֹנִים; see 3 above) rather than to maximize מִשְׁלוֹחַ מָנוֹת.
5. סְעוּדַת פּוּרִים *se'udat purim.* The joyous Purim feast takes place in the afternoon, extending into the evening. It features food and drink, as well as "Purim Torah" (parodies of Torah lessons) and a Purim *shpil* (consisting of humorous performances and skits on Purim themes).

### Procedure for Chanting Megillat Ester

**Before Chanting the Megillah**

1. The reader unrolls the מְגִלָּה and folds it like a letter.
2. The congregation stands as the reader recites three בְּרָכוֹת *berakhot* (both evening and morning): S220 W194

בָּרוּךְ אַתָּה יי, אֱ·לֹהֵינוּ מֶלֶךְ הָעוֹלָם, אֲשֶׁר קִדְּשָׁנוּ בְּמִצְוֹתָיו
וְצִוָּנוּ עַל מִקְרָא מְגִלָּה.

בָּרוּךְ אַתָּה יי, אֱ·לֹהֵינוּ מֶלֶךְ הָעוֹלָם,
שֶׁעָשָׂה נִסִּים לַאֲבוֹתֵינוּ בַּיָּמִים הָהֵם וּבַזְּמַן הַזֶּה.

בָּרוּךְ אַתָּה יי, אֱ·לֹהֵינוּ מֶלֶךְ הָעוֹלָם,
שֶׁהֶחֱיָנוּ וְקִיְּמָנוּ וְהִגִּיעָנוּ לַזְּמַן הַזֶּה.

**Chanting the M^e^gillah**

1. The reader and congregation observe the following customs:
   - When the reader reaches each of אַרְבָּעָה פְּסוּקִים שֶׁל גְּאֻלָּה *arba'ah p^e^sukim shel g^e^'ullah* ("the 4 redemption verses")—2:5, 8:15, 8:16, and 10:3:
     The reader pauses while the congregation recites the verse.
     When the congregation finishes, the reader chants the verse and continues.
   - Whenever the reader chants the name הָמָן *haman,* the congregation makes noise to drown out the name.
     We do so in response to the commandment תִּמְחֶה אֶת־זֵכֶר עֲמָלֵק *timḥeh et zekher amalek* ("blot out the memory of Amalek"; D^e^varim 25:19). According to tradition, Haman was a descendant of Amalek.
2. To reflect the frequent changes in the mood of the story, the reader adjusts the cantillation by chanting:
   - Traditional enhancements to positive turning points in the story, celebratory moments, and other special verses, including: 1:22, 2:4, 2:17, 5:7, 6:1, 6:10, 7:10, 8:14, 8:15, 8:16, 10:2, and 10:3.
   - Sad and threatening verses using the cantillation system of אֵיכָה *eykhah* (Lamentations): 1:7 (only the 3 words וְכֵלִים מִכֵּלִים שׁוֹנִים), 3:15, 4:1, 4:3 (beginning אֲבָל גָּדוֹל), and 4:16 (last 3 words only).
     This selection of verses reflects the rabbinic tradition that chapter 6 records God's intervention on behalf of the Jews. After this, no further lamenting is appropriate.
3. The reader chants the names of Haman's 10 sons (9:7–10) in 1 breath.

**After Chanting the M^e^gillah**

- The reader quickly closes the מְגִלָּה.
- The congregation stands for the concluding בְּרָכָה *berakhah:* S220 W194

בָּרוּךְ אַתָּה יי, אֱ־לֹהֵינוּ מֶלֶךְ הָעוֹלָם,
הָרָב אֶת־רִיבֵנוּ, וְהַדָּן אֶת־דִּינֵנוּ, וְהַנּוֹקֵם אֶת־נִקְמָתֵנוּ,
וְהַמְשַׁלֵּם גְּמוּל לְכָל־אוֹיְבֵי נַפְשֵׁנוּ, וְהַנִּפְרָע לָנוּ מִצָּרֵינוּ.
בָּרוּךְ אַתָּה יי, הַנִּפְרָע לְעַמּוֹ יִשְׂרָאֵל מִכָּל־צָרֵיהֶם, הָאֵ־ל הַמּוֹשִׁיעַ.

- In the evening, some add the poem אֲשֶׁר הֵנִיא *asher heni.* W195
- Evening and morning, recite שׁוֹשַׁנַּת יַעֲקֹב *shoshanat ya'^a^kov.* S220 W195

| | | 2nd Adar 5779 | Mar \| Apr 2019 | |
|---|---|---|---|---|
| ✚ Add | ✖ Omit | | 1 2 | 8 9 אֲדָר ב׳ 14 Mar 20 |
| **Siddurim** | | 3 4 5 6 7 8 9 | 10 11 12 13 14 15 16 | Mar 21 |
| **L** Lev Shalem for Shabbat and Festivals | | 10 11 12 13 14 15 16 | 17 18 19 20 21 22 23 | |
| **S** Shabbat and Festival Sim Shalom | | 17 18 19 20 21 22 23 | 24 25 26 27 28 29 30 | |
| **W** Weekday Sim Shalom | | 24 25 26 27 28 29 | 31 \| 1 2 3 4 5 | |
| **F** Full Sim Shalom (both editions) | | | | |
| **P** Personal Edition of Full Sim Shalom | | | | |

## Purim פּוּרִים אֲדָר ב׳ 14 **2nd Adar**
**Wed 20 Mar** (evening)

| **DURING** Purim | **Birkat Hamazon:** |
|---|---|
| | ✚ עַל הַנִּסִּים Al Hanissim for Purim  **L**431 **W**232\|238 **F**760 |

For information about mitsvot and procedures for Purim, see pp. 117–118.

עַרְבִית Weekday Arvit as usual  **L**264 **S**281 **W**137 **F**200
until the Amidah

**Weekday Amidah:**
✚ עַל הַנִּסִּים Al Hanissim for Purim  **L**431 **S**290 **W**146 **F**218

☞ קַדִּישׁ שָׁלֵם Full Kaddish  **L**280 **S**294 **W**149 **F**222

✚ **Megillah reading:**
מְגִלַּת אֶסְתֵּר Megillat Ester (Scroll of Esther)
Follow the procedure described on pp. 117–118.

☞ 8:11 Read וְלַהֲרֹג even if your megillah has לַהֲרֹג.
9:2 Read לִפְנֵיהֶם even if your megillah has בִּפְנֵיהֶם.
Do **not** repeat words, phrases, or verses in an effort to reflect supposed variant readings, which in fact are printer/scribal errors.

✚ וְאַתָּה קָדוֹשׁ Ve'attah kadosh  **L**216 **S**293 **W**159 **F**684

☞ קַדִּישׁ שָׁלֵם Full Kaddish, but omit sentence:  **L**280 **S**294 **W**160 **F**688
✖ תִּתְקַבַּל ~~Titkabbal~~ . . .

Conclude as on a usual weeknight.

**Thu 21 Mar** שַׁחֲרִית **Weekday Amidah:**
✚ עַל הַנִּסִּים Al Hanissim for Purim  **W**42 **F**118

✖ ~~תַּחֲנוּן Taḥanun~~

☞ Do not recite הַלֵּל Hallel.
חֲצִי קַדִּישׁ Short Kaddish  **W**64 **F**136

✚ **TORAH SERVICE**  **W**65 **F**138
Remove **1** Torah scroll from ark.

> **Torah** 3 aliyot from בְּשַׁלַּח Beshallaḥ
> שְׁמוֹת Shemot (Exodus) 17:8–16
> ¹17:8–10  ²11–13  ³14–16                    **W**337 **P**955

חֲצִי קַדִּישׁ Short Kaddish W71 F146
Open, raise, display, and wrap scroll.
Return scroll to ark. W76 F150

+ **Megillah reading:**
Follow the procedure described on pp. 117–118.

☞ 8:11 Read וְלַהֲרֹג even if your megillah has לַהֲרֹג.
9:2 Read לִפְנֵיהֶם even if your megillah has בִּפְנֵיהֶם.
Do **not** repeat words, phrases, or verses in an effort to reflect supposed variant readings, which in fact are printer/scribal errors.

אַשְׁרֵי Ashrey W78 F152
✕ ~~לַמְנַצֵּחַ Lamenatse·aḥ (Psalm 20)~~
וּבָא לְצִיּוֹן Uva letsiyyon W80 F156

קַדִּישׁ שָׁלֵם Full Kaddish W82 F158
עָלֵינוּ Aleynu W83 F160

Conclude as on a usual weekday.

מִנְחָה **Weekday Amidah:**
+ עַל הַנִּסִּים Al Hanissim for Purim W129 F182

✕ ~~תַּחֲנוּן Taḥanun~~

## 2nd Adar 15 אֲדָר ב׳ פּוּרִים שׁוּשָׁן Shushan Purim

Thu 21 Mar

עַרְבִית Weekday Arvit as usual
☞ Do not recite עַל הַנִּסִּים Al Hanissim.

Fri 22 Mar שַׁחֲרִית Weekday Shaḥarit as usual
☞ Do not recite עַל הַנִּסִּים Al Hanissim.

✕ ~~תַּחֲנוּן Taḥanun~~
✕ ~~לַמְנַצֵּחַ Lamenatse·aḥ (Psalm 20)~~

מִנְחָה Weekday Minḥah as usual
☞ Do not recite עַל הַנִּסִּים Al Hanissim.

✕ ~~תַּחֲנוּן Taḥanun~~ (as on all Friday afternoons)

פּוּרִים Purim

## 2nd Adar 16 אֲדָר ב׳ שַׁבָּת Shabbat פָּרָשַׁת צַו Parashat Tsav
Sat **23** Mar

**Torah** 7 aliyot (minimum): צַו Tsav
וַיִּקְרָא Vayikra (Leviticus) 6:1–8:36

| | | | | |
|---|---|---|---|---|
| Annual: | [1] 6:1–11 | [2] 6:12–7:10 | [3] 7:11–38 | [4] 8:1–13 |
| | [5] 8:14–21 | [6] 8:22–29° | [7] 8:30–36 | [M] 8:33–36 |
| Triennial: | [1] 8:1–5 | [2] 8:6–9 | [3] 8:10–13 | [4] 8:14–17 |
| | [5] 8:18–21 | [6] 8:22–29° | [7] 8:30–36 | [M] 8:33–36 |

☞ °8:23 Note the rare ta'am (trope) | שַׁלְשֶׁלֶת (|꙳ ): | וַיִּשְׁחָט

**Haftarah** יִרְמְיָהוּ Yirmeyahu (Jeremiah) 7:21–8:3, 9:22–23

מִנְחָה

**Torah** 3 aliyot from שְׁמִינִי Shemini
וַיִּקְרָא Vayikra (Leviticus) 9:1–16
[1] 9:1–6 [2] 7–10 [3] 11–16 W289 P909

This is also the reading for the coming Monday and Thursday.

## 2nd Adar 23 אֲדָר ב׳ שַׁבָּת Shabbat פָּרָשַׁת שְׁמִינִי Parashat Shemini
Sat **30** Mar (morning)

שַׁבַּת פָּרָה Shabbat Parah
שַׁבַּת מְבָרְכִים הַחֹדֶשׁ Shabbat Mevarekhim Haḥodesh

**Shabbat Parah** is the 3rd of 4 special Shabbatot before Pesaḥ. It falls on the Shabbat before Shabbat Haḥodesh and represents the beginning of preparation for Pesaḥ. The special *maftir aliyah* reading (Bemidbar 19:1–22), in the 2nd Torah scroll, details the matter of the פָּרָה אֲדֻמָּה *parah adummah* (red heifer). In the days of the Temple, the priest would use the ashes of the פָּרָה אֲדֻמָּה to purify people who were in a ritually impure state, which would have prevented them from being eligible to eat of the Pesaḥ sacrifice.

**TORAH SERVICE** L168 S139 F394

Remove **2** Torah scrolls from ark.

**1st scroll** 7 aliyot (minimum): שְׁמִינִי Shemini
וַיִּקְרָא Vayikra (Leviticus) 9:1–11:47

| | | | | |
|---|---|---|---|---|
| Annual: | [1] 9:1–16 | [2] 9:17–23 | [3] 9:24–10:11° | [4] 10:12–15 |
| | [5] 10:16–20 | [6] 11:1–32 | [7] 11:33–47 | |
| Triennial: | [1] 11:1–8 | [2] 11:9–12 | [3] 11:13–19 | [4] 11:20–28 |
| | [5] 11:29–32 | [6] 11:33–38 | [7] 11:39–47 | |

*(Notes for the Torah reading are on the next page.)*

☞°10:1 Note the rare ta'am (trope) מֵירְכָא־כְפוּלָה ( ֦ ): אֲשֶׁ֦ר לֹ֦א צִוָּה Connect לֹ֦א to the preceding and following words without a pause; then pause after the טִפְּחָא (צִוָּ֖ה), as usual.

☞°10:4 Note rare occurrence of the teʼamim (tropes) גֵּרְשַׁ֞יִם ( ֞ ) and תְּלִישָׁא־גְדוֹלָה ( ֠ ) on the same word קָרְבַ֞֠ו. Chant first the melody of גֵּרְשַׁ֞יִם and then the melody of תְּלִישָׁא־גְדוֹלָה consecutively on the last syllable of the word (בו). Do **not** chant the word twice.

☞°10:6 Note the unusual use of the ta'am | מֻנַּח־לְגַרְמֵיהּ (= | מֻנַּח־מַפְסִיק): | אַל־תִּפְרָעוּ

☞°10:8 Note the unusual consecutive occurrences of the ta'am | מֻנַּח־לְגַרְמֵיהּ (= | מֻנַּח־מַפְסִיק): אַל־תֵּ֣שְׁתְּ | אַתָּ֣ה | וּבָנֶ֣יךָ אִתָּךְ

Place 2nd scroll on table next to 1st scroll.
חֲצִי קַדִּישׁ Short Kaddish L174 S146 F408
Open, raise, display, and wrap 1st scroll.

+ **2nd scroll** Maftir aliyah from חֻקַּת Hukkat
בְּמִדְבַּר[M] Bemidbar (Numbers) 19:1–22

Open, raise, display, and wrap 2nd scroll.

☞**Haftarah** for Shabbat Parah
Ashkenazic: יְחֶזְקֵאל Yeḥezkel (Ezekiel) 36:16–38
Sephardic: יְחֶזְקֵאל Yeḥezkel (Ezekiel) 36:16–36

+ **Birkat Haḥodesh:** L180 S150 F418
Announce Rosh Ḥodesh Nisan:
רֹאשׁ חֹדֶשׁ נִיסָן יִהְיֶה בְּיוֹם שַׁבַּת קֹדֶשׁ . . .
Rosh ḥodesh Nisan yihyeh beyom shabbat kodesh . . .
(Friday night and Saturday)

✕ ~~אַב הָרַחֲמִים Av Haraḥamim~~

אַשְׁרֵי Ashrey L181 S151 F420
Return scrolls to ark. L183 S153 F422

חֲצִי קַדִּישׁ Short Kaddish L184 S155 F428

Continue as on a usual Shabbat.

מִנְחָה

**Torah** 3 aliyot from תַזְרִיעַ Tazria
וַיִּקְרָא Vayikra (Leviticus) 12:1–13:5
¹12:1–4 ²5–8 ³13:1–5 W290 P910

This is also the reading for the coming Monday and Thursday.

☞צִדְקָתְךָ צֶדֶק Tsidkatekha tsedek L230 S239 W183 F584

**DURING Nisan** ✕ ~~תַּחֲנוּן Taḥanun~~

## Nisan 1 נִיסָן
Fri 5 Apr (evening)

**שַׁבָּת Shabbat פָּרָשַׁת תַּזְרִיעַ Parashat Tazria**
**רֹאשׁ חֹדֶשׁ נִיסָן Rosh Ḥodesh Nisan**
**שַׁבַּת הַחֹדֶשׁ Shabbat Haḥodesh**

**Shabbat Haḥodesh** is the last of 4 special Shabbatot before Pesaḥ. It falls on the Shabbat before Nisan begins, unless Nisan begins on Shabbat, as it does this year. In that case, Shabbat Haḥodesh coincides with Rosh Ḥodesh.

The special *maftir aliyah* reading for Shabbat Haḥodesh (Shemot 12:1–20) describes the night of the 1st Pesaḥ. Notable features include eating the Pesaḥ lamb sacrifice with unleavened bread and bitter herbs, and painting the blood of the sacrificed lamb on the doorposts of Israelite houses. The passage, containing both the story and various laws of Pesaḥ, connects us to our ancient past and prods us to accelerate preparations for Pesaḥ, which is only a few weeks away.

**DURING Rosh Ḥodesh**

Birkat Hamazon:

+ יַעֲלֶה וְיָבוֹא Ya'aleh veyavo for Rosh Ḥodesh L90|95 S340|347 W233|239 F762|780

+ הָרַחֲמָן Haraḥaman for Rosh Ḥodesh L92|96 S343|348 W235|240 F768

**עַרְבִית**

Shabbat Amidah:

+ יַעֲלֶה וְיָבוֹא Ya'aleh veyavo for Rosh Ḥodesh L50 S36 F298

**Sat 6 Apr** **שַׁחֲרִית**

Before מִזְמוֹר שִׁיר Mizmor shir (Psalm 30) L120 S81 F50
or after Aleynu, recite:

Psalm for Shabbat (Psalm 92) L112 S72 F32
קַדִּישׁ יָתוֹם Mourner's Kaddish (some omit) L121 S82 F52
+ Psalm 104 for Rosh Ḥodesh L114 S78 F34
קַדִּישׁ יָתוֹם Mourner's Kaddish L121 S82 F52

Shabbat Amidah:

+ יַעֲלֶה וְיָבוֹא Ya'aleh veyavo for Rosh Ḥodesh L163 S118 F360

+ חֲצִי הַלֵּל Short Hallel L316 S133 F380

קַדִּישׁ שָׁלֵם Full Kaddish L167 S138 F392

**TORAH SERVICE** L168 S139 F394

☞ Remove **3** Torah scrolls from ark.

| Nisan 5779 | | | | | | |
| --- | --- | --- | --- | --- | --- | --- |
| | | | | | | 1 |
| 2 | 3 | 4 | 5 | 6 | 7 | 8 |
| 9 | 10 | 11 | 12 | 13 | 14 | 15 |
| 16 | 17 | 18 | 19 | 20 | 21 | 22 |
| 23 | 24 | 25 | 26 | 27 | 28 | 29 |
| 30 | | | | | | |

| Apr \| May 2019 | | | | | | |
| --- | --- | --- | --- | --- | --- | --- |
| | | | | | | 6 |
| 7 | 8 | 9 | 10 | 11 | 12 | 13 |
| 14 | 15 | 16 | 17 | 18 | 19 | 20 |
| 21 | 22 | 23 | 24 | 25 | 26 | 27 |
| 28 | 29 | 30 \| 1 | 2 | 3 | 4 | |
| 5 | | | | | | |

+ Add ✕ Omit ☞ Take note!

**Siddurim**
- **L** Lev Shalem for Shabbat and Festivals
- **S** Shabbat and Festival Sim Shalom
- **W** Weekday Sim Shalom
- **F** Full Sim Shalom (both editions)
- **P** Personal Edition of Full Sim Shalom

**1st scroll** 6 aliyot (minimum): תַּזְרִיעַ Tazria
וַיִּקְרָא Vayikra (Leviticus) 12:1–13:59

Annual: [1]12:1–13:5 [2]13:6–17 [3]13:18–23 [4]13:24–28 [5]13:29–39 [6]13:40–59

Triennial: [1]12:1–4 [2]12:5–8 [3]13:1–5 [4]13:6–8 [5]13:9–17 [6]13:18–28

Place 2nd scroll on table next to 1st scroll.
Open, raise, display, and wrap 1st scroll.

+ **2nd scroll** 7th aliyah from פִּינְחָס Pineḥas
[7]בְּמִדְבַּר Bemidbar (Numbers) 28:9–15

Place 3rd scroll on table next to 2nd scroll.
Place or hold 1st scroll near other scrolls at table.
(Some do not return the 1st scroll to table.)

חֲצִי קַדִּישׁ Short Kaddish L174 S146 F408
Open, raise, display, and wrap 2nd scroll.

+ **3rd scroll** Maftir aliyah for Shabbat Haḥodesh
[M]שְׁמוֹת Shemot (Exodus 12:1–20)

Open, raise, display, and wrap 3rd scroll.

☞ **Haftarah** for Shabbat Haḥodesh
Ashkenazic: יְחֶזְקֵאל Yeḥezkel (Ezekiel) 45:16–46:18
Sephardic: יְחֶזְקֵאל Yeḥezkel (Ezekiel) 45:18–46:15

☞ Most Ashkenazic congregations do **not** add verses from the Shabbat Rosh Ḥodesh haftarah. Sephardic congregations add the first and last verses at the end.

✕ ~~אַב הָרַחֲמִים Av Haraḥamim~~

אַשְׁרֵי Ashrey L181 S151 F420
Return scrolls to ark. L183 S153 F422

חֲצִי קַדִּישׁ Short Kaddish L184 S155 F428

מוּסָף **Rosh Ḥodesh Amidah for Shabbat:** L193 S166 F486
Shabbat קְדֻשָּׁה Kedushah L195 S167 F490
Continuation of Amidah L196 S168 F496
✕ ~~וּלְכַפָּרַת פָּשַׁע Ulkhapparat pasha~~
Beginning with Rosh Ḥodesh Nisan, we do not add these words.

קַדִּישׁ שָׁלֵם Full Kaddish L203 S181 F506
אֵין כֵּא·לֹהֵינוּ Eyn keloheynu L204 S182 F507
עָלֵינוּ Aleynu L205 S183 F508

**If psalms for the day were not recited at Shaharit, add here:**

קַדִּישׁ יָתוֹם Mourner's Kaddish (some omit) L207 S184 F512
Psalm for Shabbat (Psalm 92) L112 S72 F32
קַדִּישׁ יָתוֹם Mourner's Kaddish (some omit) L121 S82 F52
+ Psalm 104 for Rosh Hodesh L114 S78 F34
קַדִּישׁ יָתוֹם Mourner's Kaddish L207|121 S184|82 F512|52

מִנְחָה

**Torah** 3 aliyot from מְצֹרָע Metsora
וַיִּקְרָא Vayikra (Leviticus) 14:1–12
¹14:1–5 ²6–9 ³10–12 W291 P911

This is also the reading for the coming Monday and Thursday.

**Shabbat Amidah:**
+ יַעֲלֶה וְיָבוֹא Ya'aleh veyavo for Rosh Hodesh L227 S237 F580
✕ ~~צִדְקָתְךָ צֶדֶק Tsidkatekha tsedek~~

---

## Nisan 8 נִיסָן
**Sat 13 Apr (morning)**

## שַׁבָּת Shabbat פָּרָשַׁת מְצֹרָע Parashat Metsora
## שַׁבָּת הַגָּדוֹל Shabbat Hagadol

**Shabbat Hagadol** is the name of the Shabbat preceding Pesah. Some rabbis explain that this Shabbat takes its name from the end of the special haftarah for this day (Mal'akhi 3:23): "I will send the prophet Eliyahu to you before the coming of *the great* [הַגָּדוֹל], fearful day of the Lord." This is a foreshadowing of the role Eliyahu plays at the Pesah seder as a harbinger of the coming of the messianic age. A number of alternative explanations for the name are offered by other rabbis.

We do not add a special Torah reading for Shabbat Hagadol.

**Torah** 7 aliyot (minimum): מְצֹרָע Metsora
וַיִּקְרָא Vayikra (Leviticus) 14:1–15:33

| | | | | |
|---|---|---|---|---|
| Annual: | ¹14:1–12 | ²14:13–20 | ³14:21–32 | ⁴14:33–53 |
| | ⁵14:54–15:15 | ⁶15:16–28 | ⁷15:29–33 | ᴹ15:31–33 |
| Triennial: | ¹14:33–38 | ²14:39–47 | ³14:48–53 | ⁴14:54–15:7 |
| | ⁵15:8–15 | ⁶15:16–28 | ⁷15:29–33 | ᴹ15:31–33 |

☞ **Haftarah** for Shabbat Hagadol
מַלְאָכִי Mal'akhi (Malachi) 3:4–24°

☞ °After 3:24, repeat 3:23 so that the haftarah ends on a positive note.

✕ ~~אַב הָרַחֲמִים Av Harahamim~~

מִנְחָה

**Torah** 3 aliyot from אַחֲרֵי מוֹת Aḥarey mot
וַיִּקְרָא Vayikra (Leviticus) 16:1–17
¹16:1–6 ²7–11 ³12–17 W292 P912

This is also the reading for the coming Monday and Thursday.

✕ ~~צִדְקָתְךָ צֶדֶק Tsidkatekha tsedek~~

---

**Nisan 9 נִיסָן**
**Sat 13 Apr**

## מוֹצָאֵי שַׁבָּת Motsa'ey Shabbat Conclusion of Shabbat

עַרְבִית

Saturday night Arvit as usual through the Amidah L264 S281 W137 F200

☞ חֲצִי קַדִּישׁ Short Kaddish L269 S292 W158 F682

☞ וִיהִי נֹעַם Vihi no'am L279 S292 W158 F684
יוֹשֵׁב בְּסֵתֶר עֶלְיוֹן Yoshev beseter elyon L279 S292 W158 F684
וְאַתָּה קָדוֹשׁ Ve'attah kadosh L216 S293 W159 F684

קַדִּישׁ שָׁלֵם Full Kaddish L280 S294 W160 F688

Conclude as on a usual Saturday night.

---

**Nisan 14 נִיסָן**
**Thu 18 Apr** (evening)

## עֶרֶב פֶּסַח Erev Pesaḥ Day before Pesaḥ
## בְּדִיקַת חָמֵץ Bedikat Ḥamets The Search for Ḥamets

## Pesaḥ

### In Preparation

**Searching for Ḥamets**

The search is performed the evening before Pesaḥ by the light of a candle (traditionally) or a flashlight. Before the search begins, most people distribute token pieces of bread around the home so that the search is successful. (Some wrap the pieces of bread to prevent inadvertent spilling of crumbs.) Brush any חָמֵץ *ḥamets* found into a wooden spoon using a feather. (Alternately, collect any wrapped חָמֵץ.)

The associated בְּרָכָה *berakhah* and nullification formula appear at the beginning of the הַגָּדָה *haggadah*.

1. Recite the בְּרָכָה.
2. Search darkened rooms of the home by the light of a candle or flashlight.
3. Collect all token pieces of bread and any חָמֵץ not designated for sale or for consumption in the morning.
4. Recite the first formula for nullification of חָמֵץ in a language you understand.
5. Set aside the חָמֵץ you found until morning.

|   |   |   |
|---|---|---|
| ✚ Add  ✘ Omit  ☞ Take note! | **Nisan 5779** | Apr \| May 2019 | נִיסָן 14 **Apr 19** |

|   |   |
|---|---|
| | Siddurim |
| L | Lev Shalem for Shabbat and Festivals |
| S | Shabbat and Festival Sim Shalom |
| W | Weekday Sim Shalom |
| F | Full Sim Shalom (both editions) |
| P | Personal Edition of Full Sim Shalom |

| | | | | | | | | | | | | | |
|---|---|---|---|---|---|---|---|---|---|---|---|---|---|
|   |   |   |   |   | 1 |   |   |   |   |   |   | 6 |   |
| 2 | 3 | 4 | 5 | 6 | 7 | 8 | 7 | 8 | 9 | 10 | 11 | 12 | 13 |
| 9 | 10 | 11 | 12 | 13 | 14 | 15 | 14 | 15 | 16 | 17 | 18 | 19 | 20 |
| 16 | 17 | 18 | 19 | 20 | 21 | 22 | 21 | 22 | 23 | 24 | 25 | 26 | 27 |
| 23 | 24 | 25 | 26 | 27 | 28 | 29 | 28 | 29 | 30 | 1 | 2 | 3 | 4 |
| 30 |   |   |   |   |   |   | 5 |   |   |   |   |   |   |

**Fri 19 Apr** (morning)  בְּעוּר חָמֵץ  **Bi'ur Ḥamets**   Destruction of the Ḥamets

### Disposing of Ḥamets

We are allowed to possess חָמֵץ *hamets* only during the early part of the daylight hours. Consult your rabbi for the exact time limit in your community. At or before that time, any remaining חָמֵץ in your possession must be destroyed. The associated nullification formula appears at the beginning of the הַגָּדָה *haggadah*.

1. Do not recite a בְּרָכָה *berakhah*.
2. Destroy the remaining חָמֵץ, including the חָמֵץ found during the search the previous night. Traditionally, this is accomplished by burning. Other methods are also acceptable (e.g., flushing it down the toilet, crumbling and scattering it to the wind, disposing of it in a *public* waste receptacle).
3. Immediately afterward, recite the second formula for the nullification of חָמֵץ in a language you understand.

**Fri 19 Apr** (morning)  תַּעֲנִית בְּכוֹרִים  **Taʿanit Bekhorim**
Fast of the Firstborn (individual fast, begins at dawn)

### Fast of the Firstborn

A firstborn male of a mother or a father observes this daytime fast on the eve of Pesaḥ, recognizing that in Egypt the firstborn of Israel were saved, while the firstborn Egyptians died in the 10th plague.

If the firstborn male is a minor, the father fasts in his place. However, if the father is also a firstborn, the mother fasts in the child's place.

Fast of the Firstborn is an *individual* fast. Unlike a *communal* fast, it does not introduce liturgical changes or a special Torah reading.

### Siyyum and Seʿudat Mitsvah

If possible, hold a סִיּוּם *siyyum* (completion of study of a tractate of rabbinic literature) to exempt those attending from the obligation to fast.

1. Conduct the סִיּוּם after Shaḥarit.
2. Conclude the סִיּוּם with the special prayers and expanded קַדִּישׁ דְּרַבָּנָן *kaddish derabbanan* for this occasion. Texts can be found at the end of a tractate in many editions of the Talmud and in the *Moreh Derekh* rabbi's manual.
3. Hold a סְעוּדַת מִצְוָה *seʿudat mitsvah* (festive meal celebrating the performance of a *mitsvah*, in this case, the סִיּוּם).

As participants in the סִיּוּם, all firstborns present are permitted to eat at the festive meal and during the rest of the day as well.

פֶּסַח Pesaḥ

| Nisan 5779 | | | | | | | Apr \| May 2019 | | | | | | |
|---|---|---|---|---|---|---|---|---|---|---|---|---|---|
| | | | | | | 1 | | | | | | | 6 |
| 2 | 3 | 4 | 5 | 6 | 7 | 8 | 7 | 8 | 9 | 10 | 11 | 12 | 13 |
| 9 | 10 | 11 | 12 | 13 | 14 | 15 | 14 | 15 | 16 | 17 | 18 | 19 | 20 |
| 16 | 17 | 18 | 19 | 20 | 21 | 22 | 21 | 22 | 23 | 24 | 25 | 26 | 27 |
| 23 | 24 | 25 | 26 | 27 | 28 | 29 | 28 | 29 | 30 \| 1 | 2 | 3 | 4 | |
| 30 | | | | | | | 5 | | | | | | |

+ Add ✕ Omit ☞ Take note!

**Siddurim**
- **L** Lev Shalem for Shabbat and Festivals
- **S** Shabbat and Festival Sim Shalom
- **W** Weekday Sim Shalom
- **F** Full Sim Shalom (both editions)
- **P** Personal Edition of Full Sim Shalom

**שַׁחֲרִית** Shaḥarit as on a usual weekday W1 F2

✕ ~~מִזְמוֹר לְתוֹדָה Mizmor letodah (Psalm 100)~~

✕ ~~לַמְנַצֵּחַ Lamenatse·aḥ (Psalm 20)~~

+ סִיּוּם Siyyum after Shaḥarit (see blue box, above)

+ סְעוּדַת מִצְוָה Se'udat mitsvah (see blue box, above)

**Fri 19 Apr** (afternoon)

### Preparing a Flame for Yom Tov

On Yom Tov, kindling a *new* fire is not permitted; however, the use of an *existing* fire for cooking or other purposes is permitted.

To light candles for Day 2 of Yom Tov (Saturday night), ensure that you have a fire burning before candle-lighting time for Shabbat that will continue to burn until after dark on Saturday. For example:

- A burning candle that lasts for more than 25 hours
- A pilot light on a gas range (*not* a gas range with an electronic starter)

## Pesaḥ — Days 1 and 2

### Candle Lighting for Shabbat and Yom Tov — Day 1

1. Before lighting candles, prepare a flame. See above.
2. Light the candles at least 18 minutes before sunset.
3. Recite 2 בְּרָכוֹת *berakhot*: L79 S303 F718

בָּרוּךְ אַתָּה יי, אֱ־לֹהֵינוּ מֶלֶךְ הָעוֹלָם, אֲשֶׁר קִדְּשָׁנוּ בְּמִצְוֹתָיו
וְצִוָּנוּ לְהַדְלִיק נֵר שֶׁל שַׁבָּת וְשֶׁל יוֹם טוֹב.

Barukh attah adonay, eloheynu melekh ha'olam, asher kiddeshanu bemitsvotav vetsivvanu lehadlik ner shel shabbat veshel yom tov.

בָּרוּךְ אַתָּה יי, אֱ־לֹהֵינוּ מֶלֶךְ הָעוֹלָם, שֶׁהֶחֱיָנוּ וְקִיְּמָנוּ וְהִגִּיעָנוּ לַזְּמַן הַזֶּה.

Barukh attah adonay, eloheynu melekh ha'olam,
sheheḥeyanu vekiyyemanu vehiggi'anu lazeman hazeh.

### Candle Lighting for Yom Tov — Day 2

See instructions in the blue box, p. 133.

### Shabbat and Yom Tov Meals — Day 1 and Day 2

Each evening the Pesaḥ סֵדֶר *seder* tantalizes all 5 of our senses as we celebrate, relive, enjoy, and learn from the events and teachings found in the *haggadah*. In addition to these meals, the afternoon meal each day is also a festive occasion, celebrated in the manner of Shabbat meals with:

- Yom Tov daytime קִדּוּשׁ *kiddush* (Day 1: with Shabbat additions) L81 S335 F746
- הַמּוֹצִיא *hamotsi* recited over 2 whole מַצּוֹת *matsot* L81 S313–14 F746
- בִּרְכַּת הַמָּזוֹן *birkat hamazon* with Pesaḥ additions (Day 1: with Shabbat additions as well); see yellow box, p. 129
- Festive singing

פֶּסַח Pesaḥ

\+ Add ✕ Omit ☞ Take note!

**Siddurim**
- **L** Lev Shalem for Shabbat and Festivals
- **S** Shabbat and Festival Sim Shalom
- **W** Weekday Sim Shalom
- **F** Full Sim Shalom (both editions)
- **P** Personal Edition of Full Sim Shalom

| Nisan 5779 | | | | | | | Apr \| May 2019 | | | | | | |
|---|---|---|---|---|---|---|---|---|---|---|---|---|---|
| | | | | | | 1 | | | | | | | 6 |
| 2 | 3 | 4 | 5 | 6 | 7 | 8 | 7 | 8 | 9 | 10 | 11 | 12 | 13 |
| 9 | 10 | 11 | 12 | 13 | 14 | 15 | 14 | 15 | 16 | 17 | 18 | 19 | 20 |
| 16 | 17 | 18 | 19 | 20 | 21 | 22 | 21 | 22 | 23 | 24 | 25 | 26 | 27 |
| 23 | 24 | 25 | 26 | 27 | 28 | 29 | 28 | 29 | 30 \| 1 | 2 | 3 | 4 | |
| 30 | | | | | | | 5 | | | | | | |

**DURING Pesaḥ** — **Birkat Hamazon:**

All days + יַעֲלֶה וְיָבוֹא Ya'aleh veyavo for Pesaḥ L90|95 S340|347 W233|239 F762|780

Days 1, 2, 7, and 8 + הָרַחֲמָן Haraḥaman for Yom Tov L92|96 S343|348 W236|240 F768

**Every Shaḥarit, Minḥah, and Arvit Amidah:**

All days + יַעֲלֶה וְיָבוֹא Ya'aleh veyavo for Pesaḥ

## Nisan 15 נִיסָן — שַׁבָּת Shabbat פֶּסַח Pesaḥ — Day 1

Fri 19 Apr (evening)

**קַבָּלַת שַׁבָּת**

✕ ~~Kabbalat Shabbat~~
through
✕ ~~לְכָה דוֹדִי Lekhah dodi~~

Begin with מִזְמוֹר שִׁיר לְיוֹם הַשַּׁבָּת Mizmor shir leyom hashabbat (Psalm 92). L27 S23 F266

**עַרְבִית**

Arvit for Yom Tov L39 S28 F279

\+ וְשָׁמְרוּ Veshameru L46 S34 F294
\+ וַיְדַבֵּר מֹשֶׁה Vaydabber mosheh (Vayikra 23:44) L46 S34 F294

חֲצִי קַדִּישׁ Short Kaddish L46 S34 F294

**Yom Tov Amidah:** L306 S41 F304
\+ מַשִּׁיב הָרוּחַ Mashiv haruaḥ L307 S41 F304
\+ Additions for Shabbat
\+ Insertions for Pesaḥ

\+ וַיְכֻלּוּ Vaykhullu L53 S47 F314

✕ ~~בָּרוּךְ אַתָּה . . . וָאָרֶץ Barukh attah . . . va'arets~~
✕ ~~מָגֵן אָבוֹת . . . בְּרֵאשִׁית Magen avot . . . bereshit~~
✕ ~~אֱלֹהֵינוּ . . . הַשַּׁבָּת Eloheynu . . . hashabbat~~

Some congregations add
הַלֵּל שָׁלֵם Full Hallel with בְּרָכוֹת berakhot. L316 S133 F380

Some congregations add selections from
הַלֵּל שָׁלֵם without בְּרָכוֹת. L316 S133 F380

קַדִּישׁ שָׁלֵם Full Kaddish L54 S48 F316

✕ ~~קִדּוּשׁ Kiddush~~

עָלֵינוּ Aleynu L56 S51 F320
קַדִּישׁ יָתוֹם Mourner's Kaddish L58 S52 F324

Nisan 5779

| | | | | | | |
|---|---|---|---|---|---|---|
| | | | | | | 1 |
| 2 | 3 | 4 | 5 | 6 | 7 | 8 |
| 9 | 10 | 11 | 12 | 13 | 14 | 15 |
| 16 | 17 | 18 | 19 | 20 | 21 | 22 |
| 23 | 24 | 25 | 26 | 27 | 28 | 29 |
| 30 | | | | | | |

Apr | May 2019

| | | | | | | |
|---|---|---|---|---|---|---|
| | | | | | | 6 |
| 7 | 8 | 9 | 10 | 11 | 12 | 13 |
| 14 | 15 | 16 | 17 | 18 | 19 | 20 |
| 21 | 22 | 23 | 24 | 25 | 26 | 27 |
| 28 | 29 | 30 \| 1 | 2 | 3 | 4 | |
| 5 | | | | | | |

+ Add ✕ Omit ☞ Take note!

**Siddurim**
- **L** Lev Shalem for Shabbat and Festivals
- **S** Shabbat and Festival Sim Shalom
- **W** Weekday Sim Shalom
- **F** Full Sim Shalom (both editions)
- **P** Personal Edition of Full Sim Shalom

**At home** + **1st Seder**
Follow the procedures in the haggadah.

**Sat 20 Apr** שַׁחֲרִית

At the end of the preliminary service,
begin formal chanting at
הָאֵ·ל בְּתַעֲצוּמוֹת עֻזֶּךָ Ha'el beta'atsumot uzzekha. L147 S105 F336
+ הַכֹּל יוֹדוּךָ Hakol yodukha L150 S107 F340
+ אֵ·ל אָדוֹן El adon L151 S108 F342
+ לָאֵ·ל אֲשֶׁר שָׁבַת La'el asher shavat L152 S109 F342
✕ ~~הַמֵּאִיר לָאָרֶץ Hame'ir la'arets~~

Immediately preceding בָּרוּךְ אַתָּה יי גָּאַל יִשְׂרָאֵל L158 S114
some congregations add
בְּרַח דּוֹדִי עַד שֶׁתֶּחְפָּץ Beraḥ dodi ad shetehpats. L409 S221

**Yom Tov Amidah:** L306 S123 F366
+ מַשִּׁיב הָרוּחַ Mashiv haruaḥ L307 S123 F366
+ Additions for Shabbat
+ Insertions for Pesaḥ

+ הַלֵּל שָׁלֵם Full Hallel L316 S133 F380
קַדִּישׁ שָׁלֵם Full Kaddish L321 S138 F392

**SHABBAT TORAH SERVICE** L322 S139 F394
✕ ~~יי יי אֵ·ל רַחוּם וְחַנּוּן Adonay adonay el raḥum veḥannun~~
✕ ~~רִבּוֹנוֹ שֶׁל עוֹלָם Ribbono shel olam~~
✕ ~~וַאֲנִי תְפִלָּתִי לְךָ Va'ani tefillati lekha~~
Remove **2** Torah scrolls from ark.

**1st scroll** 7 aliyot from בֹּא Bo
שְׁמוֹת Shemot (Exodus) 12:21–51
1 12:21–24 2 25–28 3 29–32 4 33–36 5 37–42 6 43–47 7 48–51

Place 2nd scroll on table next to 1st scroll.
חֲצִי קַדִּישׁ Short Kaddish L327 S146 F408
Open, raise, display, and wrap 1st scroll.

**2nd scroll** Maftir aliyah from פִּינְחָס Pineḥas
M בְּמִדְבַּר Bemidbar (Numbers) 28:16–25

Open, raise, display, and wrap 2nd scroll.

פסח Pesaḥ

**Haftarah** for Pesaḥ — Day 1
Ashkenazic: יְהוֹשֻׁעַ Yehoshua (Joshua) 3:5–7, 5:2–6:1, 6:27
(alternate tradition, 5:2–6:1)
Sephardic: יְהוֹשֻׁעַ Yehoshua (Joshua) 5:2–6:1, 6:27

**Haftarah blessings:**

✕ ~~Concluding Shabbat בְּרָכָה berakhah~~
+ Concluding Yom Tov בְּרָכָה berakhah with insertions for Shabbat and Pesaḥ L329 S147 F412

יְקוּם פֻּרְקָן Yekum purkan L176 S148 F412
✕ ~~אַב הָרַחֲמִים Av Haraḥamim~~

אַשְׁרֵי Ashrey L339 S151 F420
Return scrolls to ark. L340 S153 F422

☞ שְׁלִיחַ/שְׁלִיחַת צִבּוּר sheliaḥ/sheliḥat tsibbur customarily wears a *kittel* (plain white robe) for Musaf.

☞ חֲצִי קַדִּישׁ Short Kaddish L342 S155 F428
The distinctive traditional melody of this Kaddish anticipates the opening melody of the repetition of the Amidah.

**Morid Hatal**
For congregations that follow the tradition of Erets Yisra'el to add מוֹרִיד הַטָּל *morid hatal,* announce before the silent Amidah:
"In the silent Amidah:
Replace מַשִּׁיב הָרוּחַ וּמוֹרִיד הַגָּשֶׁם *mashiv haruaḥ umorid hagashem*
with מוֹרִיד הַטָּל *morid hatal.*"

מוּסָף

**Silent Yom Tov Amidah:** L343 S166 F456
☞ מַשִּׁיב הָרוּחַ Mashiv haruaḥ L344 S166 F456
(For congregations that add מוֹרִיד הַטָּל Morid hatal, see the blue box, above.)
+ Additions for Shabbat
+ Insertions for Pesaḥ

Open ark.
**Repetition of the Yom Tov Amidah:** L374 S217 F478
+ תְּפִלַּת טַל Tefillat tal L375 S219 F478
Close ark.
Continue with מְכַלְכֵּל חַיִּים Mekhalkel ḥayyim L344 S166 F456
+ Additions for Shabbat
+ Insertions for Pesaḥ

Apr 20   15 נִיסָן

| | Nisan 5779 | | | Apr \| May 2019 | | | + Add    ✕ Omit    ☞ Take note! |
|---|---|---|---|---|---|---|---|
| | | | 1 | | | 6 | **Siddurim** |
| 2 | 3 | 4 | 5 | 6 | 7 | 8 | 7 8 9 10 11 12 13   **L** Lev Shalem for Shabbat and Festivals |
| 9 | 10 | 11 | 12 | 13 | 14 | 15 | 14 15 16 17 18 19 20   **S** Shabbat and Festival Sim Shalom |
| 16 | 17 | 18 | 19 | 20 | 21 | 22 | 21 22 23 24 25 26 27   **W** Weekday Sim Shalom |
| 23 | 24 | 25 | 26 | 27 | 28 | 29 | 28 29 30 \| 1 2 3 4   **F** Full Sim Shalom (both editions) |
| 30 | | | | | | | 5   **P** Personal Edition of Full Sim Shalom |

Some congregations include in the repetition of the Amidah the Priestly Blessing by the Koh<sup>a</sup>nim (*dukhenen*). בִּרְכַּת כֹּהֲנִים Birkat koh<sup>a</sup>nim   **L**353 **S**177 **F**472 (Some of these congregations omit it on Shabbat.) For procedures, see p. 213.

קַדִּישׁ שָׁלֵם Full Kaddish   **L**203 **S**181 **F**506
Continue with אֵין כֵּא־לֹהֵינוּ Eyn keloheynu.   **L**204 **S**182 **F**508

קִדּוּשָׁא רַבָּא    **Daytime Kiddush for Shabbat and Yom Tov:**   **L**81 **S**335 **F**746
וְשָׁמְרוּ V<sup>e</sup>shameru
זָכוֹר Zakhor (many omit)
עַל־כֵּן בֵּרַךְ Al ken berakh
+ וַיְדַבֵּר מֹשֶׁה Vaydabber mosheh (Vayikra 23:44)
בּוֹרֵא פְּרִי הַגָּפֶן Bo·re p<sup>e</sup>ri hagafen

**UNTIL Sh<sup>e</sup>mini Atseret**    **Every Amidah:**
✕ מַשִּׁיב הָרוּחַ וּמוֹרִיד הַגָּשֶׁם ~~Mashiv haruaḥ umorid hagashem~~

מִנְחָה    אַשְׁרֵי Ashrey   **L**214 **S**226 **W**170 **F**558
וּבָא לְצִיּוֹן Uva l<sup>e</sup>tsiyyon   **L**216 **S**227 **W**171 **F**560
חֲצִי קַדִּישׁ Short Kaddish   **L**217 **S**229 **W**173 **F**564

**Torah** 3 aliyot from אַחֲרֵי מוֹת Aḥarey mot
וַיִּקְרָא Vayikra (Leviticus) 16:1–17
¹16:1–6   ²7–11   ³12–17       **W**292 **P**912

☞ These verses are not read publicly again until next Shabbat.

**Yom Tov Amidah:**   **L**306 **S**242 **W**184 **F**586
✕ מַשִּׁיב הָרוּחַ וּמוֹרִיד הַגָּשֶׁם ~~Mashiv haruaḥ umorid hagashem~~
+ Additions for Shabbat
+ Insertions for Pesaḥ

✕ צִדְקָתְךָ צֶדֶק ~~Tsidkat<sup>e</sup>kha tsedek~~

קַדִּישׁ שָׁלֵם Full Kaddish   **L**230 **S**247 **W**189 **F**596
עָלֵינוּ Aleynu   **L**231 **S**248 **W**190 **F**598
קַדִּישׁ יָתוֹם Mourner's Kaddish   **L**232 **S**249 **W**191 **F**600

**Candle Lighting for Yom Tov after Shabbat**

Shabbat (Day 1 of Pesaḥ) ends after dark: when 3 stars appear, or at least 25 minutes after sunset (at least 43 minutes after the time set for lighting candles on Day 1). Some wait longer. For the appropriate time in your community, consult your rabbi.

1. Wait until Shabbat ends.
2. Do not *strike* a match. Instead, transfer fire to the candles from an *existing* flame (see p. 128) by inserting a match or other stick into the flame.
3. Do not *extinguish* the match or stick. Instead, place it on a non-flammable tray or dish, and let it self-extinguish. Alternately, a wood *safety* match held vertically (flame up) usually self-extinguishes quickly.
4. Recite 2 בְּרָכוֹת *berakhot*: L79 S303 F718

בָּרוּךְ אַתָּה יי, אֱ·לֹהֵינוּ מֶלֶךְ הָעוֹלָם, אֲשֶׁר קִדְּשָׁנוּ בְּמִצְוֹתָיו
וְצִוָּנוּ לְהַדְלִיק נֵר שֶׁל יוֹם טוֹב.

Barukh attah adonay, eloheynu melekh ha'olam, asher kiddeshanu bemitsvotav vetsivvanu lehadlik ner shel yom tov.

בָּרוּךְ אַתָּה יי, אֱ·לֹהֵינוּ מֶלֶךְ הָעוֹלָם, שֶׁהֶחֱיָנוּ וְקִיְּמָנוּ וְהִגִּיעָנוּ לַזְּמַן הַזֶּה.

Barukh attah adonay, eloheynu melekh ha'olam,
sheheḥeyanu vekiyyemanu vehiggi'anu lazeman hazeh.

## Nisan 16 נִיסָן — פֶּסַח Pesaḥ — Day 2

Sat 20 Apr

עַרְבִית

Arvit for Yom Tov L39 S28 F279

+ וַיְדַבֵּר מֹשֶׁה Vaydabber mosheh (Vayikra 23:44) L46 S34 F294

חֲצִי קַדִּישׁ Short Kaddish L46 S34 F294

**Yom Tov Amidah:** L306 S41 F304

+ וַתּוֹדִיעֵנוּ Vatodi'eynu S41 F306

+ Insertions for Pesaḥ

Some congregations add
הַלֵּל שָׁלֵם Full Hallel with בְּרָכוֹת berakhot. L316 S133 F380

Some congregations add selections from
הַלֵּל שָׁלֵם without בְּרָכוֹת. L316 S133 F380

קַדִּישׁ שָׁלֵם Full Kaddish L54 S48 F316

✕ ~~קִדּוּשׁ Kiddush~~

☞ Some count Omer at the seder. Others count here. L63 S55 F237
Day **1** (see instructions, p. 212)

| Nisan 5779 | | | | | | | Apr \| May 2019 | | | | | | |
|---|---|---|---|---|---|---|---|---|---|---|---|---|---|
| | | | | | | 1 | | | | | | | 6 |
| 2 | 3 | 4 | 5 | 6 | 7 | 8 | 7 | 8 | 9 | 10 | 11 | 12 | 13 |
| 9 | 10 | 11 | 12 | 13 | 14 | 15 | 14 | 15 | 16 | 17 | 18 | 19 | 20 |
| 16 | 17 | 18 | 19 | 20 | 21 | 22 | 21 | 22 | 23 | 24 | 25 | 26 | 27 |
| 23 | 24 | 25 | 26 | 27 | 28 | 29 | 28 | 29 | 30 \| 1 | 2 | 3 | 4 | |
| 30 | | | | | | | 5 | | | | | | |

+ Add ✕ Omit ☞ Take note!

**Siddurim**
L Lev Shalem for Shabbat and Festivals
S Shabbat and Festival Sim Shalom
W Weekday Sim Shalom
F Full Sim Shalom (both editions)
P Personal Edition of Full Sim Shalom

עָלֵינוּ Aleynu L56 S51 F320
קַדִּישׁ יָתוֹם Mourner's Kaddish L58 S52 F324

**At home** For candle lighting for Day 2, see p. 133.

+ **2nd Seder**
Follow the procedures in the haggadah.
+ Include Havdalah as part of Kiddush, as indicated.

For those who did not count Omer at Arvit, count here.
Day **1** (see instructions, p. 212)

**Sun 21 Apr** **שַׁחֲרִית** At the end of the preliminary service,
begin formal chanting at
הָאֵ·ל בְּתַעֲצוּמוֹת עֻזֶּךָ Ha'el beta'atsumot uzzekha. L147 S105 F336

✕ ~~הַכֹּל יוֹדוּךָ Hakol yodukha~~
✕ ~~אֵ·ל אָדוֹן El adon~~
✕ ~~לָאֵ·ל אֲשֶׁר שָׁבַת La'el asher shavat~~
+ הַמֵּאִיר לָאָרֶץ Hame'ir la'arets L152 S109 F342

Immediately preceding בָּרוּךְ אַתָּה יי גָּאַל יִשְׂרָאֵל L158 S114
some congregations add בְּרַח דּוֹדִי אֶל מָכוֹן לְשִׁבְתָּךְ
Beraḥ dodi el makhon leshivtakh. L409 S221

**Yom Tov Amidah:** L306 S123 F366
+ Insertions for Pesaḥ

+ הַלֵּל שָׁלֵם Full Hallel L316 S133 F380
קַדִּישׁ שָׁלֵם Full Kaddish L321 S138 F392

**YOM TOV TORAH SERVICE** L322 S139 F394
+ יי יי אֵ·ל רַחוּם וְחַנּוּן
Adonay adonay el raḥum veḥannun (3 times) L323 S140 F394
+ רִבּוֹנוֹ שֶׁל עוֹלָם Ribbono shel olam L323 S140 F396
+ וַאֲנִי תְפִלָּתִי לְךָ Va'ani tefillati lekha (3 times) L323 S140 F396

Remove **2** Torah scrolls from ark.

**1st scroll** 5 aliyot from אֱמֹר Emor
וַיִּקְרָא Vayikra (Leviticus) 22:26–23:44
[1]22:26–23:3 [2]23:4–14 [3]15–22 [4]23–32 [5]33–44

Place 2nd scroll on table next to 1st scroll.
חֲצִי קַדִּישׁ Short Kaddish L327 S146 F408
Open, raise, display, and wrap 1st scroll.

פסח Pesaḥ

**2nd scroll** Maftir aliyah from פִּינְחָס Pineḥas
[M]בְּמִדְבַּר Bemidbar (Numbers) 28:16–25

Open, raise, display, and wrap 2nd scroll.

**Haftarah** for Pesaḥ — Day 2
מְלָכִים ב׳ 2 Melakhim (2 Kings) 23:1–9, 21–25

**Haftarah blessings:**

✕ ~~Concluding Shabbat בְּרָכָה berakhah~~
\+ Concluding Yom Tov בְּרָכָה berakhah with insertions for Pesaḥ L329 S147 F412

✕ ~~יְקוּם פֻּרְקָן Yekum purkan~~
✕ ~~אַב הָרַחֲמִים Av Haraḥamim~~

אַשְׁרֵי Ashrey L339 S151 F420
Return scrolls to ark. L340 S153 F422
חֲצִי קַדִּישׁ Short Kaddish L342 S155 F428

מוּסָף

**Yom Tov Amidah:** L343 S166 F456
\+ Insertions for Pesaḥ

Some congregations include in the repetition of the Amidah the Priestly Blessing by the Kohanim (*dukhenen*).
בִּרְכַּת כֹּהֲנִים Birkat kohanim L353 S177 F472
For procedures, see p. 213.

קַדִּישׁ שָׁלֵם Full Kaddish L203 S181 F506
Continue with אֵין כֵּא·לֹהֵינוּ Eyn keloheynu. L204 S182 F508

קִדּוּשָׁא רַבָּא

**Daytime Kiddush for Yom Tov:** L81 S335 F746
וַיְדַבֵּר מֹשֶׁה Vaydabber mosheh (Vayikra 23:44)
בּוֹרֵא פְּרִי הַגָּפֶן Bo·re peri hagafen

מִנְחָה

אַשְׁרֵי Ashrey L214 S226 W170 F558
וּבָא לְצִיּוֹן Uva letsiyyon L216 S227 W171 F560
חֲצִי קַדִּישׁ Short Kaddish L217 S229 W173 F564

**Yom Tov Amidah:** L306 S242 W184 F586
\+ Insertions for Pesaḥ

קַדִּישׁ שָׁלֵם Full Kaddish L230 S247 W189 F596
עָלֵינוּ Aleynu L231 S248 W190 F598
קַדִּישׁ יָתוֹם Mourner's Kaddish L232 S249 W191 F600

| Nisan 5779 | | | | | | | Apr \| May 2019 | | | | | | |
|---|---|---|---|---|---|---|---|---|---|---|---|---|---|
| | | | | | | 1 | | | | | | | 6 |
| 2 | 3 | 4 | 5 | 6 | 7 | 8 | 7 | 8 | 9 | 10 | 11 | 12 | 13 |
| 9 | 10 | 11 | 12 | 13 | 14 | 15 | 14 | 15 | 16 | 17 | 18 | 19 | 20 |
| 16 | 17 | 18 | 19 | 20 | 21 | 22 | 21 | 22 | 23 | 24 | 25 | 26 | 27 |
| 23 | 24 | 25 | 26 | 27 | 28 | 29 | 28 | 29 | 30 \| 1 | 2 | 3 | 4 | |
| 30 | | | | | | | 5 | | | | | | |

+ Add ✕ Omit ☞ Take note!

**Siddurim**
L Lev Shalem for Shabbat and Festivals
S Shabbat and Festival Sim Shalom
W Weekday Sim Shalom
F Full Sim Shalom (both editions)
P Personal Edition of Full Sim Shalom

---

**17 Nisan THROUGH Dec. 4 at מִנְחָה**

**Every weekday Amidah:**
✕ ~~וְתֵן טַל וּמָטָר לִבְרָכָה Veten tal umatar livrakhah~~
+ וְתֵן בְּרָכָה Veten berakhah

עַרְבִית W144 F214
שַׁחֲרִית W39 F112
מִנְחָה W125 F174

---

## Nisan 17 נִיסָן Sun 21 Apr (evening) through Nisan 20 נִיסָן Thu 25 Apr (daytime)

## חֹל הַמּוֹעֵד פֶּסַח Ḥol Hamo'ed Pesaḥ — Weekdays
### Ḥol Hamo'ed (ḤH) — Days 1–4

---

ḤH Day 1 Sun 21 Apr (evening)
ḤH Day 2 Mon 22 Apr (evening)
ḤH Day 3 Tue 23 Apr (evening)
ḤH Day 4 Wed 24 Apr (evening)

עַרְבִית Arvit for weekdays L264 S281 W137 F200

**Weekday Amidah:**

ḤH Day 1 Sun 21 Apr + אַתָּה חוֹנַנְתָּנוּ Attah ḥonantanu L272 S287 W143 F212
All days + יַעֲלֶה וְיָבוֹא Ya'aleh veyavo for Pesaḥ L277 S289 W145 F216

All days קַדִּישׁ שָׁלֵם Full Kaddish L280 S294 W160 F222

+ Count Omer. L63 S55 W152 F237
ḤH Day 1 Sun 21 Apr Day **2** (see instructions, p. 212)
ḤH Day 2 Mon 22 Apr Day **3** (see instructions, p. 212)
ḤH Day 3 Tue 23 Apr Day **4** (see instructions, p. 212)
ḤH Day 4 Wed 24 Apr Day **5** (see instructions, p. 212)

ḤH Day 1 Sun 21 Apr Some recite הַבְדָּלָה Havdalah here. L283 S299 W165 F700
For instructions, see below.

All days עָלֵינוּ Aleynu L281 S297 W163 F696
קַדִּישׁ יָתוֹם Mourner's Kaddish L282 S298 W164 F698

**ḤH Day 1 Sun 21 Apr**

+ **Havdalah:** L283 S299 W165 F700

✕ ~~הִנֵּה אֵ-ל יְשׁוּעָתִי Hinneh el yeshu'ati~~

בּוֹרֵא פְּרִי הַגָּפֶן Bo·re peri hagafen

✕ ~~בּוֹרֵא מִינֵי בְשָׂמִים Bo·re miney vesamim~~

✕ ~~בּוֹרֵא מְאוֹרֵי הָאֵשׁ Bo·re me'orey ha'esh~~

הַמַּבְדִּיל בֵּין קֹדֶשׁ לְחֹל Hamavdil beyn kodesh leḥol

### Tefillin during Ḥol Hamo'ed

Whether or not to wear תְּפִלִּין *tefillin* during Ḥol Hamo'ed is a long-standing controversy. Ashkenazic Jews tend to wear תְּפִלִּין; Sephardic and Hasidic Jews tend not to wear תְּפִלִּין. The practice in Israel is not to wear them. Some who wear תְּפִלִּין do not recite the בְּרָכוֹת *berakhot*.

1. Determine your individual practice according to the following instructions:
   - If there is an established custom in your family, follow it.
   - If there is no established custom in your family, consult your rabbi.
   - Regardless of your custom, when you are in Israel, do not wear תְּפִלִּין.
2. If you wear תְּפִלִּין, remove them just before the beginning of Hallel.

**ḤH Day 1 Mon 22 Apr (morning)**
**ḤH Day 2 Tue 23 Apr (morning)**
**ḤH Day 3 Wed 24 Apr (morning)**
**ḤH Day 4 Thu 25 Apr (morning)**

**שַׁחֲרִית** Shaḥarit for weekdays W1 F2

✕ ~~מִזְמוֹר לְתוֹדָה Mizmor letodah (Psalm 100)~~

**Weekday Amidah:** W36 F106

✕ ~~וְתֵן טַל וּמָטָר לִבְרָכָה Veten tal umatar livrakhah~~

+ וְתֵן בְּרָכָה Veten berakhah W39 F112

+ יַעֲלֶה וְיָבוֹא Ya'aleh veyavo for Pesaḥ W41 F114

✕ ~~תַּחֲנוּן Taḥanun~~

☞ Those wearing תְּפִלִּין tefillin now remove and pack them.

+ חֲצִי הַלֵּל Short Hallel W50 F380

קַדִּישׁ שָׁלֵם Full Kaddish W56 F392

| Nisan 5779 | | | | | | |
|---|---|---|---|---|---|---|
| | | | | | | 1 |
| 2 | 3 | 4 | 5 | 6 | 7 | 8 |
| 9 | 10 | 11 | 12 | 13 | 14 | 15 |
| 16 | 17 | 18 | 19 | 20 | 21 | 22 |
| 23 | 24 | 25 | 26 | 27 | 28 | 29 |
| 30 | | | | | | |

| Apr \| May 2019 | | | | | | |
|---|---|---|---|---|---|---|
| | | | | | | 6 |
| 7 | 8 | 9 | 10 | 11 | 12 | 13 |
| 14 | 15 | 16 | 17 | 18 | 19 | 20 |
| 21 | 22 | 23 | 24 | 25 | 26 | 27 |
| 28 | 29 | 30 \| 1 | 2 | 3 | 4 | |
| 5 | | | | | | |

+ Add ✗ Omit ☞ Take note!

**Siddurim**
- **L** Lev Shalem for Shabbat and Festivals
- **S** Shabbat and Festival Sim Shalom
- **W** Weekday Sim Shalom
- **F** Full Sim Shalom (both editions)
- **P** Personal Edition of Full Sim Shalom

**TORAH SERVICE** W65 F138
Remove **2** Torah scrolls from ark.

**ḤH Day 1 Mon 22 Apr**
**1st scroll** 3 aliyot from בֹּא Bo
שְׁמוֹת Shemot (Exodus) 13:1–16
[1]13:1–4 [2]5–10 [3]11–16 W325 P957

**ḤH Day 2 Tue 23 Apr**
**1st scroll** 3 aliyot from מִּשְׁפָּטִים Mishpatim
שְׁמוֹת Shemot (Exodus) 22:24–23:19
[1]22:24–26 [2]22:27–23:5 [3]23:6–19 W326 P959

**ḤH Day 3 Wed 24 Apr**
**1st scroll** 3 aliyot from כִּי תִשָּׂא Ki tissa
שְׁמוֹת Shemot (Exodus) 34:1–26
[1]34:1–3 [2]4–10 [3]11–26 W328 P961

**ḤH Day 4 Thu 25 Apr**
**1st scroll** 3 aliyot from בְּהַעֲלֹתְךָ Beha'alotekha
בְּמִדְבַּר Bemidbar (Numbers) 9:1–14
[1]9:1–5 [2]6–8 [3]9–14 W329 P964

**All days**
Place 2nd scroll on table next to 1st scroll.
Open, raise, display, and wrap 1st scroll.

+ **2nd scroll** 1 aliyah from פִּינְחָס Pineḥas
[4]בְּמִדְבַּר Bemidbar (Numbers) 28:19–25 W326 F958

Place 1st scroll on table next to 2nd scroll.
חֲצִי קַדִּישׁ Short Kaddish W71 F146
Open, raise, display, and wrap 2nd scroll.

Return scrolls to ark. W76 F150

אַשְׁרֵי Ashrey W78 F152
✗ ~~לַמְנַצֵּחַ Lamenatse·aḥ (Psalm 20)~~
וּבָא לְצִיּוֹן Uva letsiyyon W80 F156

+ חֲצִי קַדִּישׁ Short Kaddish W103 F428

**מוּסָף**
+ **Yom Tov Amidah:** W104+110 F456+462
Weekday קְדֻשָּׁה Kedushah W105 F460
+ Insertions for Pesaḥ
+ וְהִקְרַבְתֶּם Vehikravtem for Ḥol Hamo'ed Pesaḥ W111 F466

+ קַדִּישׁ שָׁלֵם Full Kaddish W82 F158
עָלֵינוּ Aleynu W83 F160
Conclude as on a usual weekday.

מִנְחָה Minḥah for weekdays L289 S1 W120 F164

**Weekday Amidah:**

✕ ~~וְתֵן טַל וּמָטָר לִבְרָכָה Veten tal umatar livrakhah~~

+ וְתֵן בְּרָכָה Veten berakhah L295 S5 W144 F214

+ יַעֲלֶה וְיָבוֹא Ya'aleh veyavo for Pesaḥ L298 S7 W127 F178

✕ ~~תַּחֲנוּן Taḥanun~~

**ḤH Day 4 Thu 25 Apr**

**At home**

Prepare an Eruv Tavshilin. See blue box, below.
Prespare a flame for Yom Tov. See blue box, p. 140.
Light Yom Tov candles. See blue box, p. 140.

## Before Pesaḥ — Day 7

### Preparing an Eruv Tavshilin

On any Yom Tov that falls on a weekday, cooking is permitted, but only to prepare food for that particular day. On Shabbat it is forbidden to cook.

Therefore, preparing food for a Shabbat that follows a Friday Yom Tov presents a difficulty. To allow cooking on a Friday Yom Tov for the following Shabbat, perform the ritual of עֵרוּב תַּבְשִׁילִין *eruv tavshilin*, the combining (עֵרוּב *eruv*) of the cooking for Yom Tov and Shabbat.

Start the Shabbat cooking Thursday afternoon, following this procedure:

1. Before Yom Tov begins, take two prepared foods, customarily a baked food (e.g., מַצָּה *matsah*) and a cooked food (e.g., a hard-cooked egg or a piece of cooked chicken or fish).
2. Recite the בְּרָכָה *berakhah*: L78 S306 F716

   בָּרוּךְ אַתָּה יי, אֱ·לֹהֵינוּ מֶלֶךְ הָעוֹלָם, אֲשֶׁר קִדְּשָׁנוּ בְּמִצְוֹתָיו
   וְצִוָּנוּ עַל מִצְוַת עֵרוּב.

   Barukh attah adonay, eloheynu melekh ha'olam,
   asher kiddeshanu bemitsvotav vetsivvanu al mitsvat eruv.
3. In a language you understand, recite a declaration that cooking for Shabbat was begun before—and will be completed on—Yom Tov. L78 S306 F716

   בְּעֵרוּב הַזֶּה יְהִי מֻתָּר לָנוּ לַאֲפוֹת וּלְבַשֵּׁל וּלְהַטְמִין,
   וּלְהַדְלִיק נֵר, וְלַעֲשׂוֹת כָּל־צָרְכֵינוּ מִיּוֹם טוֹב לְשַׁבָּת,
   לָנוּ וּלְכָל־יִשְׂרָאֵל הַדָּרִים בָּעִיר הַזֹּאת.

   By means of this combining (*eruv*), we are permitted to bake, cook, warm, kindle lights, and make all the necessary preparations for Shabbat during the festival (*yom tov*), we and all who live in this city/locale.
4. Set aside the two foods for eating on Shabbat during the day.

The cooking for Shabbat may now be completed on Yom Tov.

פֶּסַח Pesaḥ

| Nisan 5779 | | | | | | | Apr \| May 2019 | | | | | | |
|---|---|---|---|---|---|---|---|---|---|---|---|---|---|
| | | | | | | 1 | | | | | | | 6 |
| 2 | 3 | 4 | 5 | 6 | 7 | 8 | 7 | 8 | 9 | 10 | 11 | 12 | 13 |
| 9 | 10 | 11 | 12 | 13 | 14 | 15 | 14 | 15 | 16 | 17 | 18 | 19 | 20 |
| 16 | 17 | 18 | 19 | 20 | 21 | 22 | 21 | 22 | 23 | 24 | 25 | 26 | 27 |
| 23 | 24 | 25 | 26 | 27 | 28 | 29 | 28 | 29 | 30 | 1 | 2 | 3 | 4 |
| 30 | | | | | | | 5 | | | | | | |

+ Add ✕ Omit ☞ Take note!

**Siddurim**

**L** Lev Shalem for Shabbat and Festivals
**S** Shabbat and Festival Sim Shalom
**W** Weekday Sim Shalom
**F** Full Sim Shalom (both editions)
**P** Personal Edition of Full Sim Shalom

**Preparing a Flame for Yom Tov**

On Yom Tov, kindling a *new* fire is not permitted; however, the use of an *existing* fire for cooking or other purposes is permitted.

To light candles for Day 8 (Shabbat), ensure that you have a fire burning before candle-lighting time for Day 7 (Thursday evening) that will continue to burn until sunset on Friday. For example:

- A burning candle that lasts for more than 25 hours
- A pilot light on a gas range (*not* a gas range with an electronic starter)

## Pesaḥ — Day 7 and Day 8

**Candle Lighting for Pesaḥ — Day 7**

1. Before lighting candles, prepare a flame. See above.
2. Light the candles at least 18 minutes before sunset.
3. Recite only 1 בְּרָכָה *berakhah*: L79 S303 F718

בָּרוּךְ אַתָּה יי, אֱ‑לֹהֵינוּ מֶלֶךְ הָעוֹלָם, אֲשֶׁר קִדְּשָׁנוּ בְּמִצְוֹתָיו
וְצִוָּנוּ לְהַדְלִיק נֵר שֶׁל יוֹם טוֹב.

Barukh attah adonay, eloheynu melekh ha'olam,
asher kiddeshanu bemitsvotav vetsivvanu lehadlik ner shel yom tov.

**Candle Lighting for Shabbat and Pesaḥ — Day 8**

See instructions in the blue box, p. 143.

**Shabbat and Pesaḥ Meals — Day 7 and Day 8**

Enjoy festive meals evening and daytime, in the manner of Shabbat meals, with:

- Yom Tov קִדּוּשׁ *kiddush* (Day 8: with Shabbat additions):
  Evening L79 S334 F742 Daytime L81 S335 F746
  הַמּוֹצִיא *hamotsi* recited over 2 whole מַצּוֹת *matsot* L81 S313–14 F744|746
- בִּרְכַּת הַמָּזוֹן *birkat hamazon* with Pesaḥ additions; see yellow box, p. 129 (Day 8: with Shabbat additions)
- Festive singing

פֶּסַח Pesaḥ

## Nisan 21 נִיסָן
Thu 25 Apr

## פֶּסַח Pesaḥ — Day 7

**עַרְבִית**

Arvit for Yom Tov L39 S28 F279

+ וַיְדַבֵּר מֹשֶׁה Vaydabber mosheh (Vayikra 23:44) L46 S34 F294

חֲצִי קַדִּישׁ Short Kaddish L46 S34 F294

**Yom Tov Amidah:** L306 S41 F304

+ Insertions for Pesaḥ

קַדִּישׁ שָׁלֵם Full Kaddish L54 S48 F316

+ קִדּוּשׁ Kiddush for Yom Tov with insertions for Pesaḥ L79 S50 F318

✕ ~~שֶׁהֶחֱיָנוּ Sheheḥeyanu~~

+ Count Omer. L63 S55 W152 F237
Day **6** (see instructions, p. 212)

עָלֵינוּ Aleynu L56 S51 F320
קַדִּישׁ יָתוֹם Mourner's Kaddish L58 S52 F324

**Fri 26 Apr** שַׁחֲרִית

At the end of the preliminary service, begin formal chanting at
הָאֵ·ל בְּתַעֲצוּמוֹת עֻזֶּךָ Ha'el beta'atsumot uzzekha. L147 S105 F336

✕ ~~הַכֹּל יוֹדוּךָ Hakol yodukha~~
✕ ~~אֵ·ל אָדוֹן El adon~~
✕ ~~לָאֵ·ל אֲשֶׁר שָׁבַת La'el asher shavat~~

+ הַמֵּאִיר לָאָרֶץ Hame'ir la'arets L152 S109 F342

**Yom Tov Amidah:** L306 S123 F366
+ Insertions for Pesaḥ

+ חֲצִי הַלֵּל Short Hallel L316 S133 F380
קַדִּישׁ שָׁלֵם Full Kaddish L321 S138 F392

**YOM TOV TORAH SERVICE** L322 S139 F394

+ יי יי אֵ·ל רַחוּם וְחַנּוּן
Adonay adonay raḥum veḥannun (3 times) L323 S140 F394
+ רִבּוֹנוֹ שֶׁל עוֹלָם Ribbono shel olam L323 S140 F396
+ וַאֲנִי תְפִלָּתִי לְךָ Va'ani tefillati lekha (3 times) L323 S140 F396

Remove **2** Torah scrolls from ark.

**1st scroll** 5 aliyot from בְּשַׁלַּח Beshallaḥ
שְׁמוֹת Shemot (Exodus) 13:17–15:26
1 13:17–22  2 14:1–8  3 14:9–14  4 14:15–25°  5 14:26–15:26°

☞ °14:22, 29, 31; 15:1–21 For instructions for the special chanting of שִׁירַת הַיָּם Shirat Hayam and of parts of the preceding sections, see p. 94.

☞ °15:11, 16 To preserve the sense of these phrases, maintain the proper pauses after the te'amim (tropes) פַּשְׁטָא ( ) and טִפְחָא ( ):

15:11 מִי־כָמֹכָה בָּאֵלִם | יי מִי כָּמֹכָה | נֶאְדָּר בַּקֹּדֶשׁ . . .
15:16 . . . עַד־יַעֲבֹר עַמְּךָ | יי עַד־יַעֲבֹר | עַם־זוּ קָנִיתָ׃

Place 2nd scroll on table next to 1st scroll.
חֲצִי קַדִּישׁ Short Kaddish L327 S146 F408
Open, raise, display, and wrap 1st scroll.

**2nd scroll** Maftir aliyah from פִּינְחָס Pineḥas
בְּמִדְבַּר[M] Bemidbar (Numbers) 28:19–25

Open, raise, display, and wrap 2nd scroll.

**Haftarah** for Pesaḥ — Day 7
שְׁמוּאֵל ב׳ 2 Shemu'el (2 Samuel) 22:1–51

**Haftarah blessings:**
✕ ~~Concluding Shabbat בְּרָכָה berakhah~~
+ Concluding Yom Tov בְּרָכָה berakhah
with insertions for Pesaḥ L329 S147 F412

✕ ~~יְקוּם פֻּרְקָן Yekum purkan~~
✕ ~~אַב הָרַחֲמִים Av Haraḥamim~~

אַשְׁרֵי Ashrey L339 S151 F420
Return scrolls to ark. L340 S153 F422
חֲצִי קַדִּישׁ Short Kaddish L342 S155 F428

מוּסָף **Yom Tov Amidah:** L343 S166 F456
+ Insertions for Pesaḥ

Some congregations include in the repetition of the Amidah the Priestly Blessing by the Kohanim (*dukhenen*).
בִּרְכַּת כֹּהֲנִים Birkat kohanim L353 S177 F472
For procedures, see p. 213.

קַדִּישׁ שָׁלֵם Full Kaddish L203 S181 F506
Continue with אֵין כֵּא·לֹהֵינוּ Eyn keloheynu. L204 S182 F508

קִדּוּשָׁא רַבָּא **Daytime Kiddush for Yom Tov:** L81 S335 F746
וַיְדַבֵּר מֹשֶׁה Vaydabber mosheh (Vayikra 23:44)
בּוֹרֵא פְּרִי הַגָּפֶן Bo·re peri hagafen

|   |   |   |   |   |   |   |   |
|---|---|---|---|---|---|---|---|
| ✚ Add | ✗ Omit | ☞ Take note! | Nisan 5779 | | Apr \| May 2019 | נִיסָן **21** | Apr 26 |
| | Siddurim | | 1 | | 6 | נִיסָן **22** | Apr 26 |
| **L** | Lev Shalem for Shabbat and Festivals | | 2 3 4 5 6 7 8 | | 7 8 9 10 11 12 13 | | |
| **S** | Shabbat and Festival Sim Shalom | | 9 10 11 12 13 14 15 | | 14 15 16 17 18 19 20 | | |
| **W** | Weekday Sim Shalom | | 16 17 18 19 20 21 22 | | 21 22 23 24 25 26 27 | | |
| **F** | Full Sim Shalom (both editions) | | 23 24 25 26 27 28 29 | | 28 29 30\|1 2 3 4 | | |
| **P** | Personal Edition of Full Sim Shalom | | 30 | | 5 | | |

מִנְחָה · אַשְׁרֵי Ashrey  **L**214 **S**226 **W**170 **F**558
· וּבָא לְצִיּוֹן Uva leʦiyyon  **L**216 **S**227 **W**171 **F**560
· חֲצִי קַדִּישׁ Short Kaddish  **L**217 **S**229 **W**173 **F**564

Yom Tov Amidah:  **L**306 **S**242 **W**184 **F**586
✚ Insertions for Pesaḥ

קַדִּישׁ שָׁלֵם Full Kaddish  **L**230 **S**247 **W**189 **F**596
עָלֵינוּ Aleynu  **L**231 **S**248 **W**190 **F**598
קַדִּישׁ יָתוֹם Mourner's Kaddish  **L**232 **S**249 **W**191 **F**600

**Candle Lighting for Shabbat and Pesaḥ — Day 8**
At least 18 minutes before sunset, follow this procedure:
1. Do not *strike* a match. Instead, transfer fire to the candles from an *existing* flame (see p. 140) by inserting a match or other stick into the flame.
2. Do not *extinguish* the match or stick. Instead, place it on a non-flammable tray or dish, and let it self-extinguish. Alternately, a wood *safety* match held vertically (flame up) usually self-extinguishes quickly.
3. Recite only 1 בְּרָכָה *berakhah*:  **L**79 **S**303 **F**718

בָּרוּךְ אַתָּה יי, אֱ־לֹהֵינוּ מֶלֶךְ הָעוֹלָם, אֲשֶׁר קִדְּשָׁנוּ בְּמִצְוֹתָיו וְצִוָּנוּ לְהַדְלִיק נֵר שֶׁל שַׁבָּת וְשֶׁל יוֹם טוֹב.

Barukh attah adonay, eloheynu melekh ha'olam, asher kiddeshanu bemitsvotav vetsivvanu lehadlik ner shel shabbat veshel yom tov.

**Nisan 22** נִיסָן  שַׁבָּת Shabbat  פֶּסַח Pesaḥ — Day 8
Fri **26** Apr

קַבָּלַת שַׁבָּת  ✗ ~~Kabbalat Shabbat~~
through
✗ ~~Lekhah dodi~~ לְכָה דּוֹדִי

Begin with מִזְמוֹר שִׁיר לְיוֹם הַשַּׁבָּת
Mizmor shir leyom hashabbat (Psalm 92).  **L**27 **S**23 **F**266

עַרְבִית  Arvit for Yom Tov  **L**39 **S**28 **F**279

✚ וְשָׁמְרוּ Veshameru  **L**46 **S**34 **F**294
✚ וַיְדַבֵּר מֹשֶׁה Vaydabber mosheh (Vayikra 23:44)  **L**46 **S**34 **F**294
חֲצִי קַדִּישׁ Short Kaddish  **L**46 **S**34 **F**294

Yom Tov Amidah:  **L**306 **S**41 **F**304
✚ Additions for Shabbat
✚ Insertions for Pesaḥ

*Pesaḥ* פסח

+ וַיְכֻלּוּ Vaykhullu L53 S47 F314

☞ בָּרוּךְ אַתָּה . . . וָאָרֶץ Barukh attah . . . va'arets L53 S47 F314
מָגֵן אָבוֹת . . . בְּרֵאשִׁית Magen avot . . . bereshit L53 S47 F314
אֱ·לֹהֵינוּ . . . הַשַּׁבָּת Eloheynu . . . hashabbat L54 S47 F314

קַדִּישׁ שָׁלֵם Full Kaddish L54 S48 F316

+ קִדּוּשׁ Kiddush for Yom Tov
with additions for Shabbat and
insertions for Pesaḥ L79 S50 F318
✕ ~~שֶׁהֶחֱיָנוּ Sheheḥeyanu~~

+ Count Omer. L63 S55 W152 F237
Day **7** (see instructions, p. 212)

עָלֵינוּ Aleynu L56 S51 F320
קַדִּישׁ יָתוֹם Mourner's Kaddish L58 S52 F324

**At home** For candle lighting for Day 8, see blue box, p. 143.

**Sat 27 Apr** **שַׁחֲרִית** At the end of the preliminary service,
begin formal chanting at
הָאֵ·ל בְּתַעֲצוּמוֹת עֻזֶּךָ Ha'el beta'atsumot uzzekha. L147 S105 F336

+ הַכֹּל יוֹדוּךָ Hakol yodukha L150 S107 F340
+ אֵ·ל אָדוֹן El adon L151 S108 F342
+ לָאֵ·ל אֲשֶׁר שָׁבַת La'el asher shavat L152 S109 F342

✕ ~~הַמֵּאִיר לָאָרֶץ Hame'ir la'arets~~

**Yom Tov Amidah:** L306 S123 F366
+ Additions for Shabbat
+ Insertions for Pesaḥ

+ חֲצִי הַלֵּל Short Hallel L316 S133 F380
קַדִּישׁ שָׁלֵם Full Kaddish L321 S138 F392

+ **Megillah reading:**
Some congregations read מְגִלַּת שִׁיר הַשִּׁירִים
Megillat Shir Hashirim (Scroll of Song of Songs),
without reciting a בְּרָכָה berakhah.
Some read selections in English. L7 S377 F788
קַדִּישׁ יָתוֹם Mourner's Kaddish L121 S82 F52

| ✚ Add | ✘ Omit | ☞ Take note! | **Nisan 5779** | | **Apr \| May 2019** | | **נִיסָן 22** Apr 27 |

| | Siddurim | | | | | 1 | | | | | 6 | | |
|---|---|---|---|---|---|---|---|---|---|---|---|---|---|

## SHABBAT TORAH SERVICE L322 S139 F394

✕ ~~יי יי אֵ-ל רַחוּם וְחַנּוּן Adonay adonay el raḥum veḥannun~~

✕ ~~רִבּוֹנוֹ שֶׁל עוֹלָם Ribbono shel olam~~

✕ ~~וַאֲנִי תְפִלָּתִי לְךָ Va'ani tefillati lekha~~

Remove **2** Torah scrolls from ark.

**1st scroll** 7 aliyot from רְאֵה Re'eh
דְּבָרִים Devarim (Deuteronomy) 14:22–16:17
[1] 14:22–29 [2] 15:1–18 [3] 19–23 [4] 16:1–3 [5] 4–8 [6] 9–12 [7] 13–17

Place 2nd scroll on table next to 1st scroll.
חֲצִי קַדִּישׁ Short Kaddish L327 S146 F408
Open, raise, display, and wrap 1st scroll.

**2nd scroll** Maftir aliyah from פִּינְחָס Pineḥas
M בְּמִדְבַּר Bemidbar (Numbers) 28:19–25

Open, raise, display, and wrap 2nd scroll.

**Haftarah** for Pesaḥ — Day 8
יְשַׁעְיָהוּ Yesha'yahu (Isaiah) 10:32–12:6

**Haftarah blessings:**

✕ ~~Concluding Shabbat בְּרָכָה berakhah~~

+ Concluding Yom Tov בְּרָכָה berakhah with additions for Shabbat and insertions for Pesaḥ L329 S147 F412

☞ יְקוּם פֻּרְקָן Yekum purkan L176 S148 F412

+ יִזְכֹּר Yizkor L330 S188 F516

☞ אַב הָרַחֲמִים Av haraḥamim L446 S151 F420

אַשְׁרֵי Ashrey L339 S151 F420
Return scrolls to ark. L340 S153 F422
חֲצִי קַדִּישׁ Short Kaddish L342 S155 F428

| Nisan 5779 | | | | | | | Apr \| May 2019 | | | | | | |
|---|---|---|---|---|---|---|---|---|---|---|---|---|---|
| | | | | | | 1 | | | | | | | 6 |
| 2 | 3 | 4 | 5 | 6 | 7 | 8 | 7 | 8 | 9 | 10 | 11 | 12 | 13 |
| 9 | 10 | 11 | 12 | 13 | 14 | 15 | 14 | 15 | 16 | 17 | 18 | 19 | 20 |
| 16 | 17 | 18 | 19 | 20 | 21 | 22 | 21 | 22 | 23 | 24 | 25 | 26 | 27 |
| 23 | 24 | 25 | 26 | 27 | 28 | 29 | 28 | 29 | 30 \| | 1 | 2 | 3 | 4 |
| 30 | | | | | | | 5 | | | | | | |

+ Add ✕ Omit ☞ Take note!

**Siddurim**
- **L** Lev Shalem for Shabbat and Festivals
- **S** Shabbat and Festival Sim Shalom
- **W** Weekday Sim Shalom
- **F** Full Sim Shalom (both editions)
- **P** Personal Edition of Full Sim Shalom

---

## מוּסָף

**Yom Tov Amidah:** L343 S166 F456

+ Additions for Shabbat
+ Insertions for Pesaḥ

Some congregations include in the repetition of the Amidah the Priestly Blessing by the Kohanim (*dukhenen*).
בִּרְכַּת כֹּהֲנִים Birkat kohanim L353 S177 F472
(Some congregations omit on Shabbat.)
For procedures, see p. 213.

קַדִּישׁ שָׁלֵם Full Kaddish L203 S181 F506
Continue with אֵין כֵּא·לֹהֵינוּ Eyn keloheynu. L204 S182 F508

## קִדּוּשָׁא רַבָּא

**Daytime Kiddush for Shabbat and Yom Tov:** L81 S335 F746

וְשָׁמְרוּ Veshameru
זָכוֹר Zakhor (many omit)
עַל־כֵּן בֵּרַךְ Al ken berakh
+ וַיְדַבֵּר מֹשֶׁה Vaydabber mosheh (Vayikra 23:44)
בּוֹרֵא פְּרִי הַגָּפֶן Bo·re peri hagafen

## מִנְחָה

אַשְׁרֵי Ashrey L214 S226 W170 F558
וּבָא לְצִיּוֹן Uva letsiyyon L216 S227 W171 F560
חֲצִי קַדִּישׁ Short Kaddish L217 S229 W173 F564

**Torah** 3 aliyot from אַחֲרֵי מוֹת Aḥarey mot
וַיִּקְרָא Vayikra (Leviticus) 16:1–17
[1]16:1–6 [2]7–11 [3]12–17 W292 P912

This is also the reading for the coming Monday and Thursday.

**Yom Tov Amidah:** L306 S242 W184 F586

+ Additions for Shabbat
+ Insertions for Pesaḥ

✕ ~~צִדְקָתְךָ צֶדֶק Tsidkatekha tsedek~~

קַדִּישׁ שָׁלֵם Full Kaddish L230 S247 W189 F596
עָלֵינוּ Aleynu L231 S248 W190 F598
קַדִּישׁ יָתוֹם Mourner's Kaddish L232 S249 W191 F600

| + Add | ✗ Omit | ☞ Take note! | Nisan 5779 | Apr \| May 2019 | נִיסָן 23 | Apr 27 |
|---|---|---|---|---|---|---|
| | Siddurim | | 1 | 6 | | Apr 28 |
| L | Lev Shalem for Shabbat and Festivals | | 2 3 4 5 6 7 8 | 7 8 9 10 11 12 13 | נִיסָן 24 | Apr 28 |
| S | Shabbat and Festival Sim Shalom | | 9 10 11 12 13 14 15 | 14 15 16 17 18 19 20 | | |
| W | Weekday Sim Shalom | | 16 17 18 19 20 21 22 | 21 22 23 24 25 26 27 | | |
| F | Full Sim Shalom (both editions) | | 23 24 25 26 27 28 29 | 28 29 30 \| 1 2 3 4 | | |
| P | Personal Edition of Full Sim Shalom | | 30 | 5 | | |

## Nisan 23 נִיסָן
### Sat 27 Apr

**מוֹצָאֵי שַׁבָּת וְיוֹם טוֹב** Motsa'ey Shabbat Veyom Tov
Conclusion of Shabbat and Yom Tov

**אִסְרוּ חַג** Isru Ḥag   The Day after Yom Tov

עַרְבִית   Saturday night Arvit as usual   **L**264 **S**281 **W**137 **F**200
through the Amidah

☞ **חֲצִי קַדִּישׁ** Short Kaddish   **L**269 **S**292 **W**158 **F**682
☞ **וִיהִי נֹעַם** Vihi no'am   **L**279 **S**292 **W**158 **F**684
☞ **יוֹשֵׁב בְּסֵתֶר עֶלְיוֹן** Yoshev beseter elyon   **L**279 **S**292 **W**158 **F**684
☞ **וְאַתָּה קָדוֹשׁ** Ve'attah kadosh   **L**216 **S**293 **W**159 **F**684

**קַדִּישׁ שָׁלֵם** Full Kaddish   **L**280 **S**294 **W**160 **F**688
+ Count Omer.   **L**63 **S**55 **W**152 **F**237
Day **8** (see instructions, p. 212)

Some recite **הַבְדָּלָה** Havdalah here.   **L**283 **S**299 **W**165 **F**700
For instructions, see below.

**עָלֵינוּ** Aleynu   **L**281 **S**297 **W**163 **F**696
**קַדִּישׁ יָתוֹם** Mourner's Kaddish   **L**282 **S**298 **W**164 **F**698

**Havdalah:**   **L**283 **S**299 **W**165 **F**700

**הִנֵּה אֵל יְשׁוּעָתִי** Hinneh el yeshu'ati
**בּוֹרֵא פְּרִי הַגָּפֶן** Bo·re peri hagafen
**בּוֹרֵא מִינֵי בְשָׂמִים** Bo·re miney vesamim
**בּוֹרֵא מְאוֹרֵי הָאֵשׁ** Bo·re me'orey ha'esh
**הַמַּבְדִּיל בֵּין קֹדֶשׁ לְחֹל** Hamavdil beyn kodesh leḥol

**DURING Nisan**   Continue:
✗ ~~תַּחֲנוּן~~ ~~Taḥanun~~

### Sun 28 Apr
שַׁחֲרִית   Shaḥarit for weekdays   **W**1 **F**2

☞ **מִזְמוֹר לְתוֹדָה** Mizmor letodah   **W**20 **F**60
✗ ~~תַּחֲנוּן~~ ~~Taḥanun~~
☞ **לַמְנַצֵּחַ** Lamenatse·aḥ (Psalm 20)   **W**79 **F**154

מִנְחָה   ✗ ~~תַּחֲנוּן~~ ~~Taḥanun~~

## Nisan 24 נִיסָן
### Sun 28 Apr
עַרְבִית   + Before **עָלֵינוּ** Aleynu, count Omer.   **L**63 **S**55 **W**152 **F**237
Day **9** (see instructions, p. 212)

Apr 29 25 נִיסָן
Apr 30 26 נִיסָן
May 1 27 נִיסָן

| Nisan 5779 | | | | | | | Apr \| May 2019 | | | | | | |
|---|---|---|---|---|---|---|---|---|---|---|---|---|---|
| | | | | | | 1 | | | | | | | 6 |
| 2 | 3 | 4 | 5 | 6 | 7 | 8 | 7 | 8 | 9 | 10 | 11 | 12 | 13 |
| 9 | 10 | 11 | 12 | 13 | 14 | 15 | 14 | 15 | 16 | 17 | 18 | 19 | 20 |
| 16 | 17 | 18 | 19 | 20 | 21 | 22 | 21 | 22 | 23 | 24 | 25 | 26 | 27 |
| 23 | 24 | 25 | 26 | 27 | 28 | 29 | 28 | 29 | 30 \| 1 | 2 | 3 | 4 | |
| 30 | | | | | | | 5 | | | | | | |

+ Add  ✕ Omit  ☞ Take note!

**Siddurim**
- **L** Lev Shalem for Shabbat and Festivals
- **S** Shabbat and Festival Sim Shalom
- **W** Weekday Sim Shalom
- **F** Full Sim Shalom (both editions)
- **P** Personal Edition of Full Sim Shalom

**Nisan 25 נִיסָן**
**Mon 29 Apr** עַרְבִית + Before עָלֵינוּ Aleynu, count Omer. L63 S55 W152 F237
Day **10** (see instructions, p. 212)

**Nisan 26 נִיסָן**
**Tue 30 Apr** עַרְבִית + Before עָלֵינוּ Aleynu, count Omer. L63 S55 W152 F237
Day **11** (see instructions, p. 212)

## Nisan 27 נִיסָן — יוֹם הַשּׁוֹאָה וְהַגְּבוּרָה Yom Hasho'ah Vehagevurah

**Wed 1 May** (evening) **Holocaust and Heroism Remembrance Day**

### Yom Hasho'ah Vehagevurah

The Knesset in Israel has officially designated 27 Nisan as a day to commemorate the Holocaust and to honor the heroes of the resistance movements during the period of the Holocaust.

Although no fixed liturgy for the occasion has yet emerged, many congregations mark the occasion with changes in the service. The following are customs practiced and resources used in various congregations:

- Reading all of (or selections from) *Megillat Hashoah: The Shoah Scroll.* This work, comprising six chapters in memory of the six million, is available from The Rabbinical Assembly at www.rabbinicalassembly.org/resources-ideas/publications).
- Reading additional texts appropriate to Holocaust commemoration and the heroic efforts of resistance fighters. Modern *siddurim* offer a selection of such readings. L450 S387 W198 F828
- Reciting a נַחֵם *naḥem* prayer for Yom Hasho'ah in each Amidah, such as the one found in *Siddur Sim Shalom for Weekdays.* W40, 127, 145
- Lighting a single memorial candle, or lighting six *yortsayt* candles.
  Yellow memorial candles have become a powerful symbol for this purpose through the efforts of the Federation of Jewish Men's Clubs. For more details, visit www.yellowcandles.org.
- Reciting אֵ-ל מָלֵא רַחֲמִים *El ma-le raḥamim.* L336 S196 W198 F522
  For the text of a Holocaust remembrance אֵ-ל מָלֵא רַחֲמִים prayer from the Chief Rabbinate of the State of Israel, with translation and explanation, visit www.milesbcohen.com/LuahResources.
- Adding a קַדִּישׁ כְּלָלִי *kaddish kelali,* a general Mourner's Kaddish (recited by those who have lost at least one parent).

עַרְבִית Arvit for weekdays L264 S281 W137 F200
+ Additions for יוֹם הַשּׁוֹאָה Yom Hasho'ah (see box, above)
+ Before עָלֵינוּ Aleynu, count Omer. L63 S55 W152 F237
Day **12** (see instructions, p. 212)

+ Add   ✕ Omit   ☞ Take note!

**Siddurim**

- **L** Lev Shalem for Shabbat and Festivals
- **S** Shabbat and Festival Sim Shalom
- **W** Weekday Sim Shalom
- **F** Full Sim Shalom (both editions)
- **P** Personal Edition of Full Sim Shalom

| Nisan 5779 | | | | | | |
|---|---|---|---|---|---|---|
| | | | | | | 1 |
| 2 | 3 | 4 | 5 | 6 | 7 | 8 |
| 9 | 10 | 11 | 12 | 13 | 14 | 15 |
| 16 | 17 | 18 | 19 | 20 | 21 | 22 |
| 23 | 24 | 25 | 26 | 27 | 28 | 29 |
| 30 | | | | | | |

| Apr \| May 2019 | | | | | | |
|---|---|---|---|---|---|---|
| | | | | | | 6 |
| 7 | 8 | 9 | 10 | 11 | 12 | 13 |
| 14 | 15 | 16 | 17 | 18 | 19 | 20 |
| 21 | 22 | 23 | 24 | 25 | 26 | 27 |
| 28 | 29 | 30 \| | 1 | 2 | 3 | 4 |
| 5 | | | | | | |

27 נִיסָן May 2
28 נִיסָן May 2
29 נִיסָן May 3
May 4

---

**Thu 2 May** שַׁחֲרִית

Shaḥarit for weekdays   W1 F2

+ Additions for יוֹם הַשּׁוֹאָה Yom Hasho'ah (see box, p. 148)

Some omit לַמְנַצֵּחַ Lamenatse·aḥ (Psalm 20).

---

**Nisan 28 נִיסָן**

**Thu 2 May** עַרְבִית

+ Before עָלֵינוּ Aleynu, count Omer.   L63 S55 W152 F237
Day **13** (see instructions, p. 212)

---

## Nisan 29 נִיסָן

**Fri 3 May**

**שַׁבָּת Shabbat** **פָּרָשַׁת אַחֲרֵי מוֹת Parashat Aḥarey mot**
**שַׁבַּת מָחָר חֹדֶשׁ Shabbat Maḥar Ḥodesh**
**שַׁבַּת מְבָרְכִים הַחֹדֶשׁ Shabbat Mevarekhim Haḥodesh**

עַרְבִית

+ Before עָלֵינוּ Aleynu, count Omer.   L63 S55 W152 F237
Day **14** (see instructions, p. 212)

**Sat 4 May**

**Torah** 7 aliyot (minimum): אַחֲרֵי מוֹת Aḥarey mot
וַיִּקְרָא Vayikra (Leviticus) 16:1–18:30

| | | | | |
|---|---|---|---|---|
| Annual: | [1]16:1–17 | [2]16:18–24 | [3]16:25–34 | [4]17:1–7 |
| | [5]17:8–18:5 | [6]18:6–21 | [7]18:22–30 | [M]18:28–30 |
| Triennial: | [1]16:1–3 | [2]16:4–6 | [3]16:7–11 | [4]16:12–17 |
| | [5]16:18–24 | [6]16:25–30 | [7]16:31–34 | [M]16:31–34 |

☞ **Haftarah** for Shabbat Maḥar Ḥodesh
שְׁמוּאֵל א׳ 1 Shemu'el (1 Samuel) 20:18–42

+ **Birkat Haḥodesh:**   L180 S150 F418
Announce Rosh Ḥodesh Iyyar:
רֹאשׁ חֹדֶשׁ אִיָּר יִהְיֶה בְּיוֹם רִאשׁוֹן וּבְיוֹם שֵׁנִי . . .
Rosh ḥodesh Iyyar yihyeh beyom rishon uvyom sheni . . .
(Saturday night, Sunday, and Monday)

☞ Recite אַב הָרַחֲמִים Av haraḥamim   L446 S151 F420
during the Omer period, even if the usual custom of the congregation is to omit it.

מִנְחָה

**Torah** 3 aliyot from קְדֹשִׁים Kedoshim
וַיִּקְרָא Vayikra (Leviticus) 19:1–14
[1]19:1–4   [2]5–10   [3]11–14   W293 P914

☞ These verses are not read publicly again until next Shabbat.

✕ ~~צִדְקָתְךָ צֶדֶק Tsidkatekha tsedek~~

| Nisan 5779 | | | | | | | Apr \| May 2019 | | | | | | |
|---|---|---|---|---|---|---|---|---|---|---|---|---|---|
| | | | | | | 1 | | | | | | | 6 |
| 2 | 3 | 4 | 5 | 6 | 7 | 8 | 7 | 8 | 9 | 10 | 11 | 12 | 13 |
| 9 | 10 | 11 | 12 | 13 | 14 | 15 | 14 | 15 | 16 | 17 | 18 | 19 | 20 |
| 16 | 17 | 18 | 19 | 20 | 21 | 22 | 21 | 22 | 23 | 24 | 25 | 26 | 27 |
| 23 | 24 | 25 | 26 | 27 | 28 | 29 | 28 | 29 | 30 | 1 | 2 | 3 | 4 |
| 30 | | | | | | | 5 | | | | | | |

+ Add ✕ Omit ☞ Take note!

**Siddurim**
- **L** Lev Shalem for Shabbat and Festivals
- **S** Shabbat and Festival Sim Shalom
- **W** Weekday Sim Shalom
- **F** Full Sim Shalom (both editions)
- **P** Personal Edition of Full Sim Shalom

## Nisan 30 ניסן — ראש חדֶשׁ אִיָּר Rosh Ḥodesh Iyyar — Day 1

Sat 4 May (evening) — מוֹצָאֵי שַׁבָּת Motsa'ey Shabbat — Conclusion of Shabbat

**DURING Rosh Ḥodesh**

**Birkat Hamazon:**

+ יַעֲלֶה וְיָבוֹא Ya'aleh veyavo for Rosh Ḥodesh L90|95 S340|347 W233|239 F762|780

+ הָרַחֲמָן Haraḥaman for Rosh Ḥodesh L92|96 S343|348 W235|240 F768

**עַרְבִית**

Saturday night Arvit as usual until the Amidah L264 S281 W137 F200

**Weekday Amidah:**

+ אַתָּה חוֹנַנְתָּנוּ Attah ḥonantanu L272 S287 W143 F212

+ יַעֲלֶה וְיָבוֹא Ya'aleh veyavo for Rosh Ḥodesh L277 S289 W145 F216

Continue as on a usual Saturday night through
קַדִּישׁ שָׁלֵם Full Kaddish L280 S294 W160 F688

+ Count Omer. L63 S55 W152 F237
Day **15** (see instructions, p. 212)

Some recite הַבְדָּלָה Havdalah here. L283 S299 W165 F700

עָלֵינוּ Aleynu L281 S297 W163 F696
קַדִּישׁ יָתוֹם Mourner's Kaddish L282 S298 W164 F698

הַבְדָּלָה Havdalah L283 S299 W165 F700

**Sun 5 May — שַׁחֲרִית**

**Before מִזְמוֹר שִׁיר Mizmor shir (Psalm 30)** W14 F50
**or at end of service, recite:**
Psalm for Sunday (Psalm 24) W85 F22
קַדִּישׁ יָתוֹם Mourner's Kaddish (some omit) W100 F52
+ Psalm 104 for Rosh Ḥodesh W90 F34
קַדִּישׁ יָתוֹם Mourner's Kaddish W100 F52

**Weekday Amidah:**

+ יַעֲלֶה וְיָבוֹא Ya'aleh veyavo for Rosh Ḥodesh W41 F114

✕ ~~תַּחֲנוּן Taḥanun~~

+ חֲצִי הַלֵּל Short Hallel W50 F380
קַדִּישׁ שָׁלֵם Full Kaddish W56 F392

+ **TORAH SERVICE** W65 F138
Remove **1** Torah scroll from ark.

**Torah** 4 aliyot: פִּינְחָס Pineḥas
בְּמִדְבַּר Bemidbar (Numbers) 28:1–15
¹28:1–3 ²3–5 ³6–10 ⁴11–15 W320 P943

חֲצִי קַדִּישׁ Short Kaddish W71 F146
Open, raise, display, and wrap scroll.
Return scroll to ark. W76 F150

אַשְׁרֵי Ashrey W78 F152
✕ ~~לַמְנַצֵּחַ Lamenatse·aḥ (Psalm 20)~~
וּבָא לְצִיּוֹן Uva letsiyyon W80 F156

**Some congregations:**
Remove and pack tefillin at this point.
+ חֲצִי קַדִּישׁ Short Kaddish W103 F428

**Other congregations:**
+ חֲצִי קַדִּישׁ Short Kaddish W103 F428
Remove and cover—but do not pack—tefillin, so that all begin Musaf Amidah at the same time, as soon after Kaddish as possible.

מוּסָף

+ **Rosh Ḥodesh Amidah for weekdays:** W104 F486
Weekday קְדֻשָּׁה Kedushah W105 F488
✕ ~~וּלְכַפָּרַת פָּשַׁע Ulkhapparat pasha~~
Beginning with Rosh Ḥodesh Nisan, we do not add these words.

+ קַדִּישׁ שָׁלֵם Full Kaddish W82 F158
עָלֵינוּ Aleynu W83 F160

**If psalms for the day were not recited at Shaḥarit, add here:**
קַדִּישׁ יָתוֹם Mourner's Kaddish (some omit) W84 F162
Psalm for Sunday (Psalm 24) W85 F22
קַדִּישׁ יָתוֹם Mourner's Kaddish (some omit) W100 F52
+ Psalm 104 for Rosh Ḥodesh W90 F34

קַדִּישׁ יָתוֹם Mourner's Kaddish W84|100 F162|52

מִנְחָה

**Weekday Amidah:**
+ יַעֲלֶה וְיָבוֹא Ya'aleh veyavo for Rosh Ḥodesh W127 F178

✕ ~~תַּחֲנוּן Taḥanun~~

| Iyyar 5779 | | | | | | | May \| Jun 2019 | | | | | | |
|---|---|---|---|---|---|---|---|---|---|---|---|---|---|
| | 1 | 2 | 3 | 4 | 5 | 6 | | 6 | 7 | 8 | 9 | 10 | 11 |
| 7 | 8 | 9 | 10 | 11 | 12 | 13 | 12 | 13 | 14 | 15 | 16 | 17 | 18 |
| 14 | 15 | 16 | 17 | 18 | 19 | 20 | 19 | 20 | 21 | 22 | 23 | 24 | 25 |
| 21 | 22 | 23 | 24 | 25 | 26 | 27 | 26 | 27 | 28 | 29 | 30 | 31 \| | 1 |
| 28 | 29 | | | | | | 2 | 3 | | | | | |

+ Add ✕ Omit ☞ Take note!

**Siddurim**
- **L** Lev Shalem for Shabbat and Festivals
- **S** Shabbat and Festival Sim Shalom
- **W** Weekday Sim Shalom
- **F** Full Sim Shalom (both editions)
- **P** Personal Edition of Full Sim Shalom

## Iyyar 1 אִיָּר 1 — ראשׁ חֹדֶשׁ אִיָּר Rosh Ḥodesh Iyyar — Day 2

Sun **5** May (evening)

**DURING Rosh Ḥodesh**

**Birkat Hamazon:**

+ יַעֲלֶה וְיָבוֹא Ya'aleh veyavo for Rosh Ḥodesh L90|95 S340|347 W233|239 F762|780

+ הָרַחֲמָן Haraḥaman for Rosh Ḥodesh L92|96 S343|348 W235|240 F768

**עַרְבִית**

**Weekday Amidah:**

+ יַעֲלֶה וְיָבוֹא Ya'aleh veyavo for Rosh Ḥodesh W145 F216

+ Before עָלֵינוּ Aleynu, count Omer. L63 S55 W152 F237
Day **16** (see instructions, p. 212)

---

Mon **6** May **שַׁחֲרִית**

TEFILLIN

**Before מִזְמוֹר שִׁיר Mizmor shir (Psalm 30) or at end of service, recite:** W14 F50

Psalm for Monday (Psalm 48) W86 F24
קַדִּישׁ יָתוֹם Mourner's Kaddish (some omit) W100 F52
+ Psalm 104 for Rosh Ḥodesh W90 F34
קַדִּישׁ יָתוֹם Mourner's Kaddish W100 F52

**Weekday Amidah:**

+ יַעֲלֶה וְיָבוֹא Ya'aleh veyavo for Rosh Ḥodesh W41 F114

✕ ~~תַּחֲנוּן Taḥanun~~

+ חֲצִי הַלֵּל Short Hallel W50 F380
קַדִּישׁ שָׁלֵם Full Kaddish W56 F392

**TORAH SERVICE** W65 F138
Remove **1** Torah scroll from ark.

**Torah** 4 aliyot: פִּינְחָס Pineḥas
בְּמִדְבַּר Bemidbar (Numbers) 28:1–15
¹28:1–3 ²3–5 ³6–10 ⁴11–15 W320 P943

חֲצִי קַדִּישׁ Short Kaddish W71 F146
Open, raise, display, and wrap scroll.
Return scroll to ark. W76 F150

אַשְׁרֵי Ashrey W78 F152
✕ ~~לַמְנַצֵּחַ Lamenatseaḥ (Psalm 20)~~
וּבָא לְצִיּוֹן Uva letsiyyon W80 F156

**Some congregations:**
Remove and pack tefillin at this point.
+ חֲצִי קַדִּישׁ Short Kaddish W103 F428

**Other congregations:**
+ חֲצִי קַדִּישׁ Short Kaddish W103 F428
Remove and cover—but do not pack—tefillin, so that all begin Musaf Amidah at the same time, as soon after Kaddish as possible.

מוּסָף
+ **Rosh Hodesh Amidah for weekdays:** W104 F486
Weekday קְדֻשָּׁה Kedushah W105 F488
✕ ~~וּלְכַפָּרַת פָּשַׁע Ulkhapparat pasha~~
Beginning with Rosh Hodesh Nisan, we do not add these words.

+ קַדִּישׁ שָׁלֵם Full Kaddish W82 F158
עָלֵינוּ Aleynu W83 F160

**If psalms for the day were not recited at Shaharit, add here:**
קַדִּישׁ יָתוֹם Mourner's Kaddish (some omit) W84 F162
Psalm for Monday (Psalm 48) W86 F24
קַדִּישׁ יָתוֹם Mourner's Kaddish (some omit) W100 F52
+ Psalm 104 for Rosh Hodesh W90 F34

קַדִּישׁ יָתוֹם Mourner's Kaddish W84|100 F162|52

מִנְחָה
**Weekday Amidah:**
+ יַעֲלֶה וְיָבוֹא Ya'aleh veyavo for Rosh Hodesh W127 F178

✕ ~~תַּחֲנוּן Tahanun~~

**Iyyar 2 אִיָּר**
**Mon 6 May**

עַרְבִית
+ Before עָלֵינוּ Aleynu, count Omer. L63 S55 W152 F237
Day **17** (see instructions, p. 212)

**BEGINNING 2 Iyyar** Resume reciting תַּחֲנוּן Tahanun.

May 7 3 אִיָּר
May 8
May 8 4 אִיָּר

| Iyyar 5779 | | | | | | |
|---|---|---|---|---|---|---|
| | 1 | 2 | 3 | 4 | 5 | 6 |
| 7 | 8 | 9 | 10 | 11 | 12 | 13 |
| 14 | 15 | 16 | 17 | 18 | 19 | 20 |
| 21 | 22 | 23 | 24 | 25 | 26 | 27 |
| 28 | 29 | | | | | |

| May \| Jun 2019 | | | | | | |
|---|---|---|---|---|---|---|
| | 6 | 7 | 8 | 9 | 10 | 11 |
| 12 | 13 | 14 | 15 | 16 | 17 | 18 |
| 19 | 20 | 21 | 22 | 23 | 24 | 25 |
| 26 | 27 | 28 | 29 | 30 | 31 | 1 |
| 2 | 3 | | | | | |

+ Add ✕ Omit ☞ Take note!

**Siddurim**
- **L** Lev Shalem for Shabbat and Festivals
- **S** Shabbat and Festival Sim Shalom
- **W** Weekday Sim Shalom
- **F** Full Sim Shalom (both editions)
- **P** Personal Edition of Full Sim Shalom

## Iyyar 3 אִיָּר
Tue 7 May (evening)

## יוֹם הַזִּכָּרוֹן Yom Hazikkaron
**Remembrance Day**

### Yom Hazikkaron

The Knesset in Israel has officially designated the day before Yom Ha'atsma'ut as יוֹם הַזִּכָּרוֹן, Remembrance Day for Fallen Soldiers and Victims of Terrorism. Appropriate observances include:

- Adding relevant readings to the service
- Lighting a *yortsayt* candle
- Reciting אֵ·ל מָלֵא רַחֲמִים *El ma·le raḥamim* W73 F522
- Reciting a communal קַדִּישׁ יָתוֹם Mourner's Kaddish W84 F524

עַרְבִית + Additions for יוֹם הַזִּכָּרוֹן Yom Hazikkaron (see box, above)

+ Before עָלֵינוּ Aleynu, count Omer. L63 S55 W152 F237
Day **18** (see instructions, p. 212)

Wed **8** May שַׁחֲרִית + Additions for יוֹם הַזִּכָּרוֹן Yom Hazikkaron (see box, above)

מִנְחָה ✕ ~~תַּחֲנוּן Taḥanun~~ REGULAR SHACHARIT
✓ TEFILLIN

## Iyyar 4 אִיָּר
Wed 8 May (evening)

## יוֹם הָעַצְמָאוּת Yom Ha'atsma'ut
**Independence Day**

### Yom Ha'atsma'ut

The Knesset in Israel has officially designated 5 Iyyar as יוֹם הָעַצְמָאוּת, Independence Day. When that date falls on Thursday night and Friday, as it does this year, Yom Ha'atsma'ut is moved up to 4 Iyyar so that festivities do not interfere with the beginning of Shabbat.

In addition to the ritual observances, the following are customary:

- Eating a festive meal that includes foods from Israel
- Singing songs related to Israel

Also, all mourning practices associated with the Omer period are suspended. For example:

- Weddings and other communal celebrations are permitted.
- Haircuts are permitted.

**DURING Yom Ha'atsma'ut**

**Birkat Hamazon:**
+ עַל הַנִּסִּים Al Hanissim for Yom Ha'atsma'ut W232|238 F760

עַרְבִית

**Weekday Amidah:**

+ עַל הַנִּסִּים Al Hanissim for Yom Ha'atsma'ut W147 F218

Some recite הַלֵּל שָׁלֵם Full Hallel. W50 F380

קַדִּישׁ שָׁלֵם Full Kaddish W149 F222

+ Prayers, readings, and songs for Yom Ha'atsma'ut W205–8

+ Before עָלֵינוּ Aleynu, count Omer. L63 S55 W152 F237
Day **19** (see instructions, p. 212)

---

**Thu 9 May** שַׁחֲרִית

Weekday Shaharit as usual through
מִזְמוֹר לְתוֹדָה Mizmor letodah (Psalm 100) W20 F60

TEFILLIN
BUT NO MUSAF

+ Psalms recited on Shabbat and Yom Tov:
☞ Psalms 19, 34, 90, 91, 135, 136, 33, 92, 93 L127–34 S87–95 F60–78
Use weekday minor nusah for the psalms.

Continue with the usual weekday service from
יְהִי כְבוֹד יי Yehi khevod adonay. W20 F80

**Weekday Amidah:**

+ עַל הַנִּסִּים Al hanissim for Yom Ha'atsma'ut W42 F118

✕ ~~תַּחֲנוּן Tahanun~~

הַלֵּל שָׁלֵם Full Hallel W50 F380

חֲצִי קַדִּישׁ Short Kaddish W56 F390

**TORAH SERVICE** W65 F138

Remove **1** Torah scroll from ark.

3 aliyot from עֵקֶב Ekev
°דְּבָרִים Devarim (Deuteronomy) 7:12–8:18
1 7:12–21 2 7:22–8:6 M 8:7–18 W343 P983

☞ °If your congregation does not read the Yom Ha'atsma'ut reading:
1. Read the regular weekday reading (קְדֹשִׁים Kedoshim; see p. 149).
2. Continue with the haftarah below, **omitting** all בְּרָכוֹת berakhot.
3. Recite תְּפִלָּה לִשְׁלוֹם הַמְּדִינָה Prayer for the State of Israel.

חֲצִי קַדִּישׁ Short Kaddish W71 F146
Open, raise, display, and wrap scroll.

Iyyar 5779

| | | | | | | |
|---|---|---|---|---|---|---|
| | 1 | 2 | 3 | 4 | 5 | 6 |
| 7 | 8 | 9 | 10 | 11 | 12 | 13 |
| 14 | 15 | 16 | 17 | 18 | 19 | 20 |
| 21 | 22 | 23 | 24 | 25 | 26 | 27 |
| 28 | 29 | | | | | |

May | Jun 2019

| | | | | | | |
|---|---|---|---|---|---|---|
| | 6 | 7 | 8 | 9 | 10 | 11 |
| 12 | 13 | 14 | 15 | 16 | 17 | 18 |
| 19 | 20 | 21 | 22 | 23 | 24 | 25 |
| 26 | 27 | 28 | 29 | 30 | 31 | 1 |
| 2 | 3 | | | | | |

+ Add ✕ Omit ☞ Take note!

**Siddurim**
- **L** Lev Shalem for Shabbat and Festivals
- **S** Shabbat and Festival Sim Shalom
- **W** Weekday Sim Shalom
- **F** Full Sim Shalom (both editions)
- **P** Personal Edition of Full Sim Shalom

---

+ Recite the בְּרָכָה berakhah before the haftarah. W74 F410 P989

**Haftarah** יְשַׁעְיָהוּ Yesha'yahu (Isaiah) 10:32–12:6 W345 P987

+ Recite the 3 concluding haftarah blessings, through מָגֵן דָּוִד. W74 F410 P989.

+ תְּפִלָּה לִשְׁלוֹם הַמְּדִינָה Prayer for the State of Israel W75 F416

Return scroll to ark. W76 F150

אַשְׁרֵי Ashrey W78 F152

✕ ~~לַמְנַצֵּחַ Lamenatseah (Psalm 20)~~

וּבָא לְצִיּוֹן Uva letsiyyon W80 F156

+ קַדִּישׁ שָׁלֵם Full Kaddish W82 F158

+ Prayers, readings, and songs for Yom Ha'atsma'ut W205–8

Conclude weekday Shaharit as usual.

---

מִנְחָה

**Weekday Amidah:**

+ עַל הַנִּסִּים Al hanissim for Yom Ha'atsma'ut W129 F182

✕ ~~תַּחֲנוּן Tahanun~~

---

**Iyyar 5 אִיָּר**
**Thu 9 May**

עַרְבִית

+ Before עָלֵינוּ Aleynu, count Omer. L63 S55 W152 F237
Day **20** (see instructions, p. 212)

---

**Iyyar 6 אִיָּר**
**Fri 10 May**

## שַׁבָּת Shabbat פָּרָשַׁת קְדֹשִׁים Parashat Kedoshim

עַרְבִית

+ Before עָלֵינוּ Aleynu, count Omer. L63 S55 W152 F237
Day **21** (see instructions, p. 212)

**Sat 11 May**

**Torah** 7 aliyot (minimum): קְדֹשִׁים Kedoshim
וַיִּקְרָא Vayikra (Leviticus) 19:1–20:27

| | | | | |
|---|---|---|---|---|
| Annual: | 1 19:1–14 | 2 19:15–22 | 3 19:23–32 | 4 19:33–37 |
| | 5 20:1–7 | 6 20:8–22 | 7 20:23–27 | M 20:25–27 |
| Triennial: | 1 19:15–18 | 2 19:19–22 | 3 19:23–32 | 4 19:33–37 |
| | 5 20:1–7 | 6 20:8–22 | 7 20:23–27 | M 20:25–27 |

**Haftarah**
☞ Ashkenazic: עָמוֹס Amos (Amos) 9:7–15
Sephardic: יְחֶזְקֵאל Yehezkel (Ezekiel) 20:2–20

☞ Recite אַב הָרַחֲמִים Av haraḥamim L446 S151 F420 during the Omer period, even if the usual custom of the congregation is to omit it.

**מִנְחָה**

**Torah** 3 aliyot: אֱמֹר Emor
וַיִּקְרָא Vayikra (Leviticus) 21:1–15
¹21:1–6 ²7–12° ³13–15 W294 P914

This is also the reading for the coming Monday and Thursday.

☞ °21:10 Note the unusual use of the ta'am (trope) | מֻנַּח־לְגַרְמֵיהּ (= | מֻנַּח־מַפְסִיק): | עַל־רֹאשׁוֹ

---

**Iyyar 7 אִיָּר**
**Sat 11 May**

**מוֹצָאֵי שַׁבָּת Motsa'ey Shabbat — Conclusion of Shabbat**

**עַרְבִית**

Saturday night Arvit as usual through L264 S281 W137 F200
קַדִּישׁ שָׁלֵם Full Kaddish L280 S294 W160 F688

+ Count Omer. L63 S55 W152 F237
Day **22** (see instructions, p. 212)

Some recite הַבְדָּלָה Havdalah here. L283 S299 W165 F700

עָלֵינוּ Aleynu L281 S297 W163 F696
קַדִּישׁ יָתוֹם Mourner's Kaddish L282 S298 W164 F698

הַבְדָּלָה Havdalah L283 S299 W165 F700

---

**Iyyar 8 אִיָּר**
**Sun 12 May** **עַרְבִית**

+ Before עָלֵינוּ Aleynu, count Omer. L63 S55 W152 F237
Day **23** (see instructions, p. 212)

---

**Iyyar 9 אִיָּר**
**Mon 13 May** **עַרְבִית**

+ Before עָלֵינוּ Aleynu, count Omer. L63 S55 W152 F237
Day **24** (see instructions, p. 212)

---

**Iyyar 10 אִיָּר**
**Tue 14 May** **עַרְבִית**

+ Before עָלֵינוּ Aleynu, count Omer. L63 S55 W152 F237
Day **25** (see instructions, p. 212)

| Iyyar 5779 | | | | | | |
|---|---|---|---|---|---|---|
| | 1 | 2 | 3 | 4 | 5 | 6 |
| 7 | 8 | 9 | 10 | 11 | 12 | 13 |
| 14 | 15 | 16 | 17 | 18 | 19 | 20 |
| 21 | 22 | 23 | 24 | 25 | 26 | 27 |
| 28 | 29 | | | | | |

| May \| Jun 2019 | | | | | | |
|---|---|---|---|---|---|---|
| | 6 | 7 | 8 | 9 | 10 | 11 |
| 12 | 13 | 14 | 15 | 16 | 17 | 18 |
| 19 | 20 | 21 | 22 | 23 | 24 | 25 |
| 26 | 27 | 28 | 29 | 30 | 31 \| | 1 |
| 2 | 3 | | | | | |

+ Add ✕ Omit ☞ Take note!

**Siddurim**
- **L** Lev Shalem for Shabbat and Festivals
- **S** Shabbat and Festival Sim Shalom
- **W** Weekday Sim Shalom
- **F** Full Sim Shalom (both editions)
- **P** Personal Edition of Full Sim Shalom

---

**Iyyar 11 אִיָּר**
**Wed 15 May**

עַרְבִית + Before עָלֵינוּ Aleynu, count Omer. L63 S55 W152 F237
Day **26** (see instructions, p. 212)

---

**Iyyar 12 אִיָּר**
**Thu 16 May**

עַרְבִית + Before עָלֵינוּ Aleynu, count Omer. L63 S55 W152 F237
Day **27** (see instructions, p. 212)

---

**Iyyar 13 אִיָּר**
**Fri 17 May**

## שַׁבָּת Shabbat פָּרָשַׁת אֱמֹר Parashat Emor

עַרְבִית + Before עָלֵינוּ Aleynu, count Omer. L63 S55 W152 F237
Day **28** (see instructions, p. 212)

**Sat 18 May**

**Torah** 7 aliyot (minimum): אֱמֹר Emor
וַיִּקְרָא Vayikra (Leviticus) 21:1–24:23

Annual: 1 21:1–15° 2 21:16–22:16 3 22:17–33 4 23:1–22
5 23:23–32 6 23:33–44 7 24:1–23 M 24:21–23

Triennial: 1 23:23–25 2 23:26–32 3 23:33–44 4 24:1–4
5 24:5–9 6 24:10–12 7 24:13–23 M 24:21–23

☞ °21:10 Note the unusual use of the ta'am (trope) | מְנַח־לְגַרְמֵיהּ
(= | מְנַח־מַפְסִיק): | עַל־רֹאשׁוֹ

**Haftarah** יְחֶזְקֵאל Yeḥezkel (Ezekiel) 44:15–31

☞ Recite אַב הָרַחֲמִים Av haraḥamim L446 S151 F420
during the Omer period, even if the usual custom of the congregation is to omit it.

מִנְחָה **Torah** 3 aliyot from בְּהַר Behar
וַיִּקְרָא Vayikra (Leviticus) 25:1–13
1 25:1–3 2 4–7 3 8–13 W295 P915

This is also the reading for the coming Monday and Thursday.

☞ צִדְקָתְךָ צֶדֶק Tsidkatekha tsedek L230 S239 W183 F584

## Iyyar 14 אִיָּר — Sat 18 May (evening)

## פֶּסַח שֵׁנִי Pesaḥ Sheni — The 2nd Pesaḥ

### מוֹצָאֵי שַׁבָּת Motsa'ey Shabbat — Conclusion of Shabbat

**Pesaḥ Sheni** is described in B<sup></sup>emidbar 9:6–14. People who were unable to partake of the Pesaḥ offering because of a particular ritual impurity or because of distant travel were obligated to perform a "make-up" Pesaḥ offering a month later. Pesaḥ Sheni is, therefore, a somewhat festive occasion.

As a reminder of this 2nd Pesaḥ offering, some eat מַצָּה *matsah* on this day.

**עַרְבִית**

Saturday night Arvit as usual through L264 S281 W137 F200
קַדִּישׁ שָׁלֵם Full Kaddish L280 S294 W160 F688

+ Count Omer. L63 S55 W152 F237
Day **29** (see instructions, p. 212)

Some recite הַבְדָּלָה Havdalah here. L283 S299 W165 F700

עָלֵינוּ Aleynu L281 S297 W163 F696
קַדִּישׁ יָתוֹם Mourner's Kaddish L282 S298 W164 F698

הַבְדָּלָה Havdalah L283 S299 W165 F700

**Sun 19 May** — **שַׁחֲרִית**

✕ ~~תַּחֲנוּן Taḥanun~~
☞ לַמְנַצֵּחַ Lamenatse·aḥ (Psalm 20) W79 F154

**מִנְחָה**

✕ ~~תַּחֲנוּן Taḥanun~~

---

## Iyyar 15 אִיָּר — Sun 19 May

**עַרְבִית**

+ Before עָלֵינוּ Aleynu, count Omer. L63 S55 W152 F237
Day **30** (see instructions, p. 212)

---

## Iyyar 16 אִיָּר — Mon 20 May

**עַרְבִית**

+ Before עָלֵינוּ Aleynu, count Omer. L63 S55 W152 F237
Day **31** (see instructions, p. 212)

---

## Iyyar 17 אִיָּר — Tue 21 May

### עֶרֶב לַ״ג בָּעֹמֶר Erev Lag Ba'omer
Day before Lag Ba'omer

**עַרְבִית**

+ Before עָלֵינוּ Aleynu, count Omer. L63 S55 W152 F237
Day **32** (see instructions, p. 212)

**Wed 22 May** — **מִנְחָה**

✕ ~~תַּחֲנוּן Taḥanun~~

| Iyyar 5779 | | | | | | |
|---|---|---|---|---|---|---|
| | 1 | 2 | 3 | 4 | 5 | 6 |
| 7 | 8 | 9 | 10 | 11 | 12 | 13 |
| 14 | 15 | 16 | 17 | 18 | 19 | 20 |
| 21 | 22 | 23 | 24 | 25 | 26 | 27 |
| 28 | 29 | | | | | |

| May \| Jun 2019 | | | | | | |
|---|---|---|---|---|---|---|
| | 6 | 7 | 8 | 9 | 10 | 11 |
| 12 | 13 | 14 | 15 | 16 | 17 | 18 |
| 19 | 20 | 21 | 22 | 23 | 24 | 25 |
| 26 | 27 | 28 | 29 | 30 | 31 \| | 1 |
| 2 | 3 | | | | | |

+ Add ✕ Omit ☞ Take note!

**Siddurim**
- **L** Lev Shalem for Shabbat and Festivals
- **S** Shabbat and Festival Sim Shalom
- **W** Weekday Sim Shalom
- **F** Full Sim Shalom (both editions)
- **P** Personal Edition of Full Sim Shalom

## Iyyar 18 אִיָּר — Wed 22 May (evening)

## לַ״ג בָּעֹמֶר Lag Ba'omer — Day 33 of the Omer

### Lag Ba'omer

Although there are no specific rituals or additions to the service, Lag Ba'omer is a festive occasion, celebrating happy events from the rabbinic period. It is customary to celebrate with outdoor activities or picnics.

Mourning practices associated with the Omer period are suspended. For example:

- Weddings and other communal celebrations are permitted.
- Haircuts are permitted. (In a year when Lag Ba'omer falls immediately after Shabbat, a haircut is permitted on Friday prior to Shabbat.)

עַרְבִית + Before עָלֵינוּ Aleynu, count Omer. L63 S55 W152 F237
Day **33** (see instructions, p. 212)

Thu 23 May שַׁחֲרִית ✕ ~~תַּחֲנוּן Taḥanun~~
☞ לַמְנַצֵּחַ Lamenatse·aḥ (Psalm 20) W79 F154

מִנְחָה ✕ ~~תַּחֲנוּן Taḥanun~~

## Iyyar 19 אִיָּר — Thu 23 May

עַרְבִית + Before עָלֵינוּ Aleynu, count Omer. L63 S55 W152 F237
Day **34** (see instructions, p. 212)

## Iyyar 20 אִיָּר — Fri 24 May

## שַׁבָּת Shabbat פָּרָשַׁת בְּהַר Parashat Behar

עַרְבִית + Before עָלֵינוּ Aleynu, count Omer. L63 S55 W152 F237
Day **35** (see instructions, p. 212)

Sat 25 May

**Torah** 7 aliyot (minimum): בְּהַר Behar
וַיִּקְרָא Vayikra (Leviticus) 25:1–26:2

| | | | | |
|---|---|---|---|---|
| Annual: | 1 25:1–13 | 2 25:14–18 | 3 25:19–24 | 4 25:25–28 |
| | 5 25:29–38 | 6 25:39–46 | 7 25:47–26:2 | M 25:55–26:2 |
| Triennial: | 1 25:1–3 | 2 25:4–7 | 3 25:8–10 | 4 25:11–13 |
| | 5 25:14–18 | 6 25:19–24 | 7 25:25–28 | M 25:25–28 |

**Haftarah**
Ashkenazic: יִרְמְיָהוּ Yirmeyahu (Jeremiah) 32:6–27
Sephardic: יִרְמְיָהוּ Yirmeyahu (Jeremiah) 32:6–22

☞ Recite אַב הָרַחֲמִים Av haraḥamim L446 S151 F420 during the Omer period, even if the usual custom of the congregation is to omit it.

מִנְחָה

**Torah** 3 aliyot from בְּחֻקֹּתַי Beḥukkotay
וַיִּקְרָא Vayikra (Leviticus) 26:3–13°
¹26:3–5 ²6–9 ³10–13 W296 P916

This is also the reading for the coming Monday and Thursday.

☞ °26:3–13 The reading extends through verse 13, which enables the correct configuration of the 3 aliyot.

---

**Iyyar 21 אִיָּר**
**Sat 25 May**

## מוֹצָאֵי שַׁבָּת Motsa'ey Shabbat Conclusion of Shabbat

עַרְבִית

Saturday night Arvit as usual through L264 S281 W137 F200
קַדִּישׁ שָׁלֵם Full Kaddish L280 S294 W160 F688

+ Count Omer. L63 S55 W152 F237
Day **36** (see instructions, p. 212)

Some recite הַבְדָּלָה Havdalah here. L283 S299 W165 F700

עָלֵינוּ Aleynu L281 S297 W163 F696
קַדִּישׁ יָתוֹם Mourner's Kaddish L282 S298 W164 F698

הַבְדָּלָה Havdalah L283 S299 W165 F700

---

**Iyyar 22 אִיָּר**
**Sun 26 May** עַרְבִית

+ Before עָלֵינוּ Aleynu, count Omer. L63 S55 W152 F237
Day **37** (see instructions, p. 212)

---

**Iyyar 23 אִיָּר**
**Mon 27 May** עַרְבִית

+ Before עָלֵינוּ Aleynu, count Omer. L63 S55 W152 F237
Day **38** (see instructions, p. 212)

---

**Iyyar 24 אִיָּר**
**Tue 28 May** עַרְבִית

+ Before עָלֵינוּ Aleynu, count Omer. L63 S55 W152 F237
Day **39** (see instructions, p. 212)

---

**Iyyar 25 אִיָּר**
**Wed 29 May** עַרְבִית

+ Before עָלֵינוּ Aleynu, count Omer. L63 S55 W152 F237
Day **40** (see instructions, p. 212)

| Iyyar 5779 | | | | | | |
|---|---|---|---|---|---|---|
| | 1 | 2 | 3 | 4 | 5 | 6 |
| 7 | 8 | 9 | 10 | 11 | 12 | 13 |
| 14 | 15 | 16 | 17 | 18 | 19 | 20 |
| 21 | 22 | 23 | 24 | 25 | 26 | 27 |
| 28 | 29 | | | | | |

| May \| Jun 2019 | | | | | | |
|---|---|---|---|---|---|---|
| | 6 | 7 | 8 | 9 | 10 | 11 |
| 12 | 13 | 14 | 15 | 16 | 17 | 18 |
| 19 | 20 | 21 | 22 | 23 | 24 | 25 |
| 26 | 27 | 28 | 29 | 30 | 31 \| | 1 |
| 2 | 3 | | | | | |

+ Add ✕ Omit ☞ Take note!

**Siddurim**
**L** Lev Shalem for Shabbat and Festivals
**S** Shabbat and Festival Sim Shalom
**W** Weekday Sim Shalom
**F** Full Sim Shalom (both editions)
**P** Personal Edition of Full Sim Shalom

---

**Iyyar 26 אִיָּר**
**Thu 30 May**

עַרְבִית + Before עָלֵינוּ Aleynu, count Omer. L63 S55 W152 F237
Day **41** (see instructions, p. 212)

---

**Iyyar 27 אִיָּר**
**Fri 31 May**

**שַׁבָּת Shabbat פָּרָשַׁת בְּחֻקֹּתַי Parashat Beḥukkotay**
**שַׁבַּת מְבָרְכִים הַחֹדֶשׁ Shabbat Mevarekhim Haḥodesh**

עַרְבִית + Before עָלֵינוּ Aleynu, count Omer. L63 S55 W152 F237
Day **42** (see instructions, p. 212)

**Sat 1 Jun**

**Torah** 7 aliyot (minimum): בְּחֻקֹּתַי Beḥukkotay
וַיִּקְרָא Vayikra (Leviticus) 26:3–27:34

| | | | | |
|---|---|---|---|---|
| Annual: | 1 26:3–5 | 2 26:6–9 | 3 26:10–46° | 4 27:1–15 |
| | 5 27:16–21 | 6 27:22–28 | 7 27:29–34▮ | M 27:32–34 |
| Triennial: | 1 27:1–4 | 2 27:5–8 | 3 27:9–15 | 4 27:16–21 |
| | 5 27:22–25 | 6 27:26–28 | 7 27:29–34▮ | M 27:32–34 |

☞°26:14–44 This is the תּוֹכֵחָה tokheḥah, verses of rebuke and warning. Because of the ominous nature of these verses, do not divide this lengthy passage into shorter aliyot. However, the chanting may be divided among multiple readers. All the readers must be present at the Torah when the oleh/olah recites the first berakhah. This serves as an implicit appointment of all the readers as sheliḥim (agents) of the oleh/olah.
Chant this section in a somewhat **subdued** voice to symbolically minimize the trepidation the congregation experiences upon hearing the message of these verses. Be sure that all words and te'amim (tropes, cantillations) remain clearly audible to the congregation.
For the verses voicing promise of God's protection and reward (10–13, 42, and 45) and for the concluding summary verse (46), chant as usual.

▮ חזק When the Torah reader concludes a book of the Torah:

1. Close the Torah scroll.
2. **For Oleh:** Congregation chants חֲזַק חֲזַק וְנִתְחַזֵּק ḥazak ḥazak venitḥazzek; oleh remains silent.
   **For Olah:** Congregation chants חִזְקִי חִזְקִי וְנִתְחַזֵּק ḥizki ḥizki venitḥazzek; olah remains silent.
3. Torah reader repeats congregation's words (oleh/olah remains silent; if Torah reader is the oleh/olah, omit this repetition).
4. Open the Torah scroll.
5. The oleh/olah kisses the Torah scroll, closes it, and continues with the usual concluding berakhah.

**Haftarah** יִרְמְיָהוּ Yirmeyahu (Jeremiah) 16:19–17:14

+ **Birkat Haḥodesh:** L180 S150 F418
Announce Rosh Ḥodesh Sivan:
רֹאשׁ חֹדֶשׁ סִיוָן יִהְיֶה בְּיוֹם שְׁלִישִׁי . . .
Rosh ḥodesh Sivan yihyeh beyom shelishi . . .
(Monday night and Tuesday)

☞ Recite אַב הָרַחֲמִים Av haraḥamim L446 S151 F420
during the Omer period, even if the usual custom of the congregation is to omit it.

מִנְחָה

**Torah** 3 aliyot from בְּמִדְבַּר Bemidbar
בְּמִדְבַּר Bemidbar (Numbers) 1:1–19
¹1:1–4 ²5–16 ³17–19 W297 P917

This is also the reading for the coming Monday and Thursday.

✕ ~~צִדְקָתְךָ צֶדֶק Tsidkatekha tsedek~~

---

**Iyyar 28 אִיָּר**
**Sat 1 Jun (evening)**

## יוֹם יְרוּשָׁלַיִם Yom Yerushalayim
**Jerusalem Day**
**מוֹצָאֵי שַׁבָּת Motsa'ey Shabbat Conclusion of Shabbat**

### Yom Yerushalayim

The Knesset in Israel established the annual observance of יוֹם יְרוּשָׁלַיִם to celebrate the reunification of Jerusalem during the Six-Day War in 1967. Celebratory psalms and readings are added to the service.

Mourning practices associated with the Omer period are suspended. For example:

- Weddings and other communal celebrations are permitted.
- Haircuts are permitted.

עַרְבִית

Saturday night Arvit as usual through L264 S281 W137 F200
קַדִּישׁ שָׁלֵם Full Kaddish L280 S294 W160 F688

+ Prayers, readings, and songs for Yom Yerushalayim W209–14

+ Count Omer. L63 S55 W152 F237
Day **43** (see instructions, p. 212)

| Iyyar 5779 | | | | | | |
|---|---|---|---|---|---|---|
| | 1 | 2 | 3 | 4 | 5 | 6 |
| 7 | 8 | 9 | 10 | 11 | 12 | 13 |
| 14 | 15 | 16 | 17 | 18 | 19 | 20 |
| 21 | 22 | 23 | 24 | 25 | 26 | 27 |
| 28 | 29 | | | | | |

| May \| Jun 2019 | | | | | | |
|---|---|---|---|---|---|---|
| | 6 | 7 | 8 | 9 | 10 | 11 |
| 12 | 13 | 14 | 15 | 16 | 17 | 18 |
| 19 | 20 | 21 | 22 | 23 | 24 | 25 |
| 26 | 27 | 28 | 29 | 30 | 31 \| | 1 |
| 2 | 3 | | | | | |

+ Add ✕ Omit ☞ Take note!

**Siddurim**
- **L** Lev Shalem for Shabbat and Festivals
- **S** Shabbat and Festival Sim Shalom
- **W** Weekday Sim Shalom
- **F** Full Sim Shalom (both editions)
- **P** Personal Edition of Full Sim Shalom

---

Some recite הַבְדָּלָה Havdalah here. L283 S299 W165 F700

עָלֵינוּ Aleynu L281 S297 W163 F696
קַדִּישׁ יָתוֹם Mourner's Kaddish L282 S298 W164 F698

הַבְדָּלָה Havdalah L283 S299 W165 F700

**Sun 2 Jun** שַׁחֲרִית

Weekday Shaharit as usual through
מִזְמוֹר לְתוֹדָה Mizmor letodah (Psalm 100) W20 F60

+ Psalms recited on Shabbat and Yom Tov:
☞ Psalms 19, 34, 90, 91, 135, 136, 33, 92, 93 S87–95 F60–78
Use weekday minor nusaḥ for the psalms.

Continue with the usual weekday service from
יְהִי כְבוֹד יי Yehi khevod adonay W20 F80
through the weekday Amidah.

✕ ~~תַּחֲנוּן Taḥanun~~

+ הַלֵּל שָׁלֵם Full Hallel W50 F380

חֲצִי קַדִּישׁ Short Kaddish W56 F390

+ תְּפִלָּה לִשְׁלוֹם הַמְּדִינָה Prayer for the State of Israel W75 F416
+ Other additions for Yom Yerushalayim W209–14

אַשְׁרֵי Ashrey W78 F152
✕ ~~לַמְנַצֵּחַ Lamenatseaḥ (Psalm 20)~~
וּבָא לְצִיּוֹן Uva letsiyyon W80 F156
קַדִּישׁ שָׁלֵם Full Kaddish W82 F158

Conclude as on a usual weekday.

מִנְחָה ✕ ~~תַּחֲנוּן Taḥanun~~

---

**Iyyar 29 אִיָּר**
**Sun 2 Jun**

**עֶרֶב ראֹשׁ חֹדֶשׁ Erev Rosh Ḥodesh**
**Day before Rosh Ḥodesh**

עַרְבִית + Before עָלֵינוּ Aleynu, count Omer. L63 S55 W152 F237
Day **44** (see instructions, p. 212)

**Mon 3 Jun** מִנְחָה ✕ ~~תַּחֲנוּן Taḥanun~~

## Sivan 1 סִיוָן
Mon 3 Jun (evening)

## רֹאשׁ חֹדֶשׁ סִיוָן Rosh Ḥodesh Sivan

**DURING Rosh Ḥodesh**

Birkat Hamazon:

+ יַעֲלֶה וְיָבוֹא Ya'aleh veyavo for Rosh Ḥodesh L90|95 S340|347 W233|239 F762|780

+ הָרַחֲמָן Haraḥaman for Rosh Ḥodesh L92|96 S343|348 W235|240 F768

**עַרְבִית**

Weekday Amidah:

+ יַעֲלֶה וְיָבוֹא Ya'aleh veyavo for Rosh Ḥodesh W145 F216

+ Before עָלֵינוּ Aleynu, count Omer. L63 S55 W152 F237
Day **45** (see instructions, p. 212)

**Tue 4 Jun** **שַׁחֲרִית**

Before מִזְמוֹר שִׁיר Mizmor shir (Psalm 30) W14 F50
or at end of service, recite:
Psalm for Tuesday (Psalm 82) W87 F26
קַדִּישׁ יָתוֹם Mourner's Kaddish (some omit) W100 F52
+ Psalm 104 for Rosh Ḥodesh W90 F34
קַדִּישׁ יָתוֹם Mourner's Kaddish W100 F52

Weekday Amidah:

+ יַעֲלֶה וְיָבוֹא Ya'aleh veyavo for Rosh Ḥodesh W41 F114

✕ ~~תַּחֲנוּן Taḥanun~~

+ חֲצִי הַלֵּל Short Hallel W50 F380
קַדִּישׁ שָׁלֵם Full Kaddish W56 F392

+ **TORAH SERVICE** W65 F138
Remove **1** Torah scroll from ark.

Torah 4 aliyot: פִּינְחָס Pineḥas
בְּמִדְבַּר Bemidbar (Numbers) 28:1–15
[1]28:1–3 [2]3–5 [3]6–10 [4]11–15 W320 P943

חֲצִי קַדִּישׁ Short Kaddish W71 F146
Open, raise, display, and wrap scroll.
Return scroll to ark. W76 F150

אַשְׁרֵי Ashrey W78 F152
✕ ~~לַמְנַצֵּחַ Lamenatseaḥ (Psalm 20)~~
וּבָא לְצִיּוֹן Uva letsiyyon W80 F156

| Jun 4 | 1 סִיוָן | | Sivan 5779 | | | | | Jun \| Jul 2019 | | | | | ➕ Add | ✖ Omit | ☞ Take note! |
|---|---|---|---|---|---|---|---|---|---|---|---|---|---|---|---|
| Jun 4 | 2 סִיוָן | | 1 | 2 | 3 | 4 | 5 | | 4 | 5 | 6 | 7 | 8 | **Siddurim** | |
| Jun 5 | | | 6 | 7 | 8 | 9 | 10 | 11 | 12 | 9 | 10 | 11 | 12 | 13 | 14 | 15 | **L** Lev Shalem for Shabbat and Festivals |
| Jun 5 | 3 סִיוָן | | 13 | 14 | 15 | 16 | 17 | 18 | 19 | 16 | 17 | 18 | 19 | 20 | 21 | 22 | **S** Shabbat and Festival Sim Shalom |
| | | | 20 | 21 | 22 | 23 | 24 | 25 | 26 | 23 | 24 | 25 | 26 | 27 | 28 | 29 | **W** Weekday Sim Shalom |
| | | | 27 | 28 | 29 | 30 | | | | 30 \| 1 | 2 | 3 | | | | **F** Full Sim Shalom (both editions) |
| | | | | | | | | | | | | | | | | **P** Personal Edition of Full Sim Shalom |

**Some congregations:**
Remove and pack tᵉfillin at this point.
➕ חֲצִי קַדִּישׁ Short Kaddish  ᵂ103 ᶠ428

**Other congregations:**
➕ חֲצִי קַדִּישׁ Short Kaddish  ᵂ103 ᶠ428
Remove and cover—but do not pack—tᵉfillin, so that all begin Musaf Amidah at the same time, as soon after Kaddish as possible.

מוּסָף ➕ **Rosh Ḥodesh Amidah for weekdays:**  ᵂ104 ᶠ486
Weekday קְדֻשָּׁה Kᵉdushah  ᵂ105 ᶠ488
✖ ~~וּלְכַפָּרַת פָּשַׁע Ulkhapparat pasha~~
Beginning with Rosh Ḥodesh Nisan, we do not add these words.

➕ קַדִּישׁ שָׁלֵם Full Kaddish  ᵂ82 ᶠ158
עָלֵינוּ Aleynu  ᵂ83 ᶠ160

**If psalms for the day were not recited at Shaḥarit, add here:**
קַדִּישׁ יָתוֹם Mourner's Kaddish (some omit)  ᵂ84 ᶠ162
Psalm for Tuesday (Psalm 82)  ᵂ87 ᶠ26
קַדִּישׁ יָתוֹם Mourner's Kaddish (some omit)  ᵂ100 ᶠ52
➕ Psalm 104 for Rosh Ḥodesh  ᵂ90 ᶠ34

קַדִּישׁ יָתוֹם Mourner's Kaddish  ᵂ84\|100 ᶠ162\|52

מִנְחָה **Weekday Amidah:**
➕ יַעֲלֶה וְיָבוֹא Ya'ᵃleh vᵉyavo for Rosh Ḥodesh  ᵂ127 ᶠ178

✖ ~~תַּחֲנוּן Taḥᵃnun~~

---

**Sivan 2 סִיוָן**
Tue **4** Jun  עַרְבִית ➕ Before עָלֵינוּ Aleynu, count Omer.  ᴸ63 ˢ55 ᵂ152 ᶠ237
Day **46** (see instructions, p. 212)

Wed **5** Jun  שַׁחֲרִית ✖ ~~תַּחֲנוּן Taḥᵃnun~~
☞ לַמְנַצֵּחַ Lamᵉnatse·aḥ (Psalm 20)  ᵂ79 ᶠ154

מִנְחָה ✖ ~~תַּחֲנוּן Taḥᵃnun~~

---

**Sivan 3 סִיוָן**
Wed **5** Jun  עַרְבִית ➕ Before עָלֵינוּ Aleynu, count Omer.  ᴸ63 ˢ55 ᵂ152 ᶠ237
Day **47** (see instructions, p. 212)

**Thu 6 Jun** שַׁחֲרִית ✕ ~~תַּחֲנוּן Taḥanun~~
☞ לַמְנַצֵּחַ Lamenatse·aḥ (Psalm 20) W79 F154

מִנְחָה ✕ ~~תַּחֲנוּן Taḥanun~~

**Sivan 4 סִיוָן**
**Thu 6 Jun** עַרְבִית + Before עָלֵינוּ Aleynu, count Omer. L63 S55 W152 F237
Day **48** (see instructions, p. 212)

**Fri 7 Jun** שַׁחֲרִית ✕ ~~תַּחֲנוּן Taḥanun~~
☞ לַמְנַצֵּחַ Lamenatse·aḥ (Psalm 20) W79 F154

מִנְחָה ✕ ~~תַּחֲנוּן Taḥanun~~ (as on all Friday afternoons)

## Shavu'ot
### Before Shabbat

**Preparing a Flame for Yom Tov**

On Yom Tov, kindling a *new* fire is not permitted; however, the use of an *existing* fire for cooking or other purposes is permitted.

To light candles for Yom Tov (Saturday night), ensure you have a fire burning before candle-lighting time for Shabbat that will continue to burn until after dark on Saturday. For example:

- A burning candle that lasts for more than 25 hours
- A pilot light on a gas range (*not* a gas range with an electronic starter)

**Sivan 5 סִיוָן** שַׁבָּת **Shabbat** פָּרָשַׁת בְּמִדְבַּר **Parashat Bemidbar**
**Fri 7 Jun**

עַרְבִית + Before עָלֵינוּ Aleynu, count Omer. L63 S55 W152 F237
Day **49** (see instructions, p. 212)

**Sat 8 Jun**

**Torah** 7 aliyot (minimum): בְּמִדְבַּר Bemidbar
בְּמִדְבַּר Bemidbar (Numbers) 1:1–4:20

| | | | | |
|---|---|---|---|---|
| Annual: | 1 1:1–19 | 2 1:20–54 | 3 2:1–34 | 4 3:1–13 |
| | 5 3:14–39 | 6 3:40–51 | 7 4:1–20 | M 4:17–20 |
| Triennial: | 1 3:14–20 | 2 3:21–26 | 3 3:27–39 | 4 3:40–43 |
| | 5 3:44–51 | 6 4:1–10 | 7 4:11–20 | M 4:17–20 |

**Haftarah** הוֹשֵׁעַ Hoshe·a (Hosea) 2:1–22

| Sivan 5779 | | | | | | |
|---|---|---|---|---|---|---|
| | | 1 | 2 | 3 | 4 | 5 |
| 6 | 7 | 8 | 9 | 10 | 11 | 12 |
| 13 | 14 | 15 | 16 | 17 | 18 | 19 |
| 20 | 21 | 22 | 23 | 24 | 25 | 26 |
| 27 | 28 | 29 | 30 | | | |

| Jun \| Jul 2019 | | | | | | |
|---|---|---|---|---|---|---|
| | | 4 | 5 | 6 | 7 | 8 |
| 9 | 10 | 11 | 12 | 13 | 14 | 15 |
| 16 | 17 | 18 | 19 | 20 | 21 | 22 |
| 23 | 24 | 25 | 26 | 27 | 28 | 29 |
| 30 | 1 | 2 | 3 | | | |

+ Add ✕ Omit ☞ Take note!

**Siddurim**
**L** Lev Shalem for Shabbat and Festivals
**S** Shabbat and Festival Sim Shalom
**W** Weekday Sim Shalom
**F** Full Sim Shalom (both editions)
**P** Personal Edition of Full Sim Shalom

☞ Recite אַב הָרַחֲמִים Av haraḥamim L446 S151 F420 during the Omer period, even if the usual custom of the congregation is to omit it.

מִנְחָה

**Torah** 3 aliyot from נָשֹׂא Naso
בְּמִדְבַּר Bemidbar (Numbers) 4:21–4:33°
1 4:21–24 2 25–28 3 29–33° W298 P918

This is also the reading for the coming Thursday.

☞ °4:21–33 Some continue reading through 4:37. This is not necessary.

✕ ~~צִדְקָתְךָ צֶדֶק Tsidkatekha tsedek~~

## Shavu'ot — Day 1 and Day 2

### Candle Lighting for Yom Tov

Both Shabbat and Yom Tov end after dark: when 3 stars appear or at least 25 minutes after sunset (43 minutes after the time set for Shabbat candle lighting). Some wait longer. For the appropriate time in your community, consult your rabbi.

1. **Shavu'ot — Day 1:** Wait until Shabbat ends.
   **Shavu'ot — Day 2:** Wait until Day 1 ends.
2. Do *not strike* a match. Instead, transfer fire to the candles from an *existing* flame (see p. 167) by inserting a match or other stick into the flame.
3. Do *not extinguish* the match or stick. Instead, place it on a non-flammable tray or dish, and let it self-extinguish. Alternately, a wood *safety* match held vertically (flame up) usually self-extinguishes quickly.
4. Recite 2 בְּרָכוֹת *berakhot* (both nights): L79 S303 F718

   בָּרוּךְ אַתָּה יי, אֱ־לֹהֵינוּ מֶלֶךְ הָעוֹלָם, אֲשֶׁר קִדְּשָׁנוּ בְּמִצְוֹתָיו
   וְצִוָּנוּ לְהַדְלִיק נֵר שֶׁל יוֹם טוֹב.

   Barukh attah adonay, eloheynu melekh ha'olam,
   asher kiddeshanu bemitsvotav vetsivvanu lehadlik ner shel yom tov.

   בָּרוּךְ אַתָּה יי, אֱ־לֹהֵינוּ מֶלֶךְ הָעוֹלָם, שֶׁהֶחֱיָנוּ וְקִיְּמָנוּ וְהִגִּיעָנוּ לַזְּמַן הַזֶּה.

   Barukh attah adonay, eloheynu melekh ha'olam,
   sheheḥeyanu vekiyyemanu vehiggi'anu lazeman hazeh.
5. **Shavu'ot — Day 1:** To light candles for Yom Tov — Day 2 (Sunday night), you must have a fire that will continue to burn until after dark on Sunday. If this necessitates lighting another long-burning candle, follow instructions 2 and 3 above for transferring the flame.

**Yom Tov Meals — Day 1 and Day 2**

Enjoy festive meals evening and afternoon, in the manner of Shabbat meals, with:

- Yom Tov קִדּוּשׁ *kiddush* (after dark):
  Night L79 S334 F742 (Day 1: add Havdalah L80 S335 F744) Daytime L81 S335 F746
- הַמּוֹצִיא *hamotsi* recited over 2 whole חַלָּה *ḥallah* loaves or rolls L81 S313–14 F744|746
- בִּרְכַּת הַמָּזוֹן *birkat hamazon* with Shavu'ot additions (see yellow box, below)
- Festive singing

Meals consisting of dairy foods are customary on Shavu'ot. Some follow this practice only for the first day of Shavu'ot.

**Tikkun Leyl Shavu'ot**

On the first night, some follow the kabbalistic tradition of participating in a תִּקּוּן לֵיל שָׁבוּעוֹת *tikkun leyl shavu'ot,* a night of Torah study, to thoroughly prepare for reliving God's revelation at Sinai during the morning Torah service.

## Sivan 6 סִיוָן — שָׁבוּעוֹת Shavu'ot — Day 1

Sat 8 Jun (evening)

**DURING Shavu'ot**

**Birkat Hamazon:**

+ יַעֲלֶה וְיָבוֹא Ya'aleh veyavo for Shavu'ot L90|95 S340|347 W233|239 F762|780

+ הָרַחֲמָן Haraḥaman for Yom Tov L92|96 S343|348 W236|240 F768

**עַרְבִית**

Arvit for Yom Tov L39 S28 F279

+ וַיְדַבֵּר מֹשֶׁה Vaydabber mosheh (Vayikra 23:44) L46 S34 F294

חֲצִי קַדִּישׁ Short Kaddish L46 S34 F294

**Yom Tov Amidah:** L306 S41 F304

+ וַתּוֹדִיעֵנוּ Vatodi'eynu L309 S41 F306

+ Insertions for Shavu'ot

קַדִּישׁ שָׁלֵם Full Kaddish L54 S48 F316

+ קִדּוּשׁ Kiddush for Yom Tov
with insertions for Shavu'ot L79 S50 F318

+ with Havdalah L80 S50 F320

+ שֶׁהֶחֱיָנוּ Sheheḥeyanu L80 S50 F319

עָלֵינוּ Aleynu L56 S51 F320

קַדִּישׁ יָתוֹם Mourner's Kaddish L58 S52 F324

**At home**

Light candles after dark.
See "Candle Lighting for Yom Tov," p. 168.
Recite קִדּוּשׁ Kiddush after dark, including Havdalah.
See "Yom Tov Meals — Day 1 and Day 2," above.

| Sivan 5779 | | | | | | |
|---|---|---|---|---|---|---|
| | | 1 | 2 | 3 | 4 | 5 |
| 6 | 7 | 8 | 9 | 10 | 11 | 12 |
| 13 | 14 | 15 | 16 | 17 | 18 | 19 |
| 20 | 21 | 22 | 23 | 24 | 25 | 26 |
| 27 | 28 | 29 | 30 | | | |

| Jun \| Jul 2019 | | | | | | |
|---|---|---|---|---|---|---|
| | | 4 | 5 | 6 | 7 | 8 |
| 9 | 10 | 11 | 12 | 13 | 14 | 15 |
| 16 | 17 | 18 | 19 | 20 | 21 | 22 |
| 23 | 24 | 25 | 26 | 27 | 28 | 29 |
| 30 | 1 | 2 | 3 | | | |

+ Add ✕ Omit ☞ Take note!

**Siddurim**
**L** Lev Shalem for Shabbat and Festivals
**S** Shabbat and Festival Sim Shalom
**W** Weekday Sim Shalom
**F** Full Sim Shalom (both editions)
**P** Personal Edition of Full Sim Shalom

**Sun 9 Jun** שַׁחֲרִית

At the end of the preliminary service, begin formal chanting at
הָאֵ־ל בְּתַעֲצוּמוֹת עֻזֶּךָ Ha'el beta'atsumot uzzekha. L147 S105 F336

✕ ~~הַכֹּל יוֹדוּךָ Hakol yodukha~~
✕ ~~אֵ־ל אָדוֹן El adon~~
✕ ~~לָאֵ־ל אֲשֶׁר שָׁבַת La'el asher shavat~~
+ הַמֵּאִיר לָאָרֶץ Hame'ir la'arets L152 S109 F342

**Yom Tov Amidah:** L306 S123 F366
+ Insertions for Shavu'ot

+ הַלֵּל שָׁלֵם Full Hallel L316 S133 F380

קַדִּישׁ שָׁלֵם Full Kaddish L321 S138 F392

**YOM TOV TORAH SERVICE** L322 S139 F394

+ יי יי אֵ־ל רַחוּם וְחַנּוּן
Adonay adonay el raḥum veḥannun (3 times) L323 S140 F394
+ רִבּוֹנוֹ שֶׁל עוֹלָם Ribbono shel olam L323 S140 F396
+ וַאֲנִי תְפִלָּתִי לְךָ Va'ani tefillati lekha (3 times) L323 S140 F396

Remove **2** Torah scrolls from ark.

+ Just before the person called for the 1st aliyah begins the 1st בְּרָכָה berakhah, recite אַקְדָּמוּת Akdamut. L413 S222 F526
Torah reader and congregation chant alternate couplets.

**1st scroll** 5 aliyot from יִתְרוֹ Yitro
שְׁמוֹת Shemot (Exodus) 19:1–°20:22
¹19:1–6 ²19:7–13 ³19:14–19 °⁴19:20–20:13 °⁵20:14–22

☞ °**Verse numbers in chapter 20:** The verses are misnumbered in many editions. Use these guidelines to properly divide the reading:
Aliyah **4**: ends לְרֵעֶךָ (20:14 in many books).
Aliyah **5**: וְכָל־הָעָם through עָלָיו (20:15–23 in many books)

☞ °20:1–13 Follow the te'amim (tropes) for the public reading of עֲשֶׂרֶת הַדִּבְּרוֹת, on p. 97. For additional instructions for this passage, see p. 96.

Place 2nd scroll on table next to 1st scroll.

חֲצִי קַדִּישׁ Short Kaddish L327 S146 F408
Open, raise, display, and wrap 1st scroll.

**2nd scroll** Maftir aliyah from פִּינְחָס Pinehas
בְּמִדְבַּר^M^ Bemidbar (Numbers) 28:26–31

Open, raise, display, and wrap 2nd scroll.

**Haftarah** for Shavu'ot — Day 1
יְחֶזְקֵאל Yehezkel (Ezekiel) 1:1–28; 3:12

**Haftarah blessings:**
✕ ~~Concluding Shabbat בְּרָכָה berakhah~~
+ Concluding Yom Tov בְּרָכָה berakhah with insertions for Shavu'ot L329 S147 F412

✕ ~~יְקוּם פֻּרְקָן Yekum purkan~~
✕ ~~אַב הָרַחֲמִים Av Harahamim~~

אַשְׁרֵי Ashrey L339 S151 F420
Return scrolls to ark. L340 S153 F422
חֲצִי קַדִּישׁ Short Kaddish L342 S155 F428

מוּסָף

**Yom Tov Amidah:** L343 S166 F456
+ Insertions for Shavu'ot

Some congregations include in the repetition of the Amidah the Priestly Blessing by the Kohanim (*dukhenen*).
בִּרְכַּת כֹּהֲנִים Birkat kohanim L353 S177 F472
For procedures, see p. 213.

קַדִּישׁ שָׁלֵם Full kaddish L203 S181 F506
Continue with אֵין כֵּא·לֹהֵינוּ Eyn keloheynu. L204 S182 F508

קִדּוּשָׁא רַבָּא

**Daytime Kiddush for Yom Tov:** L81 S335 F746
וַיְדַבֵּר מֹשֶׁה Vaydabber mosheh (Vayikra 23:44)
בּוֹרֵא פְּרִי הַגָּפֶן Bo·re peri hagafen

מִנְחָה

אַשְׁרֵי Ashrey L214 S226 W170 F558
וּבָא לְצִיּוֹן Uva letsiyyon L216 S227 W171 F560
חֲצִי קַדִּישׁ Short Kaddish L217 S229 W173 F564

**Yom Tov Amidah:** L306 S242 W184 F586
+ Insertions for Shavu'ot

קַדִּישׁ שָׁלֵם Full Kaddish L230 S247 W189 F596
עָלֵינוּ Aleynu L231 S248 W190 F598
קַדִּישׁ יָתוֹם Mourner's Kaddish L232 S249 W191 F600

Sivan 5779

| | | | | | | |
|---|---|---|---|---|---|---|
| | | 1 | 2 | 3 | 4 | 5 |
| 6 | 7 | 8 | 9 | 10 | 11 | 12 |
| 13 | 14 | 15 | 16 | 17 | 18 | 19 |
| 20 | 21 | 22 | 23 | 24 | 25 | 26 |
| 27 | 28 | 29 | 30 | | | |

Jun | Jul 2019

| | | | | | | |
|---|---|---|---|---|---|---|
| | | 4 | 5 | 6 | 7 | 8 |
| 9 | 10 | 11 | 12 | 13 | 14 | 15 |
| 16 | 17 | 18 | 19 | 20 | 21 | 22 |
| 23 | 24 | 25 | 26 | 27 | 28 | 29 |
| 30 | 1 | 2 | 3 | | | |

+ Add ✕ Omit ☞ Take note!

**Siddurim**
- **L** Lev Shalem for Shabbat and Festivals
- **S** Shabbat and Festival Sim Shalom
- **W** Weekday Sim Shalom
- **F** Full Sim Shalom (both editions)
- **P** Personal Edition of Full Sim Shalom

## Sivan 7 סִיוָן — Sun 9 Jun

## שָׁבוּעוֹת Shavu'ot — Day 2

**עַרְבִית**

Arvit for Yom Tov L39 S28 F279

+ וַיְדַבֵּר מֹשֶׁה Vaydabber mosheh (Vayikra 23:44) L46 S34 F294

חֲצִי קַדִּישׁ Short Kaddish L46 S34 F294

**Yom Tov Amidah:** L306 S41 F304

+ Insertions for Shavu'ot

קַדִּישׁ שָׁלֵם Full Kaddish L54 S48 F316

+ קִדּוּשׁ Kiddush for Yom Tov
with insertions for Shavu'ot L79 S50 F318

+ שֶׁהֶחֱיָנוּ Sheheḥeyanu L80 S50 F319

עָלֵינוּ Aleynu L56 S51 F320

קַדִּישׁ יָתוֹם Mourner's Kaddish L58 S52 F324

**At home**

For candle-lighting instructions for Day 2, see blue box, p. 168.
For Yom Tov meals, see blue box, p. 169.

**Mon 10 Jun שַׁחֲרִית**

At the end of the preliminary service,
begin formal chanting at הָאֵ·ל בְּתַעֲצוּמוֹת עֻזֶּךָ Ha'el beta'atsumot uzzekha. L147 S105 F336

✕ ~~הַכֹּל יוֹדוּךָ Hakol yodukha~~
✕ ~~אֵ·ל אָדוֹן El adon~~
✕ ~~לָאֵ·ל אֲשֶׁר שָׁבַת La'el asher shavat~~

+ הַמֵּאִיר לָאָרֶץ Hame'ir la'arets L152 S109 F342

**Yom Tov Amidah:** L306 S123 F366

+ Insertions for Shavu'ot

+ הַלֵּל שָׁלֵם Full Hallel L316 S133 F380

קַדִּישׁ שָׁלֵם Full Kaddish L321 S138 F392

+ **Megillah reading:**
Some congregations read
מְגִלַּת רוּת Megillat Rut (Scroll of Ruth),
without reciting a בְּרָכָה berakhah.
Some read selections in English. L333 S383 F790

קַדִּישׁ יָתוֹם Mourner's Kaddish L338 S82 F52

## YOM TOV TORAH SERVICE L322 S139 F394

+ יי יי אֵ-ל רַחוּם וְחַנּוּן
Adonay adonay el raḥum veḥannun (3 times) L323 S140 F394

+ רִבּוֹנוֹ שֶׁל עוֹלָם Ribbono shel olam L323 S140 F396

+ וַאֲנִי תְפִלָּתִי לְךָ Va'ani tefillati lekha (3 times) L323 S140 F396

Remove **2** Torah scrolls from ark.

**1st scroll** 5 aliyot from רְאֵה Re'eh
דְּבָרִים Devarim (Deuteronomy) 15:19–16:17
1 15:19–23 2 16:1–3 3 4–8 4 9–12 5 13–17

Place 2nd scroll on table next to 1st scroll.
חֲצִי קַדִּישׁ Short Kaddish L327 S146 F408
Open, raise, display, and wrap 1st scroll.

**2nd scroll** Maftir aliyah from פִּינְחָס Pineḥas
M בְּמִדְבַּר Bemidbar (Numbers) 28:26–31

Open, raise, display, and wrap 2nd scroll.

**Haftarah** for Shavu'ot — Day 2
Ashkenazic: חֲבַקּוּק Ḥavakkuk (Habakkuk) 3:1–19°
Sephardic: חֲבַקּוּק Ḥavakkuk (Habakkuk) 2:20–3:19°

☞ °3:19 יֱהוִֹה אֲ-דֹנָי — Read: elohim adonay.

**Haftarah blessings:**

✕ ~~Concluding Shabbat בְּרָכָה berakhah~~

+ Concluding Yom Tov בְּרָכָה berakhah
with insertions for Shavu'ot L329 S147 F412

✕ ~~יְקוּם פֻּרְקָן Yekum purkan~~

+ יִזְכֹּר Yizkor L330 S188 F516

☞ אַב הָרַחֲמִים Av Haraḥamim L446 S151 F420

אַשְׁרֵי Ashrey L339 S151 F420
Return scrolls to ark. L340 S153 F422
חֲצִי קַדִּישׁ Short Kaddish L342 S155 F428

| Sivan 5779 | | | | | | |
|---|---|---|---|---|---|---|
| | | 1 | 2 | 3 | 4 | 5 |
| 6 | 7 | 8 | 9 | 10 | 11 | 12 |
| 13 | 14 | 15 | 16 | 17 | 18 | 19 |
| 20 | 21 | 22 | 23 | 24 | 25 | 26 |
| 27 | 28 | 29 | 30 | | | |

| Jun \| Jul 2019 | | | | | | |
|---|---|---|---|---|---|---|
| | | 4 | 5 | 6 | 7 | 8 |
| 9 | 10 | 11 | 12 | 13 | 14 | 15 |
| 16 | 17 | 18 | 19 | 20 | 21 | 22 |
| 23 | 24 | 25 | 26 | 27 | 28 | 29 |
| 30 \| 1 | 2 | 3 | | | | |

+ Add ✕ Omit ☞ Take note!

**Siddurim**
- **L** Lev Shalem for Shabbat and Festivals
- **S** Shabbat and Festival Sim Shalom
- **W** Weekday Sim Shalom
- **F** Full Sim Shalom (both editions)
- **P** Personal Edition of Full Sim Shalom

**מוּסָף**

**Yom Tov Amidah:** L343 S166 F456

+ Insertions for Shavu'ot

Some congregations include in the repetition of the Amidah the Priestly Blessing by the Kohanim (*dukhenen*).
בִּרְכַּת כֹּהֲנִים Birkat kohanim L353 S177 F472
For procedures, see p. 213.

קַדִּישׁ שָׁלֵם Full kaddish L203 S181 F506
Continue with אֵין כֵּא·לֹהֵינוּ Eyn keloheynu. L204 S182 F508

**קִדּוּשָׁא רַבָּא**

**Daytime Kiddush for Yom Tov:** L81 S335 F746
וַיְדַבֵּר מֹשֶׁה Vaydabber mosheh (Vayikra 23:44)
בּוֹרֵא פְּרִי הַגָּפֶן Bo·re peri hagafen

**מִנְחָה**

אַשְׁרֵי Ashrey L214 S226 W170 F558
וּבָא לְצִיּוֹן Uva letsiyyon L216 S227 W171 F560
חֲצִי קַדִּישׁ Short Kaddish L217 S229 W173 F564

**Yom Tov Amidah:** L306 S242 W184 F586

+ Insertions for Shavu'ot

קַדִּישׁ שָׁלֵם Full Kaddish L230 S247 W189 F596
עָלֵינוּ Aleynu L231 S248 W190 F598
קַדִּישׁ יָתוֹם Mourner's Kaddish L232 S249 W191 F600

---

**Sivan 8 סִיוָן**
**Mon 10 Jun**

**מוֹצָאֵי יוֹם טוֹב Motsa'ey Yom Tov**
**Conclusion of Yom Tov**
**אִסְרוּ חַג Isru Ḥag The Day after Yom Tov**

**עַרְבִית**

Arvit for weekdays L264 S281 W137 F200

**Weekday Amidah:**

+ אַתָּה חוֹנַנְתָּנוּ Attah ḥonantanu L272 S281 W143 F212

קַדִּישׁ שָׁלֵם Full Kaddish L280 S294 W160 F222

Some recite הַבְדָּלָה Havdalah here. L283 S299 W165 F700
For instructions, see below.

עָלֵינוּ Aleynu L281 S297 W163 F696
קַדִּישׁ יָתוֹם Mourner's Kaddish L282 S298 W164 F698

| ✚ Add  ✘ Omit  ☞ Take note! | **Sivan 5779** | **Jun \| Jul 2019** | סִיוָן **8** Jun 10 |
| **Siddurim** | 1 2 3 4 5 | 4 5 6 7 8 | Jun 11 |
| **L** Lev Shalem for Shabbat and Festivals | 6 7 8 9 10 11 12 | 9 10 11 12 13 14 15 | סִיוָן **9** Jun 12 |
| **S** Shabbat and Festival Sim Shalom | 13 14 15 16 17 18 19 | 16 17 18 19 20 21 22 | סִיוָן **12** Jun 15 |
| **W** Weekday Sim Shalom | 20 21 22 23 24 25 26 | 23 24 25 26 27 28 29 | |
| **F** Full Sim Shalom (both editions) | 27 28 29 30 | 30 \| 1 2 3 | |
| **P** Personal Edition of Full Sim Shalom | | | |

+ **Havdalah:** L283 S299 W165 F700

✕ ~~הִנֵּה אֵ-ל יְשׁוּעָתִי Hinneh el yeshu'ati~~

בּוֹרֵא פְּרִי הַגָּפֶן Bo·re peri hagafen

✕ ~~בּוֹרֵא מִינֵי בְשָׂמִים Bo·re miney vesamim~~

✕ ~~בּוֹרֵא מְאוֹרֵי הָאֵשׁ Bo·re me'orey ha'esh~~

הַמַּבְדִּיל בֵּין קֹדֶשׁ לְחֹל Hamavdil beyn kodesh leḥol

**Tue 11 Jun** שַׁחֲרִית Shaḥarit for weekdays W1 F2

✕ ~~תַּחֲנוּן Taḥanun~~

☞ לַמְנַצֵּחַ Lamenatse·aḥ (Psalm 20) W79 F154

מִנְחָה ✕ ~~תַּחֲנוּן Taḥanun~~

---

**Sivan 9 סִיוָן**
**Wed 12 Jun**

**BEGINNING 9 Sivan** Resume reciting תַּחֲנוּן Taḥanun.
(Some congregations do not resume until 13 Sivan.)

---

**Sivan 12 סִיוָן**
**Sat 15 Jun**

## שַׁבָּת Shabbat פָּרָשַׁת נָשֹׂא Parashat Naso

**Torah** 7 aliyot (minimum): נָשֹׂא Naso
בְּמִדְבַּר Bemidbar (Numbers) 4:21–7:89

| | | | | |
|---|---|---|---|---|
| Annual: | 1 4:21–37° | 2 4:38–49 | 3 5:1–10 | 4 5:11–6:27 |
| | 5 7:1–41 | 6 7:42–71 | 7 7:72–89 | M 7:87–89 |
| Triennial: | 1 7:1–11 | 2 7:12–23 | 3 7:24–35 | 4 7:36–47 |
| | 5 7:48–59 | 6 7:60–71 | 7 7:72–89 | M 7:87–89 |

☞ °4:26 Note the unusual consecutive occurrences of the ta'am | מֻנַּח־לְגַרְמֵיהּ (= | מֻנַּח־מַפְסִיק): וְאֶת־מָסַךְ | פֶּתַח | שַׁעַר הֶחָצֵר

**Haftarah** שׁוֹפְטִים Shofetim (Judges) 13:2–25

מִנְחָה **Torah** 3 aliyot from בְּהַעֲלֹתְךָ Beha'alotekha
בְּמִדְבַּר Bemidbar (Numbers) 8:1–14
1 8:1–4 2 5–9 3 10–14 W299 P919

This is also the reading for the coming Monday and Thursday.

☞ Congregations that resume reciting תַּחֲנוּן Taḥanun after 8 Sivan recite צִדְקָתְךָ צֶדֶק Tsidkatekha tsedek.

Jun 16 13 סִיוָן
Jun 22 19 סִיוָן

| Sivan 5779 | | | | | | |
|---|---|---|---|---|---|---|
| | 1 | 2 | 3 | 4 | 5 | |
| 6 | 7 | 8 | 9 | 10 | 11 | 12 |
| 13 | 14 | 15 | 16 | 17 | 18 | 19 |
| 20 | 21 | 22 | 23 | 24 | 25 | 26 |
| 27 | 28 | 29 | 30 | | | |

| Jun \| Jul 2019 | | | | | | |
|---|---|---|---|---|---|---|
| | | 4 | 5 | 6 | 7 | 8 |
| 9 | 10 | 11 | 12 | 13 | 14 | 15 |
| 16 | 17 | 18 | 19 | 20 | 21 | 22 |
| 23 | 24 | 25 | 26 | 27 | 28 | 29 |
| 30 | 1 | 2 | 3 | | | |

\+ Add ✕ Omit ☞ Take note!

**Siddurim**
**L** Lev Shalem for Shabbat and Festivals
**S** Shabbat and Festival Sim Shalom
**W** Weekday Sim Shalom
**F** Full Sim Shalom (both editions)
**P** Personal Edition of Full Sim Shalom

## Sivan 13 סִיוָן
Sun 16 Jun

**BEGINNING 13 Sivan** Congregations that have not yet resumed reciting תַּחֲנוּן Taḥanun resume now.

## Sivan 19 סִיוָן
Sat 22 Jun

### שַׁבָּת Shabbat פָּרָשַׁת בְּהַעֲלֹתְךָ Parashat Beha'alotekha

**Torah** 7 aliyot (minimum): בְּהַעֲלֹתְךָ Beha'alotekha
בְּמִדְבַּר Bemidbar (Numbers) 8:1–12:16

| | | | | |
|---|---|---|---|---|
| Annual: | 1 8:1–14 | 2 8:15–26 | 3 9:1–14 | 4 9:15–10:10 |
| | 5 10:11–34° | 6 10:35–11:29° | 7 11:30–12:16 | M 12:14–16 |
| Triennial: | 1 10:35–11:9° | 2 11:10–18 | 3 11:19–22 | 4 11:23–29 |
| | 5 11:30–35 | 6 12:1–13 | 7 12:14–16 | M 12:14–16 |

☞ °10:15–16, 19–20, 23–24, 26–27 Chant these 4 pairs of verses using the "desert traveling melody," based on Shirat Hayam melody.

☞ °10:35–36 This pair of verses is marked before and after with the "twisted nun" symbol. No special treatment is required.

☞ °11:1–6 Chant in a somewhat **subdued** voice to symbolically minimize the embarrassment the congregants experience upon hearing the terrible misdeeds of their ancestors. Be sure that all words and te'amim (tropes, cantillations) remain clearly audible to the congregation.

**Haftarah** זְכַרְיָה Zekharyah (Zechariah) 2:14–4:7°

☞ °3:2 Note the rare ta'am (trope) מֵירְכָא־כְפוּלָה ( ֦ ): הֲלוֹא זֶה אוּד Connect זֶה to the preceding and following words, without a pause; then pause after the טִפְּחָא (אוּד), as usual.

מִנְחָה

**Torah** 3 aliyot from שְׁלַח־לְךָ Shelaḥ lekha
בְּמִדְבַּר Bemidbar (Numbers) 13:1–20
1 13:1–3 2 4–16 3 17–20 W300 P920

This is also the reading for the coming Monday and Thursday.

## Sivan 26 סִיוָן
## Sat 29 Jun

## שַׁבָּת Shabbat פָּרָשַׁת שְׁלַח־לְךָ Parashat Shelaḥ lekha
## שַׁבַּת מְבָרְכִים הַחֹדֶשׁ Shabbat Mevarekhim Haḥodesh

**Torah** 7 aliyot (minimum): שְׁלַח־לְךָ Shelaḥ lekha
בְּמִדְבַּר Bemidbar (Numbers) 13:1–15:41

| | | | | |
|---|---|---|---|---|
| Annual: | [1]13:1–20 | [2]13:21–14:7° | [3]14:8–25 | [4]14:26–15:7 |
| | [5]15:8–16 | [6]15:17–26 | [7]15:27–41 | [M]15:37–41 |
| Triennial: | [1]15:8–10 | [2]15:11–16 | [3]15:17–21 | [4]15:22–26 |
| | [5]15:27–31 | [6]15:32–36 | [7]15:37–41 | [M]15:37–41 |

☞ °14:3 Note the rare ta'am (trope) מֵירְכָא־כְפוּלָה (֦):
הֲלוֹא טוֹב לָנוּ Connect טוֹב to the preceding and following words, without a pause; then pause after the טִפְּחָא (לָנוּ), as usual.

**Haftarah** יְהוֹשֻׁעַ Yehoshua (Joshua) 2:1–24

+ **Birkat Haḥodesh:** L180 S150 F418
Announce Rosh Ḥodesh Tammuz:
רֹאשׁ חֹדֶשׁ תַּמּוּז יִהְיֶה בְּיוֹם רְבִיעִי וּבְיוֹם חֲמִישִׁי . . .
Rosh ḥodesh Tammuz yihyeh beyom revi'i uvyom ḥamishi . . .
(Tuesday night, Wednesday, and Thursday)

✕ ~~אַב הָרַחֲמִים Av Haraḥamim~~

מִנְחָה

**Torah** 3 aliyot from קֹרַח Koraḥ
בְּמִדְבַּר Bemidbar (Numbers) 16:1–13
[1]16:1–3 [2]4–7 [3]8–13 W301 P921

This is also the reading for the coming Monday.

---

## Sivan 29 סִיוָן
## Tue 2 Jul

## עֶרֶב רֹאשׁ חֹדֶשׁ Erev Rosh Ḥodesh
## Day before Rosh Ḥodesh

מִנְחָה ✕ ~~תַּחֲנוּן Taḥanun~~

| Sivan 5779 | | | | | | |
|---|---|---|---|---|---|---|
| | | 1 | 2 | 3 | 4 | 5 |
| 6 | 7 | 8 | 9 | 10 | 11 | 12 |
| 13 | 14 | 15 | 16 | 17 | 18 | 19 |
| 20 | 21 | 22 | 23 | 24 | 25 | 26 |
| 27 | 28 | 29 | 30 | | | |

| Jun \| Jul 2019 | | | | | | |
|---|---|---|---|---|---|---|
| | | 4 | 5 | 6 | 7 | 8 |
| 9 | 10 | 11 | 12 | 13 | 14 | 15 |
| 16 | 17 | 18 | 19 | 20 | 21 | 22 |
| 23 | 24 | 25 | 26 | 27 | 28 | 29 |
| 30 \| | 1 | 2 | 3 | | | |

+ Add ✕ Omit ☞ Take note!

**Siddurim**
- **L** Lev Shalem for Shabbat and Festivals
- **S** Shabbat and Festival Sim Shalom
- **W** Weekday Sim Shalom
- **F** Full Sim Shalom (both editions)
- **P** Personal Edition of Full Sim Shalom

## Sivan 30 סִיוָן — רֹאשׁ חֹדֶשׁ תַּמּוּז Rosh Ḥodesh Tammuz — Day 1

Tue **2** Jul (evening)

**DURING Rosh Ḥodesh** — **Birkat Hamazon:**

+ יַעֲלֶה וְיָבוֹא Ya'aleh veyavo for Rosh Ḥodesh L90|95 S340|347 W233|239 F762|780

+ הָרַחֲמָן Haraḥaman for Rosh Ḥodesh L92|96 S343|348 W235|240 F768

**עַרְבִית** — **Weekday Amidah:**

+ יַעֲלֶה וְיָבוֹא Ya'aleh veyavo for Rosh Ḥodesh W145 F216

Wed **3** Jul **שַׁחֲרִית**

**Before מִזְמוֹר שִׁיר Mizmor shir (Psalm 30)** W14 F50
**or at end of service, recite:**

Psalm for Wednesday (Psalms 94:1–95:3) W87 F26
קַדִּישׁ יָתוֹם Mourner's Kaddish (some omit) W100 F52
+ Psalm 104 for Rosh Ḥodesh W90 F34
קַדִּישׁ יָתוֹם Mourner's Kaddish W100 F52

**Weekday Amidah:**

+ יַעֲלֶה וְיָבוֹא Ya'aleh veyavo for Rosh Ḥodesh W41 F114

✕ ~~תַּחֲנוּן Taḥanun~~

+ חֲצִי הַלֵּל Short Hallel W50 F380
קַדִּישׁ שָׁלֵם Full Kaddish W56 F392

+ **TORAH SERVICE** W65 F138
Remove **1** Torah scroll from ark.

**Torah** 4 aliyot: פִּינְחָס Pineḥas
בְּמִדְבַּר Bemidbar (Numbers) 28:1–15
[1]28:1–3 [2]3–5 [3]6–10 [4]11–15 W320 P943

חֲצִי קַדִּישׁ Short Kaddish W71 F146
Open, raise, display, and wrap scroll.
Return scroll to ark. W76 F150

אַשְׁרֵי Ashrey W78 F152
✕ ~~לַמְנַצֵּחַ Lamenatse·aḥ (Psalm 20)~~
וּבָא לְצִיּוֹן Uva letsiyyon W80 F156

**Some congregations:**
Remove and pack tefillin at this point.
+ חֲצִי קַדִּישׁ Short Kaddish W103 F428

| ✚ Add  ✗ Omit  ☞ Take note! | **Sivan 5779** | Jun \| Jul 2019 | סִיוָן 30 Jul 3 |
|---|---|---|---|
| **Siddurim** | 1 2 3 4 5 | 4 5 6 7 8 | |
| **L** Lev Shalem for Shabbat and Festivals | 6 7 8 9 10 11 12 | 9 10 11 12 13 14 15 | |
| **S** Shabbat and Festival Sim Shalom | 13 14 15 16 17 18 19 | 16 17 18 19 20 21 22 | |
| **W** Weekday Sim Shalom | 20 21 22 23 24 25 26 | 23 24 25 26 27 28 29 | |
| **F** Full Sim Shalom (both editions) | 27 28 29 30 | 30\| 1 2 3 | |
| **P** Personal Edition of Full Sim Shalom | | | |

**Other congregations:**

+ חֲצִי קַדִּישׁ Short Kaddish W103 F428

Remove and cover—but do not pack—tefillin, so that all begin Musaf Amidah at the same time, as soon after Kaddish as possible.

**מוּסָף**

+ **Rosh Ḥodesh Amidah for weekdays:** W104 F486

Weekday קְדֻשָּׁה Kedushah W105 F488

✕ ~~וּלְכַפָּרַת פָּשַׁע Ulkhapparat pasha~~

Beginning with Rosh Ḥodesh Nisan, we do not add these words.

+ קַדִּישׁ שָׁלֵם Full Kaddish W82 F158

עָלֵינוּ Aleynu W83 F160

**If psalms for the day were not recited at Shaḥarit, add here:**

קַדִּישׁ יָתוֹם Mourner's Kaddish (some omit) W84 F162

Psalm for Wednesday (Psalms 94:1–95:3) W87 F26

קַדִּישׁ יָתוֹם Mourner's Kaddish (some omit) W100 F52

+ Psalm 104 for Rosh Ḥodesh W90 F34

קַדִּישׁ יָתוֹם Mourner's Kaddish W84|100 F162|52

**מִנְחָה**

**Weekday Amidah:**

+ יַעֲלֶה וְיָבוֹא Ya'aleh veyavo for Rosh Ḥodesh W127 F178

✕ ~~תַּחֲנוּן Taḥanun~~

| Tammuz 5779 | | | | | | | Jul \| Aug 2019 | | | | | | |
|---|---|---|---|---|---|---|---|---|---|---|---|---|---|
| | | | | 1 | 2 | 3 | | | | | 4 | 5 | 6 |
| 4 | 5 | 6 | 7 | 8 | 9 | 10 | 7 | 8 | 9 | 10 | 11 | 12 | 13 |
| 11 | 12 | 13 | 14 | 15 | 16 | 17 | 14 | 15 | 16 | 17 | 18 | 19 | 20 |
| 18 | 19 | 20 | 21 | 22 | 23 | 24 | 21 | 22 | 23 | 24 | 25 | 26 | 27 |
| 25 | 26 | 27 | 28 | 29 | | | 28 | 29 | 30 | 31 \| 1 | | | |

+ Add ✕ Omit ☞ Take note!

**Siddurim**
- **L** Lev Shalem for Shabbat and Festivals
- **S** Shabbat and Festival Sim Shalom
- **W** Weekday Sim Shalom
- **F** Full Sim Shalom (both editions)
- **P** Personal Edition of Full Sim Shalom

## Tammuz 1 תַּמּוּז
Wed 3 Jul (evening)

## רֹאשׁ חֹדֶשׁ תַּמּוּז Rosh Hodesh Tammuz — Day 2

**DURING Rosh Hodesh**

**Birkat Hamazon:**
+ יַעֲלֶה וְיָבוֹא Ya'aleh veyavo for Rosh Hodesh L90|95 S340|347 W233|239 F762|780
+ הָרַחֲמָן Harahaman for Rosh Hodesh L92|96 S343|348 W235|240 F768

**עַרְבִית**

**Weekday Amidah:**
+ יַעֲלֶה וְיָבוֹא Ya'aleh veyavo for Rosh Hodesh W145 F216

**Thu 4 Jul שַׁחֲרִית**

**Before מִזְמוֹר שִׁיר Mizmor shir (Psalm 30)** W14 F50
**or at end of service, recite:**
Psalm for Thursday (Psalm 81) W89 F30
קַדִּישׁ יָתוֹם Mourner's Kaddish (some omit) W100 F52
+ Psalm 104 for Rosh Hodesh W90 F34
קַדִּישׁ יָתוֹם Mourner's Kaddish W100 F52

**Weekday Amidah:**
+ יַעֲלֶה וְיָבוֹא Ya'aleh veyavo for Rosh Hodesh W41 F114

✕ ~~תַּחֲנוּן Tahanun~~

+ חֲצִי הַלֵּל Short Hallel W50 F380
קַדִּישׁ שָׁלֵם Full Kaddish W56 F392

**TORAH SERVICE** W65 F138
Remove **1** Torah scroll from ark.

**Torah** 4 aliyot: פִּינְחָס Pinehas
בְּמִדְבַּר Bemidbar (Numbers) 28:1–15
[1]28:1–3 [2]3–5 [3]6–10 [4]11–15 W320 P943

חֲצִי קַדִּישׁ Short Kaddish W71 F146
Open, raise, display, and wrap scroll.
Return scroll to ark. W76 F150

אַשְׁרֵי Ashrey W78 F152
✕ ~~לַמְנַצֵּחַ Lamenatse-ah (Psalm 20)~~
וּבָא לְצִיּוֹן Uva letsiyyon W80 F156

**Some congregations:**
Remove and pack tefillin at this point.
+ חֲצִי קַדִּישׁ Short Kaddish W103 F428

**Other congregations:**
+ חֲצִי קַדִּישׁ Short Kaddish W103 F428
Remove and cover—but do not pack—tefillin, so that all begin Musaf Amidah at the same time, as soon after Kaddish as possible.

מוּסָף
+ **Rosh Ḥodesh Amidah for weekdays:** W104 F486
Weekday קְדֻשָּׁה Kedushah W105 F488
✕ ~~וּלְכַפָּרַת פָּשַׁע Ulkhapparat pasha~~
Beginning with Rosh Ḥodesh Nisan, we do not add these words.

+ קַדִּישׁ שָׁלֵם Full Kaddish W82 F158
עָלֵינוּ Aleynu W83 F160

**If psalms for the day were not recited at Shaḥarit, add here:**
קַדִּישׁ יָתוֹם Mourner's Kaddish (some omit) W84 F162
Psalm for Thursday (Psalm 81) W89 F30
קַדִּישׁ יָתוֹם Mourner's Kaddish (some omit) W100 F52
+ Psalm 104 for Rosh Ḥodesh W90 F34

קַדִּישׁ יָתוֹם Mourner's Kaddish W84|100 F162|52

מִנְחָה
**Weekday Amidah:**
+ יַעֲלֶה וְיָבוֹא Ya'aleh veyavo for Rosh Ḥodesh W127 F178

✕ ~~תַּחֲנוּן Taḥanun~~

## Tammuz 3 תַּמּוּז Sat 6 Jul

## שַׁבָּת Shabbat פָּרָשַׁת קֹרַח Parashat Koraḥ

**Torah** 7 aliyot (minimum): קֹרַח Koraḥ
בְּמִדְבַּר Bemidbar (Numbers) 16:1–18:32

| | | | | |
|---|---|---|---|---|
| Annual: | 1 16:1–13 | 2 16:14–19 | 3 16:20–17:8 | 4 17:9–15 |
| | 5 17:16–24 | 6 17:25–18:20 | 7 18:21–32 | M 18:30–32 |
| Triennial: | 1 17:25–18:7 | 2 18:8–10 | 3 18:11–13 | 4 18:14–20 |
| | 5 18:21–24 | 6 18:25–29 | 7 18:30–32 | M 18:30–32 |

**Haftarah** שְׁמוּאֵל א׳ 1 Shemu'el (1 Samuel) 11:14–12:22

מִנְחָה
**Torah** 3 aliyot from חֻקַּת Ḥukkat
בְּמִדְבַּר Bemidbar (Numbers) 19:1–17
1 19:1–6 2 7–9 3 10–17 W302 P922

This is also the reading for the coming Monday and Thursday.

Tammuz 5779

| | | | | | | |
|---|---|---|---|---|---|---|
| | | | | 1 | 2 | 3 |
| 4 | 5 | 6 | 7 | 8 | 9 | 10 |
| 11 | 12 | 13 | 14 | 15 | 16 | 17 |
| 18 | 19 | 20 | 21 | 22 | 23 | 24 |
| 25 | 26 | 27 | 28 | 29 | | |

Jul | Aug 2019

| | | | | | | |
|---|---|---|---|---|---|---|
| | | | | 4 | 5 | 6 |
| 7 | 8 | 9 | 10 | 11 | 12 | 13 |
| 14 | 15 | 16 | 17 | 18 | 19 | 20 |
| 21 | 22 | 23 | 24 | 25 | 26 | 27 |
| 28 | 29 | 30 | 31 \| 1 | | | |

+ Add ✕ Omit ☞ Take note!

**Siddurim**
- **L** Lev Shalem for Shabbat and Festivals
- **S** Shabbat and Festival Sim Shalom
- **W** Weekday Sim Shalom
- **F** Full Sim Shalom (both editions)
- **P** Personal Edition of Full Sim Shalom

## Tammuz 10 תַּמּוּז
Sat 13 Jul

## שַׁבָּת Shabbat פָּרָשַׁת חֻקַּת Parashat Ḥukkat

**Torah** 7 aliyot (minimum): חֻקַּת Ḥukkat
בְּמִדְבַּר Bemidbar (Numbers) 19:1–22:1

| | | | | |
|---|---|---|---|---|
| Annual: | [1]19:1–17 | [2]19:18–20:6 | [3]20:7–13 | [4]20:14–21 |
| | [5]20:22–21:9 | [6]21:10–20° | [7]21:21–22:1 | [M]21:34–22:1 |
| Triennial: | [1]21:11–13 | [2]21:14–16 | [3]21:17–20° | [4]21:21–25 |
| | [5]21:26–28 | [6]21:29–33 | [7]21:34–22:1 | [M]21:34–22:1 |

☞ °21:19 Chant this verse using the "desert traveling melody," based on the Shirat Hayam melody.

**Haftarah** שׁוֹפְטִים Shofetim (Judges) 11:1–33

מִנְחָה

**Torah** 3 aliyot from בָּלָק Balak
בְּמִדְבַּר Bemidbar (Numbers) 22:2–12
[1]22:2–4 [2]5–7° [3]8–12° W303 P923

This is also the reading for the coming Monday and Thursday.

☞ The following notes apply to readers using Israeli pronunciation:
°22:6 אָרָה־לִּי Read: ora-li (vowel of א is kamets katan)
°22:11 קָבָה־לִּי Read: kova-li (vowel of ק is kamets katan)

Because 17 Tammuz falls on Shabbat, we delay the fast-day observance one day. See p. 183.

## Tammuz 17 תַּמּוּז
Sat 20 Jul

## שַׁבָּת Shabbat פָּרָשַׁת בָּלָק Parashat Balak

**Torah** 7 aliyot (minimum): בָּלָק Balak
בְּמִדְבַּר Bemidbar (Numbers) 22:2–25:9

| | | | | |
|---|---|---|---|---|
| Annual: | [1]22:2–12° | [2]22:13–20° | [3]22:21–38 | [4]22:39–23:12° |
| | [5]23:13–26° | [6]23:27–24:13 | [7]24:14–25:9 | [M]25:7–9 |
| Triennial: | [1]23:27–30 | [2]24:1–9 | [3]24:10–13 | [4]24:14–19 |
| | [5]24:20–25 | [6]25:1–6 | [7]25:7–9 | [M]25:7–9 |

☞ The following notes apply to readers using Israeli pronunciation:
°22:6 אָרָה־לִּי Read: ora-li (vowel of א is kamets katan)
°22:11 קָבָה־לִּי Read: kova-li (vowel of ק is kamets katan)
°22:17 קָבָה־לִּי Read: kova-li (vowel of ק is kamets katan)
°23:7 אָרָה־לִּי Read: ora-li (vowel of א is kamets katan)
°23:13 וְקָבְנוֹ־לִי Read: vekovno-li (vowel of ק is kamets katan)
°23:25 תִקֳּבֶנּוּ Read: tikkovennu (every ֳ [ḥataf kamets] is pronounced "o")

**Haftarah** מִיכָה Mikhah (Micah) 5:6–6:8

מִנְחָה

**Torah** 3 aliyot from פִּינְחָס Pineḥas
בְּמִדְבַּר Bemidbar (Numbers) 25:10–26:4
1 25:10–12 2 25:13–15 3 25:16–26:4° W304 P924

This is also the reading for the coming Monday and Thursday.

☞ °26:1 (sometimes incorrectly marked as 25:19)
וַיְהִי אַחֲרֵי הַמַּגֵּפָה וַיֹּאמֶר . . .
Despite the break in the text after הַמַּגֵּפָה, this is a single verse until לֵאמֹר. Chant the אֶתְנַחְתָּא of הַמַּגֵּפָה as usual, and continue with the rest of the verse.

☞ צִדְקָתְךָ צֶדֶק Tsidkatekha tsedek L230 S239 W183 F584

## The 3 Weeks

Shiv'ah Asar Betammuz inaugurates a 3-week mourning period, which concludes on Tish'ah Be'av.

During these weeks, avoid concerts and public celebrations such as weddings. Some refrain from haircuts.

---

**Tammuz 18 תַּמּוּז**
**Sat 20 Jul**

## שִׁבְעָה עָשָׂר בְּתַמּוּז Shiv'ah Asar Betammuz

**17th of Tammuz** (communal fast, begins at dawn)

**מוֹצָאֵי שַׁבָּת Motsa'ey Shabbat Conclusion of Shabbat**

עַרְבִית Saturday night Arvit as usual L264 S281 W137 F200

## Shiv'ah Asar Betammuz

On this date in 70 C.E., soldiers of the Roman army broke through the walls of Jerusalem. Three weeks later, on the 9th of Av, they destroyed the Second Temple.

This year the 17th of Tammuz falls on Shabbat. Therefore, we delay the fast until the 18th of Tammuz.

- This is a minor fast day, so called because the fast does not begin until dawn.
- The fast (from both eating and drinking) lasts until dark (a minimum of 25 minutes after sunset).
- *Sheliḥey tsibbur*, Torah readers, and those called for *aliyot* should be fasting.
- The preferred fast-day procedures apply when at least 6 of those who are counted for a *minyan* are fasting.
- If it is ascertained (without causing embarrassment) that fewer than 6 are fasting, follow the procedures printed in gray and marked with ✦.

| Tammuz 5779 | | | | | | | Jul \| Aug 2019 | | | | | | |
|---|---|---|---|---|---|---|---|---|---|---|---|---|---|
| | | | 1 | 2 | 3 | | | | | | 4 | 5 | 6 |
| 4 | 5 | 6 | 7 | 8 | 9 | 10 | 7 | 8 | 9 | 10 | 11 | 12 | 13 |
| 11 | 12 | 13 | 14 | 15 | 16 | 17 | 14 | 15 | 16 | 17 | 18 | 19 | 20 |
| 18 | 19 | 20 | 21 | 22 | 23 | 24 | 21 | 22 | 23 | 24 | 25 | 26 | 27 |
| 25 | 26 | 27 | 28 | 29 | | | 28 | 29 | 30 | 31 \| | 1 | | |

+ Add ✕ Omit ☞ Take note!

**Siddurim**
- **L** Lev Shalem for Shabbat and Festivals
- **S** Shabbat and Festival Sim Shalom
- **W** Weekday Sim Shalom
- **F** Full Sim Shalom (both editions)
- **P** Personal Edition of Full Sim Shalom

## Sun 21 Jul שַׁחֲרִית

**Silent weekday Amidah:**
Do not add עֲנֵנוּ Anenu.

**Repetition of the weekday Amidah:**

**6 or more fasting** + עֲנֵנוּ Anenu, before רְפָאֵנוּ Refa'enu W38 F110

**Fewer than 6 fasting** ✦ Add עֲנֵנוּ Anenu in שׁוֹמֵעַ תְּפִלָּה Shome·a tefillah. Replace תַּעֲנִיתֵנוּ ta'anitenu (6th word) with הַתַּעֲנִית הַזֶּה hata'anit hazeh. W38 F110

**6 or more fasting** + אָבִינוּ מַלְכֵּנוּ Avinu malkenu W57 F124

**Fewer than 6 fasting** ✦ Those fasting recite אָבִינוּ מַלְכֵּנוּ individually.

☞ תַּחֲנוּן Tahanun W62 F132
חֲצִי קַדִּישׁ Short Kaddish W64 F136

**Fewer than 6 fasting** ✦ Omit the entire Torah service. Continue with אַשְׁרֵי Ashrey.

**6 or more fasting** + **TORAH SERVICE** W65 F138

Remove **1** Torah scroll from ark.

**Torah** 3 aliyot from כִּי תִשָּׂא Ki tissa
שְׁמוֹת Shemot (Exodus) 32:11–14, 34:1–10
¹32:11–14° ²34:1–3 ³4–10° W341 P979

☞ °At each of the 3 passages indicated below, follow this procedure:
1. The reader pauses before the indicated text.
2. The congregation recites the indicated text.
3. Afterward, the reader chants the indicated text in the manner of the cantillation of High Holiday Torah reading.

32:12 שׁוּב מֵחֲרוֹן אַפֶּךָ וְהִנָּחֵם עַל־הָרָעָה לְעַמֶּךָ׃

34:6–7 יי | יי אֵ·ל רַחוּם וְחַנּוּן אֶרֶךְ אַפַּיִם וְרַב־חֶסֶד וֶאֱמֶת׃
נֹצֵר חֶסֶד לָאֲלָפִים נֹשֵׂא עָוֺן וָפֶשַׁע וְחַטָּאָה וְנַקֵּה

34:9 וְסָלַחְתָּ לַעֲוֺנֵנוּ וּלְחַטָּאתֵנוּ | וּנְחַלְתָּנוּ׃

To preserve the sense of this passage, maintain the appropriate pause after the טִפְּחָא (וּלְחַטָּאתֵנוּ).

חֲצִי קַדִּישׁ Short Kaddish W71 F146
Open, raise, display, and wrap scroll.
Return scroll to ark. W76 F150

**All minyanim** אַשְׁרֵי Ashrey W78 F152
☞ לַמְנַצֵּחַ Lamenatse·ah (Psalm 20) W79 F154
Conclude the service in the usual manner.

| + Add    ✗ Omit    ☞ Take note! | **Tammuz 5779** | **Jul | Aug 2019** | **18 תַּמּוּז** **Jul 21** |
|---|---|---|---|
| **Siddurim** | 1 2 3 | 4 5 6 | |
| L  Lev Shalem for Shabbat and Festivals | 4 5 6 7 8 9 10 | 7 8 9 10 11 12 13 | |
| S  Shabbat and Festival Sim Shalom | 11 12 13 14 15 16 17 | 14 15 16 17 18 19 20 | |
| W  Weekday Sim Shalom | 18 19 20 21 22 23 24 | 21 22 23 24 25 26 27 | |
| F  Full Sim Shalom (both editions) | 25 26 27 28 29 | 28 29 30 31 | 1 | |
| P  Personal Edition of Full Sim Shalom | | | |

**מִנְחָה** אַשְׁרֵי Ashrey W120 F164
חֲצִי קַדִּישׁ Short Kaddish W121 F166

Fewer than 6 fasting ✦ Omit the entire Torah service.
Continue with the silent Amidah.

**6 or more fasting** + **TORAH SERVICE** W65 F138

Remove **1** Torah scroll from ark.

**Torah** 3 aliyot from כִּי תִשָּׂא Ki tissa
שְׁמוֹת Shemot (Exodus) 32:11–14, 34:1–10
1 32:11–14° 2 34:1–3 M 4–10° W341 P979

☞ °Follow the same procedure as for the morning reading. See p. 184.

☞ Do not recite חֲצִי קַדִּישׁ Short Kaddish after maftir aliyah.

Open, raise, display, and wrap scroll.

Recite the בְּרָכָה berakhah before the haftarah. W74 F410 P989

**Haftarah** יְשַׁעְיָהוּ Yesha'yahu (Isaiah) 55:6–56:8 W342 P980

Recite the 3 concluding haftarah blessings,
through מָגֵן דָּוִד Magen david. W74 F410 P989.

Return scroll to ark. W76 F150
חֲצִי קַדִּישׁ Short Kaddish W121 F166

**All minyanim** **Silent weekday Amidah:**
**If fasting** + עֲנֵנוּ Anenu, in שׁוֹמֵעַ תְּפִלָּה Shome·a tefillah W127 F178
**All** ✕ ~~שָׁלוֹם רָב Shalom rav~~
+ שִׂים שָׁלוֹם Sim shalom W131 F184

**Repetition of the weekday Amidah:**
**6 or more fasting** + עֲנֵנוּ Anenu, before רְפָאֵנוּ Refa'enu W124 F172
Fewer than 6 fasting ✦ Add עֲנֵנוּ Anenu in שׁוֹמֵעַ תְּפִלָּה Shome·a tefillah.
Replace תַּעֲנִיתֵנוּ ta'anitenu (6th word) with
הַתַּעֲנִית הַזֶּה hata'anit hazeh. W127 F172
**All minyanim** + בִּרְכַּת כֹּהֲנִים Birkat kohanim W131 F184
✕ ~~שָׁלוֹם רָב Shalom rav~~
+ שִׂים שָׁלוֹם Sim shalom W131 F184

**6 or more fasting** + אָבִינוּ מַלְכֵּנוּ Avinu malkenu W57 F188
Fewer than 6 fasting ✦ Those fasting recite אָבִינוּ מַלְכֵּנוּ individually.

☞ תַּחֲנוּן Tahanun W132 F192

| Tammuz 5779 | | | | | | |
|---|---|---|---|---|---|---|
| | | | | 1 | 2 | 3 |
| 4 | 5 | 6 | 7 | 8 | 9 | 10 |
| 11 | 12 | 13 | 14 | 15 | 16 | 17 |
| 18 | 19 | 20 | 21 | 22 | 23 | 24 |
| 25 | 26 | 27 | 28 | 29 | | |

| Jul \| Aug 2019 | | | | | | |
|---|---|---|---|---|---|---|
| | | | | 4 | 5 | 6 |
| 7 | 8 | 9 | 10 | 11 | 12 | 13 |
| 14 | 15 | 16 | 17 | 18 | 19 | 20 |
| 21 | 22 | 23 | 24 | 25 | 26 | 27 |
| 28 | 29 | 30 | 31 \| | 1 | | |

+ Add ✕ Omit ☞ Take note!

**Siddurim**
- **L** Lev Shalem for Shabbat and Festivals
- **S** Shabbat and Festival Sim Shalom
- **W** Weekday Sim Shalom
- **F** Full Sim Shalom (both editions)
- **P** Personal Edition of Full Sim Shalom

---

קַדִּישׁ שָׁלֵם Full Kaddish W134 F194
עָלֵינוּ Aleynu W135 F196
קַדִּישׁ יָתוֹם Mourner's Kaddish W136 F198

---

## Tammuz 24 תַּמּוּז
Sat 27 Jul

## שַׁבָּת Shabbat פָּרָשַׁת פִּינְחָס Parashat Pineḥas
## שַׁבַּת מְבָרְכִים הַחֹדֶשׁ Shabbat Mevarekhim Haḥodesh

**Torah** 7 aliyot (minimum): פִּינְחָס Pineḥas
בְּמִדְבַּר Bemidbar (Numbers) 25:10–30:1

| | | | | |
|---|---|---|---|---|
| Annual: | [1]25:10–26:4° | [2]26:5–51 | [3]26:52–27:5 | [4]27:6–23 |
| | [5]28:1–15 | [6]28:16–29:11 | [7]29:12–30:1 | [M]29:35–30:1 |
| Triennial: | [1]28:16–25 | [2]28:26–31 | [3]29:1–6 | [4]29:7–11 |
| | [5]29:12–16 | [6]29:17–28 | [7]29:29–30:1 | [M]29:35–30:1 |

☞ °26:1 (in some books incorrectly marked as 25:19)
וַיְהִי אַחֲרֵי הַמַּגֵּפָה וַיֹּאמֶר . . .
Despite the break in the text after הַמַּגֵּפָה, this is a single verse until לֵאמֹר. Chant the אֶתְנַחְתָּא of הַמַּגֵּפָה as usual, and continue with the rest of the verse.

☞ **Haftarah** יִרְמְיָהוּ Yirmeyahu (Jeremiah) 1:1–2:3
(1st of 3 haftarot of rebuke preceding Tish'ah Be'av)

+ **Birkat Haḥodesh:** L180 S150 F418
Announce Rosh Ḥodesh Menaḥem Av:
Do not announce the month as "Av."
רֹאשׁ חֹדֶשׁ מְנַחֵם אָב יִהְיֶה בְּיוֹם שִׁשִּׁי . . .
Rosh ḥodesh Menaḥem Av yihyeh beyom shishi . . .
(Thursday night and Friday)

✕ ~~אַב הָרַחֲמִים Av Haraḥamim~~

מִנְחָה

**Torah** 3 aliyot from מַטּוֹת Mattot
בְּמִדְבַּר Bemidbar (Numbers) 30:2–17
[1]30:2–9 [2]10–13 [3]14–17 W305 P925

This is also the reading for the coming Monday and Thursday.

---

## Tammuz 29 תַּמּוּז
Thu 1 Aug

## עֶרֶב רֹאשׁ חֹדֶשׁ Erev Rosh Ḥodesh
## Day before Rosh Ḥodesh

מִנְחָה ✕ ~~תַּחֲנוּן Taḥanun~~

| | | | Av 5779 | | Aug 2019 | | אָב 1 | Aug 1 |
|---|---|---|---|---|---|---|---|---|
| + Add | ✗ Omit | ☞ Take note! | | 1  2 | | 2  3 | | Aug 2 |
| **F** | Full Sim Shalom (both editions) | | | | | | | |
| **P** | Personal Edition of Full Sim Shalom | | | | | | | |

## The 9 Days

### Restrictions

The Rabbis instructed: מִשֶּׁנִּכְנַס אָב מְמַעֲטִין בְּשִׂמְחָה *mishenikhnas av mema'atin besimḥah* "From the moment Av arrives, we are to diminish our rejoicing."

As Tish'ah Be'av nears, the mourning that began with Shiv'ah Asar Betammuz (see p. 183) intensifies. From Rosh Ḥodesh Av through Tish'ah Be'av, we observe additional restrictions. For example, we refrain from:

- Eating meat
- Drinking wine
- Purchasing or wearing new clothes
- Getting a haircut

Restrictions on meat and wine are suspended on Shabbat and also for a סְעוּדַת מִצְוָה *se'udat mitsvah* (mandatory festive meal), celebrating events such as:

- בְּרִית מִילָה *berit milah* (ritual circumcision)
- פִּדְיוֹן הַבֵּן *pidyon haben* (redemption of a male firstborn child
- סִיּוּם *siyyum* (completion of study of a tractate of rabbinic literature)

This year the 9th of Av falls on Shabbat. Therefore, we delay the observance of Tish'ah Be'av until the 10th of Av.

We continue to refrain from eating meat and drinking wine throughout the night following the fast.

## Av 1 אָב — רֹאשׁ חֹדֶשׁ אָב Rosh Ḥodesh Av

Thu 1 Aug (evening)

**DURING Rosh Ḥodesh** — **Birkat Hamazon:**

+ יַעֲלֶה וְיָבוֹא Ya'aleh veyavo for Rosh Ḥodesh L90|95 S340|347 W233|239 F762|780

+ הָרַחֲמָן Haraḥaman for Rosh Ḥodesh L92|96 S343|348 W235|240 F768

**עַרְבִית** — **Weekday Amidah:**

+ יַעֲלֶה וְיָבוֹא Ya'aleh veyavo for Rosh Ḥodesh W145 F216

Fri 2 Aug — **שַׁחֲרִית**

**Before מִזְמוֹר שִׁיר Mizmor shir (Psalm 30)** W14 F50 **or at end of service, recite:**

Psalm for Friday (Psalm 93) W90 F32

קַדִּישׁ יָתוֹם Mourner's Kaddish (some omit) W100 F52

+ Psalm 104 for Rosh Ḥodesh W90 F34

קַדִּישׁ יָתוֹם Mourner's Kaddish W100 F52

| Av 5779 | | | | | | |
|---|---|---|---|---|---|---|
| | | | | | 1 | 2 |
| 3 | 4 | 5 | 6 | 7 | 8 | 9 |
| 10 | 11 | 12 | 13 | 14 | 15 | 16 |
| 17 | 18 | 19 | 20 | 21 | 22 | 23 |
| 24 | 25 | 26 | 27 | 28 | 29 | 30 |

| Aug 2019 | | | | | | |
|---|---|---|---|---|---|---|
| | | | | | 2 | 3 |
| 4 | 5 | 6 | 7 | 8 | 9 | 10 |
| 11 | 12 | 13 | 14 | 15 | 16 | 17 |
| 18 | 19 | 20 | 21 | 22 | 23 | 24 |
| 25 | 26 | 27 | 28 | 29 | 30 | 31 |

+ Add ✕ Omit ☞ Take note!

**Siddurim**
- **L** Lev Shalem for Shabbat and Festivals
- **S** Shabbat and Festival Sim Shalom
- **W** Weekday Sim Shalom
- **F** Full Sim Shalom (both editions)
- **P** Personal Edition of Full Sim Shalom

**Weekday Amidah:**
+ יַעֲלֶה וְיָבוֹא Ya'aleh veyavo for Rosh Hodesh W41 F114

✕ ~~תַּחֲנוּן Tahanun~~

+ חֲצִי הַלֵּל Short Hallel W50 F380
קַדִּישׁ שָׁלֵם Full Kaddish W56 F392

+ **TORAH SERVICE** W65 F138
Remove **1** Torah scroll from ark.

**Torah** 4 aliyot: פִּינְחָס Pinehas
בְּמִדְבַּר Bemidbar (Numbers) 28:1–15
¹28:1–3 ²3–5 ³6–10 ⁴11–15 W320 P943

חֲצִי קַדִּישׁ Short Kaddish W71 F146
Open, raise, display, and wrap scroll.
Return scroll to ark. W76 F150

אַשְׁרֵי Ashrey W78 F152
✕ ~~לַמְנַצֵּחַ Lamenatse·ah (Psalm 20)~~
וּבָא לְצִיּוֹן Uva letsiyyon W80 F156

**Some congregations:**
Remove and pack tefillin at this point.
+ חֲצִי קַדִּישׁ Short Kaddish W103 F428

**Other congregations:**
+ חֲצִי קַדִּישׁ Short Kaddish W103 F428
Remove and cover—but do not pack—tefillin, so that all begin Musaf Amidah at the same time, as soon after Kaddish as possible.

מוּסָף + **Rosh Hodesh Amidah for weekdays:** W104 F486
Weekday קְדֻשָּׁה Kedushah W105 F488
✕ ~~וּלְכַפָּרַת פָּשַׁע Ulkhapparat pasha~~
Beginning with Rosh Hodesh Nisan, we do not add these words.

+ קַדִּישׁ שָׁלֵם Full Kaddish W82 F158
עָלֵינוּ Aleynu W83 F160

**If psalms for the day were not recited at Shaharit, add here:**
קַדִּישׁ יָתוֹם Mourner's Kaddish (some omit) W84 F162
Psalm for Friday (Psalm 93) W90 F32
קַדִּישׁ יָתוֹם Mourner's Kaddish (some omit) W100 F52
+ Psalm 104 for Rosh Hodesh W90 F34
קַדִּישׁ יָתוֹם Mourner's Kaddish W84|100 F162|52

## מִנְחָה

**Weekday Amidah:**

+ יַעֲלֶה וְיָבוֹא Ya'aleh veyavo for Rosh Ḥodesh W127 F178

✕ ~~תַּחֲנוּן Taḥanun~~

---

**Av 2 אָב**
**Sat 3 Aug**

## שַׁבָּת Shabbat

### פָּרָשׁוֹת מַטּוֹת + מַסְעֵי Parashot Mattot + Mas'ey

**Torah** 7 aliyot (minimum): מַטּוֹת + מַסְעֵי Mattot + Mas'ey
בְּמִדְבַּר Bemidbar (Numbers) 30:2–36:13

| | | | | |
|---|---|---|---|---|
| Annual: | 1 30:2–31:12 | 2 31:13–54 | 3 32:1–19 | 4 32:20–33:49° |
| | 5 33:50–34:15 | 6 34:16–35:8° | 7 35:9–36:13▮ | M 36:11–13 |
| Triennial: | 1 33:50–34:15 | 2 34:16–29 | 3 35:1–8° | 4 35:9–15 |
| | 5 35:16–29 | 6 35:30–34 | 7 36:1–13▮ | M 36:10–13 |

☞ °32:42 Note the rare ta'am (trope) מֵירְכָא־כְפוּלָה ( ֦ ):
וַיִּקְרָא לָה נֹבַח Connect לָה to the preceding and following words, without a pause; then pause after the טִפְחָא (נֹבַח), as usual.

☞ °33:9–49 Chant 14 (others: 13) pairs of verses using the "desert traveling melody," based on the Shirat Hayam melody:
33:10–11 12–13 (others: 11–12 instead) 15–16 17–18 19–20 21–22 23–24 25–26 27–28 29–30 31–32 33–34 41–42 45–46

☞ °35:5 Note the rare te'amim (tropes) יֶרַח־בֶּן־יוֹמוֹ ( ֪ ) and קַרְנֵי־פָרָה ( ֟ ):
אַלְפַּיִם בָּאַמָּה Connect אַלְפַּיִם to the preceding and following words, without a pause; then pause after בָּאַמָּה.

▮ חזק When the Torah reader concludes a book of the Torah:

1. Close the Torah scroll.
2. **For Oleh:** Congregation chants חֲזַק חֲזַק וְנִתְחַזֵּק ḥazak ḥazak venitḥazzek; oleh remains silent.
   **For Olah:** Congregation chants חִזְקִי חִזְקִי וְנִתְחַזֵּק ḥizki ḥizki venitḥazzek; olah remains silent.
3. Torah reader repeats congregation's words (oleh/olah remains silent; if Torah reader is the oleh/olah, omit this repetition).
4. Open the Torah scroll.
5. The oleh/olah kisses the Torah scroll, closes it, and continues with the usual concluding berakhah.

☞ **Haftarah**
Ashkenazic: יִרְמְיָהוּ Yirmeyahu (Jeremiah) 2:4–28; 3:4
Sephardic: יִרְמְיָהוּ Yirmeyahu (Jeremiah) 2:4–28; 4:1–2
(2nd of 3 haftarot of rebuke preceding Tish'ah Be'av)

| Av 5779 | | | | | | |
|---|---|---|---|---|---|---|
| | | | | | 1 | 2 |
| 3 | 4 | 5 | 6 | 7 | 8 | 9 |
| 10 | 11 | 12 | 13 | 14 | 15 | 16 |
| 17 | 18 | 19 | 20 | 21 | 22 | 23 |
| 24 | 25 | 26 | 27 | 28 | 29 | 30 |

| Aug 2019 | | | | | | |
|---|---|---|---|---|---|---|
| | | | | | 2 | 3 |
| 4 | 5 | 6 | 7 | 8 | 9 | 10 |
| 11 | 12 | 13 | 14 | 15 | 16 | 17 |
| 18 | 19 | 20 | 21 | 22 | 23 | 24 |
| 25 | 26 | 27 | 28 | 29 | 30 | 31 |

+ Add ✕ Omit ☞ Take note!

**Siddurim**
**L** Lev Shalem for Shabbat and Festivals
**S** Shabbat and Festival Sim Shalom
**W** Weekday Sim Shalom
**F** Full Sim Shalom (both editions)
**P** Personal Edition of Full Sim Shalom

---

מִנְחָה

**Torah** 3 aliyot from דְּבָרִים Devarim
דְּבָרִים Devarim (Deuteronomy) 1:1–10 (or 11)
¹1:1–3 ²4–7 ³8–10 (or ³8–11) W307 P927

This is also the reading for the coming Monday and Thursday.

---

**Av 8 אָב**
**Fri 9 Aug** (daytime)

## עֶרֶב שַׁבָּת Erev Shabbat
## Day before Shabbat

Because 9 Av falls on Shabbat, we delay the fast-day observance one day. See p. 193.

### Preparing Shoes for Tish'ah Be'av

Wearing leather shoes is prohibited on Tish'ah Be'av. This year Tish'ah Be'av begins on Saturday night, immediately after the end of Shabbat. We do not diminish the joy of Shabbat by preparing during Shabbat for the mournful day that is coming. Therefore:

- Leave non-leather shoes at the synagogue *before* Shabbat begins.
- Do *not* take non-leather shoes with you to the synagogue on Shabbat.

---

**Av 9 אָב**
**Fri 9 Aug** (evening)

## שַׁבָּת Shabbat פָּרָשַׁת דְּבָרִים Parashat Devarim
## שַׁבַּת חֲזוֹן Shabbat Ḥazon

**Shabbat Ḥazon**, named after the 1st word of the haftarah, is the Shabbat immediately preceding Tish'ah Be'av. The mood of this mourning period intrudes upon the joyous spirit of Shabbat as some of the synagogue music foreshadows the upcoming day of destruction.

קַבָּלַת שַׁבָּת

Chant לְכָה דוֹדִי L23 S21 F262
to the melody of אֱלִי צִיּוֹן Eli tsiyyon
(Tish'ah Be'av lamentation poem)

**Sat 10 Aug**

**Torah** 7 aliyot (minimum): דְּבָרִים Devarim
דְּבָרִים Devarim (Deuteronomy) 1:1–3:22

| | | | | |
|---|---|---|---|---|
| Annual: | ¹1:1–10° | ²1:11–21° | ³1:22–38 | ⁴1:39–2:1 |
| | ⁵2:2–30 | ⁶2:31–3:14 | ⁷3:15–3:22 | ᴹ3:20–22 |
| Triennial: | ¹2:31–34 | ²2:35–37 | ³3:1–3 | ⁴3:4–7 |
| | ⁵3:8–11 | ⁶3:12–14 | ⁷3:15–22 | ᴹ3:20–22 |

☞ °1:10 Although some books extend the 1st aliyah to 1:11, it is preferable to end at 1:10 so that the second aliyah does not begin with the melody of אֵיכָה (see note to 1:12).

☞ °1:12 Because the first word of this verse is אֵיכָה and this parashah is always read the Shabbat before Tish'ah Be'av, this verse is traditionally chanted using the cantillation of the book of אֵיכָה.

**Haftarah** יְשַׁעְיָהוּ Y^e^sha'yahu (Isaiah) 1:1–27°
(3rd of 3 haftarot of rebuke preceding Tish'ah Be'av)

☞°The cantillation changes twice from haftarah melody to אֵיכָה melody and back, reflecting the content of the verses:

| | | |
|---|---|---|
| verse | 1 | regular haftarah melody |
| verses | 2–15 | אֵיכָה melody |
| verses | 16–19 | regular haftarah melody |
| verses | 20–23 | אֵיכָה melody |
| verses | 24–27 | regular haftarah melody |

☞Recite אַב הָרַחֲמִים Av harahamim L446 S151 F420
even if the usual custom of the congregation is to omit it.

מִנְחָה

**Torah** 3 aliyot from וָאֶתְחַנַּן Va'et·hannan
דְּבָרִים Devarim (Deuteronomy) 3:23–4:8°
1 3:23–25 2 3:26–4:4 3 4:5–8 W308 P927

This is also the reading for the coming Monday and Thursday.

☞°3:23–4:8 The reading ends with 4:8, which enables the correct configuration of the 3 aliyot.

✕ ~~צִדְקָתְךָ צֶדֶק Tsidkatekha tsedek~~

Although פִּרְקֵי אָבוֹת Pirkey Avot is commonly studied on Shabbat afternoon, do not study it on this Shabbat, the eve of Tish'ah Be'av.

## Tish'ah Be'av

The 3-week period of mourning culminates in Tishah Be'av, the commemoration of the destruction of both the First and Second Temples in Jerusalem. Over the centuries, other catastrophes that befell the Jewish people also came to be associated with this day of mourning.

In contrast to the 4 minor fast days (see pp. 13, 87, 114, and 183), this fast, like Yom Kippur, lasts the full day. It begins immediately at sunset and ends after dark the next day. Some wait until 3 stars appear, or at least 25 minutes after sunset. Others wait longer. For the proper waiting time in your community, consult your rabbi.

### Se'udah Shelishit before Tish'ah Be'av

- Eating meat and drinking wine are permitted.
- If three or more have eaten together, precede בִּרְכַּת הַמָּזוֹן *birkat hamazon* as usual with בִּרְכַּת זִמּוּן *birkat zimmun* (i.e., רַבּוֹתַי נְבָרֵךְ *rabbotay nevarekh*).
- The meal must be completed before sunset.

## Tish'ah Be'av Prohibitions

Beginning at Arvit, wearing leather shoes is prohibited. The other prohibitions take effect at sunset.

The following are not permitted throughout Tish'ah Be'av:

- Eating and drinking
- Wearing leather shoes
- Sexual relations
- Bathing (except for minimal washing to remove dirt or after using the toilet)
- Applying skin or bath oils
- Studying Jewish religious texts

  Exceptions are texts that support the mood of the day, e.g., מְגִלַּת אֵיכָה *megillat eykhah* (Lamentations), אִיּוֹב *iyyov* (Job), certain other biblical texts, and rabbinic or other texts dealing with catastrophes in Jewish history.
- Greeting one another, especially with the word שָׁלוֹם *shalom*

## Procedures in the Synagogue

### Creating the Tish'ah Be'av Mood

Most congregations remove the table cover, as well as the פָּרֹכֶת *parokhet* (decorative ark curtain) if the ark has doors or if a plain curtain is available.

- On Saturday night, remove the table cover and the פָּרֹכֶת after the Kaddish following the Amidah of Arvit.
- Sit like mourners—on the floor or on low seats—especially during the reading of מְגִלַּת אֵיכָה and קִינוֹת *kinot* (liturgical lamentation poetry). See below.
- Keep lights low; candles or flashlights can provide just enough light for reading.

If it is ascertained (without causing embarrassment) that fewer than 6 are fasting, follow the procedures printed in gray and marked with ✦.

Most congregations restore table cover and פָּרֹכֶת immediately before Minḥah.

### Chanting Megillat Eykhah

- Sit on the floor or on low seats or benches.
- Chant מְגִלַּת אֵיכָה *megillat eykhah* (Lamentations).
- When the reader reaches the second-to-last verse, the congregation chants the verse (5:21) with the reader: . . . הֲשִׁיבֵנוּ *hashivenu* . . .
- The reader concludes the final verse (5:22).
- The congregation chants the previous verse (5:21) aloud.
- The reader alone repeats the same verse (5:21).

### Reciting Kinot

- Sit on the floor or on low seats or benches.
- Recite קִינוֹת *kinot* using melodies suitable for liturgical lamentation poetry.

**Av 10 אָב**
**Sat 10 Aug (evening)**

# תִּשְׁעָה בְּאָב Tish'ah Be'av

**9th of Av (full-day communal fast, begins at sunset)**

## מוֹצָאֵי שַׁבָּת Motsa'ey Shabbat Conclusion of Shabbat

Wait until Shabbat ends.

**Before עַרְבִית**

For the sheliaḥ/sheliḥat tsibbur:
End your Shabbat by reciting: בָּרוּךְ הַמַּבְדִּיל בֵּין קֹדֶשׁ לְחֹל
Barukh hamavdil beyn kodesh leḥol.

Change to non-leather shoes.
If possible, do not touch the leather shoes.

Do not remove the table cloth or the פָּרֹכֶת parokhet (decorative ark curtain) at this time.

**עַרְבִית**

For the sheliaḥ/sheliḥat tsibbur:
Begin Arvit with וְהוּא רַחוּם vehu raḥum. L264 S281 W137 F200

☞ Chant Arvit in a subdued voice, using melodies appropriate for the mournful mood.

☞ Pause before בָּרְכוּ barekhu.

**Before בָּרְכוּ**

For the congregation:
Change to non-leather shoes.
If possible, do not touch the leather shoes

If you neglected to bring non-leather shoes to the synagogue before Shabbat, remove your shoes.

Continue Saturday night Arvit as usual through the Amidah.

קַדִּישׁ שָׁלֵם Full Kaddish L280 S294 W160 F688

☞ Most congregations remove the table cover and the פָּרֹכֶת parokhet.
See "Procedures in the Synagogue," p. 192.

✕ ~~הַבְדָּלָה Havdalah~~

☞ Upon seeing a flame (light a candle if necessary), recite only the בְּרָכָה berakhah over a flame. (It is preferred not to recite the בְּרָכָה over electric lights.)

\+ Megillah reading:
Chant מְגִלַּת אֵיכָה Megillat Eykhah and קִינוֹת kinot following the procedures in the blue box on p. 192.

| Av 5779 | | | | | | |
|---|---|---|---|---|---|---|
| | | | | | 1 | 2 |
| 3 | 4 | 5 | 6 | 7 | 8 | 9 |
| 10 | 11 | 12 | 13 | 14 | 15 | 16 |
| 17 | 18 | 19 | 20 | 21 | 22 | 23 |
| 24 | 25 | 26 | 27 | 28 | 29 | 30 |

| Aug 2019 | | | | | | |
|---|---|---|---|---|---|---|
| | | | | | 2 | 3 |
| 4 | 5 | 6 | 7 | 8 | 9 | 10 |
| 11 | 12 | 13 | 14 | 15 | 16 | 17 |
| 18 | 19 | 20 | 21 | 22 | 23 | 24 |
| 25 | 26 | 27 | 28 | 29 | 30 | 31 |

+ Add ✗ Omit ☞ Take note!

**Siddurim**

- **L** Lev Shalem for Shabbat and Festivals
- **S** Shabbat and Festival Sim Shalom
- **W** Weekday Sim Shalom
- **F** Full Sim Shalom (both editions)
- **P** Personal Edition of Full Sim Shalom

---

✗ ~~וִיהִי נֹעַם Vihi no'am~~
✗ ~~יֹשֵׁב בְּסֵתֶר עֶלְיוֹן Yoshev beseter elyon~~
☞ וְאַתָּה קָדוֹשׁ Ve'attah kadosh L216 S293 W159 F684
☞ קַדִּישׁ שָׁלֵם Full Kaddish, but omit sentence: L280 S294 W160 F688
✗ ~~תִּתְקַבַּל Titkabbal . . .~~
עָלֵינוּ Aleynu L281 S297 W163 F696
קַדִּישׁ יָתוֹם Mourner's Kaddish L282 S298 W164 F698
✗ ~~הַבְדָּלָה Havdalah~~

**After עַרְבִית** ☞ If you did not wear non-leather shoes:
Put on your shoes to return home.
Wear non-leather shoes for the remainder of the fast.

**Sun 11 Aug שַׁחֲרִית** ☞ Do not wear tallit or tefillin.

If you wear a טַלִּית קָטָן tallit katan,
put it on, but do not recite the בְּרָכָה berakhah.

Weekday Shaharit as usual through the silent Amidah, except:
✗ ~~Psalm for Sunday~~
☞ Chant the service in a subdued voice, using melodies appropriate for the mournful mood.

**Silent weekday Amidah:**
Do not add עֲנֵנוּ Anenu.

**Repetition of the weekday Amidah:**
**6 or more fasting** + עֲנֵנוּ Anenu, before רְפָאֵנוּ Refa'enu W38 F110
**Fewer than 6 fasting** ✦ Add עֲנֵנוּ Anenu in שׁוֹמֵעַ תְּפִלָּה Shome·a tefillah.
Replace תַּעֲנִיתֵנוּ ta'anitenu (6th word) with
הַתַּעֲנִית הַזֶּה hata'anit hazeh. W38 F110
**All minyanim** ✗ ~~בִּרְכַּת כֹּהֲנִים Birkat kohanim~~

✗ ~~אָבִינוּ מַלְכֵּנוּ Avinu malkenu~~
✗ ~~תַּחֲנוּן Tahanun~~
חֲצִי קַדִּישׁ Short Kaddish W64 F136

**Fewer than 6 fasting** ✦ Omit the entire Torah service.
Continue with קִינוֹת Kinot.

**6 or more fasting** + **TORAH SERVICE** W65 F138
Remove **1** Torah scroll from ark.

☞ Before placing the Torah scroll on the table, spread a טַלִּית tallit as a temporary table cover.

**Torah** 3 aliyot from וָאֶתְחַנַּן Va'et·ḥannan
דְּבָרִים Devarim (Deuteronomy) 4:25–40
¹4:25–29 ²30–35 ᴹ36–40 W338 P973

חֲצִי קַדִּישׁ Short Kaddish W71 F146
Open, raise, display, and wrap scroll.

Recite the בְּרָכָה berakhah before the haftarah. W74 F410 P989
This בְּרָכָה may be chanted using אֵיכָה melody.

**Haftarah** יִרְמְיָהוּ Yirmeyahu (Jeremiah) 8:13–9:23° W339 P975

☞ °This haftarah is chanted with אֵיכָה melody, except for the last two verses (9:22–23), which are chanted with the regular haftarah melody. (Some chant also the last verses with אֵיכָה melody.)

Recite the 3 concluding haftarah blessings, through מָגֵן דָּוִד Magen david. W74 F410 P989.

Return scroll to ark. W76 F150

**All minyanim** Sit on the floor or on low seats or benches.
Recite קִינוֹת kinot.
Some chant מְגִלַּת אֵיכָה Megillat Eykhah, either at this point or at the end of the service.
Follow the procedures in the blue box on p. 192.

אַשְׁרֵי Ashrey W78 F152
✕ ~~לַמְנַצֵּחַ Lamenatse·aḥ (Psalm 20)~~

☞ וּבָא לְצִיּוֹן Uva letsiyyon, but omit 2nd verse: W80 F156
✕ ~~וַאֲנִי זֹאת בְּרִיתִי אוֹתָם Va'ani zot beriti otam . . .~~

☞ קַדִּישׁ שָׁלֵם Full Kaddish, but omit sentence: W82 F158
✕ ~~תִּתְקַבַּל Titkabbal . . .~~

עָלֵינוּ Aleynu W83 F160
✕ ~~Psalm for Sunday~~
קַדִּישׁ יָתוֹם Mourner's Kaddish W84 F162

**מִנְחָה** ☞ Immediately before Minḥah, most congregations that removed the table cover and the פָּרֹכֶת restore them.

☞ Wear טַלִּית tallit and תְּפִלִּין tefillin, reciting the בְּרָכוֹת berakhot in the usual manner. W2–3 F4

Av 5779

| | | | | | | |
|---|---|---|---|---|---|---|
| | | | | | 1 | 2 |
| 3 | 4 | 5 | 6 | 7 | 8 | 9 |
| 10 | 11 | 12 | 13 | 14 | 15 | 16 |
| 17 | 18 | 19 | 20 | 21 | 22 | 23 |
| 24 | 25 | 26 | 27 | 28 | 29 | 30 |

Aug 2019

| | | | | | | |
|---|---|---|---|---|---|---|
| | | | | | 2 | 3 |
| 4 | 5 | 6 | 7 | 8 | 9 | 10 |
| 11 | 12 | 13 | 14 | 15 | 16 | 17 |
| 18 | 19 | 20 | 21 | 22 | 23 | 24 |
| 25 | 26 | 27 | 28 | 29 | 30 | 31 |

+ Add ✕ Omit ☞ Take note!

**Siddurim**

- **L** Lev Shalem for Shabbat and Festivals
- **S** Shabbat and Festival Sim Shalom
- **W** Weekday Sim Shalom
- **F** Full Sim Shalom (both editions)
- **P** Personal Edition of Full Sim Shalom

---

☞ Use regular weekday melodies throughout this service.

+ Psalm for Sunday (Psalm 24) W85 F22

+ קַדִּישׁ יָתוֹם Mourner's Kaddish W100 F52

אַשְׁרֵי Ashrey W120 F164

חֲצִי קַדִּישׁ Short Kaddish W121 F166

Fewer than 6 fasting ✦ Omit the entire Torah service.
Continue with the silent Amidah.

6 or more fasting + **TORAH SERVICE** W65 F138

Remove **1** Torah scroll from ark.
If the table cover was removed and has not yet been restored, spread a טַלִּית tallit as a temporary table cover.

**Torah** 3 aliyot from כִּי תִשָּׂא Ki tissa
שְׁמוֹת Shemot (Exodus) 32:11–14, 34:1–10
1 32:11–14° 2 34:1–3 M 4–10° W341 P979

☞ °At each of the 3 passages indicated below, follow this procedure:

1. The reader pauses before the indicated text.
2. The congregation recites the indicated text.
3. Afterward, the reader chants the indicated text in the manner of the cantillation of High Holiday Torah reading.

32:12 שׁוּב מֵחֲרוֹן אַפֶּךָ וְהִנָּחֵם עַל־הָרָעָה לְעַמֶּךָ׃

34:6–7 יְיָ | יְיָ אֵ·ל רַחוּם וְחַנּוּן אֶרֶךְ אַפַּיִם וְרַב־חֶסֶד וֶאֱמֶת׃
נֹצֵר חֶסֶד לָאֲלָפִים נֹשֵׂא עָוֺן וָפֶשַׁע וְחַטָּאָה וְנַקֵּה

34:9 וְסָלַחְתָּ לַעֲוֺנֵנוּ וּלְחַטָּאתֵנוּ | וּנְחַלְתָּנוּ׃

To preserve the sense of this passage, maintain the appropriate pause after the טִפְחָא (וּלְחַטָּאתֵנוּ).

Do not recite חֲצִי קַדִּישׁ Short Kaddish after maftir aliyah.

Open, raise, display, and wrap scroll.

Recite the בְּרָכָה berakhah before the haftarah. W74 F410 P989

**Haftarah** יְשַׁעְיָהוּ Yesha'yahu (Isaiah) 55:6–56:8 W342 P980

☞ Chant this haftarah using the regular haftarah melody.

Recite the 3 concluding haftarah blessings, through מָגֵן דָּוִד Magen david. W74 F410 P989.

Return scroll to ark. W76 F150

חֲצִי קַדִּישׁ Short Kaddish W121 F166

| | | Av 5779 | Aug 2019 | אָב 10 | Aug 11 |
|---|---|---|---|---|---|
| ✚ Add ✘ Omit ☞ Take note! | | | | אָב 11 | Aug 11 |
| **Siddurim** | | 1 2 | 2 3 | אָב 14 | Aug 15 |
| L Lev Shalem for Shabbat and Festivals | | 3 4 5 6 7 8 9 | 4 5 6 7 8 9 10 | | |
| S Shabbat and Festival Sim Shalom | | 10 11 12 13 14 15 16 | 11 12 13 14 15 16 17 | | |
| W Weekday Sim Shalom | | 17 18 19 20 21 22 23 | 18 19 20 21 22 23 24 | | |
| F Full Sim Shalom (both editions) | | 24 25 26 27 28 29 30 | 25 26 27 28 29 30 31 | | |
| P Personal Edition of Full Sim Shalom | | | | | |

**All minyanim** — **Silent weekday Amidah:**
+ נַחֵם Naḥem W126 F176

**If fasting** + עֲנֵנוּ Anenu, in שׁוֹמֵעַ תְּפִלָּה Shome·a tefillah W127 F178

**All** ✕ ~~שָׁלוֹם רָב Shalom rav~~
+ שִׂים שָׁלוֹם Sim shalom W131 F184

**Repetition of the weekday Amidah:**

**6 or more fasting** + עֲנֵנוּ Anenu, before רְפָאֵנוּ Refa'enu W124 F172

**All minyanim** + נַחֵם Naḥem W126 F176

**Fewer than 6 fasting** ✦ Add עֲנֵנוּ Anenu in שׁוֹמֵעַ תְּפִלָּה Shome·a tefillah. Replace תַּעֲנִיתֵנוּ ta'anitenu (6th word) with הַתַּעֲנִית הַזֶּה hata'anit hazeh. W127 F172

**All minyanim** + בִּרְכַּת כֹּהֲנִים Birkat kohanim W131 F184
✕ ~~שָׁלוֹם רָב Shalom rav~~
+ שִׂים שָׁלוֹם Sim shalom W131 F184

✕ ~~אָבִינוּ מַלְכֵּנוּ Avinu malkenu~~
✕ ~~תַּחֲנוּן Taḥanun~~

☞ קַדִּישׁ שָׁלֵם Full Kaddish *with* תִּתְקַבַּל Titkabbal W134 F194
עָלֵינוּ Aleynu W135 F196
קַדִּישׁ יָתוֹם Mourner's Kaddish W136 F198

---

**Av 11 אָב**
**Sun 11 Aug**

**עַרְבִית** If the table cover and פָּרֹכֶת were removed and have not yet been restored, restore them before beginning Arvit.

Weekday Arvit as usual

+ **Havdalah (delayed from Saturday night)** S299 W165 F700
✕ ~~הִנֵּה אֵ-ל יְשׁוּעָתִי Hinneh el yeshu'ati~~
+ בּוֹרֵא פְּרִי הַגָּפֶן Bo·re peri hagafen
✕ ~~בּוֹרֵא מִינֵי בְשָׂמִים Bo·re miney vesamim~~
✕ ~~בּוֹרֵא מְאוֹרֵי הָאֵשׁ Bo·re me'orey ha'esh~~
+ הַמַּבְדִּיל בֵּין קֹדֶשׁ לְחֹל Hamavdil beyn kodesh leḥol

**At home** ☞ Do not eat meat or drink wine until morning.

---

**Av 14 אָב**
**Thu 15 Aug**

עֶרֶב ט"ו בְּאָב Erev Tu Be'av Day before Tu Be'av

**מִנְחָה** ✕ ~~תַּחֲנוּן Taḥanun~~

Av 5779

| | | | | | | |
|---|---|---|---|---|---|---|
| | | | | | 1 | 2 |
| 3 | 4 | 5 | 6 | 7 | 8 | 9 |
| 10 | 11 | 12 | 13 | 14 | 15 | 16 |
| 17 | 18 | 19 | 20 | 21 | 22 | 23 |
| 24 | 25 | 26 | 27 | 28 | 29 | 30 |

Aug 2019

| | | | | | | |
|---|---|---|---|---|---|---|
| | | | | | 2 | 3 |
| 4 | 5 | 6 | 7 | 8 | 9 | 10 |
| 11 | 12 | 13 | 14 | 15 | 16 | 17 |
| 18 | 19 | 20 | 21 | 22 | 23 | 24 |
| 25 | 26 | 27 | 28 | 29 | 30 | 31 |

+ Add ✕ Omit ☞ Take note!

**Siddurim**
- **L** Lev Shalem for Shabbat and Festivals
- **S** Shabbat and Festival Sim Shalom
- **W** Weekday Sim Shalom
- **F** Full Sim Shalom (both editions)
- **P** Personal Edition of Full Sim Shalom

## Av 15 אָב — ט"ו בְּאָב Tu Be'av

Fri 16 Aug (daytime)

**15th of Av (day of communal celebration)**

**Tu Be'av**, according to the Talmud, is one of the most joyous days of the Jewish year. Various happy events in Jewish history are associated with this day.

During the time of the Second Temple in Jerusalem, the 15th of Av marked the beginning of the grape harvest. The Talmud explains that the daughters of Israel used to dress in white and go out to the vineyards to dance. Young unmarried men would follow after them in the hope of finding a bride.

שַׁחֲרִית ✕ ~~תַּחֲנוּן Taḥanun~~

☞ לַמְנַצֵּחַ Lamenatse·aḥ (Psalm 20) W79 F154

מִנְחָה ✕ ~~תַּחֲנוּן Taḥanun~~

## Chanting Aseret Hadibberot

### Parashat Va'et·ḥannan

Parashat Va'et·ḥannan has a second version of עֲשֶׂרֶת הַדִּבְּרוֹת *aseret hadibberot.* Although usually translated "the 10 commandments," the phrase actually means "the 10 pronouncements."

The congregants stand as they hear this section read, just as the people Israel stood at the foot of Mount Sinai and listened to the voice of God.

The proper chanting of עֲשֶׂרֶת הַדִּבְּרוֹת requires exceptional attention because this passage is marked with 2 sets of verse divisions and 2 sets of *te'amim* (tropes, cantillation marks). One set, for private study, divides the passage into verses of usual length, suitable for study. The 2nd set, for public reading, divides the passage into exactly *10* verses. Each verse corresponds to 1 of the 10 pronouncements. The congregation listens to exactly *10* pronouncements, reenacting the events experienced by the people Israel at Mount Sinai.

For further discussion of the verse divisions of עֲשֶׂרֶת הַדִּבְּרוֹת, see p. 96.

Over the centuries, the complexity of the task of separating 2 sets of verse divisions and 2 sets of *te'amim* resulted in countless errors in printed *ḥumashim.* The confusing verse divisions led to a confusion in verse *numbers,* which in fact should follow the private reading. There are 29 verses in the chapter, but many editions erroneously count 30. This leads to confusing *aliyah* divisions, which are clarified on p. 200.

The correct verse divisions and *te'amim* for the public reading appear on p. 199. Only this version presents *10* pronouncements in *10* verses.

# עֲשֶׂרֶת הַדִּבְּרוֹת — פָּרָשַׁת וָאֶתְחַנַּן

**FOR PUBLIC READING –** טַעֲמָא תְּנִינָא (טַעַם עֶלְיוֹן)

דִּבְּרוֹת

1 אָנֹכִי יְהוָה אֱלֹהֶיךָ אֲשֶׁר
2 הוֹצֵאתִיךָ מֵאֶרֶץ מִצְרַיִם מִבֵּית עֲבָדִים: לֹא יִהְיֶה־
לְךָ אֱלֹהִים אֲחֵרִים עַל־פָּנַי לֹא תַעֲשֶׂה־לְךָ פֶסֶל |
כָּל־תְּמוּנָה אֲשֶׁר בַּשָּׁמַיִם | מִמַּעַל וַאֲשֶׁר בָּאָרֶץ
מִתָּחַת וַאֲשֶׁר בַּמַּיִם | מִתַּחַת לָאָרֶץ לֹא־תִשְׁתַּחֲוֶה
לָהֶם וְלֹא תָעָבְדֵם° כִּי אָנֹכִי יְהוָה אֱלֹהֶיךָ אֵל קַנָּא
°Read: **to'ovdem**
פֹּקֵד עֲוֺן אָבוֹת עַל־בָּנִים וְעַל־שִׁלֵּשִׁים וְעַל־רִבֵּעִים
לְשֹׂנְאָי וְעֹשֶׂה חֶסֶד לַאֲלָפִים לְאֹהֲבַי וּלְשֹׁמְרֵי
3 מִצְוֺתָי°: לֹא תִשָּׂא אֶת־שֵׁם־יְהוָה
°Read: **mitsvotay**
כְּתִיב: מצותו
אֱלֹהֶיךָ לַשָּׁוְא כִּי לֹא יְנַקֶּה יְהוָה אֵת אֲשֶׁר־יִשָּׂא
4 אֶת־שְׁמוֹ לַשָּׁוְא: שָׁמוֹר אֶת־יוֹם
הַשַּׁבָּת לְקַדְּשׁוֹ כַּאֲשֶׁר צִוְּךָ | יְהוָה אֱלֹהֶיךָ שֵׁשֶׁת
יָמִים תַּעֲבֹד וְעָשִׂיתָ כָּל־מְלַאכְתֶּךָ וְיוֹם הַשְּׁבִיעִי
שַׁבָּת | לַיהוָה אֱלֹהֶיךָ לֹא תַעֲשֶׂה כָל־מְלָאכָה
אַתָּה וּבִנְךָ־וּבִתֶּךָ וְעַבְדְּךָ־וַאֲמָתֶךָ וְשׁוֹרְךָ וַחֲמֹרְךָ
וְכָל־בְּהֶמְתֶּךָ וְגֵרְךָ אֲשֶׁר בִּשְׁעָרֶיךָ לְמַעַן יָנוּחַ
עַבְדְּךָ וַאֲמָתְךָ כָּמוֹךָ וְזָכַרְתָּ כִּי־עֶבֶד הָיִיתָ | בְּאֶרֶץ
מִצְרַיִם וַיֹּצִאֲךָ יְהוָה אֱלֹהֶיךָ מִשָּׁם בְּיָד חֲזָקָה וּבִזְרֹעַ
נְטוּיָה עַל־כֵּן צִוְּךָ יְהוָה אֱלֹהֶיךָ לַעֲשׂוֹת אֶת־יוֹם
5 הַשַּׁבָּת: כַּבֵּד אֶת־אָבִיךָ וְאֶת־
אִמֶּךָ כַּאֲשֶׁר צִוְּךָ יְהוָה אֱלֹהֶיךָ לְמַעַן | יַאֲרִיכֻן יָמֶיךָ
וּלְמַעַן יִיטַב לָךְ עַל הָאֲדָמָה אֲשֶׁר־יְהוָה אֱלֹהֶיךָ נֹתֵן
7 | 6 לָךְ: לֹא תִרְצָח: וְלֹא
9 | 8 תִנְאָף: וְלֹא תִגְנֹב: וְלֹא־
10 תַעֲנֶה בְרֵעֲךָ עֵד שָׁוְא: וְלֹא תַחְמֹד
אֵשֶׁת רֵעֶךָ וְלֹא תִתְאַוֶּה בֵּית
רֵעֶךָ שָׂדֵהוּ וְעַבְדּוֹ וַאֲמָתוֹ שׁוֹרוֹ וַחֲמֹרוֹ וְכֹל אֲשֶׁר
לְרֵעֶךָ:

| Av 5779 | | | | | | |
|---|---|---|---|---|---|---|
| | | | | | 1 | 2 |
| 3 | 4 | 5 | 6 | 7 | 8 | 9 |
| 10 | 11 | 12 | 13 | 14 | 15 | 16 |
| 17 | 18 | 19 | 20 | 21 | 22 | 23 |
| 24 | 25 | 26 | 27 | 28 | 29 | 30 |

| Aug 2019 | | | | | | |
|---|---|---|---|---|---|---|
| | | | | | 2 | 3 |
| 4 | 5 | 6 | 7 | 8 | 9 | 10 |
| 11 | 12 | 13 | 14 | 15 | 16 | 17 |
| 18 | 19 | 20 | 21 | 22 | 23 | 24 |
| 25 | 26 | 27 | 28 | 29 | 30 | 31 |

+ Add ✕ Omit ☞ Take note!

**Siddurim**
- **L** Lev Shalem for Shabbat and Festivals
- **S** Shabbat and Festival Sim Shalom
- **W** Weekday Sim Shalom
- **F** Full Sim Shalom (both editions)
- **P** Personal Edition of Full Sim Shalom

## Aseret Hadibberot and Shema in the Triennial Cycle

- **Triennial Option A:** A fuller reading. The congregation thus experiences עֲשֶׂרֶת הַדִּבְּרוֹת every year, and hears שְׁמַע *shema* in years 2 and 3 of the cycle.
- **Triennial Option B:** A more abbreviated reading. The congregation experiences עֲשֶׂרֶת הַדִּבְּרוֹת only in year 2 and hears שְׁמַע only in year 3 of the cycle.

For details, see below.

## Av 16 אָב Sat 17 Aug

## שַׁבָּת Shabbat פָּרָשַׁת וָאֶתְחַנַּן Parashat Va'et·ḥannan
## שַׁבַּת נַחֲמוּ Shabbat Naḥamu

**Shabbat Naḥamu**, the Shabbat after Tish'ah Be'av, is the 1st of the 7 *shabbatot* of consolation leading to Rosh Hashanah. This Shabbat takes its name from the 1st word of the haftarah, "Console yourselves."

This parashah contains עֲשֶׂרֶת הַדִּבְּרוֹת *aseret hadibberot.* For the correct text and *te'amim* (tropes, cantillation marks), see p. 199. For special instructions for the chanting of this passage, see p. 198 and below.

**Torah** 7 aliyot (minimum): וָאֶתְחַנַּן Va'et·ḥannan
דְּבָרִים Devarim (Deuteronomy) 3:23–7:11

| | | | | |
|---|---|---|---|---|
| Annual: | 1 3:23–4:4 | 2 4:5–40 | 3 4:41–49 | °4 5:1–17 |
| | °5 5:18–6:3 | 6 6:4–25 | 7 7:1–11 | M 7:9–11 |

Triennial:

°Option A (includes both Aseret Hadibberot and Shema)

| | | | |
|---|---|---|---|
| °1 5:1–17 | °2 5:18–23 | °3 5:24–6:3 | 4 6:4–9 |
| 5 6:10–19 | 6 6:20–25 | 7 7:1–11 | M 7:9–11 |

°Option B (excludes Aseret Hadibberot, but includes Shema):

| | | | |
|---|---|---|---|
| 1 6:4–9 | 2 6:10–19 | 3 6:20–22 | 4 6:23–25 |
| 5 7:1–5 | 6 7:6–8 | 7 7:9–11 | M 7:9–11 |

☞ °**Verse numbers in chapter 5:** The verses are misnumbered in many editions. Use these guidelines to properly divide the reading:

**Annual Reading**
Aliyah **4**: ends לְרֵעֶךָ (5:18 in many books).
Aliyah **5**: begins אֶת־הַדְּבָרִים (5:19 in many books)

**Triennial Option A**
Aliyah **1**: ends לְרֵעֶךָ (5:18 in many books).
Aliyah **2**: אֶת־הַדְּבָרִים through וְעָשִׂינוּ (5:19–24 in many books)
Aliyah **3**: וַיִּשְׁמַע through תִּירָשׁוּן (5:25–30 in many books)

☞ °5:6–17 (5:7–18 in many books) Follow the te'amim (tropes) for the public reading of עֲשֶׂרֶת הַדִּבְּרוֹת, found on p. 199. For additional instructions for chanting this passage, see the blue box on p. 198.

☞ °**Triennial Option A** excludes Shema in year 1 (next year).
°**Triennial Option B** includes Aseret Hadibberot only in year 2 (last year) and Shema only in year 3 (this year).

**Haftarah** יְשַׁעְיָהוּ Yesha'yahu (Isaiah) 40:1–26°
(1st of 7 haftarot of consolation following Tish'ah Be'av)

☞ °40:12 For readers using Sephardic/Israeli pronunciation:
וְכָל Read: vekhal (**not** vekhol; this is **not** kamets katan).

מִנְחָה

**Torah** 3 aliyot from עֵקֶב Ekev
דְּבָרִים Devarim (Deuteronomy) 7:12–8:10
¹7:12–21 ²7:22–8:3 ³8:4–10 W309 P929

This is also the reading for the coming Monday and Thursday.

---

**Av 23 אָב**
**Sat 24 Aug**

## שַׁבָּת Shabbat פָּרָשַׁת עֵקֶב Parashat Ekev
## שַׁבַּת מְבָרְכִים הַחֹדֶשׁ Shabbat Mevarekhim Haḥodesh

**Torah** 7 aliyot (minimum): עֵקֶב Ekev
דְּבָרִים Devarim (Deuteronomy) 7:12–11:25

| | | | | |
|---|---|---|---|---|
| Annual: | ¹7:12–8:10 | ²8:11–9:3 | ³9:4–29 | ⁴10:1–11 |
| | ⁵10:12–11:9 | ⁶11:10–21 | ⁷11:22–25 | M11:22–25 |
| Triennial: | ¹10:12–15 | ²10:16–22 | ³11:1–9 | ⁴11:10–12 |
| | ⁵11:13–15 | ⁶11:16–21 | ⁷11:22–25 | M11:22–25 |

**Haftarah** יְשַׁעְיָהוּ Yesha'yahu (Isaiah) 49:14–51:3
(2nd of 7 haftarot of consolation following Tish'ah Be'av)

+ **Birkat Haḥodesh:** L180 S150 F418
Announce Rosh Ḥodesh Elul:
רֹאשׁ חֹדֶשׁ אֱלוּל יִהְיֶה בְּיוֹם שַׁבַּת קֹדֶשׁ
וּלְמָחֳרָתוֹ בְּיוֹם רִאשׁוֹן . . .
Rosh ḥodesh Elul yihyeh beyom shabbat kodesh
ulmoḥorato beyom rishon . . .
(Friday night, Saturday, and Sunday)

✕ ~~אַב הָרַחֲמִים Av Haraḥamim~~

מִנְחָה

**Torah** 3 aliyot from רְאֵה Re'eh
דְּבָרִים Devarim (Deuteronomy) 11:26–12:10
¹11:26–31 ²11:32–12:5 ³12:6–10 W311 P931

This is also the reading for the coming Monday and Thursday.

| Av 5779 | | | | | | | Aug 2019 | | | | | | |
|---|---|---|---|---|---|---|---|---|---|---|---|---|---|
| | | | | | 1 | 2 | | | | | | 2 | 3 |
| 3 | 4 | 5 | 6 | 7 | 8 | 9 | 4 | 5 | 6 | 7 | 8 | 9 | 10 |
| 10 | 11 | 12 | 13 | 14 | 15 | 16 | 11 | 12 | 13 | 14 | 15 | 16 | 17 |
| 17 | 18 | 19 | 20 | 21 | 22 | 23 | 18 | 19 | 20 | 21 | 22 | 23 | 24 |
| 24 | 25 | 26 | 27 | 28 | 29 | 30 | 25 | 26 | 27 | 28 | 29 | 30 | 31 |

+ Add ✕ Omit ☞ Take note!

**Siddurim**
- **L** Lev Shalem for Shabbat and Festivals
- **S** Shabbat and Festival Sim Shalom
- **W** Weekday Sim Shalom
- **F** Full Sim Shalom (both editions)
- **P** Personal Edition of Full Sim Shalom

## Av 30 אָב
Fri 30 Aug (evening)

## שַׁבָּת Shabbat פָּרָשַׁת רְאֵה Parashat Re'eh
## רֹאשׁ חֹדֶשׁ אֱלוּל Rosh Ḥodesh Elul — Day 1

**DURING Rosh Ḥodesh**

**Birkat Hamazon:**
+ יַעֲלֶה וְיָבוֹא Ya'aleh veyavo for Rosh Ḥodesh L90|95 S340|347 W233|239 F762|780
+ הָרַחֲמָן Haraḥaman for Rosh Ḥodesh L92|96 S343|348 W235|240 F768

**עַרְבִית**

**Shabbat Amidah:**
+ יַעֲלֶה וְיָבוֹא Ya'aleh veyavo for Rosh Ḥodesh L50 S36 F298

**Sat 31 Aug שַׁחֲרִית**

**Before מִזְמוֹר שִׁיר Mizmor shir (Psalm 30)** L120 S81 F50
**or after Aleynu, recite:**
Psalm for Shabbat (Psalm 92) L112 S72 F32
קַדִּישׁ יָתוֹם Mourner's Kaddish (some omit) L121 S82 F52
+ Psalm 104 for Rosh Ḥodesh L114 S78 F34
קַדִּישׁ יָתוֹם Mourner's Kaddish L121 S82 F52

**Shabbat Amidah:**
+ יַעֲלֶה וְיָבוֹא Ya'aleh veyavo for Rosh Ḥodesh L163 S118 F360

+ חֲצִי הַלֵּל Short Hallel L316 S133 F380
קַדִּישׁ שָׁלֵם Full Kaddish L167 S138 F392

**TORAH SERVICE** L168 S139 F394

Remove **2** Torah scrolls from ark.

**1st scroll** 7 aliyot (minimum): רְאֵה Re'eh
דְּבָרִים Devarim (Deuteronomy) 11:26–16:17

| | | | | |
|---|---|---|---|---|
| Annual: | 1 11:26–12:10 | 2 12:11–28 | 3 12:29–13:19 | 4 14:1–21 |
| | 5 14:22–29 | 6 15:1–18 | 7 15:19–16:17 | |
| Triennial: | 1 15:1–6 | 2 15:7–11 | 3 15:12–18 | 4 15:19–23 |
| | 5 16:1–8 | 6 16:9–12 | 7 16:13–17 | |

Place 2nd scroll on table next to 1st scroll.
חֲצִי קַדִּישׁ Short Kaddish L174 S146 F408
Open, raise, display, and wrap 1st scroll.

+ **2nd scroll** Maftir aliyah from פִּינְחָס Pineḥas
בְּמִדְבַּר M Bemidbar (Numbers) 28:9–15

Open, raise, display, and wrap 2nd scroll.

☞ **Haftarah** for Shabbat Rosh Ḥodesh
°יְשַׁעְיָהוּ Yesha'yahu (Isaiah) 66:1–24°

☞ °The haftarah for Shabbat Rosh Ḥodesh serves appropriately as the 3rd of 7 haftarot of consolation following Tish'ah Be'av. Then, in 2 weeks, append the usual 3rd haftarah to the 5th. See p. 207.

☞ °After 66:24, repeat 66:23 so the haftarah ends on a positive note.

☞ Most Ashkenazic congregations do **not** add verses from the Shabbat Maḥar Ḥodesh haftarah. Sephardic congregations add the first and last verses at the end.

✕ ~~אַב הָרַחֲמִים Av Haraḥamim~~

אַשְׁרֵי Ashrey L181 S151 F420
Return scrolls to ark. L183 S153 F422

חֲצִי קָדִישׁ Short Kaddish L184 S155 F428

מוּסָף

**Rosh Ḥodesh Amidah for Shabbat:** L193 S166 F486
Shabbat קְדֻשָּׁה Kedushah L195 S167 F490
Continuation of Amidah L196 S168 F496
✕ ~~וּלְכַפָּרַת פָּשַׁע Ulkhapparat pasha~~
Beginning with Rosh Ḥodesh Nisan, we do not add these words.

קַדִּישׁ שָׁלֵם Full Kaddish L203 S181 F506
אֵין כֵּא·לֹהֵינוּ Eyn keloheynu L204 S182 F507
עָלֵינוּ Aleynu L205 S183 F508

**If psalms for the day were not recited at Shaḥarit, add here:**
קַדִּישׁ יָתוֹם Mourner's Kaddish (some omit) L207 S184 F512
Psalm for Shabbat (Psalm 92) L112 S72 F32
קַדִּישׁ יָתוֹם Mourner's Kaddish (some omit) L121 S82 F52
+ Psalm 104 for Rosh Ḥodesh L114 S78 F34

קַדִּישׁ יָתוֹם Mourner's Kaddish L207|121 S184|82 F512|52

מִנְחָה

**Torah** 3 aliyot from שֹׁפְטִים Shofetim
דְּבָרִים Devarim (Deuteronomy) 16:18–17:13
1 16:18–20 2 16:21–17:10 3 17:11–13 W312 P932

This is also the reading for the coming Monday and Thursday.

**Shabbat Amidah:**
+ יַעֲלֶה וְיָבוֹא Ya'aleh veyavo for Rosh Ḥodesh L227 S237 F580

✕ ~~צִדְקָתְךָ צֶדֶק Tsidkatekha tsedek~~

| Elul 5779 | | | | | | |
|---|---|---|---|---|---|---|
| 1 | 2 | 3 | 4 | 5 | 6 | 7 |
| 8 | 9 | 10 | 11 | 12 | 13 | 14 |
| 15 | 16 | 17 | 18 | 19 | 20 | 21 |
| 22 | 23 | 24 | 25 | 26 | 27 | 28 |
| 29 | | | | | | |

| Sep 2019 | | | | | | |
|---|---|---|---|---|---|---|
| 1 | 2 | 3 | 4 | 5 | 6 | 7 |
| 8 | 9 | 10 | 11 | 12 | 13 | 14 |
| 15 | 16 | 17 | 18 | 19 | 20 | 21 |
| 22 | 23 | 24 | 25 | 26 | 27 | 28 |
| 29 | | | | | | |

+ Add ✕ Omit ☞ Take note!

**Siddurim**

**L** Lev Shalem for Shabbat and Festivals
**S** Shabbat and Festival Sim Shalom
**W** Weekday Sim Shalom
**F** Full Sim Shalom (both editions)
**P** Personal Edition of Full Sim Shalom

## DURING Elul

### MORNINGS

**If psalm(s) for the day recited early in the service:**

**Every day** Recite psalm(s) for the day, followed by:
קַדִּישׁ יָתוֹם Mourner's Kaddish (some omit) L58 S82 W100 F52
+ Psalm 27 for the Season of Repentance L59 S80 W92 F40
קַדִּישׁ יָתוֹם Mourner's Kaddish L58 S82 W100 F52

**Weekdays** + At the end of the service, sound the shofar* (except on 29 Elul).

**If psalm(s) for the day recited at the end of the service:**

**Every day** Recite psalm(s) for the day, followed by:
קַדִּישׁ יָתוֹם Mourner's Kaddish (some omit) L58 S82 W100 F52

**Weekdays** + Sound the shofar* (except on 29 Elul). (Some sound the shofar instead after the last קַדִּישׁ יָתוֹם Mourner's Kaddish.)

**Every day** + Psalm 27 for the Season of Repentance L59 S80 W92 F40
קַדִּישׁ יָתוֹם Mourner's Kaddish L58 S82 W100 F52

### EVENINGS

**After עָלֵינוּ Aleynu:**

קַדִּישׁ יָתוֹם Mourner's Kaddish (some omit) L58 S82 W100 F52
+ Psalm 27 for the Season of Repentance L59 S80 W92 F40
קַדִּישׁ יָתוֹם Mourner's Kaddish L58 S82 W100 F52

---

*Without anyone reciting a בְּרָכָה berakhah or calling out *teki'ah, shevarim,* etc., sound the shofar:
תְּקִיעָה ← שְׁבָרִים ← תְּרוּעָה ← תְּקִיעָה Teki'ah → Shevarim → Teru'ah → Teki'ah

## Elul 1 אֱלוּל 1 — ראֹשׁ חֹדֶשׁ אֱלוּל Rosh Hodesh Elul — Day 2

Sat 31 Aug (evening) — מוֹצָאֵי שַׁבָּת Motsa'ey Shabbat — Conclusion of Shabbat

**DURING Rosh Hodesh**

**Birkat Hamazon:**

+ יַעֲלֶה וְיָבוֹא Ya'aleh veyavo for Rosh Hodesh L90|95 S340|347 W233|239 F762|780

+ הָרַחֲמָן Harahaman for Rosh Hodesh L92|96 S343|348 W235|240 F768

**עַרְבִית**

Saturday night Arvit as usual until the Amidah L264 S281 W137 F200

**Weekday Amidah:**

+ אַתָּה חוֹנַנְתָּנוּ Attah honantanu L272 S287 W143 F212
+ יַעֲלֶה וְיָבוֹא Ya'aleh veyavo for Rosh Hodesh L277 S289 W145 F216

Continue as on a usual Saturday night through
קַדִּישׁ שָׁלֵם Full Kaddish L280 S294 W160 F688

Some recite הַבְדָּלָה Havdalah here. L283 S299 W165 F700

עָלֵינוּ Aleynu L281 S297 W163 F696
קַדִּישׁ יָתוֹם Mourner's Kaddish (some omit) L282 S298 W164 F698
+ Psalm 27 for the Season of Repentance L59 S80 W92 F40
קַדִּישׁ יָתוֹם Mourner's Kaddish L58 S82 W100 F52

הַבְדָּלָה Havdalah L283 S299 W165 F700

**Sun 1 Sep — שַׁחֲרִית**

**Before מִזְמוֹר שִׁיר Mizmor shir (Psalm 30) W14 F50 or at end of service, recite:**

Psalm for Sunday (Psalm 24) W85 F22
קַדִּישׁ יָתוֹם Mourner's Kaddish (some omit) W100 F52
+ Psalm 104 for Rosh Hodesh W90 F34
קַדִּישׁ יָתוֹם Mourner's Kaddish (some omit) W100 F52
+ Psalm 27 for the Season of Repentance W92 F40
קַדִּישׁ יָתוֹם Mourner's Kaddish W100 F52"

**Weekday Amidah:**

+ יַעֲלֶה וְיָבוֹא Ya'aleh veyavo for Rosh Hodesh W41 F114

✕ ~~תַּחֲנוּן Tahanun~~

+ חֲצִי הַלֵּל Short Hallel W50 F380
קַדִּישׁ שָׁלֵם Full Kaddish W56 F392

Elul 5779

| | | | | | | |
|---|---|---|---|---|---|---|
| 1 | 2 | 3 | 4 | 5 | 6 | 7 |
| 8 | 9 | 10 | 11 | 12 | 13 | 14 |
| 15 | 16 | 17 | 18 | 19 | 20 | 21 |
| 22 | 23 | 24 | 25 | 26 | 27 | 28 |
| 29 | | | | | | |

Sep 2019

| | | | | | | |
|---|---|---|---|---|---|---|
| 1 | 2 | 3 | 4 | 5 | 6 | 7 |
| 8 | 9 | 10 | 11 | 12 | 13 | 14 |
| 15 | 16 | 17 | 18 | 19 | 20 | 21 |
| 22 | 23 | 24 | 25 | 26 | 27 | 28 |
| 29 | | | | | | |

+ Add ✕ Omit ☞ Take note!

**Siddurim**

- **L** Lev Shalem for Shabbat and Festivals
- **S** Shabbat and Festival Sim Shalom
- **W** Weekday Sim Shalom
- **F** Full Sim Shalom (both editions)
- **P** Personal Edition of Full Sim Shalom

---

+ **TORAH SERVICE** W65 F138

Remove **1** Torah scroll from ark.

**Torah** 4 aliyot: פִּינְחָס Pineḥas
בְּמִדְבַּר Bemidbar (Numbers) 28:1–15
[1]28:1–3 [2]3–5 [3]6–10 [4]11–15 W320 P943

חֲצִי קַדִּישׁ Short Kaddish W71 F146
Open, raise, display, and wrap scroll.
Return scroll to ark. W76 F150

אַשְׁרֵי Ashrey W78 F152
✕ ~~לַמְנַצֵּחַ Lamenatse·aḥ (Psalm 20)~~
וּבָא לְצִיּוֹן Uva letsiyyon W80 F156

**Some congregations:**
Remove and pack tefillin at this point.
+ חֲצִי קַדִּישׁ Short Kaddish W103 F428

**Other congregations:**
+ חֲצִי קַדִּישׁ Short Kaddish W103 F428
Remove and cover—but do not pack—tefillin, so that all begin Musaf Amidah at the same time, as soon after Kaddish as possible.

מוּסָף + **Rosh Ḥodesh Amidah for weekdays:** W104 F486
Weekday קְדֻשָּׁה Kedushah W105 F488
✕ ~~וּלְכַפָּרַת פָּשַׁע Ulkhapparat pasha~~
Beginning with Rosh Ḥodesh Nisan, we do not add these words.

+ קַדִּישׁ שָׁלֵם Full Kaddish W82 F158
עָלֵינוּ Aleynu W83 F160

**If psalms for the day were recited at Shaḥarit:**
קַדִּישׁ יָתוֹם Mourner's Kaddish W84 F162
+ Sound the shofar (see procedure on p. 204).

**If psalms for the day were not recited at Shaḥarit, add here:**
קַדִּישׁ יָתוֹם Mourner's Kaddish (some omit) W84 F162
Psalm for Sunday (Psalm 24) W85 F22
קַדִּישׁ יָתוֹם Mourner's Kaddish (some omit) W100 F52
+ Psalm 104 for Rosh Ḥodesh W90 F34
קַדִּישׁ יָתוֹם Mourner's Kaddish (some omit) W100 F52
+ Sound the shofar (see procedure on p. 204).
+ Psalm 27 for the Season of Repentance W92 F40
קַדִּישׁ יָתוֹם Mourner's Kaddish W84|100 F162|52

מִנְחָה

**Weekday Amidah:**

+ יַעֲלֶה וְיָבוֹא Ya'aleh veyavo for Rosh Ḥodesh W127 F178

✕ ~~תַּחֲנוּן Taḥanun~~

## Elul 7 אֱלוּל
**Sat 7 Sep**

## שַׁבָּת Shabbat פָּרָשַׁת שֹׁפְטִים Parashat Shofetim

**Torah** 7 aliyot (minimum): שֹׁפְטִים Shofetim
דְּבָרִים Devarim (Deuteronomy) 16:18–21:9

| | | | | |
|---|---|---|---|---|
| Annual: | ¹16:18–17:13 | ²17:14–20 | ³18:1–5 | ⁴18:6–13 |
| | ⁵18:14–19:13 | ⁶19:14–20:9 | ⁷20:10–21:9 | ᴹ21:7–9 |
| Triennial: | ¹19:14–21 | ²20:1–4 | ³20:5–9 | ⁴20:10–14 |
| | ⁵20:15–20 | ⁶21:1–6 | ⁷21:7–9 | ᴹ21:7–9 |

**Haftarah** יְשַׁעְיָהוּ Yesha'yahu (Isaiah) 51:12–52:12
(4th of 7 haftarot of consolation following Tish'ah Be'av)

מִנְחָה

**Torah** 3 aliyot from כִּי־תֵצֵא Ki tetse
דְּבָרִים Devarim (Deuteronomy) 21:10–21
¹21:10–14 ²15–17 ³18–21 W313 P934

This is also the reading for the coming Monday and Thursday.

## Elul 14 אֱלוּל
**Sat 14 Sep**

## שַׁבָּת Shabbat פָּרָשַׁת כִּי־תֵצֵא Parashat Ki tetse

**Torah** 7 aliyot (minimum): כִּי־תֵצֵא Ki tetse
דְּבָרִים Devarim (Deuteronomy) 21:10–25:19

| | | | | |
|---|---|---|---|---|
| Annual: | ¹21:10–21 | ²21:22–22:7 | ³22:8–23:7 | ⁴23:8–24 |
| | ⁵23:25–24:4 | ⁶24:5–13 | ⁷24:14–25:19 | ᴹ25:17–19 |
| Triennial: | ¹24:14–16 | ²24:17–19 | ³24:20–22 | ⁴25:1–4 |
| | ⁵25:5–10 | ⁶25:11–16 | ⁷25:17–19 | ᴹ25:17–19 |

☞ **Haftarah** יְשַׁעְיָהוּ Yesha'yahu (Isaiah) 54:1–10 + °54:11–55:5
(5th + 3rd of 7 haftarot of consolation following Tish'ah Be'av)

☞°54:1–10 + 54:11–55:5 Because Shabbat Re'eh was Rosh Ḥodesh, the usual 3rd haftarah of consolation was not read. Read the haftarah of Ki tetse and then the haftarah of Re'eh as a single haftarah. In the book of Isaiah these two brief passages are adjacent.

| Elul 5779 | | | | | | |
|---|---|---|---|---|---|---|
| 1 | 2 | 3 | 4 | 5 | 6 | 7 |
| 8 | 9 | 10 | 11 | 12 | 13 | 14 |
| 15 | 16 | 17 | 18 | 19 | 20 | 21 |
| 22 | 23 | 24 | 25 | 26 | 27 | 28 |
| 29 | | | | | | |

| Sep 2019 | | | | | | |
|---|---|---|---|---|---|---|
| 1 | 2 | 3 | 4 | 5 | 6 | 7 |
| 8 | 9 | 10 | 11 | 12 | 13 | 14 |
| 15 | 16 | 17 | 18 | 19 | 20 | 21 |
| 22 | 23 | 24 | 25 | 26 | 27 | 28 |
| 29 | | | | | | |

+ Add ✕ Omit ☞ Take note!

**Siddurim**
- **L** Lev Shalem for Shabbat and Festivals
- **S** Shabbat and Festival Sim Shalom
- **W** Weekday Sim Shalom
- **F** Full Sim Shalom (both editions)
- **P** Personal Edition of Full Sim Shalom

מִנְחָה

**Torah** 3 aliyot from כִּי־תָבוֹא Ki tavo
דְּבָרִים Devarim (Deuteronomy) 26:1–15°
¹26:1–3 ²4–11 ³12–15 W314 P935

This is also the reading for the coming Monday and Thursday.

☞°26:1–15 The reading extends through verse 15, which enables the correct configuration of the 3 aliyot.

## Elul 21 אֱלוּל 21
Sat 21 Sep

## שַׁבָּת Shabbat פָּרָשַׁת כִּי־תָבוֹא Parashat Ki tavo

**Torah** 7 aliyot (minimum): כִּי־תָבוֹא Ki tavo
דְּבָרִים Devarim (Deuteronomy) 26:1–29:8

| | | | | |
|---|---|---|---|---|
| Annual: | ¹26:1–11 | ²26:12–15 | ³26:16–19 | ⁴27:1–10 |
| | ⁵27:11–28:6 | ⁶28:7–69° | ⁷29:1–8 | M29:6–8 |
| Triennial: | ¹27:11–28:3 | ²28:4–6 | ³28:7–11 | ⁴28:12–14 |
| | ⁵28:15–69° | ⁶29:1–5 | ⁷29:6–8 | M29:6–8 |

☞°28:15–69 This is the תּוֹכֵחָה tokheḥah, verses of rebuke and warning. Because of the ominous nature of these verses, do not divide this lengthy passage into shorter aliyot. However, the chanting may be divided among multiple readers. All the readers must be present at the Torah when the oleh/olah recites the first berakhah. This serves as an implicit appointment of all the readers as sheliḥim (agents) of the oleh/olah.
Chant this section in a somewhat **subdued** voice to symbolically minimize the trepidation that the congregation experiences upon hearing the message of these verses. Be sure that all words and te'amim (tropes, cantillations) remain **clearly** audible to the congregation.
However, for verses 7–14, voicing the promise of God's protection and reward, and for the conclusion, verse 69, chant as usual.

**Haftarah** יְשַׁעְיָהוּ Yesha'yahu (Isaiah) 60:1–22
(6th of 7 haftarot of consolation following Tish'ah Be'av)

מִנְחָה

**Torah** 3 aliyot from נִצָּבִים Nitsavim
דְּבָרִים Devarim (Deuteronomy) 29:9–28°
¹29:9–11 ²12–14 ³15–28 W315 P936

This is also the reading for the coming Monday and Thursday.

☞°29:9–28 The reading extends through verse 28, which enables the correct configuration of the 3 aliyot.

Elul 22 אֱלוּל
Sat 21 Sep

## מוֹצָאֵי שַׁבָּת Motsa'ey Shabbat Conclusion of Shabbat

עַרְבִית

Saturday night Arvit as usual L264 S281 W137 F200

+ Psalm 27 for the Season of Repentance L59 S80 W92 F40

קַדִּישׁ יָתוֹם Mourner's Kaddish L58 S82 W100 F52

Elul 22 אֱלוּל
Sat 21 Sep (night)

## לֵיל סְלִיחוֹת Leyl Seliḥot

Seliḥot at Night

### Seliḥot — Penitential Prayers

We recite סְלִיחוֹת *seliḥot* prayers beginning the Saturday night before Rosh Hashanah to prepare ourselves for the upcoming Days of Repentance.

In a year when Rosh Hashanah begins on a Sunday night or Monday night, as in the coming year, we begin סְלִיחוֹת a week earlier so that we have more time to prepare in advance of Rosh Hashanah.

- Recite the first סְלִיחוֹת at midnight, an expression of our eagerness to begin the process of repentance.
- On subsequent days, recite סְלִיחוֹת before Shaḥarit every morning until Yom Kippur, except Shabbat and Rosh Hashanah.

The standard סְלִיחוֹת liturgy includes:

- אַשְׁרֵי *ashrey* and חֲצִי קַדִּישׁ Short Kaddish
- Various פִּיּוּטִים *piyyutim*, distinct liturgical poems for each day
- The Thirteen Attributes of God, . . . יי יי אֵ·ל רַחוּם וְחַנּוּן *adonay adonay el raḥum veḥannun* (based on Shemot 34:6–7)
- שְׁמַע קוֹלֵנוּ *shema kolenu*, אָשַׁמְנוּ *ashamnu*, and other סְלִיחוֹת prayers that appear in the Yom Kippur liturgy
- Short תַּחֲנוּן *taḥanun*
- קַדִּישׁ שָׁלֵם Full Kaddish

Elul 28 אֱלוּל
Sat 28 Sep

## שַׁבָּת Shabbat נִצָּבִים Parashat Nitsavim

**Torah** 7 aliyot (minimum): נִצָּבִים Nitsavim
דְּבָרִים Devarim (Deuteronomy) 29:9–30:20

| | | | | |
|---|---|---|---|---|
| Annual: | 1 29:9–11 | 2 29:12–14 | 3 29:15–28 | 4 30:1–6 |
| | 5 30:7–10 | 6 30:11–14 | 7 30:15–20 | M 30:15–20 (or 18–20) |

Triennial: Read the full parashah, divided as above.

**Haftarah** יְשַׁעְיָהוּ Yesha'yahu (Isaiah) 61:10–63:9
(last of 7 haftarot of consolation following Tish'ah Be'av)

✕ ~~Birkat Haḥodesh~~

| Sep 28 | 28 אֱלוּל | Elul 5779 | Sep 2019 | ✚ Add    ✘ Omit    ☞ Take note! |
|---|---|---|---|---|
| Sep 28 | 29 אֱלוּל | 1 2 3 4 5 6 7 | 1 2 3 4 5 6 7 | **Siddurim** |
| Sep 29 | | 8 9 10 11 12 13 14 | 8 9 10 11 12 13 14 | **L** Lev Shalem for Shabbat and Festivals |
| | | 15 16 17 18 19 20 21 | 15 16 17 18 19 20 21 | **S** Shabbat and Festival Sim Shalom |
| | | 22 23 24 25 26 27 28 | 22 23 24 25 26 27 28 | **W** Weekday Sim Shalom |
| | | 29 | 29 | **F** Full Sim Shalom (both editions) |
| | | | | **P** Personal Edition of Full Sim Shalom |

מִנְחָה **Torah** 3 aliyot from וַיֵּלֶךְ Vayelekh
דְּבָרִים Dᵉvarim (Deuteronomy) 31:1–13°
¹31:1–3   ²4–6   ³7–13                                                **W**317 **P**938

This is also the reading for the coming Thursday.

☞°31:1–13   The reading extends through verse 13, which enables the correct configuration of the 3 aliyot.

**Elul 29** אֱלוּל   מוֹצָאֵי שַׁבָּת Motsa'ey Shabbat   Conclusion of Shabbat
**Sat 28 Sep** (evening)   עֶרֶב רֹאשׁ הַשָּׁנָה Erev Rosh Hashanah
Day before Rosh Hashanah

עַרְבִית   Saturday night Arvit as usual   **L**264 **S**281 **W**137 **F**200
through the Amidah

✘ חֲצִי קַדִּישׁ ~~Short Kaddish~~
✘ וִיהִי נֹעַם ~~Vihi no'am~~
✘ יוֹשֵׁב בְּסֵתֶר עֶלְיוֹן ~~Yoshev bᵉseter elyon~~
✘ וְאַתָּה קָדוֹשׁ ~~Vᵉ'attah kadosh~~

קַדִּישׁ שָׁלֵם Full Kaddish   **L**280 **S**294 **W**160 **F**688

Some recite הַבְדָּלָה Havdalah here.   **L**283 **S**299 **W**165 **F**700

עָלֵינוּ Aleynu   **L**281 **S**297 **W**163 **F**696
קַדִּישׁ יָתוֹם Mourner's Kaddish (some omit)   **L**282 **S**298 **W**164 **F**698
✚ Psalm 27 for the Season of Repentance   **L**59 **S**80 **W**92 **F**40
קַדִּישׁ יָתוֹם Mourner's Kaddish   **L**58 **S**82 **W**100 **F**52

הַבְדָּלָה Havdalah   **L**283 **S**299 **W**165 **F**700

**Sun 29 Sep** (morning)   ✚ סְלִיחוֹת Sᵉliḥot (penitential prayers)
(including תַּחֲנוּן Taḥᵃnun)

שַׁחֲרִית   ✘ תַּחֲנוּן ~~Taḥᵃnun~~
☞ לַמְנַצֵּחַ Lamᵉnatse·aḥ (Psalm 20)   **W**79 **F**154

✘ תְּקִיעַת שׁוֹפָר ~~Sounding the shofar~~

✚ Psalm 27 for the Season of Repentance   **W**92 **F**40
קַדִּישׁ יָתוֹם Mourner's Kaddish   **W**100 **F**52

מִנְחָה   ✘ תַּחֲנוּן ~~Taḥᵃnun~~

---

**Luaḥ 5780**

Order your copies at www.milesbcohen.com.

## Rosh Hashanah

### Looking Ahead to Rosh Hashanah

**Teki'at Shofar — Hearing the Sounds of the Shofar**

The *mitsvah* of hearing the sounds of the shofar on Rosh Hashanah is not restricted to the synagogue. For a person unable to attend a synagogue service, arrange a shofar blowing wherever the person is located, so the person can fulfill the *mitsvah*.

**Preparing to Celebrate with a New Fruit or with New Clothes**

The 2nd day of Rosh Hashanah is celebrated Monday evening with a "new" fruit (that is, a seasonal fruit that you have not yet tasted this season) or with new clothes, worn for the first time that evening. In preparation, obtain the new fruit or new clothes before Rosh Hashanah begins.

**THROUGH Hosha'na Rabbah (some continue through Shemini Atseret)**

**Mornings**

After Psalm for the Day:
- קַדִּישׁ יָתוֹם Mourner's Kaddish (some omit) L58 S82 W100 F52
- + Psalm 27 for the Season of Repentance L59 S80 W92 F40
- קַדִּישׁ יָתוֹם Mourner's Kaddish L58 S82 W100 F52

**Evenings**

After עָלֵינוּ Aleynu:
- קַדִּישׁ יָתוֹם Mourner's Kaddish (some omit) L58 S82 W100 F52
- + Psalm 27 for the Season of Repentance L59 S80 W92 F40
- קַדִּישׁ יָתוֹם Mourner's Kaddish L58 S82 W100 F52

### Before Rosh Hashanah

**Preparing a Flame for Yom Tov**

On Yom Tov, kindling a *new* fire is not permitted; however, the use of an *existing* fire for cooking or other purposes is permitted.

To light candles for Day 2 of Rosh Hashanah (Monday night), ensure that you have a fire burning before candle-lighting time for Day 1 (Sunday evening) that will continue to burn until after dark on Monday. For example:

- A burning candle that lasts for more than 25 hours
- A pilot light on a gas range (*not* a gas range with an electronic starter)

**Omer** is a period of seven weeks extending from Pesaḥ to Shavu'ot. Aside from its obvious agrarian references, it serves also to tie the themes of Pesaḥ to those of Shavu'ot. As we perform סְפִירַת הָעֹמֶר *sefirat ha'omer*—counting off the days one by one every night—we realize that the freedom we gained on Pesaḥ has given us the opportunity to seek out and commit to the covenant and law that we celebrate on Shavu'ot.

### Sefirat Ha'omer

Counting Omer is a two-fold counting. Each night, beginning the 2nd night of Pesaḥ, count both (1) the number of days and (2) the number of weeks and parts of weeks.

- Count Omer after nightfall, preferably at least 25 minutes after sunset.
- Precede the counting with the בְּרָכָה *berakhah*. L63 S55 W152 F237
- To ensure that you properly count the number of days, as well as the number of weeks and parts of weeks, use the formulas in a *siddur* or other text.
- In the synagogue, count during Arvit, before עָלֵינוּ Aleynu.

  If your congregation conducts Arvit before nightfall, count Omer without a בְּרָכָה. Encourage congregants to count individually with a בְּרָכָה after nightfall.

Although the rabbinic obligation is to count after nightfall, the biblical obligation can be fufilled the next day as well. Consequently, if you forgot to count one evening:

- Count during the following day.
- Refrain from reciting the בְּרָכָה because you are not performing the *mitsvah* in strict accordance with rabbinic law.
- Continue counting in the evening, reciting the בְּרָכָה as usual.

Most authorities consider the 7 weeks of counting to be a single *mitsvah*. Therefore, if you miss counting 1 of the days completely, fulfillment of the rabbinic *mitsvah* is disrupted. In that case, you continue counting until Shavu'ot as usual, but you refrain from reciting the בְּרָכָה for the remaining days of the Omer.

Some authorities consider the counting to be 49 separate *mitsvot*. According to their reasoning, if you miss a day, you have forfeited one of the *mitsvot*, but you may continue to recite the בְּרָכָה for the remaining days.

In order not to miss any days, some people have the custom of making it a point to count again every morning (without a בְּרָכָה). That way, if they forgot at night, they are likely to at least remember the next day.

It is advisable in the synagogue each morning to count Omer without a בְּרָכָה. This counting fulfills the obligation of those present who neglected to count the previous night.

# APPENDIX B: Birkat Kohanim

Many congregations have continued or reinstated the traditional practice of calling כֹּהֲנִים *kohanim* forward to ask for God's blessing upon the congregation. In doing so, we recall that long ago the descendants of Aharon, the 1st priest, asked for God's blessing upon the people Israel (see Bemidbar 6:22–27). This is one of innumerable ways we use elements of ritual to connect ourselves to our people's past.

Although in some communities, the ritual of בִּרְכַּת כֹּהֲנִים *birkat kohanim* (the blessing from the priests, referred to in Yiddish as *dukhenen*) is done daily, among Ashkenazi Jews outside of Israel, the ritual is practiced only on holidays, usually at the Musaf service.

### Birkat Kohanim

The ritual involves the following steps:

1. After the קְדֻשָּׁה *kedushah* at a holiday Musaf service (Shaḥarit on Simḥat Torah), the כֹּהֲנִים *kohanim* (descendants of Aharon) and the לְוִיִּם *leviyyim* (descendants of the tribe of Levi) proceed to the hand-washing area.
2. The לְוִיִּם perform a ritual washing of the hands of the כֹּהֲנִים.
3. The כֹּהֲנִים, each wearing a large טַלִּית *tallit,* return to the sanctuary and approach—but do not ascend—the בִּימָה *bimah.*
4. As the *sheliaḥ/sheliḥat tsibbur* nears the prayer רְצֵה *retseh,* the כֹּהֲנִים remove their shoes (without touching the shoes).
5. When the *sheliaḥ/sheliḥat tsibbur* actually begins the prayer רְצֵה, the כֹּהֲנִים ascend the בִּימָה and stand in front of the ark.
6. The כֹּהֲנִים cover their heads with their large טַלִּיּוֹת *talliyyot* and face the ark to recite the בְּרָכָה *berakhah* in advance of performing the *mitsvah:*

   בָּרוּךְ אַתָּה יי, אֱ־לֹהֵינוּ מֶלֶךְ הָעוֹלָם, אֲשֶׁר קִדְּשָׁנוּ בִּקְדֻשָּׁתוֹ שֶׁל אַהֲרֹן
   וְצִוָּנוּ לְבָרֵךְ אֶת־עַמּוֹ יִשְׂרָאֵל בְּאַהֲבָה.

   Barukh attah adonay, eloheynu melekh ha'olam,
   asher kiddeshanu bikdushato shel aharon
   vetsivvanu levarekh et ammo yisra'el be'ahavah.
7. The כֹּהֲנִים turn in a clockwise direction to face the congregation.
8. The *sheliaḥ/sheliḥat tsibbur* leads the כֹּהֲנִים in the three-part blessing, slowly chanting each word, which the כֹּהֲנִים then repeat.
9. At the end of each of the 3 verses, the congregation responds אָמֵן *amen.*

## Determining the Date of a Yortsayt

Observe a *yortsayt* on the anniversary of the date of death, calculated according to the Hebrew calendar.

Some dates do not occur every year. For a death on one of these dates, determine the *yortsayt* using these guidelines:

**Death occurred on 30 Ḥeshvan (Rosh Ḥodesh Kislev – Day 1)**

- If in the *next* year 30 Ḥeshvan does *not* occur, then *every* year:
  Observe 29 Ḥeshvan.
  (Thus, the *yortsayt* is observed on the same date each year.)
- If in the *next* year 30 Ḥeshvan *does* occur, then each year:
  Observe 30 Ḥeshvan in every year it occurs.
  In other years, observe 1 Kislev.
  (Thus, the *yortsayt* is always observed on Rosh Ḥodesh Kislev, either on Day 1 of Rosh Ḥodesh or on the only day of Rosh Ḥodesh.)

**Death occurred on 30 Kislev (Rosh Ḥodesh Tevet – Day 1)**

- If in the *next* year 30 Kislev does *not* occur, then *every* year:
  Observe 29 Kislev.
  (Thus, the *yortsayt* is observed on the same date each year.)
- If in the *next* year 30 Kislev *does* occur, then each year:
  Observe 30 Kislev in every year it occurs.
  In other years, observe 1 Tevet.
  (Thus, the *yortsayt* is always observed on Rosh Ḥodesh Tevet, either on Day 1 of Rosh Ḥodesh or on the only day of Rosh Ḥodesh.)

**Death occurred during Adar (in a non-leap year)**

- In a non-leap year, observe the date of death in Adar.
- In a leap year, observe the date in 1st Adar. (Some follow the custom of observing the date in both 1st Adar and 2nd Adar.)

**Death occurred during 1st Adar or 2nd Adar (in a leap year)**

- In a non-leap year, observe the date in Adar.
- In a leap year, observe the date in whichever Adar the death occurred.

**Death occurred on 30th of 1st Adar (Rosh Ḥodesh 2nd Adar – Day 1, in a leap year)**

- In a non-leap year, observe 30 Shevat (Rosh Ḥodesh Adar – Day 1).
- In a leap year, observe 30th of 1st Adar (Rosh Ḥodesh 2nd Adar – Day 1).